CHOOSING A WORLD-VIEW AND VALUE-SYSTEM

To the Memory of

Leo Shields,

The Friend Who Led Me to the Faith

Visit our web site at
WWW.ALBAHOUSE.ORG

CHOOSING A WORLD-VIEW AND VALUE-SYSTEM

AN ECUMENICAL APOLOGETICS

BENEDICT M. ASHLEY, OP

ALBA·HOUSE NEW·YORK

SOCIETY OF ST. PAUL, 2187 VICTORY BLVD., STATEN ISLAND, NEW YORK 10314

Library of Congress Cataloging-in-Publication Data

Ashley, Benedict M.
Choosing a world-view and value-system: an ecumenical apologetics / Benedict M. Ashley.
p. cm.
Includes bibliographical references.
ISBN 0-8189-0829-7
1. Catholic Church Apologetic works. I. Title.
BX1752.A84 2000
239—dc21 99-33773
CIP

Produced and designed in the United States of America by the Fathers and Brothers of the Society of St. Paul, 2187 Victory Boulevard, Staten Island, New York 10314-6603, as part of their communications apostolate.

ISBN: 0-8189-0829-7

Printing Information:

Current Printing - first digit 1 2 3 4 5 6 7 8 9 10

Year of Current Printing - first year shown

2000 2001 2002 2003 2004 2005 2006 2007 2008 2009

CONTENTS

Foreword vii

CHOOSING

Chapter 1: Does Everyone Need a World-View and Value-System? .. 3

1. "I Am Not a Religious Person." 3
2. Is Religion Dying? 6
3. The Functional Definition of Religion 9
4. Functional Equivalents for Religion 16
5. Choosing a Philosophy of Life 17
6. Weighing the Options 19

THE OPTIONS

Chapter 2: Humanist Philosophies of Life 25

1. Break Away from Christianity 25
2. The Humanist World-View and Value-System 33
3. The Capitalist and Socialist Versions of Humanism 37
4. Are Modern Humanisms Unique? 42
5. Questions about Humanistic Philosophies of Life 47

Chapter 3: Mythological Religions 63

1. Mythic Cultures 63
2. Prehistoric Religion 67
3. The Pre-Literary Religions 67
4. The Ancient Urban Religions 74
5. Mythic Religion vs. Humanism 82

Chapter 4: Emanation Religions 97

1. The Great Reformation 97
2. Gautama, the Buddha 100
3. Hinduism 105
4. How Absolute is the Absolute? 109

Chapter 5: Creation Religions 121

1. What is Creation? 121
2. The God of Abraham, Isaac, and Jacob 123

3. Christianity 128
4. Islam 136
5. How Is the Creator Known? 141
6. An Alternative Way to the Creator 168

THE ECUMENICAL CHOICE

Chapter 6: THE DIALOGUE OF THEISM WITH NON-THEISM 183
1. Is Such Dialogue Possible? 183
2. Why Must Revelation be Received on Faith? 188
3. Is Revelation Verifiable? 192
4. Revelation: Communication Verified by Signs 199
5. God's Intimate Self-Revelation 202
6. How Theism Includes the Other World-Views 206

Chapter 7: THE ECUMENICAL CHURCH: SIGN OF GOD'S SELF-COMMUNICATION 211
1. The Search for a Revelatory Sign 211
2. Ecumenicity as Miraculous 215
3. Catholicity, the Sign of Inclusive Care 217
4. Unity, the Sign of the Church as Community 223
5. Holiness, the Sign of the Church as Graced 228
6. The Gap between the Gospel and Popular Christianity 238
7. Conclusion 239

Chapter 8: JESUS CHRIST: GOD'S SELF-COMMUNICATION IN HISTORY 245
1. Apostolicity, the Sign of Historical Continuity 245
2. Historicity and Ecumenicity 247
3. Historical Credibility of the Church's Tradition 251
4. Did Jesus Rise from Death? 254
5. Jesus as God's Self-Revelation 260

Chapter 9: THE HISTORICAL CHRISTIAN COMMUNITY 269
1. The Organization of the Christian Community 269
2. Incarnation and Trinity 275
3. The Constantinian Establishment 279
4. The Indefectibility and Infallibility of the Church 288
5. The Presence of Jesus Christ in His Church 290

Chapter 10: COSMIC EVIL AND CHRISTIAN HOPE 297
1. The Subjective Aspects of Faith 297
2. The Origin of Evil 300
3. The Subject and Evil 310
4. Compensation and Consolation 315
5. The Greater Good 319
6. The God of Love 321
Conclusion 323

FOREWORD

Much is said these days among Christians both about "evangelization" and "ecumenism," but it is not clear how the two goals can be reconciled. Karl Rahner's important theory of "the anonymous Christian" has been mistakenly taken to imply that since the Good News has already been heard by everyone willing to hear it, evangelization is unnecessary. All that is needed is ecumenical dialogue to help all to recognize that they really are already of one faith. Hence, the function of the branch of theology formerly called "apologetics" has largely dropped out of current literature and the theological curriculum. The place of apologetics has been taken by what appears to be a newer discipline of "fundamental" theology. The distinction between the two is clearly stated by Gerald O'Collins, S.J. in his *Fundamental Theology*[1] as follows:

> Fundamental theology tackles a *twofold task* by (a) methodologically reflecting on the source of theological knowledge in the divine revelation recorded in tradition and Scripture, and (b) calling attention to the way human experience is open to receive that revelation.... [Since] the task of apologetics is to present, defend and justify rationally the Christian faith for unbelievers, its discussion with various kinds of "unbelievers" will presuppose human experience and reason but *not* faith — or at least not full Christian and Roman Catholic faith.

This situation, however, has recently become more complicated. Francis Schüssler Fiorenza in his *Foundational Theology*[2] points out that fundamental theology has tended to absorb apologetics by dealing not only with the *meaning* of the Christian tradition but also with its *truth* by one of two methods: the historical and the transcendental. The first correlates the fundamental truths of Christianity with historical facts according to a correspondence theory of truth. The second correlates them with present experience according to a coherence theory of truth. This second transcendental method has led to the absorption of fundamental theology in its turn into "foundational theology" as in Karl Rahner's great work, *Foundations of the Christian Faith.*[3] Fiorenza criticizes both fundamental and foundational theology on the philosophical assumption that there can be no absolute ground for testing the truth of any thought system, whether scientific or religious, since we are always caught in a hermeneutical circle in which experience, theory, and praxis mutually condition each other. He proposes a hermeneutic method in which a broad "reflective equilibrium" between all these elements is sought.

In this highly sophisticated, hermeneutical perspective of current theology is it not more than ever necessary to remember the apologetic task of theology in the service of ecumenism and evangelization? Evangelization is directed to those who do not believe (or do not think they believe) in Jesus Christ as their Savior (leaving open the question of their salvation through implicit faith in Him). Hence it seeks from theology a kind of guidance that is no longer thematically presented in most works or courses on fundamental or foundational theology. Ecumenism also requires us "to place ourselves in the other fellow's shoes." Thus our theological schools which seek to prepare those who will minister not only to believers but who will evangelize or enter into ecumenical dialogue with the unbelieving cannot neglect special attention to the apologetic task.

John Paul II In his encyclical *Fides et Ratio*[4] accepts the term "fundamental theology" but broadens it to include classical apologetics in a passage that explains why an apologetic is needed by priests and catechists or indeed by all Christians in witness to the Gospel. As St. Peter counsels, "always be ready to give an explanation to anyone who asks you for a reason for your hope, but do it with gentleness and reverence" (1 P 3:15-16a). Though the Pope speaks principally of the apologetic use of philosophy, by which he especially means metaphysics, what he says applies also to the apologetic use of forms of human reason.

> With its specific character as a discipline charged with giving an account of faith (cf. 1 P 3:15), the concern of *fundamental theology* will be to justify and expound the relationship between faith and philosophical thought. Recalling the teaching of Saint Paul (cf. Rm 1:19-20), the First Vatican Council pointed to the existence of truths which are naturally, and thus philosophically, knowable; and an acceptance of God's Revelation necessarily presupposes knowledge of these truths. In studying Revelation and its credibility, as well as the corresponding act of faith, fundamental theology should show how, in the light of the knowledge conferred by faith, there emerge certain truths which reason, from its own independent enquiry, already provides. Revelation endows these truths with their fullest meaning, directing them towards the richness of the revealed mystery in which they find their ultimate purpose. Consider, for example, the natural knowledge of God, the possibility of distinguishing divine Revelation from other phenomena or the recognition of its credibility, the capacity of human language to speak in a true and meaningful way even of things which transcend all human experience. From all these truths, the mind is led to acknowledge the existence of a truly propaedeutic path to faith, one that can lead to the acceptance of Revelation without in any way compromising the principles and autonomy of the mind itself.
>
> Similarly, fundamental theology should demonstrate the profound compatibility that exists between faith and its need to find expression by way of human reason fully free to give its assent. Faith will thus be able "to show fully the path to reason in a sincere search for the truth. Although faith, a gift of God, is not based on reason, it can certainly not dispense with it. At the same time, it becomes apparent that reason needs to be reinforced by faith, in order to discover horizons it cannot reach on its own."

The current neglect of apologetics, occasioned in part by the neglect of metaphysics that John Paul II deplores, is understandable when we examine the condition of this theological discipline before Vatican

II. Its presentation often suffered from two grave defects. First, it was developed in a *rationalistic* manner as if faith were the conclusion of a syllogism rather than a gift of God surpassing the mode of all human reason and involving not only the human intelligence but also the totality of the human person. Second, it was presented in a manner which neglected our pluralistic culture and contradicted our commitment to ecumenism, that is, in such a way as to demand from all who were not Catholics or even Christians the recantation of their "demonstrated" errors.

In the following work I have attempted to develop in the manner of an essay rather than an exhaustive treatise a line of apologetic or rather *evangelical* argument which is rational but not rationalistic. I have also tried to base it on an ecumenical and thus hermeneutical attitude to other religions as well as to purely secular world-views.

I will not attempt to describe religions other than Christianity in detail as do the specialists in Hans Küng's well known *Christianity and World Religions: Paths to Dialogue.*[5] Instead I supply sufficient bibliography for a reader to explore in detail the beliefs and practices of the various world-views concerning which I here only try to generalize. For the present purposes I believe it is sufficient to consider the chief *apparent* differences between these world-views that have been recognized by experts in comparative religion. It is the task of ecumenical dialogue to determine how real these differences are. What Christian apologetics is concerned about is to disclose Jesus Christ as the Truth in which all truth, from whatever source it comes, can be honestly acknowledged and reconciled.

Notes

1 New York: Paulist Press, 1981, pp. 22-23.
2 New York: Crossroad, 1984, pp. 251-310.
3 New York: Seabury/Crossroad, 1978.
4 Sept. 14, 1998, N. 67.
5 With Josef von Ess, Heinrich von Stietencron and Heinz Bechert (Maryknoll, NY: Orbis Books, 1996).

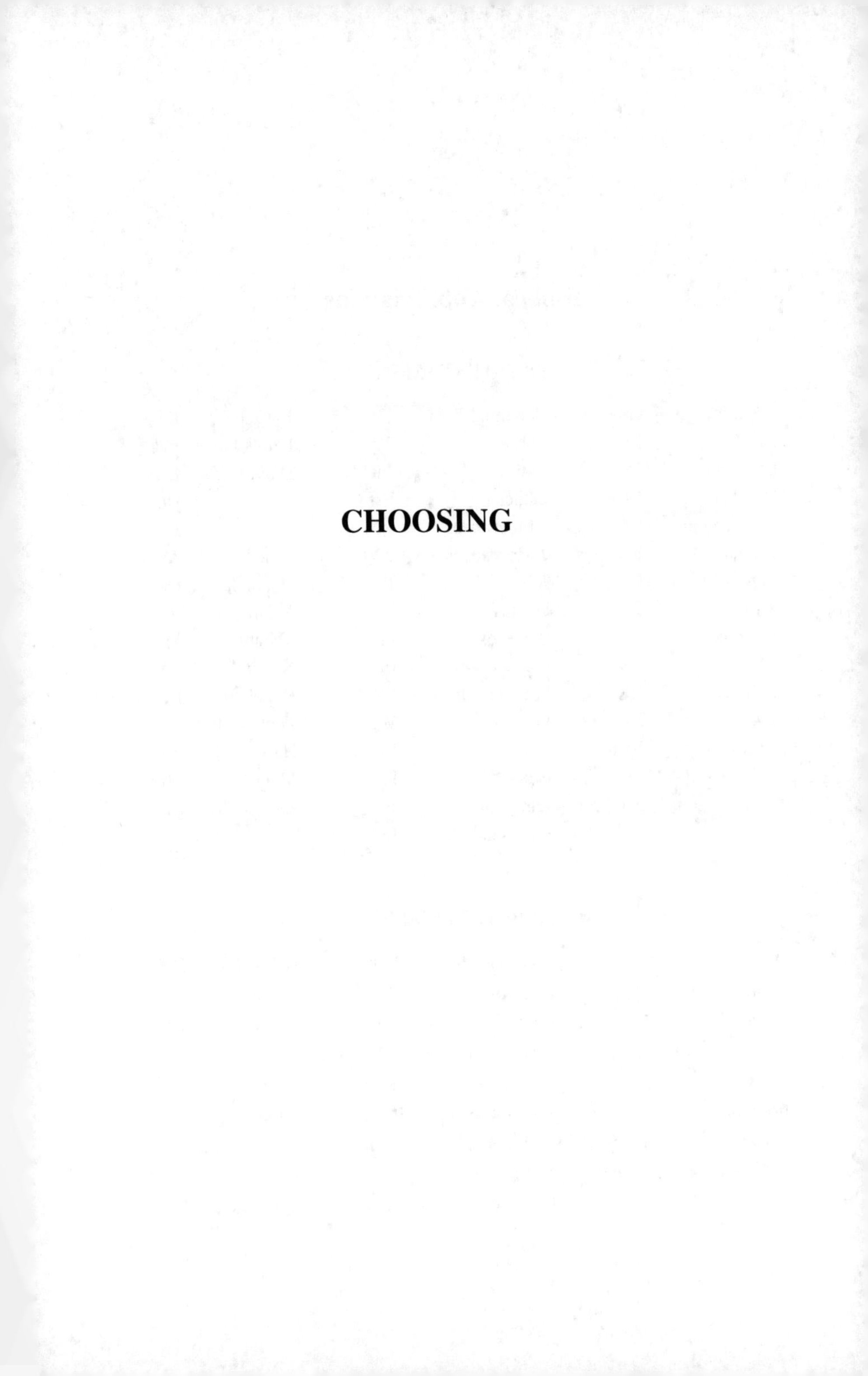

CHOOSING

Biblical Abbreviations

OLD TESTAMENT

Genesis	Gn	Nehemiah	Ne	Baruch	Ba
Exodus	Ex	Tobit	Tb	Ezekiel	Ezk
Leviticus	Lv	Judith	Jdt	Daniel	Dn
Numbers	Nb	Esther	Est	Hosea	Ho
Deuteronomy	Dt	1 Maccabees	1 M	Joel	Jl
Joshua	Jos	2 Maccabees	2 M	Amos	Am
Judges	Jg	Job	Jb	Obadiah	Ob
Ruth	Rt	Psalms	Ps	Jonah	Jon
1 Samuel	1 S	Proverbs	Pr	Micah	Mi
2 Samuel	2 S	Ecclesiastes	Ec	Nahum	Na
1 Kings	1 K	Song of Songs	Sg	Habakkuk	Hab
2 Kings	2 K	Wisdom	Ws	Zephaniah	Zp
1 Chronicles	1 Ch	Sirach	Si	Haggai	Hg
2 Chronicles	2 Ch	Isaiah	Is	Malachi	Ml
Ezra	Ezr	Jeremiah	Jr	Zechariah	Zc
		Lamentations	Lm		

NEW TESTAMENT

Matthew	Mt	Ephesians	Eph	Hebrews	Heb
Mark	Mk	Philippians	Ph	James	Jm
Luke	Lk	Colossians	Col	1 Peter	1 P
John	Jn	1 Thessalonians	1 Th	2 Peter	2 P
Acts	Ac	2 Thessalonians	2 Th	1 John	1 Jn
Romans	Rm	1 Timothy	1 Tm	2 John	2 Jn
1 Corinthians	1 Cor	2 Timothy	2 Tm	3 John	3 Jn
2 Corinthians	2 Cor	Titus	Tt	Jude	Jude
Galatians	Gal	Philemon	Phm	Revelation	Rv

CHAPTER 1

DOES EVERYONE NEED A WORLD-VIEW AND VALUE-SYSTEM?

1. "I Am Not a Religious Person."

The public discourse of our universities and other centers of culture give the impression that at the end of the twentieth century many of the elite of our day feel no need for "religion." The popular media, though they give occasional attention to religious affairs, also picture modern life in America as little concerned with issues of religious faith. Many Americans do not seem to be anti-religious but simply find the claims and practices of Christianity or Judaism or other traditional religions irrelevant to their lives. Nor does the absence of religious faith leave a void in their daily existence. Many feel their lives are full enough without bothering about theological dogmas, traditional rituals, religiously sanctioned codes of conduct or special times of prayer. Of course life has its tragic puzzles, but religious solutions to these seem illusory. Is it not more honest just to admit that for some problems, both intellectual and practical, there are no satisfactory answers?

A study by Evert C. Call, Jr. and Seymour M. Lipset, *The Divided Academy*[1] in 1975 and another by Howard R. Bowen and Jack H. Schuster, *American Professors*[2] in 1985 showed that a considerable part of the academic elite of the United States seem indifferent to religion. The latter study found that 36% did not consider themselves even "moderately religious" and 52% did not attend worship services even once a month. Moreover these figures included small colleges where faculties are probably somewhat more traditional. *The Connecticut Mutual Life Report on American Values*[3] showed that the situation was much the same for non-academic elites such as public media professionals.

What percentage of the American people feels as these individuals do about religion? In 1997 *The Gallop Poll*[4] summarized its findings on this question as follows:

> [N]ine out of ten adults both indicate a religious preference of one kind or another and say that they attend church on at least some occasions. Two-thirds maintain an affiliation with a church or synagogue, and six in ten consider religion to be very important to their personal lives. At the same time, the percentage who attend church regularly is much lower, close to four in ten ...[Most] of these patterns of religious belief and practice have held relatively steady for the past three decades, since the early 1970's. Prior to that time, religious commitment tended to be slightly higher, although frequency of church attendance has been remarkably stable for almost sixty years, with the exception of the 1950's, when churchgoing went up. Eighty-seven percent put themselves in one of four major Christian groups: 58% are Protestant, 27% Roman Catholic, 1% Mormon, and another 1% are affiliated with an Eastern Orthodox church. Judaism is embraced by 3%... A mix of other less prevalent religions comprises another 3%, leaving only 5% of respondents who have no religious preference whatsoever. Among Protestants, the most common denomination is Baptist, with 19% of respondents calling themselves either Southern Baptist or another type. Methodists at 9% are the second largest denomination, followed by other mainline Protestant groups including Lutherans (6%), Presbyterians (5%) members of the Church of Christ (9%) and Episcopalians (2%). About one-third (30%) are devout practitioners of their faith, saying they attend church or synagogue at least once per week. Another 60% indicate that they do attend, albeit with varying degrees of frequency: 13% go almost weekly, 17% about once per month. Another 30% go, but seldom. Only 9% never attend a church or synagogue. What is perhaps most telling is that two out of three (67%) of U.S. adults claim that they have made a "personal commitment to Jesus Christ that is still important in their life today."[5]

As all commentators on such data agree, the United States is remarkably "religious" compared with the countries of Western Europe. For example a recent study on Great Britain[6] found that only 31% believed in "a personal God" and only 41% in a "life after death." Another study[7] showed that in The Netherlands, which many had regarded as religiously stable, belief in "a personal God" fell from 34% in 1981 to 28% in 1990 and weekly church attendance from 26% to 20%. Other European rates are similar. Thus in France only 60% "believe in God" and 10% are convinced atheists, and only 11% attend church regularly.

Yet also in the United States, in spite of the high level of people's identification of themselves as Catholic, Protestant or Jewish, a 1988 report[8] showed that 44% of all Americans over the age of 18 (78 million adults) today are functionally "unchurched." "This means that they do not belong to any church, synagogue or temple," or, though they claim membership, "have not voluntarily worshiped in the church, synagogue or temple of their choice for six months or more, not counting funerals, weddings, Christmas, Easter or the High Holydays." Thus it is evident that in the United States by a conservative estimate there are at least 30% of the population who are secularized to the extent that their practical outlook on life is not that of any of the traditional religions. Perhaps even more significant are the statistics for the largest Christian denomination in the United States, Roman Catholicism. In this church a 1998 poll[9] shows that of members 20-29 years of age only 65% think that in their "vision of the Catholic faith" it is "essential" to believe that "God is present in the sacraments." Of the same younger Catholics only 58% believe that it is required "to make charitable efforts toward helping the poor," 58% "that Christ is really present in the Eucharist," and 53% that "devotion to Mary, the Mother of God" is required. Furthermore only 42% hold for "the teaching that Christ established the authority of the bishops by choosing Peter, 37% that there is an obligation to attend Mass once a week, or to go to confession to a priest (32%), and only 31% think that abortion is wrong. Only 30% said that they had regularly attended Mass once a week in the previous year." Another 1996 poll of the General Social Survey of the National Science Foundation[10] showed that the 30-49 group who in 1970 thought that premarital sex was wrong by 48%, now only about 20% think so. It also showed that of those who in 1970 thought homosexual relations were wrong by about 78%, only 56% now think so. Such figures certainly manifest a wide gap between official church doctrine and perhaps a majority of church members in the direction of secular influences.

2. Is Religion Dying?

How then are we to interpret this fact that in advanced countries from a third to half the people, and especially the dominating elites, find religion largely irrelevant, although the half or two-thirds still find it very important in their lives? The most obvious interpretation is the one often given by the religionless themselves. They commonly claim that *modernization* necessarily undermines religion because religion is based on an irrational, mythical view of reality supported by a static traditionalism that must inevitably yield to cultural progress[11] with the advance of science and technology and the consequent urbanization, universal communication, and social rationalization.

The former Marxist governments of Eastern Europe and that of China today, have always denounced religion as "the opiate of the people" and maintained that in a communist society religious organizations, along with the class struggle and the state, will quietly "wither away." This prediction is not only unsubstantiated, but contradicted by the fact that such governments like that of the former Soviet Union and now of China have found it necessary to continue their harassment of religion for many years. Religion may be suffering a percentage decline, but a strongly resistant religious minority remains.

"Post-moderns" disillusioned about the inevitability of human progress propose a different explanation of the percentage decline of religion. They no longer claim religion will simply melt away with the dawn of scientific rationalism. Instead these sociologists view the growth of the religionless as the consequence of *secularization*.[12] The constitutional separation of church and state adopted by most democratic governments logically commits them not only to neutrality toward denominational religion but even toward the competition between religion and irreligion. This neutrality inevitably reflects and promotes shrinkage of the sphere of the sacred to make room to enlarge the secular areas of life.

Some theologians have also accepted this secularization theory. Of these some declare that "for modern man, come of age, God is dead" and consequently the values formerly expressed by sacred symbols must now be reinterpreted in secular terms.[13] Others who are unwilling to grant the demise of God nevertheless actually welcome this desacralization of life. They argue that authentic Christianity, unlike other traditional faiths, is not a religion because it has freed us from idolatry, mythology, ritualism, and ecclesiasticism. They advocate a "non-religious" Christianity, although they have found some difficulty in making their fellow Christians understand what this might mean.[14]

In opposition to such interpretations of the growth of irreligion, other sociologists bring forward evidence that neither modernization nor secularization necessarily results in the death of religion. This "persistence of religion" in the face of rapid change, pluralism, and the secularization of modern culture, it is argued, provides strong evidence that religion will survive.[15] Indeed some religious sociologists maintain that free-market competition among religions and between religion and irreligion actually invigorates religion.[16]

Moreover, this school of thought maintains that the statistical growth of those who are unchurched indicates not so much a decline in religious commitment as the *privatization* of religion. Many people today are fed-up not with religion as such but with "organized" religion. They prefer to seek religious experience individually or in intimate informal groupings rather than in institutions which so often seem formalistic or even hypocritical and exploitative. Secularization, because it has removed religion from the public sphere of politics, has encouraged this privatization and the growth of what Thomas Luckman called the "Invisible Religion."[17] Furthermore, the religious scene is changing so rapidly that it is difficult to predict what it will soon be. George Barna[18] in a survey of recent studies concludes:

> The religious scene in America today is undergoing fundamental changes of seismic proportions. Like almost everything in

> our culture today, there is nothing sacred anymore, even in the realm of the sacred. Americans are questioning everything about religion and faith, and the long term taboos have been discarded in favor of a wholesale re-evaluation.... [T]he undeniable reality is that America is transitioning from a Christian nation to a syncretistic, spiritually diverse society. It is shifting from a denominational landscape to a domain of independent churches.... What is *not* lost in this spiritual upheaval is the new perception of religion: a personalized, customized form of faith views which meet personal needs, minimize rules and absolutes, and which bear little resemblance to the "pure" form of any of the world's major religions.

That such a "personalized, customized form of faith" really can "meet personal needs" in a way that satisfactorily fulfills the functions of a world-view and value-system that the traditional religions met is, however, questionable. Hence sociologists of religion are inclined to think that the increase of the percentage of persons who reject "organized religion" for purely individual philosophies of life is just another example of the *anomie* or *normlessness* of our complex society, along with high rates of crime, suicide, and divorce. Rapid social change, they say, disrupts human value-systems and the communities based on them. Thus while one sector of the society clings to religion as its last hope of a stable way of life transmissible from generation to generation, another loses its religious identity and just drifts. Such people have not rejected religion. They simply feel confused about it or deserted by its leaders who speak with an uncertain voice. Some theorists consider this anomie as pathological. Hence they look for a remedy in what they call "civil religion." They define this civil religion as a widespread allegiance, often expressed in our political rhetoric, to a set of common values and value-laden symbols, largely derived from our historic Protestantism, but vague enough to be acceptable to Catholics and even to Jews.[19]

Other sociologists attack the notion of civil religion and argue that modern pluralistic societies do not operate on the basis of some "public philosophy" on which there is consensus but on the acknowledged co-existence of different value-systems. Hence Americans should not vainly attempt to develop a civil religion but should seek more effective ways to bring all interests into dialogue, arbitration, and pragmatic compromise in the "culture wars." This is supported by some "deconstructionist" philosophers who believe that our times of "post-modernity" require us always to be aware of the "difference" or the "otherness" of views not our own, since no one point of view can do justice to the complexity of reality.[20]

Finally, it can be argued that the recent statistical growth of the religionless may not be as significant as some suppose, but may only represent the ups-and-downs of cultural fashion. Historians of "popular religion" have shown that even in the so-called "Ages of Faith" there was still a great gap between the teachings of the institutional Church and the actual perceptions and practices of the majority of the faithful.[21] If we could have taken a Gallup Poll in 13th-century France, would it not have showed that most people were only superficially influenced by the official theology? Of course people then lived in a world of Christian symbols, but did these symbols mean to them what they meant to the university theologians? Today secularization has largely replaced those ancient symbols with TV images, but perhaps these new secular symbols better express the values that long since have really characterized American life. Whichever of these interpretations or some combination of them we may prefer, the fact remains that our dominant elites and the very considerable sector of the population most directly influenced by them, especially in economically developed countries, are today without commitment to any one of the traditional world religions.

3. The Functional Definition of Religion

For a better understanding of the relation between those who seem to be religiously committed and those who do not, it is necessary to ask, "Exactly what is religion and what function does it fulfill in our lives, if any?" Sociologists of religion generally prefer a *functional* to a *substantive* definition of religion.[22] A substantive definition would require us to identify the content of beliefs and practices generically common to all those systems which are labeled "religion" by common usage, such as Judaism, Christianity, Islam, Hinduism, Buddhism, Confucianism, Taoism, and the tribal religions of Africa, Asia, the Pacific, and the Americas.

The problem with such a substantive definition is that it seems impossible to find beliefs and practices truly common to all these "religions." Judaism, Christianity, and Islam confess the same personal God, but it is not clear that Buddhism and Confucianism believe in such a God at all. Some "religions" are founded on belief in survival of the human person after death; others are not. Some have a priesthood; others do not. For every doctrine or practice in one religion another religion can be found which lacks or even contradicts it. The more we study the different systems labeled "religion" the more obvious it becomes that, as regards substantive content, their similarities are only analogical. Consequently, if we are to compare one religion with another fairly and objectively, without privileging one particular religion because it is the one most familiar to us, as the perfect exemplar, we must define religion not in terms of content but of *function*.[23]

What are the functions of religion in human life? W. Richard Comstock[24] cites Robert Merton's distinction between "manifest" and "latent" functions to show that social behavior often serves a social function of which the participants are not conscious. Allowing for this distinction, Comstock identifies three types of function for religion.

1. Religion by its rituals and its accompanying myths is *socially integrative* in the following ways:

   a) Religion *symbolically articulates* social relations, e.g., the relations between the gods serves as a model for human social relations.
   b) It *validates* these relations. Thus authority is attributed to the Dalai Lama as the "living Buddha" or the Pope as the "Vicar of Christ."
   c) It is *performatory*, e.g., a congregation in church or synagogue or temple performs a social act.
   d) It is *heuristic* in that it concentrates human energies on a particular social act and teaches how to carry it out. Thus the ritual of ordination prepares the brahman or priest to sacrifice.
   e) It is *creative* in helping overcome social problems. Thus a ritual may reconcile quarreling parties.

f) It is *mitigative* by enabling some social acts to be performed tactfully. Thus a ritual may be used to make a divorce less painful or going into war less terrifying.

2. Religion by managing the identity crises of birth, puberty, and death which require some initiation or "rite of passage," has a *biological-psychological* function.
3. Religion by helping us cope with and find meaning in the inescapable "limit situations" of life that cannot be overcome by pragmatic means has a *depth-psychological* function. Religion also helps us to give expression to our feelings in these situations and hence to find joy in life events which are otherwise inexpressible. Thus a funeral ritual helps us both to express our grief and find some meaning and consolation within its pain.

Since the use of rituals, myths and other symbolic forms of expression seem so typical of religions many sociologists of religion favor Clifford Geertz' *symbolic* definition of religion.[25] Semiotic theory shows that while matters of ordinary practical life can be expressed in literal language, this is more difficult for limit situations that touch on what is most primal, comprehensive, and profound in our experience. For such experiences *symbolic* expression is often more effective. To understand why this is so it is necessary to define the term "symbol," as well as the term "metaphor" which often substitutes for it.[26] "Symbol" and "metaphor" are currently used by many writers in contrast to "sign," on the grounds that a "sign" has only one meaning, while symbols and metaphors are "polyvalent," that is, they convey many meanings. It seems to me the former philosophical classification was more precise according to which "sign" is a generic term for anything that signifies something, and "symbol" was a *species* of sign characterized by polyvalence. For example in religious liturgy, a lighted candle is a sign that can have one or many meanings. It can simply say, "Be attentive, the service is about to begin" or it can raise a flood of images that signify God's presence, life, the Gospel, the coming of evening, or death, etc. A symbol can carry such a weight of meaning, while a merely literal sign cannot, because human thought tends to extend a sign having one meaning to include many similar or otherwise related meanings.

This extension of signification is called *analogy*. Since the human mind cannot grasp the whole of reality in any literal way, it is forced to use analogy when it attempts to express totality or ultimate matters. Analogy itself is subdivided into "metaphor" (an explicit metaphor is a "simile") if the point of comparison is merely superficial and "proper analogy" if it is essential. Thus to name God "The Rock" is metaphorical, but to name God "Love" is proper analogy since the comparison with our own experience of earthly love tells us something essential about our relation to God and God's relation to us.

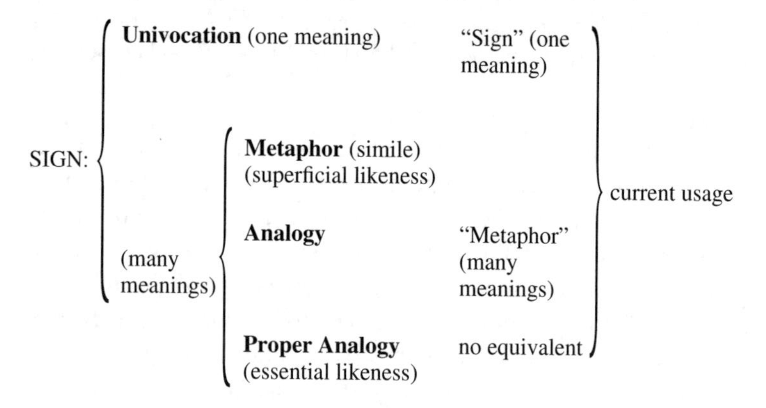

In particular, symbols and metaphors have the property of being able to serve as substitutes for what they signify. Thus we may treat a religious leader as if the reverence due to God were due the leader personally.

Because we humans are bodily beings who communicate not only by spoken and written language, but also by gesture, religious expression requires *ritual*, the performance of symbolic acts, often with the use of natural objects which have been given symbolism or artificial ones specially designed to convey such meanings. At the same time we express the meanings of these acts verbally by ritual formulae, songs, affirmations of belief, readings of sacred scriptures, etc. and often by the retelling of sacred stories or *myths* which are explanatory of our actions. Ritual and myth thus complement one another. In Catholic theology the medieval Scholastics called this twofold aspect of a sacrament its "matter" (the ritual action) and its "form" (the verbal expression). Yet as important as are these various kinds of symbols for the expression of religious beliefs — and in the rest of this book they must be given special attention — it does not seem that Geertz' symbolic definition of religion should be preferred to a functional one. This is because in Comstock's classification of religious functions quoted above the providing of symbols is only one function, though a major one, of religion. Furthermore, to assert, as do some anthropologists of religion that the symbols in question refer to the "integration of the self" and not to realities that transcend the human self is once again to insert a substantive element into the functional definition of religion. Of course these symbols may serve to integrate the self, but they also may refer to the nature of the cosmos of which the self is a part. The referential content and its truth-value of religious symbolism cannot be settled by a purely functional definition.[27]

Thus sociologically for the purposes of comparison we can classify as religions any cultural complex that helps people (1) integrate their society, (2) deal with identity crises, (3) cope with limit situations, especially by use of ritual and myth. But before we adopt such a functional definition, we must also recognize that some sociologists prefer a substantive one based on a dichotomy between the "transcendent," "supernatural" or "sacred" and the "mundane," "natural," "empirical," "profane" or "secular." One difficulty with such definitions in terms of sacred vs. secular is that in some societies (particularly those based on simple economies) the sacred is not clearly distinguished from the secular, at least in the minds of the natives. Another difficulty is the vagueness of such terms as "transcendence" or "the sacred." Rudolf Otto in a famous book *The Idea of the Holy*[28] defined the sacred as the *mysterium tremendum et fascinans* because we are fascinated by it yet are in awe of its overwhelming power. Note, however, that a definition of religion need not imply that the "transcendent" or "sacred" is outside us or absolutely beyond our control. You may stand in awe and fascination before your mirror because the depths of your own personality exceed your ordinary behavior and self-comprehension! An adolescent awakening to his own sexuality may be awestruck by this unexpected energy and may experience it as "sacred," as do artists or scientists overwhelmed with the realization of their own creative powers.

Since functionally religion deals with limit situations, it engages our awareness of the presence of a realm which exceeds ordinary, routine living, but this need not imply the existence of "supernatural" or "superempirical" powers that exceed the laws of nature or the limits of purely human experience and experiment. Hence "transcendence" is not necessarily a substantive element of the content of every religion, but simply another term for the third of Comstock's three principal functions of religion: "to cope with the limit situations of life." Yet to define religion functionally by the notion of "transcendence" taken in this merely relative sense seems to be too broad, because it does not clearly distinguish religion from esthetic and other experiences in which the humdrum and routine are also exceeded. Hence I prefer the functional definition proposed by the Protestant theologian Paul Tillich[29] according to whom religion deals with matters of "ultimate concern," i.e. our priorities or *value-systems.* A value-system, however, cannot be taken seriously unless we believe it to be grounded in a *world-view,* that is, in the actuality in which we live and its possibilities for the future.

It can be objected that religion deals not only with ultimate matters, but also with a host of others that do not seem ultimate, such as prayers for the success of a favorite football team. Tillich, however, meant that religion is concerned not only with our ultimate problems but also with everything in life as it relates to these problems. No matter how trivial some item of daily living may be, it has religious significance when viewed in the perspective of its relation to our primary goals in life, our personal identity (sometimes symbolized by our favorite sports team), our deepest personal relationships, our death. Thus Zen Buddhists teach that the one who has experienced *satori* (enlightenment) goes on living as usual, but now sees everything differently in relation to the ultimate mystery of the Void.

Therefore, in this book to make the notion of "ultimate concerns" more concrete and to make clear that it includes both cognitive and practical concerns I will define "religion" as a *world-view and value-*

system. By "world-view" I mean a conception and perception of reality as a whole, as the horizon of one's life. Each of us lives in a "world" of which we are a part and in which we have a particular location in place and time. We perceive the universe as made up of various entities acting and reacting on each other and on ourselves. For us this whole is ultimate (or appears so) although some religions consider it only phenomenal, requiring to be wiped away so that the really ultimate Whole behind it can be uncovered. By the principle of what semioticians call "the hermeneutic circle" a whole enters into the meaning of all its parts just as the parts enter into the meaning of the whole. Hence there can be no meaning in anything in our life except in relation to or at least against the background and within the horizon of the whole, the ultimate.

Our life, considered as a series of decisions and commitments, must also go on within a developing value-system in terms of which such decisions are made. This value-system for any agent or cooperating group of agents is also ultimate in the sense that it includes a whole scale of priorities and, for that agent or group, there is nothing of greater value. Anyone's world-view and value-system must be congruent, although they are not reducible to each other, just as the "ought" cannot simply be reduced to the "is," "values" to "facts," or "prescription" to "description." It is because we have a certain view of the totality of reality and of our own place in it that we can judge some things valuable, others undesirable.

Many religions believe that the human being is a *microcosm* that reflects the *macrocosm*. Certainly this is true in the broad sense that our world-view and value-system are summed up in the understanding of our own selves. Everything in the whole of reality has its meaning for me in relation to myself as part of that whole and I understand myself only in relation to that whole. Moreover, my life is part of the history of the whole and cannot be lived except through decisions made in view of the processes undergone by the whole. This is the *dynamic* aspect that I also intend to include in my functional definition. Religion thus is that aspect of human life by which it takes on an ultimate meaning through being perceived and freely lived in relation to the whole taken not only structurally but in its historical unfolding. What that Whole is, however, is precisely the question on which the different religions seem to disagree, which makes them substantively but not functionally diverse.

Yet, is it true that most people have any such totality of outlook or clear scale of values? Doesn't the ordinary person simply live from day to day, solving this or that problem as it arises, without any coherent view of life or general goal for his or her decisions? My reply to this objection would be that the commitment to some world-view and value-system is precisely the first of our "ultimate" concerns, the very point at which religion arises in human life. Our life *is* largely incoherent and unplanned, lived in the pressing confusion of the immediate and random. But this very fact raises for each of us enormous questions that, try as we will, we cannot avoid. *What does it all mean*? *Where am I going*?[30] Freud is supposed to have said that anyone who asks such questions should return to the psychoanalytic couch, but will he or she find the answers there? Or merely learn to suppress them for a time? We cannot live for long without at least some working answer to such urgent problems.

4. Functional Equivalents for Religion

I do not mean to imply by what has been said so far that those labeled "religionless" are living despairingly with no answers to these ultimate questions. No, my contention rather is that most of the "religionless" do in fact have a functional equivalent to religion. Even if they reject the label and claim to be religious, not religious, or anti-religious, they do have consistent world-views and value-systems that render for them those of the traditional religions irrelevant.

Thus I would maintain that the issue today is not to choose religion or no religion, but *which religion* (functionally defined) *to choose.* No one can escape this question because life without a world-view and value-system, either for the individual or for a community of cooperating individuals, is impossible except as a temporary transitional or chronically pathological state of personal disintegration.

In using the functional definition of religion for which I have argued, we must avoid, as Peter Berger has cautioned us,[31] any reductionist tendency to infer that therefore religion is nothing but an ideology useful for individual peace of mind and social propaganda. We must leave room for each religion to establish its own world-view and value-system. The functional definition of religion cannot of itself serve to limit the various meanings of religion, but only to identify what systems we are comparing with each other. Once we have adopted this functional definition as the basis for comparing the traditional religions, we will notice that it includes other world-views and value-systems not ordinarily labeled as religions. For example, Marxism has for many provided a world-view and value-system which, though explicitly anti-religious, nevertheless seems to have performed the function of religion for a number of societies and sub-societies and for the life projects of many well-integrated individuals.

In the *Humanist Manifesto* of 1933 a distinguished group of Humanists including the philosopher John Dewey argued convincingly that Humanism deserves the honorable title of religion, although the *Humanist Manifesto II* of 1973 repudiated that title.[32] Therefore, in order to avoid this paradox in this book I will usually speak of "philosophies of life." This term is broad enough to include both the traditional religions and also other world-views and value-systems considered not as abstract theories but as ways of life meeting the criteria of the sociologists' functional definition of "religion." In thus using the term "philosophy" I do not mean to restrict it to purely rational beliefs nor to exclude world-views and value-systems that claim to be purely scientific.

5. Choosing a Philosophy of Life

It seems, therefore, that everyone must choose or create a philosophy of life (but to create one requires genius) whether it be labeled a religion or not. Hence the 30% to 40% of our population who are "religionless" are not really so, but rather must have chosen some other philosophy of life than those offered by traditional religions. No doubt some of these persons have not definitively made their choice but are in a process of transition or confusion. Perhaps they will finally commit themselves again to the religion of their ancestors for which they still express a nominal preference, but more likely they are in the process of genuine conversion to a philosophy of life which appears to be a "secular" equivalent of that "old time religion."

Hence the choice which lies before every one of us and that is usually made in a personal way during adolescence or young adulthood is the commitment to a philosophy of life. This is either the religion of our parents or a replacement of that childhood religion by conversion to some other traditional religion (a relatively infrequent occurrence), or to a philosophy of life such as Humanism or even Satanism. The statistical reports already quoted show that today during adolescence or young adulthood (less commonly in middle age) a considerable percentage of Christians and Jews[33] give up the religion of their parents as no longer relevant. What have been less studied are the kinds of philosophy of life that they adopt to replace their childhood faith.

A peculiar feature of modern culture is the fact that a secular philosophy of life is often not named or expressed. Ask the average person who has abandoned traditional religion as irrelevant, "What philosophy of life *do* you find relevant?" and you are not likely to get an articulate response. In the following chapter I will attempt to articulate the philosophy of life which seems most common in the United States and which I myself in youth shared before my commitment to a kind of pantheism or atheism, then to Marxism, then to Roman Catholicism. Because it is the philosophy of life of many of the religionless of our country, especially of its influential elites, it seems the right place to begin for those faced here and now with the need to choose a philosophy of life or to clarify one already chosen.

In considering a philosophy of life, that is, a world-view and value-system, each of us must examine our own experience and the experiences of others that we have been able vicariously and imaginatively to share. This is so whether we reflect on the world-view and value-system to which we are already committed or one to which we might commit ourselves, or to which are committed those we love. I can enter into the philosophy of life of the Sioux or the Nur only to the degree that I can translate their perceptions and feelings into what I have perceived and felt and vice versa. In this hermeneutical effort I make explicit in my own experience many things that are already there but which I previously did not appreciate so clearly. Translation of one world-view into another is impossible unless we can identify some experience that is at least analogically common to both.

Therefore, in this book we are setting out on a search for the meaning of our lives by means of an exploration of the principal articulations that have been given to common human experience by the great religions and their secular equivalents and still have significant communities of followers today. Of course many today think that they can create their own philosophy of life and prefer not to be committed to any "organized religion." We are, however, social animals, and a world-view and scale of values that is purely idiosyncratic cannot function without being shared with at least some that are similarly committed. In fact when most people make up a purely personal religion it turns out to be an eclectic borrowing from various sources that gets such coherence as it may have from some dominate influence. Hence it seems most practical at least to first consider those philosophies of life that still function successfully for large human communities in our world today. The purpose of this exploration is to enable those who are in the process of choice to make their own choice and for those who have made a choice to deepen and enrich it.

6. Weighing the Options

My procedure in this book will be first to present the major options that someone seeking a world-view and value-system needs to consider today before making a choice. I will group these options into four chapters:

Chapter 2: Humanistic Philosophies of Life
Chapter 3: Mythological Religions
Chapter 4: Emanation Religions
Chapter 5: Creation Religions

Second, I will explore as follows how the truths found in each of these types of world-views and value-systems can be ecumenically unified in Jesus Christ.

Chapter 6: The Dialogue of Theism with Non-Theism
Chapter 7: The Ecumenical Church: Sign of God's Self-Communication
Chapter 8: Jesus Christ: God's Self-Communication in History
Chapter 9: The Historical Christian Community
Chapter 10: Cosmic Evil and Christian Hope

By a dialogue in Chapter 6 between Theism and Non-Theism I hope to show that Humanism should not deny that the Mythological Religions contain important truths that Humanism often neglects. I then hope to show that these two world-views and those of the non-theistic Emanation Religions tend to monotheism but lack an adequate conception of *creation* found in the Theistic religions. Then in Chapters 7, 8, and 9 I will go on to expound how among the theistic religions Judaism and Islam rightly show God's self-revelation in creation but to this Christianity adds God's more intimate self-revelation in Jesus Christ and his Community of Love. I will also ask how we can recognize the center with that Christian Church in which this revelation of God in Jesus Christ is so integrally maintained that it can draw all the other churches into unity. Then by its witness to Jesus it can become the global center in which all philosophies of life and religions can enter into dialogue in search of complete union in God's truth and love. In Chapter 10 I confirm this option for Catholic Christianity by showing that it does in fact give the best answer to the great problem for every religion and philosophy of life, the problem of evil and human suffering.

Notes

[1] Carnegie Foundation for the Advancement of Teaching (New York: McGraw Hill, 1975), p. 166.

[2] New York: Oxford University Press, 1985.

[3] Conducted by Research and Forecasts, Inc. and commissioned by Connecticut Mutual Life Insurance Co. (Hartford, CT, 1981), p. 186 ff.

[4] Edited by George H. Gallup (New York: Scholarly Resources, 1998), p. 44. Figures on church attendance, however, must be received with caution. Mark Chaves and James E.

Cavendish, "More Evidence on U.S. Catholic Church Attendance," *Journal for the Scientific Study of Religion*, 33 (4), 1994, pp. 376-391, say that self-reports almost double the rate of actual weekly church attendance, which for Catholics is probably about 26%.

[5] George Barna, *Index of Leading Spiritual Indicators* (Dallas: Word Publishing, 1996), pp. 3, 8, data cited from Stephen Carter, *The Culture of Disbelief* (New York: Basic Books, 1993), p. 41.

[6] Robin Gill, C. Kirk Hadaway, Penny Long Marler, "Is Religious Belief Declining in Britain?" *Journal for the Scientific Study of Religion,* 37 (3), 1998, pp. 507-515.

[7] Rodney Stark and Laurence R. Iannaccone, "A Supply-Side Reinterpretation of the 'Secularization of Europe'," *Journal for the Scientific Study of Religion,* 1994 (3): 230-252 and "Response to Lechner: Recent Religious Declines in Quebec, Poland, and the Netherlands: A Theory Vindicated," *ibid.* 1996, 38 (3), pp. 265-271.

[8] *Unchurched Americans,* a report of a study conducted by The Gallup Organization for a coalition of twenty-one Catholic and Protestant Church groups (The Paulist National Catholic Evangelization Association, Washington, DC, 1988). Also *Religion in America: The Gallup Opinion Index 1977-78* (The American Institute of Public Opinion, Princeton, NJ), p. 12 and *Religion in America: The Gallup March, 1984 Report No. 22* (The American Institute of Public Opinion: Princeton, NJ). For a fuller discussion see George D. Gallup, Jr. and David Poling, *The Search for America's Faith* (Nashville, Abingdon, 1980) and *The Search for Unchurched Americans* (The American Institute of Public Opinion: Princeton, NJ).

[9] William Dines, D.R. Hoge, Mary Johnson, J.L. Gonzales, Jr., "A Faith Loosely Held: The Institutional Allegiance of Young Catholics," *Commonweal,* July 17, 1998, pp. 13-18.

[10] Reported in Dean R. Hoge, "Catholic Generations Polarized on Gender and Sex," *America,* Nov. 12, 1998, pp. 16-18.

[11] For the distinction between modernization and secularization see Thomas G. Sanders, *Secular Consciousness and National Consciousness in Southern Europe,* A Report from the Center for Mediterranean Studies, Rome, Italy (Hanover, NH: American Universities Field Staff, 1977), pp. 10-19.

[12] See Larry Shiner, "The Meanings of Secularization" in James F. Chudress and David S. Harned, *Secularization and the Protestant Prospect* (Philadelphia: Westminster, 1970) and Peter E. Glasner, *The Sociology of Secularization: A Critique of the Concept* (London: Routledge, Kegan Paul, 1977).

[13] See Thomas J. Altizer, *The Gospel of Christian Atheism* (Philadelphia: Westminster Press, 1966).

[14] See André Dumas, *Dietrich Bonhoeffer Theologian of Reality* (London: SCM Press, 1959) for Bonhoeffer's notion of "religionless Christianity" and the various interpretations given it by those he influenced.

[15] Andrew M. Greeley, *Unsecular Man: The Persistence of Religion* (New York: Schocken Books, 1972); see also *Religion: A Secular Theology* (New York: Free Press, Macmillan, 1982) and the essays in *Unsecular America,* ed. by Richard J. Neuhaus (Grand Rapids, MI: Eerdmans, 1986). The *Connecticut Mutual Life Report* already cited comes to the same conclusion.

[16] See Rodney and Iannaccone, "A Supply-Side Reinterpretation," note 6 above.

[17] *The Invisible Religion* (New York: Macmillan, 1967).

[18] *Index of Leading Spiritual Indicators*, pp. 129-130.

[19] See Robert N. Bellah and Phillip E. Hammond, *Varieties of Civil Religion* (San Francisco: Harper and Row, 1981).

[20] For an analysis of the attack on "onto-theology" by Martin Heidegger, its deconstruction by Jacques Derrida, and the trend toward apophatic or negative theology see Kevin Hart, *The Trespass of the Sign: Deconstruction, theology, and philosophy* (New York: Cambridge University Press, 1989).

[21] See Rosalind and Christopher Brooke, *Popular Religion in the Middle Ages: Western Europe 1000-1300* (London: Thames and Hudson, 1984).

[22] See Robert D. Baird, *Category Formation and the History of Religions* (The Hague: Mouton, 1971). Some prefer a *dynamic* definition, i.e., one that recognizes that the ways a religion functions can undergo change, but this can easily be incorporated in a functional definition.

[23] There are of course scholars who attempt to find a common content to all religions such as Huston Smith, *Forgotten Truth, the Primordial Tradition* (New York: Crossroad, 1977).

[24] W. Richard Comstock et al., *Religion and Man: An Introduction* (New York: Harper and Row, 1971).

[25] See Geertz' famous article, "Religion as a Cultural System" in *Anthropological Approaches to the Study of Religion,* edited by Michael Banton (London: Tavistock, 1966), discussed by Keith A. Roberts, *Religion in Sociological Perspective* (Belmont, NY, 3rd edition 1995), pp. 3-26. Roberts concludes as follows: "Functional definitions identify religion as that which provides a sense of ultimate meaning, a system of macrosymbols, and a set of core values for life" (p. 25 f.).

[26] See Raymond Firth, *Symbols: Public and Private* (Ithaca, NY: Cornell University Press, 1973) for an extensive study of this problem with bibliography.

[27] This seems to me to be the mistake of Jacob Pandian, "The Sacred Integration of the Cultural Self: An Anthropological Approach to the Study of Religion" in Stephen D. Glazier, ed. *Anthropology of Religion: A Handbook* (Westport, CT, 1997), Chapter 19, pp. 505-516 and of most of the writers included in that book; they assume without serious discussion that religious symbols have truth value only as referring to self-integration.

[28] Translated by J.W. Harvey (2nd ed., New York: Oxford University Press, 1952).

[29] Paul Tillich, *Systematic Theology* (Chicago: University of Chicago Press), 1:8-15.

[30] Vatican II, *The Church in the Modern World* (*Gaudium et Spes,* 1965), n. 10, posed these questions to moderns as follows: "What is the human person? What is the meaning of suffering, evil, death, which have not been eliminated by all this progress? What is the purpose of these achievements purchased at so high a price? What can human beings contribute to society? What can they expect from it? What happens after this earthly life is ended?" John Paul II in the encyclical *Fides et Ratio* (1998) shows that these are the questions, summed up in the ancient Greek maxim "Know thyself!" that confront every philosopher as well as every theologian.

[31] Peter L. Berger, *The Sacred Canopy* (New York: Doubleday Anchor Books, 1969), p. 107.

[32] For *The Humanist Manifesto* (1933) and *Humanist Manifesto II* see *The Humanist* 33 (1), 1973, pp. 4-9 and 13-14 respectively. For further discussion see my *Theologies of the Body: Humanist and Christian,* 2nd edition with new Introduction (Boston: National Catholic Center for Bioethics, 1997), Chapter 3, pp. 51-100.

[33] Samuel C. Hellman in a letter to *The New York Review of Books* 45 (8), Nov. 19, 1998, p. 77 f. cites a 1996 study comparing American Jews to Israeli Jews. It showed that now only 52% of American Jews observe the Passover Seder compared to 81% of Israeli Jews, only 20% keep a kosher home compared to 46% of Israeli Jews who do, and only 54% compared to 80% of Israeli Jews consider Jewishness an important part of their self-identity.

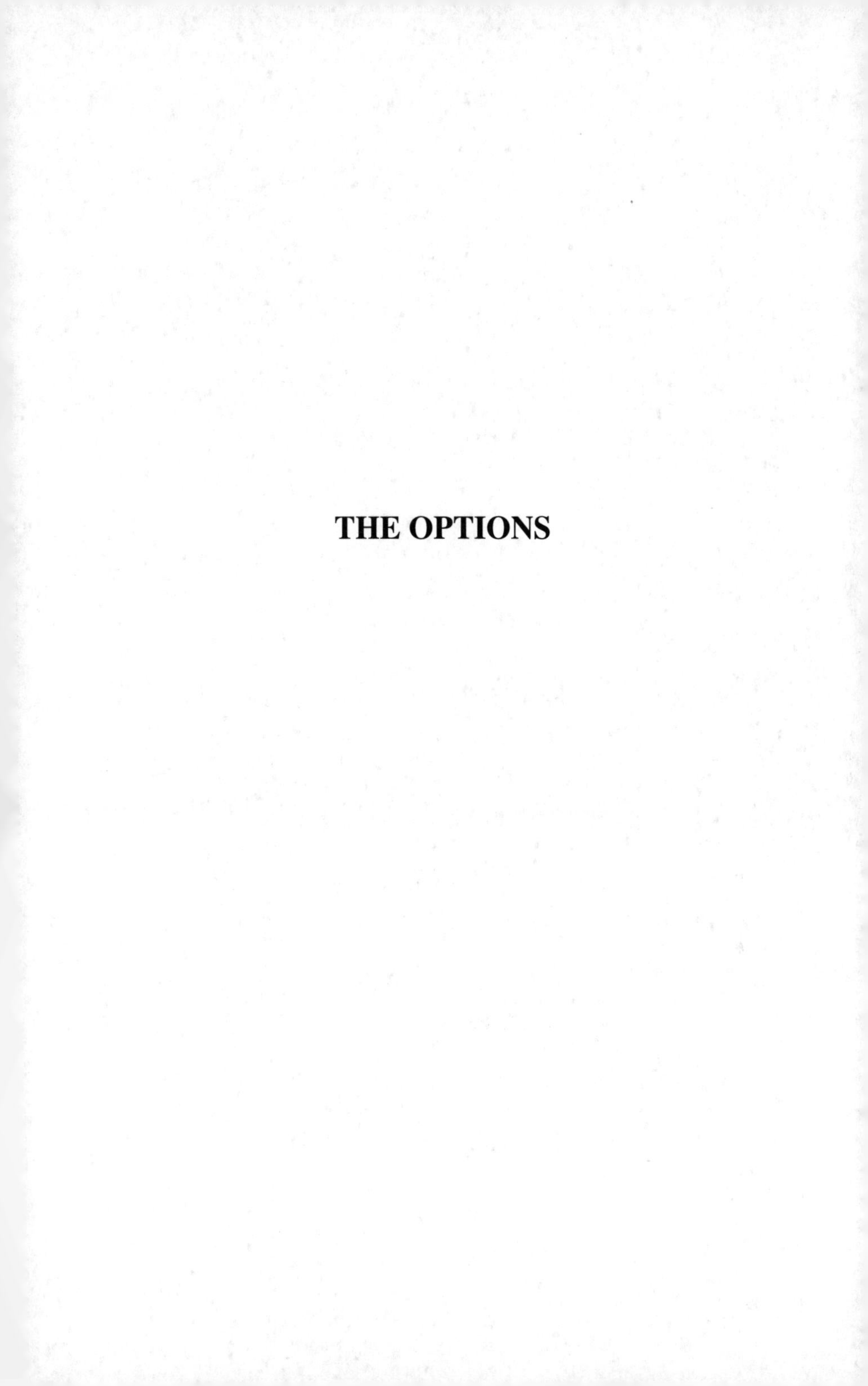

THE OPTIONS

CHAPTER 2

HUMANIST PHILOSOPHIES OF LIFE

1. Break Away from Christianity

As we begin to consider the options for a choice of a world-view and value-system, it seems best to start with the one that has a dominant position in the universities and public media in the United States and other technologically advanced countries, namely what I will call "Humanism." What are its historic origins? What are its basic ideas?

In its beginnings the Christian religion quickly spread to the whole Mediterranean world and east into Asia Minor and Persia, but in the seventh and following centuries lost much of its territory to the new rival religion of Islam. Europe, however, remained or became Christian, the northern Germanic and the eastern Slavic peoples being the last to be missionarized. Spain and Portugal, once liberated from Islam, spread Christianity throughout the Americas.

Thus, in spite of the division of Christians first into a Western and an Eastern church and then in the West into Catholics and Protestants, the civilization of Europe and its colonies remained identified with the Christian religion until about 1700. After that date a powerful new movement known as the Enlightenment gradually revealed itself as a philosophy of life, a world-view and value-system distinct from, equivalent to, and in rivalry with Christianity, just as Islam had become in the seventh century.

Islam arose at a time when the semi-nomadic Arabs were eager to enter into the cultural mainstream by replacing their tribal polytheism with some universal monotheistic religion. Yet the Christians, divided by the politico-theological quarrels that finally separated the Eastern and Western churches, neglected to missionarize these peoples who otherwise might have received the Gospel.[1] Similarly the Enlightenment breakaway from Christianity occurred because the intellectual elites of Europe were weary and disillusioned with the fratricidal religious wars between Catholics and Protestants that had concluded with the Treaty of Westphalia in 1648 after the disastrous Thirty Years War. Hence these elites saw in the seventeenth century rise of modern science a surer hope for a more rational and universalistic way of life than that offered by the Christian faith. This coincidence of disillusionment and new possibilities generated a new world-view and value-system.[2]

The Enlightenment, however, was neither the cause nor the inevitable effect of the rise of modern science and technology. Historians of the transition from medieval science based directly on ancient Greek science to the modern science of Copernicus, Galileo, Kepler, Newton, Boyle, Vesalius, and Harvey have demonstrated the continuity of scientific development first under Christian and then under Enlightenment patronage. The originators of modern science were committed Catholics or Protestants strongly motivated in their researches by their conviction that the scientific exploration of the universe would powerfully confirm the Christian world-view and value-system and that its application to technology would promote the Kingdom of God on earth.[3] Their discoveries did not shake the fundamental Christian convictions of the discoverers, nor end the patronage of the churches.

Nevertheless, as the Enlightenment came to place its own hopes in the power of scientific technology rather than in prayer to the Christian God, both Catholics and Protestants became increasingly suspicious of the new science and allowed it to be co-opted by this rival philosophy of life. Thus, when in 1859 Charles Darwin's theory of evolution by the natural selection of the fittest seemed to eliminate the need for a Creator, "The Warfare between Science and Religion"[4] seemed to many, both theologians and scientists, to demand unconditional surrender by one party or the other.[5]

The Enlightenment, unlike some philosophies of life, did not originate with a single great genius, a Buddha, Confucius, Jesus, Muhammad, or Marx, but like others (Hinduism, Gnosticism) was the work of a number of interacting sages. It originated in England and Scotland, spread to France where it was radicalized, and then to Germany, the rest of Europe, and the colonies. It taught that even if there is a Creator, once this Supreme Being has created the universe, it refrains from intervening in its creation and leaves it to operate according to its own autonomous mechanisms. Human creatures endowed by the Creator with reason have the freedom to conform to the natural moral law as this is known to them through natural instinct or discovered by rational reflection. Violation of this moral law brings its own sanctions by causing disorder in nature and society.

Out of this first phase of the Enlightenment arose the exciting dream of a utopian social order based not on tradition, nor on heavy-handed authority, but on a universal natural law. This natural law was supposed to be evident to all persons of good will. It protects the rights of all equally and — by democratic, or at least representative, republican government — safeguards against any reversion to tyranny.[6] This hope was in a measure realized at the end of the eighteenth century by the establishment of the United States of America and the more radical First Republic of France. Eventually it has led to the adoption of constitutional, democratic governments throughout the Western world.

Soon these new governments, often at the expense of violent party struggles and of cycles of reform and reaction, wrote into law the principle of the separation of church and state, establishing the toleration of all traditional religions. The leaders of the Enlightenment correctly foresaw that this reduction of the old religions to the private sphere and the institution of universal public education neutral to religion would tend to make their own "philosophy" the unifying principle of public life.

This new establishment was achieved only gradually during the nineteenth century and was slowed in mid-century by an apparent revival of Christianity. In England this revival took the form of the so-called "Victorian Compromise" and in the United States of enthusiastic evangelical movements and of a pseudo-Protestant civil religion. This revival, however, was unstable, and after the First World War it became increasingly clear that the Enlightenment had prevailed under the form of what is now called "secular humanism." Yet to avoid the bad odor this term has received from its use by some right wing extremists, I will refer to it simply as "Humanism," recognizing, however, that the term "humanism" is used for many other attitudes.[7] It seem obvious today that this secularizing Humanism has won dominant influence in Western society.

In the meantime, important internal developments within Humanism had occurred. Even in the eighteenth century some Humanists began to doubt that all aspects of human experience were amenable to scientific dissection. The mathematical, experimental, strictly objective Newtonian world-view was necessarily *value free*. The natural moral law cannot be deduced from the natural physical law, particularly when this physical law takes a purely mathematical, non-teleological form. To attempt such a deduction is to commit the "naturalistic fallacy" of inferring the "ought" from the "is," values from facts. How then can a value-system be developed exclusively on the basis of the scientific world-view? And without a value-system how could Humanism be an adequate philosophy able to supplant Christianity?[8]

It was chiefly Jean Jacques Rousseau (1712-1778) and Immanuel Kant (1724-1804) who provided Humanism with an effective answer to this dilemma.[9] Rousseau sought a foundation for an enlightened ethics in natural human instincts and sincere humane feelings, what one might call "common decency." When not distorted by the inhibitions imposed by artificial or tyrannical man-made customs and arbitrary laws, human intuitive feeling is the safest guide, free of dangerous fanaticism, by which to recognize authentic human values in personal life. In politics also the People in its instinctive wisdom and "general will," if allowed full expression through democratic, representative government, is the wisest legislator.

Kant greatly admired the ethical and political thought of Rousseau, but was aware that the subjectivism of Rousseau had dangers for the rational objectivism of Newton (1642-1727). Kant was deeply impressed by Newtonian science, and hence much troubled by the skepticism of David Hume. Hume (1711-1776) seemed to show that science is not, as Enlightenment thinkers had at first supposed, a purely objective mirror of nature revealing a chain of causes and effects governed by universal deterministic laws. He argued that in fact the "principle of causality" is nothing but an imposition of our human habits of thought on the flow of natural events whose real connections remain unknowable. All we actually observe in nature is one event following another.

Thus Kant saw his task to be the rescue of the Enlightenment scientific world-view and the romantic value-system from the deconstruction threatened by Rousseau's emotivism and Hume's skepticism. In the footsteps of Descartes (a Catholic Christian influenced by St. Augustine rather than an Enlightenment thinker) by way of Leibnitz (1646-1716) whose metaphysics dominated the German universities, Kant found a way out of his quandary by a "turn to the subject," i.e., by reducing all knowledge to self-knowledge. Yet along with this reliance on subjectivity, he also was anxious to do justice to the objectivity of Newtonian science. Hence, while Kant agreed with Hume that no human science, even psychology, can penetrate to the reality (*noumena*) of things, yet he maintained against Hume that the laws of nature are not mere projections of our habits of thought. Instead, these laws are certain and necessary because they reflect the structure of *all* human minds, not merely the prejudices of the individual formed in a particular culture.

The world, Kant argued, necessarily appears to all of us as Newtonian because we are all human. All scientists organize their data in space and time, not because they are sure that space and time are real properties of things, but because the very structure of our human senses order observed phenomena in these "schemas" or patterns. As for the relations of cause and effect and other universal principles of intelligibility these too result from the necessary structures or categories of our human intelligence. Yet the object in its reality outside our thought (*Ding an sich*) will always remain unknown to us. Hence Kant was led to advocate a "critical" *consistency* or coherence theory of truth (Truth is conformity of reality to the mind) in place of what he dismissed as the "naïve" classical *correspondence* theory (Truth is conformity of the mind to reality). This Kantian Revolution, more radical than the Copernican Revolution, was a direct consequence of the Cartesian Revolution that initiated modern philosophy.

It seems odd that this *idealism* of Kant could come to dominate Enlightenment thought that was so scornful of the traditional religions as trapped in "myths" while it prided itself on its hard-head realism. The appeal of Kant's revolution was that it seemed to promise a way to synthesize the value-free scientific world-view with the romantic construction of a value-system. The result of its wide acceptance in the universities, especially in the German universities that had the leadership in scientific advancement, was that the objectivity of science itself had to be interpreted in an idealist and therefore subjectivist fashion. Hence modern science has been deeply influenced, often unknowingly, by this Kantian idealism that emphasizes the constructive rather than the receptive work of the intelligence in trying to understand the world. This is especially evident since Einstein's relativity and the quantum theories have raised more and more problems for a realistic, physical interpretation of modern science's pragmatically successful mathematical models. Thus the "Copenhagen interpretation" of quantum physics was thought by Einstein to fall short of scientific realism.

Idealists after Kant, such as Schelling and Hegel, did not hesitate to overcome the Cartesian-Kantian dualism between thought and external reality by opting for a principally spiritual world-view to which they vainly hoped modern science could be assimilated. Kant, however, had been forced by his devotion to the empiricism of Newtonian science to limit human theoretical knowledge to the study of sensible phenomena. Thus he had to deny the possibility of a theoretical knowledge of God, of the spiritual human self, or even of the nature of material things other than their phenomenal aspects accessible to the senses. This raised a grave problem for him, since one of his chief concerns was to save morality without recourse to Christian revelation. His solution was to argue that, though we cannot theoretically prove the existence of a God who rewards and punishes human behavior, we can, for practical reasons, affirm his existence so that the moral order of society is maintained and a consistent world-view is sustained. Obviously such an exhortation to act "as if" there were a God, was not very satisfactory. Nevertheless it was widely adopted by the romantic wing of the Enlightenment as the basis of its subjectivist value-system, leaving to science the establishment of objective truth for a world-view limited to material reality.

Kant also hoped to replace the Christian notion of faith as a supernatural gift giving privileged access to a unique revelation concerning incomprehensible "mysteries" and its reliance on miracle working prayer, by a rational faith accessible to all and demanding of us humans responsibility for our own welfare. Kant therefore rejected petitionary prayer and all the *revealed* doctrines of Christianity. He did, however, approve worship of a wise Creator who cannot be bribed but leaves the laws of nature to take their course.[10] Applying the same method to dealing with esthetic values, Kant denied that nature as objectively studied by science exhibits any teleology or purposeful design. It appears to do so, he argued, because of the tendency of our minds to project such purpose into the works of nature just as we really embody them in works of human art. Beauty, meaning, relevance, value are not discovered objectively in the world but created by the human subject seeking to express feelings and desires. When these projections are in harmony with the structures of universal human reason and sensibility they deserve the approval of good taste, just as Rousseau claimed, but they remain only projections.

Subsequent criticism of Kant has led to a general abandonment of the view that the categories that according to him human thinking imposes on the data of experience are innate and universal rather than culturally determined or creatively assumed by individual choice. Likewise most Humanists today see no need to maintain even a pragmatic "as if" belief in God, since they think the moral order is sufficiently guaranteed by a social consensus based on agreement on human rights.

Within Christianity most philosophers, including Aquinas, have admitted that all world-views and value-systems have a subjective aspect. Aquinas was fond of the axiom, "A thing is received according to the mode of the recipient," and hence any human view of the world is limited by human subjective capacities for knowing. But he defended the view that our knowing powers are primarily receptive so that external reality itself impresses certain truths on the human knower that human knowers can distinguish from their mental limitations. The development of scientific, critical methodologies are designed for this very purpose. On the one hand, we all know in a common-sense way that there is a cycle of day and night. On the other hand, it required considerable scientific effort to be sure that this is so because the earth, not the sun, moves. With Descartes and above all with Kant this balance of subjectivity and objectivity was reversed to give priority in modern philosophy to the subjective. The result is an *idealism* in which what we primarily know is our own thoughts about a world that makes only a phenomenal impression on us whose meaning is so ambiguous that we must ourselves supply it. In a Humanist culture modern science has fallen under this pervasive Kantian influence. Though it confidently seeks to know objective reality and rightly prides itself on its successes, for fear it might be considered "dogmatic" it then hesitates and confusedly feels it must admit that all it really knows is its theories about the world, not the world itself.

Kant is the greatest thinker of the Enlightenment and of the Humanism that it produced, because while defending scientific truth, the Enlightenment's fundamental value, he was able to reconcile this with a deep practical concern for human values. Thus he provided a justification for *Romanticism*, the movement which at the end of the eighteenth century arose to form the counter-scientific pole of Humanism.[11] Romanticism, though more sympathetic to Christian culture as an historic achievement than Enlightenment scientism had been, was no more Christian. This fact is sometimes missed because some romantics had great enthusiasm for monasticism, chivalry, and Gothic architecture. Indeed some returned to the Church and some Christians were much influenced by this romantic sensibility. Nevertheless romantic interest in the Middle Ages was esthetic, not doctrinal. Typical romantics were more trusting in the new theories of science than in the old dogmas of orthodox Christianity. Thus fully developed Humanism as it appeared in the nineteenth century and prevails in our century is a Kantian synthesis of scientism and romanticism, of a world-view based on rigorously objective science and a value-system based on a subjective creation of values, meaning, and relevance. In this value-system the subjective happiness of the individual, protected by the social acknowledgment of human rights, is supreme.

Although Kant emphasized the universality of reason and natural law, his "turn to the subject" led romantics to a greater interest in the concrete events of history and the evolution of nature to which, somewhat later, Darwin was to give scientific form. The German idealists who were Kant's immediate successors, especially the great Hegel, struggled with this problem and developed philosophies of history in which they tried to demonstrate that history for all its concreteness is still a manifestation of reason, indeed its ultimate realization. For a time they fostered the myth of inevitable human progress which served, and still serves, as a replacement for Christian eschatology.[12] It also often goes under the name of "modernity."

The myth of progress blossomed politically in many utopian movements such as the Age of Aquarius collectives of our '60's youth culture.[13] Today toward the end of the twentieth century, Humanists, the heirs of the Enlightenment, are suffering from a disillusionment that is often called "post-modernity" that tends to the take the form of existentialism and ethical relativism. Each individual, without hope of any community consensus on values or even deeply suspicious of any apparent consensus must courageously create his or her own value-system by which to live in loneliness. The French philosopher Jacques Derrida has proclaimed that all human reason is circular since it always rests on assumptions (foundationalism), often hidden from honest examination, that are themselves the conclusions of what is claimed to be proved in their light. Hence the claim of the Enlightenment that reason can hope at least in principle to master the totality of reality is inherently unrealizable.[14]

Nevertheless, this dark mood does not necessarily signal the decline of Humanism. Rather it is probably a sign that Humanism has now reached maturity and like other great philosophies of life is finally able to acknowledge that it is not in exclusive possession of the truth. It need no longer assume as self-evident that it is the wave of the future, but can be open to dialogue with other philosophies of life, even the ancient religions.

2. The Humanist World-View and Value-System

The foregoing brief survey of the origin and maturation of Humanism as a philosophy of life has already indicated some of its features, but they must now be described in more systematic detail. How can Humanism really be considered as a single, unified philosophy of life comparable to Christianity with its hierarchical church, dogmatic creed, and uniform liturgy and moral code? Isn't the religionless sector of our society characterized precisely by its complete pluralism, freedom of thought and conscience, and by its rejection of any kind of ideological institution claiming authority over minds or wills? Who ever better expressed the faith of Humanism than Thomas Jefferson in the famous vow inscribed in his white marble shrine in Washington, "I have sworn upon the altar of God eternal hostility to every form of tyranny over the mind of man"?[15]

Of course it is true that the Enlightenment and the Humanism into which it consolidated were in vigorous reaction to the authoritarianism and doctrinal monopoly claimed by the Catholic Church but already undermined by the Reformers' demand for freedom of conscience. This fact, however, does not imply that Humanism itself is not unified by a set of theoretical and practical principles which operate as basic assumptions shared widely by Humanists who at the same time feel free to differ on many of their applications. A wide spectrum of opinions is also to be found within Christianity, Judaism, Islam, and Buddhism, yet each world-view has a basic unity.

The fundamental principle which grounds Humanism's sincere commitment to freedom of thought and respect for pluralism and which gives it the unity by which it can be named and sharply marked off from Christianity, is that *Humanism puts its faith not in God but in the human potential.* The human potential is what we can make of ourselves and our environment by the creative and cooperative use of our unaided human intelligence, imagination, will and other powers.

A Humanist is not necessarily an atheist, although from the beginning of the Enlightenment some leading Humanists such as Denis Diderot and the Baron d'Holbach explicitly denied the existence of a God. Most early Humanists, however, were deists.[16] After Kant's widely accepted deconstruction of the traditional objective arguments for God's existence, many Humanists became agnostics. There is no reason that even today a Humanist may not choose to believe in the God common to all the theistic religions, as did Franklin and Jefferson.[17]

The essential point for mature Humanism is that opinions about

God are regarded as purely personal and private, not as the necessary foundation of the rest of the system. Instead, the necessary foundation is the conviction that Humanity must solve its own problems by its own powers. Yet Humanists may still find value in prayer as a process of relaxation, psychological integration or even as esthetic expression of awe and reverence before the mystery of the cosmos.

Since Humanists put their faith not in God but in the human potential, we must ask how they conceive this potential. They are naturalists who believe that the human race is the product of a purely natural evolutionary process. Yet they do not deny that we are unique among animals in our power to gain technological control over the forces of nature and to reconstruct it, even to reconstruct our own bodies and minds.

Most Humanists today would hold that this human mind is nothing more than the functioning of our marvelously complex human brain (the "mind-body identity theory"). Deistic and idealistic Humanists, however, may still accept the notion of a human spirit of a somehow different order than the body. They may favor theories of psychophysical parallelism, panpsychism, or even reincarnation. Yet Humanists are generally agnostic about life after death and stoically ready to face death with serene courage. What is essential to Humanist anthropology is that all such questions be left open to private opinion, so that humankind may be chiefly concerned about *this* life on earth and responsibility for it.

This naturalistic anthropology need not reduce human life to materialistic determinism. Of course there are serious philosophical problems about how to reconcile the notion of human freedom with the determinism of the natural laws of physics, and how to relate nature and culture without falling into the "naturalistic fallacy" of trying to deduce values from facts. Generally Humanists accept a solution of the Kantian type according to which freedom is essentially a subjective experience of natural processes which for science are objectively law-determined. Nevertheless, Humanists are convinced that our power of reason over nature makes it possible for us to be truly creative, free to master and remake nature which they commonly regard as indifferent to human concerns.

Consequently, for Humanists human nature is not static but almost indefinitely plastic, so there really are no limits to its possible modification by history and culture. Jean-Paul Sartre's claim that "man has no nature, only a history" is a radical formulation of this Humanist conviction. Therefore, Humanists generally reject the label "materialists" if this implies they must deny that humans are truly spiritual, that is, intelligent and free.

We have seen that Humanists accept the "turn to the subject" by which Descartes initiated modern thought and by which Kant systematically made room for the romantic, counter-scientistic, aspect of Humanism. Hence they believe that thought must be "critical" in the sense that nothing is to be taken as dogma but must rest on the immediate experience of the free, autonomous subject. We have the duty "to think for ourselves." Hence ultimately no authority is to be trusted except our own reason, conscience, and intuitive feelings. In the field of public discourse, however, the only valid and relevant knowledge is that provided by the objective, empirical, experimentally tested methods of modern science.

In questions of value, on the other hand, subjective freedom is supreme. Hence consensus can only be obtained by effective communication, empathy, and persuasion. Ultimately a value can be tested and weighed only by personal esthetic experience. Above all it is in the fine arts that the power to create new values and to communicate them to others expressively is most perfectly achieved. Thus experiences sought by the religious through prayer and mystical contemplation are chiefly enjoyed by Humanists through the fine arts, including the erotic arts, and its artists and poets and passionate lovers are the best guides to the spiritual. For many Humanists the concert hall or the art museum are temples for the spiritual experiences they try to carry over into the quality of their daily lives.

Kant's emphasis on human subjectivity led to German Idealism, congenial to the Romantic aspects of Humanism. The most influential thinker of this school was George W.F. Hegel (1770-1831) who converted metaphysics into a philosophy of history. With this new romantic emphasis on human historicity Humanism largely abandoned Kant's absolute, universal, and formal ethical norms in favor of a developmental, cultural view of its value-system and more and more resigned itself to ethical relativism and pragmatism. Ethical right and wrong were seen to depend on the standards of a particular time and culture. Hence they are to be judged in terms of their consequences for that unique culture. The only ethical absolutes are the obligations to protect the creative freedom of individuals and the pursuit of objective scientific truth.[18]

3. The Capitalist and Socialist Versions of Humanism

No world-view and value-system can be understood without examining its inner tensions and the sects that these tend to generate within its overall unity. Christianity arose as a sect within Judaism; Islam as a sect within the broader Judeo-Christian tradition. It is not strange, therefore, that Humanism in spite of its general unifying features has developed inner tensions and a variety of sectarian forms. Nor is it odd, since it puts its faith in the power of human reason to control the material world by science and technology, that the inner tensions in its value-system should center on economics.

In politics Humanism favors representative democracy, but is pragmatically willing to accept even benevolent dictatorship if this is a step toward democracy. In economics the Enlightenment generally adopted the defense of private property by John Locke (1632-1704). An even more systematic defense of Capitalism and its regulation of the economy by the free market was provided by Adam Smith in his *The Wealth of Nations* (1776). Smith argued that the free-market of supply and demand favored individual freedom, creativity, initiative, productivity, and efficiency. His idea that economies operate mechanically according to laws that can be mathematically expressed has always been congenial to the objective, scientistic aspect of Humanism. Thus Capitalism largely eliminates the problem of constructing a Humanist value-system. Competitors in the market are supposed to make coldly objective, rational estimations of their subjective needs whose moral basis in individual conscience can be neglected, since the averaging-out of the free-market mechanism inevitably produces the most just possible balancing of needs and the products available to supply these needs. The producer can always excuse himself by saying that he "only makes what the public wants," while the public can excuse itself by saying that, as Rousseau had argued, the "general will" cannot be wrong since it represents the instinctive judgment of the average man.

In the nineteenth century, however, with industrialization and urbanization class conflicts between rich and poor increased so grossly that they gave rise to many proposals, generally called "Socialism," for economic and social reforms that would emphasize economic cooperation rather than competition. Many of these proposals were "utopian," and gave rise to experimental communities that soon failed.[19] A more politically effective form of socialism was developed by Karl Marx (1818-1883), a son of a German Jewish family turned Christian, but who was never seriously either a religious Jew or Christian. He came to believe that the American and French Revolutions had been co-opted by the bourgeoisie and thus prevented from running their full course to the formation of the egalitarian, classless society at which they supposedly had aimed. In place of the failed utopian forms of socialism he proposed what he claimed was a "scientific socialism" based on Hegel's "laws of history." For Hegel history was an inevitable unfolding of the World Spirit by a dialectical process of thesis, antithesis, and synthesis.

Marx "turned Hegel on his head" by interpreting this historical dialectic as a development of a purely material but dynamic world. For human history this had to take the form of a dialectic of economic production and control. Marx believed that Capitalism (thesis) contained within itself an internal contradiction in the form of Socialism (antithesis). This struggle would eventually reach a crisis point or revolution in which Socialism would conquer and form a temporary "dictatorship of the proletariat" (working class rule) which would soon construct the classless society of Communism (synthesis) in which all productive property would be held in common. Under Communism the oppressive state would "wither away" and society would become a perfect democracy, or rather an anarchistic community in which all authority and obedience would be rendered unnecessary because all citizens would be educated to cooperate in peaceful economic productivity. Then every human being would have perfect autonomy and freedom and the efforts of the communistic community would no longer be exhausted in competition and war but would be united to achieve a total technological control of nature in the interest of human desires. At last "man would create himself."

Thus Marx believed that the humanistic goal of the Enlightenment, only partially attained by Capitalism, namely, to provide a religion of Man rather than of God, would be at last realized. He argued that the internal contradiction of liberal democratic Capitalism (thesis) was to produce the socialist political parties (antithesis) that could overthrow it. Capitalism would self-destruct by reason of its great invention the factory system that inevitably educated the working class to act cooperatively in the use of complex modern technology. When the workers at last became conscious that they could run the economy without the exploiting capitalist class, they would organize politically to vote in socialism non-violently and retire the capitalists.

Yet Marx also foresaw that this peaceful process would probably result in efforts by the obsolescent capitalists to suppress change by military force so that the socialists would have to defend themselves and the revolution would become violent until this capitalist counter-revolution was overcome. Marxist socialism in various forms, some more extreme, others more moderate, played an increasing role in European countries up to World War I. At the end of the war it surprisingly triumphed in Russia, a country that was still technologically backward. The more advanced capitalist countries resisted this revolution, but throughout the twentieth century found it necessary to adopt various forms of the "welfare state" in which the central government closely regulated private business and thus mitigated many of the social ills produced by previous total reliance on the free-market. Because up to World War I, Germany had the lead in technological advancement in Europe, Marx had expected the socialist revolution to take place there first. In fact, however, Germany was disastrously defeated in the savage struggle between competing capitalist nations in Europe in World War I and its post-war democratic Weimar Republic, although it resisted the example of Russia and did not go communist, proved incompetent to restore national unity.

The result was the rise of National Socialism (the Nazis) in Germany paralleled by Fascism in Italy, and later in Spain and Portugal. As against Marxism, which always claimed to be an advocate of the international working class, National Socialism and Fascism advocated an aggressive unifying nationalism. It borrowed many of the totalitarian features of Marxism, while retaining a capitalist economy geared to support a powerful army. The Christian churches were tolerated only as a support to a unified nation. From the Romantic tradition National Socialism borrowed an emphasis on the "spirit of the Folk" and "purity of blood" and supported this racism by pseudo-Darwinian theories. Thus "alien" elements in the population, especially the Jews (though the majority of German Jews were highly assimilated to secular humanism) became the scapegoats for a fanatical nationalism that climaxed in massive genocide in the Holocaust.

The oppressive totalitarianism of Communism in Russia under Lenin and Stalin and of Nazism/Fascism under Hitler and Mussolini seem the very antithesis of the Enlightenment, but in fact they grew out of the Enlightenment and represent extreme paradoxical strategies to achieve the Enlightenment's goals. Marxist Communism hoped by its obedience to the laws of history to achieve a society in which technological progress would at last abolish all poverty and oppression and achieve the absolute autonomous freedom of individuals in a cooperative society. The Nazis dreamed of achieving the Romantic ideal of a united people whose empire would combine the rich traditions of folk culture and the high culture of Aryan Greeks, while the Italian Fascists dreamed of a revival of the splendor of the Romans. Notably in both systems it was considered imperative that the family and religion should not be permitted to interfere with social progress. The Marxists attacked the family as a source of resistant traditionalism and the Nazis saw it as merely a procreative machine. For both, as for more moderate Humanism, Christianity, and especially its concept of the family as the basis of society, was an obstacle to their social schemes. This reflected the Enlightenment attempt to control population technologically and to replace the family by state operated public education. Both movements attempted to convert God-centered religion to the worship of leaders like Hitler and Stalin by elaborate propaganda manipulation.

The struggle between the democratic, communist, and nationalist forms of the Religion of Humanity with its scientistic and romantic tendencies came to a climax in World War II that eliminated the Nazis and Fascists and in the Cold War that eliminated Communism. Today even in China, though it remains politically Communist, a reaction has set in that favors the capitalist version of Humanism, but a capitalism moderated by various forms of welfare to prevent the return to extremist movements.

An important feature of Humanism in all its forms is that it places its faith in a future of technological control over nature and human society. Ernst Bloch, himself a Marxist, has shown that Marxist eschatology was a secularization of the Jewish and Christian faith in the coming Kingdom of God.[20] Certainly the Marxist movement has a remarkable Messianism that inspires hope in the poor and in marginalized intellectuals. This eschatology now exercises important influence on Christian "liberation theology."[21] The Nazis dreamt of "the thousand year Reich" and democratic capitalist countries seem confident of a future of golden "globalization." Humanism in all its forms has promised a society that frees individuals to live their own lives while gladly cooperating in necessary social tasks. Citizens are supposed to be willing to sacrifice individual freedom for the sake of "progress" or "generations yet to come."

Nevertheless, as the twentieth century ends, this Humanist hope seems to falter. To many its seems that the ideals of the Enlightenment, like those of Christianity, have not so much failed, as never have been really put into practice. Humanism is based on trust in scientific technology, but is now terrified by the prospect of nuclear war and deeply troubled by the evidence of the devastation wrought by this technology on the environment. Moreover, its value system was supposed to be romantically constructed as a creative sharing of values by common consent, while in fact it seems to be crumbling into a pluralism that renders genuine communication and sharing extremely difficult. This post-modern disillusion with Enlightenment principles is evident in two of the most influential philosophers of the last half of this century. Martin Heidegger, sympathetic to Nazism, proclaimed the end of Western culture and its technological way of thinking. Now Jacques Derrida's "deconstructionism" seems to expose all rational thought as no more than disguised propaganda in the service of hidden self-interest. Post-modernism, however, probably does not mean the end of Humanism, which remains the dominant philosophy of life at the beginning of the twenty-first century. The elimination of its more extreme sects has led to more moderate and realistic expectations. Historically all the world religions have experienced such crises of faith and self-doubt and have often emerged the stronger.

4. Are Modern Humanisms Unique?

In contrast to the traditional religions, Humanism in all its versions is characterized by *modernism*. Traditional religion often glories in its antiquity, while the Humanistic philosophies of life, as I have indicated, seem to assume that some evolutionary law makes it probable or even guarantees that the most "modern" world-view must be the truest. Yet, as a number of important Enlightenment thinkers recognized, there is an interesting parallel between the Humanism of the West in the last three centuries and another ancient world philosophy of life, namely Confucianism, the paramount religion of China until this century.[22] It is important to look at this historic parallel in order see both the strengths and weaknesses of a humanistic type of religion, very different than modern Humanism yet sharing some of its features and suggestive of its possible developments. This is especially interesting because the most likely competition today to the dominance of Western Humanism is the Marxist Humanism of China.

The Jesuits who entered China in the sixteenth century were astonished to find a very old culture built on high moral ideals comparable to those of Christianity yet which was governed by sophisticated literati who philosophically were secular humanists, even atheists. The great Jesuit missionary and scholar Matteo Ricci (d. 1610) after careful study and discussions with leading Confucian scholars came to the conclusion that in spite of its elaborate rituals Confucianism was not a religion in the Christian sense, but a purely rational ethical system. The Dominican, Franciscan, and other Catholic missionaries more in contact with popular Confucianism disagreed. In 1742 the reigning pope finally rejected the Jesuit view with the result that the Chinese Emperor, who had supported Ricci's interpretation, indignantly instituted a persecution of the Catholic Church.[23]

In the meantime, Ricci's view has been adopted by such important Enlightenment philosophers as Leibnitz, Christian Wolff, Lessing, and the chief missionary of Humanism, Voltaire, who all saw in Confucianism a proof that a high natural morality can be maintained without the support of revelation. As a deist, Voltaire regarded revealed religion as sheer obscurantism fostering antihuman fanaticism. Thus, quite unintentionally, in their efforts at what today is generally favored as "missionary accommodation," the Jesuits made an important contribution to the development of Humanism.

The founder of Confucianism, Kung Fu Tze (d. 479 BCE) was one of those great religious reformers who appeared in many different cultures during the so-called "Axial Period" centering on 500 BCE.[24] China had already developed its own unique culture under the Shang (c. 1500 BCE) and Chou dynasties, which I will discuss in the next chapter. By Confucius' time, however, the Chou was sinking into a disorderly feudalism, although it lingered on until 221 BCE. A nobleman, scholar, and minister to the Duke of Lu, Confucius attempted to reform his people by reviving what he believed to be the high standards of the dynasty's first years. When the Duke rejected his teaching, he traveled about China seeking a more receptive patron.

Like Plato in Greece, Confucius failed to find a docile ruler who would carry out his ideas. Nevertheless he gathered many lesser disciples who recorded his teachings in the *Analects*, to which was later added *The Great Learning* and *The Doctrine of the Mean*. These works, along with the *Five Classics* (two of history, others of poetry, ceremonies, and divination) of ancient origin but re-edited under Confucian influences, constituted this religion's basic scriptures. To these were added also works of Mencius (d. 289 BCE) and Hsun Tzu (d. 238 BCE) as standard (but polarizing) commentaries.

The influence of Confucian ideas gradually increased until under the Han dynasty in 140 BCE they were made the basis of education and of promotion in the imperial bureaucracy. In 59 BCE Confucius was officially venerated in the rituals as the greatest teacher of China. Although with the decline of the Han in 200 CE Confucianism was somewhat eclipsed by Buddhism, after 700 it revived and remained the dominant religion of China until the Empire was overthrown in 1912, assimilating all other cults into its own. Then democratic Humanism on the Western model took over, only to be replaced in turn by the present Republic governed at first on radically Marxist principles and recently by a revisionist Marxism. How much of Confucian tradition survives in China today is not clear, but some Sinologists predict that Chinese Marxism will eventually be assimilated to some renewed form of Confucianism.

How can Confucianism be compared to Western Humanism? The pre-Confucian religion of China during the Shang dynasty was based on the worship of a Supreme Being called Shang Ti (Lord on High) but more impersonally called T'ien (Heaven) under the Chou. Yet Confucius himself undoubtedly understood T'ien to be a personal God. He believed that his own teaching was authorized by a "Mandate of T'ien," although he did not claim that he had learned this by revelation but simply from his reflection on ancient traditions. Hence, the Enlightenment Humanists were not entirely mistaken in supposing that the Confucian Heaven was much like their own deistic God. Confucius never discussed the nature of God or implied any intervention on its part except to maintain the perennial order of nature and the corresponding social order. Similarly, although Confucius never questioned the reality of natural or ancestral spirits or the value of their traditional cult, yet his teaching contains nothing on the mode of existence of the spirits or their activities. Although popular religion turned on seeking the aid of spirits for earthly welfare, the elite scorned such "superstitions." Thus the Eastern Han scholar Wang Fu wrote,[25] "Concerning one's happiness or misfortune, it mainly depends on his conduct, but eventually is decided by fate. Behavior is the manifestation of one's own character, fate is what heaven controls. One can certainly improve on what lies in himself, he cannot know what lies in heaven."

Confucianism, therefore, just as Ricci and Voltaire maintained, seems largely silent about anything transcending human concerns for this life and is essentially a mundane ethical system. Confucius' ethical system is based on the profound conviction that harmony in human social life can be achieved only through harmony with the natural cosmic order. He does not seem to have attained, however, the notion of a scientific-technological control over the natural order so central to the Enlightenment world-view. His two major disciples Mencius and Hsun Tzu disagreed on whether human nature as such is inherently good (Mencius) or bad (Hsun Tzu), but agreed with the principal teaching of their master that human perfection can only be achieved by careful education and discipline.

The ideal educated man (Chun Tzu), who alone is fit to educate others, is characterized by the virtue of *jen* (*humaneness*) a quality difficult to define and acquired only in a lifetime of self-discipline. *Jen* manifests itself on the one hand in a perfect balance of character according to the "Mean," and on the other by a selfless devotion to the common good and a merciful attitude toward human frailty. Its maxim is the negative Golden Rule: "Don't do to others, what you don't want done to you." *Jen* is supported by other virtues: loyalty to duty, altruism, study, courtesy, sincerity, and respect for parents and superiors. This lofty, humanistic ideal did not go uncriticized in China.[26] On the one hand the Legalists (such as Han Fei Tzu, d. 233 BCE) argued that it is unrealistic to believe society can be maintained by education, since most human beings are uneducable. Therefore, social order must be maintained by laws that are physically enforced. On the other hand, the Mohists (Mo Tzu, d. c. 376) argued that Confucius' system of education so stressed elaborate manners and ceremonies that it crushed all human spontaneity. Against Confucius' careful gradation of duties, the Mohists preached a universal and equal love for all human beings. They argued for a kind of natural, instinctive morality like that which Rousseau was to propose. Confucius is reported to have opposed such views when he said, "It is man that can make the Way (T'ao) great, and not the Way that can make man great" (*Analects* XV, 28). Hsun Tzu particularly insisted against Mencius that human perfection is not simply going the way of nature but controlling and overcoming its disorder.

Somewhat similar to Mohism's opposition to Confucianism was that of Taoism attributed to the legendary Lao Tzu and to Yang Chu (d. c. 366 BCE). Taoism's chief classics are the *Tao Te Ching* and the works of Chuang Tzu (d. 286 BCE). They combine the worship of nature spirits with magic, the alchemical search for the elixir of perpetual youth, and a philosophical system of ethics and mysticism. In its popular forms Taoism remains widespread in China. As a highly organized, hierarchical religion of a messianic type it flourished during the decline of Confucianism and then was largely absorbed into Neo-Confucianism, although it was still perpetuated by secret societies. At its height it stood in polar opposition to official socially oriented, activist, and rationalist Confucianism by its pronounced individualism, quietism, and mysticism. Philosophical Taoists taught that the state should allow affairs to take their natural course, while the individual should seek to live in harmony with nature, becoming one with it by an inward contemplative life withdrawn from the distraction of public life. We seem to have here much the same reaction to Confucianism as that of the Romantic to the Scientistic poles of Humanism.

The native opposition to Confucianism was powerfully reinforced by the introduction of missionary Buddhism, chiefly in the Mahayana form, into China about the time Christianity began to spread through the Roman Empire. Buddhism in its otherworldliness seemed a direct negation of Confucian Humanism, and, while its influence on Chinese culture was profound, it was also profoundly modified by that culture. Popular Buddhism in China has chiefly followed the teachings of the Pure Land School. This sect puts its hopes in the grace of the Amida Buddha who brings his devotees to dwell with him in the Pure Land paradise where they enjoy a continuation of life much like that of earth except free of suffering. Great trust is also placed in the help of Kuan Yin, the mother goddess of mercy and fertility (a Chinese transformation of the Indian male Buddha Avalokitesvara). At a more speculative level, however, Buddhism confronted the practical-minded Confucian scholars with cosmological and metaphysical questions that they could no longer ignore. Formerly in China such questions had been the concern only of the native Yin-Yang School of philosophy. This school attempted to explain the universe and human relations somewhat as had the Greek Pre-Socratic philosophers and Indian Samkhya School in terms of a dualism of male or active principles (*yang*) and female or passive principles (*yin*).

As a result of these encounters, official Confucianism, when it revived in the Sung dynasty (after 960 CE) as Neo-Confucianism, found it necessary to assimilate to its original almost purely ethical system a well-developed world-view. Thus it incorporated much of what it had learned from its Mohist, Yin-Yang, Taoist, and Buddhist critics. According to the historian Wingtsit Chan,[27] this development can be divided into the School of Principles (960-1279 CE) resembling the system of Plato, the School of Mind (1368-1644) favoring subjective idealism, and the Empirical School (1644-1911) which called for a return to original Confucianism, understood, however as a monistic materialism. Neo-Confucianism, while tolerating popular veneration of spirits and ancestors, was essentially atheistic and naturalistic in its world-view, while remaining a Humanism in its fundamental ethical attitudes.

In this century Western Humanism, as exemplified by John Dewey, the chief author of the *Humanist Manifesto*, entered China. So did Marxism, first in its socialist form with the revolution of 1912 and then as Communism in 1949. These modern forms of Humanism found among the literate elite much in common with native Humanism in its Confucian form. Nevertheless, there is a profound difference between Chinese humanism and Western Humanism. Confucian scholarship was rationalistic and had fostered a culture which up to about 1650 was technologically more advanced than the West. Yet, though it had developed a genuine spirit of historical criticism, it always remained, like Western medieval and Renaissance learning, a study of classical texts rather than an exploration of natural phenomena for the sake of technological control.

5. Questions about Humanistic Philosophies of Life

After this description of Humanism one might still ask how is it that Humanists, if they have so much in common, are today so inclined to reject all organized religions and to seek some purely individualistic, private world-view and value-system. Certainly recent studies of current American "spirituality" all emphasize this extreme individualism that is reflected in the Protestant "mega-churches" where even attendance at Christian worship resembles the search for a well-advertised movie. It is even more evident in the amorphous New Age Movement and in the flourishing of occult sects that seem subject to the vagaries of the free market like brands of cereal or detergent.[28] Yet this paradox is easily resolved. What makes Humanism a coherent system is that although it has not perfectly reconciled its scientistic and its romantic wings — what world religion does not exhibit similar polarization? — these two wings are complementary and thus help it fly. Humanism's reliance on the objective truth of science and technology unites it as a single world-view. Even New Agers appeal to science (or pseudo-science) to support their views. On the other hand Humanism's romantic reduction of values to subjectivity and its emphasis on the autonomy of the individual in such matters, opens the way to an extreme individualism as regards a personal spirituality. Thus in Humanist culture there is a remarkable uniformity in world-view and just as remarkable a diversity in freely chosen values, provided, of course, that the pursuit and advocacy of these values does not limit the free choice of other autonomous individuals.

Therefore in our Humanist culture the problem for the individual of choosing a world-view and value-system still remains urgent. In making this choice, moreover, one discovers that no individual can simply believe what he or she pleases without also seeking others who have made similar choices. I cannot really get through life simply "Doing my own thing." We absolutely need others who agree with us, approve us, live like us; and so we need to evangelize others to our way of thinking. That great preacher of "Self-reliance," Ralph Waldo Emerson, spent his life urging others to be like himself and to recognize him as their leader and guide to a self-reliant life that could be publicly defended.

What reasons, then, might there be to choose the Humanist world-view and value-system for one's own and in doing so choose the community in which one finds necessary support? The first reason obviously is that this, in one form or another, is the philosophy of life that dominates our modern world. One has the witness of many among our elites who have found this to be the most reasonable choice. Many of our contemporaries were born and educated as humanists and have never found what seems to them a sufficient reason to change. They are well-informed about the discoveries of science and the lessons of modern history and see no alternative that seems to accord with modern knowledge of the world and human needs. Moreover, as I have earlier argued, we are social beings and our philosophy of life cannot be a merely individual view. It must be something that can be the basis of our life with others. To share the perspectives of the majority we live with is extremely helpful in living out our life in a full and harmonious way. The life of those of a minority religion who are in a defensive posture is never very comfortable. Furthermore it is a special characteristic of Humanism that it permits a great range of life-styles and personal opinions within its general consensus, since its great value is "freedom" understood as freedom from any outside coercion that might limit individual choice in all matters that do not directly infringe on the same kind of freedom for others.

Thus the modern emphasis on human rights and freedom of conscience is largely an achievement of Humanism. To the moderate Humanist, as distinguished from Communist and Nazi extremists, it appears intolerable that the subjective freedom of self-determination in life and of personal self-fulfillment should be sacrificed to the interests of the collectivity either of church or state. Consequently, the government and "organized religion" must be restrained from intruding on personal privacy in such matters as sexual conduct between consenting adults or freedom of thought. Even in the public sphere there must be no interference with the free communication of ideas and attitudes except when these ideas and attitudes advocate some absolute standard of thought or conduct which might restrict the expression of other views. The government ought also to promote this freedom actively by public and compulsory education so that all its citizens may come to share this capacity for mutual tolerance and social cooperation. Other philosophies of life than that of the dominant Humanism are thus reduced to the private sphere. To do this it is necessary to deny that Humanism functions as a "religion" as do other world-views and value-systems.

We have seen that everywhere such moderate Humanism flourishes there is a certain polarization not only between scientism and romanticism, but also between attitudes commonly labeled "right" and "left" or "conservative" and "liberal." This last pair of terms, however, has different meanings in different countries. In Europe "conservative" usually signified sympathy for the old aristocratic culture with its close alliance of church and state, while "liberal" connoted a sympathy with middle class aspirations, capitalism, and anticlericalism. By these standards all American Humanists are liberals.[29]

Our conservatives are strong advocates of capitalism and nationalism, and our liberals, although more favorable to socialism and internationalism, prefer the freedom of capitalism to any tightly regulated socialism and are anxious to make the world "safe for democracy" as in America. The real significance of this polarization within Humanism is that its faith in scientific and technological progress as the means of solving human problems by human effort demands constant social change. Such rapid change produces tensions within the value-system that are expressed by the conservative vs. liberal polarity. Yet this polarization between liberals and conservatives over the pace of change is not so intense that such practical compromises as are worked out in the American two-party system become impossible. Thus in accepting Humanism as a philosophy of life one can still choose to favor one or the other party or be an independent.

The hopes of Humanism at its most confident are certainly pinned on constant social progress through increasing control, not only over nature but over human nature, leading to ever greater freedom and self-fulfillment for every individual. Although the glorification of the French and American revolutions and other revolutions of national independence are essential parts of the mythology of Humanism, its faithful, unlike the Marxists or Nazis, do not pin their hopes on some crucial social revolution but on gradual evolution, disagreeing only on its pace.

Humanists today often talk about the "conquest of space" and the possibility of intelligent life forms elsewhere in the universe. Nevertheless, just as they accept uncertainty about life after death, most also accept the fact that ultimately the human race will perish. We may destroy ourselves through war or environmental pollution or we may make way for some new species. Finally we must inevitably share in the entropic doom of our universe. Since nothing can prevent ultimate individual or species extinction there is no use worrying about it except to attempt to delay it indefinitely. Ultimately, however, in this world-view the existence of the human species can hardly be more than a brief episode in the long history of the universe, a universe that is indifferent to our fate.

The foregoing description of the Humanist world-view and value-system should suffice to demonstrate that it is a unique, unified system comparable to the other world religions or philosophies of life. Yet it may still be objected that it lacks two features that for many sociologists are characteristic of a religion: (1) faith in the Transcendent; (2) expression through myth and ritual.

The first requirement, however, seems satisfied if we note that for the Humanist humanity is at least *self*-transcendent because its potentiality for creativity enables it to surpass every natural or cultural limitation into an open future. As for the second feature of the traditional religions it must be conceded that the Enlightenment rejected symbols of a Christian type, but Islam and the Protestant Reformers had also done so. Avoiding metaphorical language, scientistic Humanism favored the clear, literal language of mathematics and technical description.[30] Nevertheless, romantic Humanism has fostered a keen appreciation of symbolism as a means of awakening human feeling and imagination and inculcating a sense of values. Hence it has developed its own repertoire of symbolic rituals. Placing its hopes not in divine but in human creativity, Humanism finds "the sacred" or the "awe inspiring" in great discoverers: Galileo, Newton, Einstein, and in great artists: Mozart, Beethoven, Michelangelo, Picasso.

These Promethean creators are venerated not as mere "saints" but as symbols of the human capacity to solve problems and to prophesy and create the future. This same numinosity is enshrined in the places and buildings hallowed by human genius: our great universities, museums, libraries, laboratories, space centers, monuments to the lonely struggles of these scientists, explorers and artists, their martyrdom by the inquisitorial obscurantists, censors, and philistines, and their ultimate triumphs. To support this cult of human creativity we have witnessed in recent years an extraordinary flood of exhaustively researched biographies of creative men and women, especially of complex, conflicted, and rejected ones. The fact that so many were deeply neurotic, morally ambiguous, sexually compulsive, and pathetically suicidal makes their personalities all the more mythic, each one a *mysterium tremendum et fascinans*.

Humanism also has its ritual occasions: minor ones such as university graduations, and major ones such as the inaugurations of Presidents and the apotheoses of the Nobel laureates. The magnificent pageantry of the Olympic games and superbowls, of political demonstrations and elections, the pomp of the weddings and funerals of the famous, as well as the displays of military power and space travel, rival the most ecstatic religious rituals and express the values of Humanism symbolically and mythically. Hence the recent celebration of the restoration of the Statue of Liberty was the occasion of many efforts to answer the question, "What does the U.S.A. stand for?" Thus the sociological requirements for Humanism to be a unified functional equivalent to the traditional religions able to enter into dialogue with them on the basis of equality seem sufficiently satisfied.

In terms of our human experience, how adequately does ancient Confucianism or modern Humanism answer those problems that are of ultimate concern to us? It should be obvious from the foregoing descriptions that both the older Eastern Humanism of China and the modern one of the West are remarkably complete and coherent world-views and value-systems. They have been able to win millions of adherents and to exert a powerful influence on human history, Confucianism for a millennium and a half. Chinese Marxists severely criticize Confucianism for its conservatism since this has proved an obstacle to human progress through technology. Yet they also continue to attack progressive Humanism as responsible for the cruel poverty under which most of humanity still suffers in spite of the abundance which modern technology can produce, as well as the nuclear armaments that threaten humanity with extinction. In reply to these criticisms Humanists claim their defects are largely due to the existence of the Chinese and former Marxist countries and of Islamic terrorism. Thus Humanist countries blame the persistence of poverty under capitalism on state interference with free enterprise, due to socialistic influences; while Marxists and Muslims claim that the arrogant hegemony of the capitalist countries prevents them from fully developing their own economies and has forced them to restrict human freedoms.

This exchange of criticisms makes it clear that it is not easy to subject any philosophy of life to a pragmatic test, since the same facts can be differently interpreted to fit one's own commitments. Nor is it fair to judge a philosophy of life simply by its historical exemplifications, since in each case unfaithful disciples have applied that philosophy imperfectly. Better ask whether the pragmatic consequences of a philosophy are rooted in something *essential* to it or are merely adventitious.

The achievements of Humanism tested by its own value-system are indeed remarkable. Under its global leadership there seems to have been an immense progress for humanity scientifically, economically, and politically. The "knowledge explosion" since 1750 and particularly in this twentieth century has exceeded anything known in human history. We have explored the interior of atoms and the far reaches of the cosmos. We have attained a knowledge of the evolution of the universe, of the earth, of life on earth, of the human body and psyche incomparably greater than that achieved under the dominance of the traditional religions, including Christianity.

From this scientific advance has followed a technology capable of producing economic abundance where before famine and plague were common. It has developed "miraculous" remedies for human physical and mental ills, largely eliminated contagious disease, and doubled average life expectancy. The rate of increase of knowledge and control over nature in recent decades gives promise of still greater discoveries. Humanist culture has linked all humanity through rapid transportation and broadcast communications. Now the development of computers and automation promises a tremendous extension of human powers. In principle at least we see no limits now to our possible control over natural forces. As we have already noted, politically this leadership of Humanism has also meant the advance of democracy and respect for human rights. Humanism has convinced the world of "the rights of man" proclaimed by the American and French Revolutions. Today the cruelty of former ages and the callous neglect of the lives of the powerless seem to all of us barbaric, and we accept as self-evident new claims for the rights of women, of homosexuals, of the disabled, of (postnatal) children, and even of animals. This marvelous advance in the appreciation of the value of human life must be largely credited to the influence of the ethical ideals of Humanism, and Humanists have been heroic leaders and even martyrs in fighting for these rights. Furthermore in the fine arts and literature the centuries since 1700 have been wonderfully creative and have produced works that celebrate secular life, rather than being subordinated to ecclesiastical control.

When Humanists look at the traditional religions of the world, they can largely agree with Marx's critique of religion. The traditional religions, and Christianity in particular, has so often been the source of fanatical cruelty and persecution. They have often stood in the way of scientific advance, and have frequently bolstered tyrannical governments by fostering passive obedience among the oppressed, persuading them to wait for justice in another life or assuring them that their misery is "the will of God." Moreover, China lacked that unique achievement of Greek culture, pure mathematics (as distinguished from practical mathematics in which the Chinese were quite advanced) and with it the notion of the scientific method in the natural sciences. On this mathematical science the whole dramatic technological advance made by the West after 1650 was based. It was this lack of scientific technology which made modern China feel backward when confronted by Western culture and led to its adoption of Humanism and Marxism in place of Confucianism.[31] It was this lack also that has made Confucian Humanism appear rigidly conservative and Western Humanism liberal and progressive.

What is significant for our search for answers to ultimate questions is that in China for centuries a world-view and value-system flourished that were as this-worldly and humanity-centered as those of Western Humanism. In both cases this Humanism has exhibited a certain internal polarization between a rationalist, social tendency and a romantic, individualistic tendency. Both have made relatively successful efforts to synthesize these two poles and to provide their respective ethical systems with cosmological foundations while tolerating a considerable degree of religious pluralism. Finally, both have rejected control of society by the uncultured masses and have retained decisive power in the hands of a well-educated, intensely humanistic bureaucracy and technocracy. What the Confucian parallel to Humanism can teach us is that a world-view and value-system, in which a personal God plays no significant part, can have, at least for a considerable time, genuine social success.

Furthermore, traditional religions have burdened peoples with false guilt and fear of divine retribution that has paralyzed their creative energies that could have been used for earthly progress and enjoyment. Hence Humanism, though it proclaims religious freedom, is deeply suspicious of other world-views and value-systems as irrational and dogmatic and hence ultimately dangerous to individual freedom. Those committed to traditional religions (*including* Confucianism) are obliged to face these hard questions honestly. Yet Humanists, too, have hard questions to face. As the Marxists have pointed out, these great benefits of Humanism often are much more available to elites, than to the masses. Such great wealth and power in the hands of a few that the masses cannot share is a greater injustice just because remedies for poverty are now available. Moreover, this neglect of justice cannot be excused simply as transitional, since it has persisted throughout the period since 1700 when Humanism began its rise, and no end to it is in sight. Is such injustice accidental or is it rooted in Humanism's advocacy of *individualism* based on the notion of the autonomy of the human subject?

Paradoxically this individualism leads many moderate Humanists, in spite of their insistence on human rights, in some circumstances to approve, as the Marxists and Nazis did, the sacrifice of individuals to social progress. Thus many Humanists have accepted the practice of abortion and nuclear deterrence (i.e., the destruction of the innocent) as necessary instruments of social control. At the extreme, as we have seen, this can go as far as the Marxist and Nazi extermination of the "socially undesirable." While Humanists generally abhor such extremes, their cultural and ethical relativism seem to make it difficult for them to find a consistent answer to such proposals. In fact this century of Humanist dominance has seen some of the most frightful wars and genocidal atrocities of history and the increasing threat of nuclear Armageddon.

One has only to read the literature created by our leading current writers, who represent the Humanist spirit at its best, to find that they perceive "post modernism" as a time when it is prudent to withdraw from the hopeless corruption of public life into the dubious security of privatism. It is often noted that "modernism" in literature and art fatally isolates the modern artist from the general public while, in cultures based on the traditional religions, the arts expressed a common faith.

To many today it seems that Western culture under the increasing dominance of Humanism has entered a phase of alarming decadence. Ethical relativism has led to a wide spread materialistic consumerism and hedonism, with increasing acceptance of every form of addictive indulgence in sex, drugs, and mindless self-destructive violence that governments seem helpless to correct. Especially alarming is the instability of family life with the resultant neglect and abuse of children. The sense of community in our cities has broken down so that many individuals feel isolated and lonely and rely more and more on psychotherapy or tranquilizing drugs. Popular culture as seen on TV or expressed in popular music has become irrational and violent and people seem more and more open to propaganda manipulation by special interests. Of course sensitive, responsible Humanists do not approve this moral decadence but they seem unable to oppose it effectively, because they can propose no motivation for a more disciplined life that would be consistent with the moral relativism or positivism that they have embraced.

The origin of decadence seems to be the reliance of Humanism on a morally subjective or romantic basis for ethics.[32] If ethics is not rooted in human nature but is a purely human creation, constantly changing with time and place, how can individuals be held responsible by a permissive society? Humanism has for long lived on the remnants of an ethical consensus derived from the Christianity from which it divorced itself. Once, however, this heritage has been exhausted by criticism and ridicule of Christianity this consensus evaporates. Yet it hardly seems possible to regain this consensus by a reliance on a static traditionalism as before this century Confucianism attempted to do in China, since the adoption of a progressive scientific technology tends to disrupt any such moral system. Yet this is not odd, since the resemblance of Confucianism to Humanism is based on their secularism and their guidance by intellectual elites, but they differ in the kind of knowledge that constitutes those elites.

With penetrating insight Nietzsche saw that the bourgeois morality of his day (in England "the Victorian Compromise") was sheer hypocrisy.[33] He called for the "transvaluation of all values" by an honest admission that the strong make their own moral laws for the weak. The result is that for some Humanists the only real virtue is "honesty" in the sense of the frank admission of one's own egoistic needs. Thus Jean-Paul Sartre has argued that genuine love of one human being for another is impossible. We are each inescapably imprisoned in our own self-love.[34] Humanists do not want to accept inhuman conclusions but what answer can they give, if values are nothing more than subjective creations of the individual?

Although the greatest Humanist thinker, Kant, maintained there are transcendental, absolute, and universal moral principles given by human autonomous reason, he himself undermined this doctrine by accepting an interpretation of modern science which eliminated all objectively knowable purpose from the universe. To say, as he did, that practical reason must acknowledge a God and a universal moral law in order to make human social life possible, has proved a foundation of sand for Humanism. The autonomous individual can decide to exploit society for his or her own egoistic purposes while using the art of rhetoric, given new power by the modern media of social communication, to disguise these purposes. A "hermeneutic of suspicion" then replaces all social trust. Even science becomes propaganda.

The only way out of this dilemma for Humanism would seem to be to revive the concept of natural purpose and thus give the discoveries of modern science the teleological significance which Kant, because of his Newtonian conception of science, believed he must deny. Today we realize that "science" is not given as a self-evident body of truth, but that it is subject to a variety of philosophical interpretations.

The mechanistic, anti-teleological interpretation has generally prevailed because it was favored by Humanism as a weapon against Christian theology. But this interpretation has often been protested by leading scientists themselves, and today is wide open for discussion.[35] In seeking the best option for a world-view and value-system, we ought not to abandon the objective methodology of science. Following this method we can still hold that the universe in its various natural units, whether atoms, molecules, or organisms, exhibits a teleological unity of functions. We can also hold that natural processes have produced a complex earthly environment indispensable for the evolution of intelligent life not reasonably attributable to mere chance.[36]

Teleology is not, as Kant claimed, an anthropomorphic projection of human purpose, but is an objective recognition of order and function in the world. Once such a natural teleology is admitted it becomes possible (without succumbing to the so-called "naturalistic fallacy" of confusing the "ought" with the "is") to found ethics and a prescriptive theory of human rights on an objective description of universal human nature that is empirically observable.

Why is it then that Humanism is so resistant to founding ethics on stable and universal human nature rather than on changing local culture? The real reason is the fear that this will lead to a moral absolutism contrary to human freedom of conscience. But to admit the teleological foundation of ethics is not to claim, as did some early Humanists, that the natural moral law is self-evident. Moral law is not innate but is grounded in historical experience and is subject to objective public debate just as are the findings of natural science. There will always be differences of opinion about moral as about scientific matters, but it is essential that public debate about them be possible if a "public philosophy" is to be achieved. The question is, as Jürgen Habermas has shown, whether in modern society such a "civil discourse" is really possible.[37]

The other reason that Humanists today resist the notion of a natural law foundation for ethics is that to admit an objective teleology in nature is to admit, as did Humanism in its first, deistic phase, that there is an intelligent Creator. Yet if they could bring themselves to accept the existence of God as an objective, publicly knowable fact, and not merely as a matter of private opinion, they could return to the original insights of the Enlightenment. They would not thereby be required to commit themselves to Christianity, Judaism, Islam or any of the traditional religions. Would not this gain them a decisive advantage over their atheistic rival Marxism, since as I will show in the next chapter, belief in a wise Creator has a universal appeal to the people of all cultures?

Thus, although the secular philosophies of life have a very strong case to make for themselves, they are also faced with very difficult questions about the adequacy of their world-views and value-systems to explain experience and give guidance in moral decisions. If we are to accept their own emphasis on our responsibility for honesty and dedication to objective truth we must not take these philosophies of life as self-evident merely because they are favored by the elites of our most powerful political blocs today. Nor must we accept them merely because they are the most "modern" or even because they are "post-modern." Instead we must open our minds to other possibilities, new and old. First, we must examine the claims of the oldest philosophies of life and their modern heirs that (unlike Confucianism) are strikingly different from Humanism. Is it not possible that the past had insights that our times in their progress have forgotten but which must be recovered for an adequate philosophy of life?

Notes

1 On the rise of Islam see W.M. Watt, *Muhammad at Mecca* and *Muhammad at Medina, Muhammad: Prophet and Statesman* (Oxford: Clarendon Press, 1956, 1968).

2 Peter Gay, *The Enlightenment: An Interpretation,* 2 vols. (New York: Alfred Knopf, 1967) and Ira O. Wade, *The Intellectual Origins of the French Enlightenment* (Princeton, NJ: Princeton University Press, 1971).

3 Charles Webster, *The Great Instauration; Science, Medicine and Reform 1626-1660* (New York: Holmes and Meier, 1976) and Eugene M. Kiaren, *Religious Origins of Modern Science* (Grand Rapids, MI: Eerdmans, 1977).

4 From the title of a famous old polemic by Andrew Dickson White, *A History of the Warfare of Science with Theology in Christendom* (New York: Dover, 1896, 1960), 2 vols.

5 See William A. Wallace, OP, *Causality and Scientific Explanation* (Ann Arbor, MI: University of Michigan, 1972) vol. 1, pp. 117-210 and *Galileo and His Sources* (Princeton, NJ: Princeton University Press, 1984) for recent research.

6 See Ernest L. Tuveson, *Millennium and Utopia* (Berkeley: University of California Press,

1949) and Franco Venturi, *Utopia and Reform in the Enlightenment* (Cambridge: Cambridge University Press, 1971).

[7] See Chapter 1, note 32 for references to the *Humanist Manifesto and The New Humanist Manifesto* in which the claim for this title is made by activists promoting this philosophy of life. Though this group and the magazine, *The Humanist* (The Beacon Press, Boston), and the standard *Encyclopedia of Philosophy,* edited by Paul Edwards (New York: Macmillan/Free Press, 1967) probably represent only a small group of intellectuals, they have given a very clear formulation of the views of a far wider public. Another classic of Humanism is Julian Huxley, *Religion Without Revelation,* a publisher's blurb for which says, "One of the twentieth century's great scientists and philosophers goes beyond skepticism to affirm a humanistic faith based on man, intelligence and the scientific method" (New York: Harper and Bros., 1957). Special to Huxley's version of his world-view is his panpsychism.

[8] G.E. Moore, *Principia Ethica* (London: Cambridge University Press, 1903) says this "naturalistic fallacy" is a principal topic of modern ethical discussion, but medieval thinkers also recognized the fallacy. For criticism cf. Arthur Prior, *Logic and the Basis of Ethics* (Oxford: Clarendon Press, 1965). It is of course true that the descriptive terms proper to theoretical sciences have a different logical form than do the prescriptive terms of practical sciences, but the latter presuppose the former as their necessary condition. The prescriptive rules of medicine make sense only if based on correct anatomical and physiological description. Moreover, in ethics the prescriptive norms refer to the choice of means to ends, but if these ends are not purely arbitrary, they must be derived from the needs (teleology) of human nature and these are known through a descriptive anthropology.

[9] For an introduction to the thought of Rousseau and Kant and further bibliography see the articles under their names in Paul Edwards, ed., *The Encyclopedia of Philosophy*, vol. 7, pp. 218-225 and vol. 4, pp. 305-324 respectively.

[10] Kant's *Religion within the Bounds of Mere Reason* (1793) and his essay on "What is Enlightenment?" are the most classic statements of the Enlightenment philosophy as a substitute for Christianity and Judaism. Kant, often obscure, is here brilliantly plain and eloquent.

[11] See Geoffrey Clive, *The Romantic Enlightenment* (New York: Meridian Books, 1960) and H.G. Schenck, *The Mind of the European Romantics* (New York: Frederic Ungar, 1966).

[12] See Sidney Pollard, *The Idea of Progress* (New York: Basic Books, 1968).

[13] Herbert Marcuse, *Eros and Civilization* (New York: Vintage Books, 1962) combined Marxist and Freudian theory in a seductive synthesis that provided a theoretical justification for the revolutionary hedonism of the "youth culture" of the 1960's. Cf. Neil Mclnnes, *The Western Marxists* (New York: Library Press, 1972), pp. 169-185.

[14] See Jacques Derrida, *et al., The Ear of the Other: Otobiography, Transference, Translation,* ed. by Christie V. McDonald (New York: Schocken Books, 1985).

[15] Letter to Dr. Benjamin Rush, Sept. 23, 1800 in *The Essential Jefferson,* ed. by Alfred Fried (New York: Collier Books, 1963), p. 393.

[16] Peter Gay, ed., *Deism: An Anthology* (Princeton, NJ: Van Nostrand, 1968).

[17] On the religious views of the Founding Fathers see Adolf O. Koch, *Religion of the American Enlightenment* (New York: Thomas Y. Crowell, 1968). Also Garry Wills, *Inventing America: Jefferson's Declaration of Independence* (Garden City, NY: Doubleday, 1981).

[18] See John Ladd, ed., *Ethical Relativism* (Belmont, CA: Wadsworth Publishing Co., 1973) and David Little and Sumner B. Twiss, *Comparative Religious Ethics: A New Method* (San Francisco: Harper and Row, 1978).

[19] Isaiah Berlin, *Karl Marx: His Life and Environment,* 3rd ed. (Oxford: Oxford University Press, 1963) and Werner Blomberg, *Portrait of Marx: An Illustrated Biography* (New York: Herder and Herder, 1972). For a review on Marxism see Arthur F. McGovern, *Marxism: An American Christian Perspective* (Maryknoll, NY: Orbis Books, 1980).

[20] Ernst Bloch, *Atheism in Christianity: the Religion of Exodus and the Kingdom* (New York: Herder and Herder, 1972).

[21] Cf. a representative selection of essays in Rosino Gibellini, ed., *Frontiers of Theology in Latin America* (Maryknoll, NY: Orbis Books, 1979).

[22] On Chinese Religion see A.C. Graham, "Confucianism" in Robert C. Zaehner, ed., *The Concise Encyclopedia of Living Faiths* (afterwards CE), (New York: Hawthorn Books, 1959), pp. 365-84 and W. Eichorn, "Taoism," pp. 385-401. See also with selections from sources, Wingtsit Chan, *A Source Book in Chinese Philosophy* (Princeton, NJ: Princeton University Press, 1963). Cf. also W.T. de Bary, ed., *The Unfolding of Neo-Confucianism* (New York: Columbia University Press, 1975); H.C. Creel, *Confucianism and the Chinese Way* (New York: Harper and Row, paperback, 1960); E.R. and K. Hughes, *Religion in China* (London: Hutchinson, 1950); Arthur F. Wright, *Confucianism and Chinese Civilization* (New York: Atheneum Publishers, 1964); Joseph R. Levenson, *Confucian China and Its Modern Fate* (Los Angeles: University of California Press, 1958); *Ch'ing K'un Yang, Religion in Chinese Society* (Berkeley and Los Angeles: University of California Press); Fung Yu Lan, *A Short History of Chinese Philosophy,* ed. D. Bodde (New York: Macmillan, paperback, 1966). On Confucianism as a Humanism see Wingtsit Chan, "Chinese Theory and Practice with Special Reference to Humanism" in Charles A. Moore, ed., *The Chinese Mind* (Honolulu: East West Center, University of Hawaii Press, 1967), pp. 11-30.

[23] See Jonathan D. Spence, *The Memory Palace of Matteo Ricci* (New York: Viking Press, 1984).

[24] On the notion of "Axial Period" see Karl Jaspers, *The Origin and Goal of History* (New York: Yale University Press, 1953).

[25] Quoted in Mu-Chou Poo, *In Search of Personal Welfare: A View of Ancient Chinese Religion* (Albany, NY: State University of New York Press, 1998), p. 274. This book stresses the distinction between popular and elite religion in China and the this-worldliness of both aspects of the culture.

[26] On Taoist opposition to Confucianism see W. Richard Comstock, *et al., Religion and Man: An Introduction* (New York: Harper and Row, 1971), pp. 286-316.

[27] See Wingtsit Chan, *A Sourcebook of Chinese Philosophy*, p. 573.

[28] See Richard Woods, OP, *The Occult Revolution* (New York: Herder and Herder, 1971) on the rise of this trend.

[29] See Thomas P. O'Neill, *The Rise and Decline of Liberalism* (Milwaukee: Bruce, 1953) on the meaning of the term. He shows that since both our Democratic and Republican parties champion a free-market economy and the Republicans more consistently than the Democrats, the Republicans, generally said in the U.S. to be the "conservative" party are in the original sense of the term more "liberal" than the Democrats!

[30] For recent theories on types of language see William A. Van Roo, *Man the Symbolizer* (Rome: Gregorian University Press, 1981).

[31] Joseph Needham, *The Great Titration* (London: Allen and Unwin, 1969), pp. 14-54.

[32] Alasdaire McIntyre, *After Virtue* (Notre Dame, IN: University of Notre Dame Press, 1982) discusses at length the shortcomings of current Humanist theories of ethics.

[33] Cf. Frederick Copleston, *A History of Philosophy* (Westminster, MD: Newman Press, 1965), vol. vii, pp. 390-420 for an introduction to Nietzsche's ethical thought.

[34] *Being and Nothingness,* trans. by Hazel Barnes (New York: Philosophical Library, 1965),

Part 3: Chapter 3, pp. 361-432, argues that all human relations are based on conflict. Sartre later tried to overcome this individualism; see Thomas C. Anderson, *The Foundation and Structure of Sartrean Ethics* (Lawrence: Regents Press of Kansas, 1979), pp. 67-96.

[35] See my articles "Final Causality" (vol. 5, pp. 915-19) and "Teleology" (vol. 13, pp. 979-81) in the *New Catholic Encyclopedia.*

[36] See John D. Barrow and Frank J. Tipler, *The Anthropic Cosmological Principle* (New York: Oxford University Press, 1988) who show that unless the universe was always pretty much as we find it there would never have been human life or scientific intelligence on our planet.

[37] For an introduction to Habermas' thought with a bibliography of his publications in English see the essays in Don S. Browning and Francis Schüssler Fiorenza, eds., *Habermas, Modernity, and Public Theology* (New York: Crossroad, 1992).

CHAPTER 3

MYTHOLOGICAL RELIGIONS

1. Mythic Cultures

The Humanist philosophies of life center on the natural reality directly accessible to human experience, the visible, audible, tangible. They vehemently reject the invisible, silent, and intangible as impossible to ratify rationally and therefore as distractions from human concerns and control. Belief in the reality of supernatural realities or efforts to communicate with nonhuman persons is regarded by Humanists as irrational, superstitious, foolish, an illusory projection of human fantasy and of unconscious desires.

Yet Humanist scholars recognize that not only for the so-called "primitive," or pre-literary peoples who still exist marginally, but also for the great ancient civilizations in which our own modern world is rooted, the line between nature and supernature was not clearly drawn. In these cultures direct human experience seems penetrated by a constant awareness of the effective presence of supernatural beings just as real as visible ones. Indeed, the art and poetry of these cultures make these invisible presences visible and report their frequent apparition and intervention in human affairs.

For these people the barrier between the visible and the invisible is overcome by a type of experience we can call *mythic*. A student of mythology, Joseph Campbell, says[1] that myths have three functions:

> The first function of mythology is to reconcile waking consciousness to the *mysterium tremendum et fascinans* of this universe *as it is*: the second being to render an interpretive total image of the same, as known to contemporary consciousness. Shake-

> speare's definition of the function of his art, "to hold, as it 'twere, the mirror up to nature," is thus equally a definition of mythology. It is the revelation to waking consciousness of the powers of its own sustaining source. A third function, however, is the enforcement of a moral order: the shaping of the individual to the requirements of his geographically and historically conditioned social group, and here an actual break from nature may ensue... [as in circumcision, etc. This serves] to join the merely natural human body in membership to a larger more enduring, cultural body, the mind and feelings being imprinted simultaneously with a correlative mythology.

Thus the first two of these functions provide a world-view for societies which do not take one from science as modernity does, while the third function provides a value-system derived from and reinforcing this mythic world-view. Likewise many of the human needs which are met for us by our scientific technology seem to be met for them by their sacramental and magical rites. Of course, just as some myth and magic survives in our culture, so these people also have some primitive science and rudimentary technology. Nevertheless, their world is structured primarily by mythic thinking, as ours by scientific thinking.

In the Humanist world-view the supernatural has been largely excluded from the objective realm of science and relegated to the subjective realm of romanticism. Even the romantics among the Humanists regard mythology only as a dream world of symbols whose real content is wholly reducible to the objective scientific world. Thus, in a sense, "reality" is wider for those who live in a mythic world than for Humanists, since mythical reality leaves room for some common-sense cause and effect explanations of phenomena that are still retained by science, while scientific reality excludes the objective reality of the mythical. In mythic cultures people know that the sun makes things hot, but in a scientific culture people may deny that human thinking requires a spiritual mind.

Therefore, if we are to compare the Humanist world-views to those of the mythological cultures fairly, we must not *assume* with the Humanists that the mythological view of reality is illusory, but we must describe it neutrally. Then we must ask whether in fact it has a validity of its own, irreducibly complementary to the validity of the Humanist world-view. At the outset, however, we ought to note that many Humanists today have come to recognize some value in mythological thinking. But for the sake of consistency with their own world-view they are compelled to psychologize such thought, reducing it, as Carl Gustav Jung has done,[2] to a symbolic expression of the human self. Thus many in our Humanist dominated culture understand mythical or metaphorical language only when it is used in art or literature to express subjective feelings. They do not know how to interpret such language when it is seriously intended to convey objective truth, since for Humanists objective truth is restricted to the literal, univocal language of science. This ineptitude of our culture in dealing with symbolic truth can be illustrated by two very different but current controversies.

On the conservative side, the reason that religious fundamentalists reject the scientific theory of evolution is because they try to read the Bible as if it were written in the language of science. They take little or no account of the Bible's frequent use of metaphorical and symbolic language. Nor do these fundamentalists understand why such modes of expression are necessary to express objective realities that transcend ordinary human experience. On the liberal side, the campaign for "vertical inclusive language" is also a well-meant but confused effort to accommodate the symbolism of biblical language to the mentality and concerns of our Humanist culture. Attempts in monotheistic religions to avoid naming the Divinity as male can ultimately lead only to imagining It as a monstrous androgyne or as a neuter and hence *impersonal* "Supreme Being" as did the deists of the eighteenth century. Or if the term "Goddess" is used exclusively, this is sexist exclusion in reverse, while to tack between God and Goddess is to deprive the Divinity of personal identity. Of course one may use such names as "Spirit" (New Age language), "Sophia" (theosophist language), "The Force" (the language of the film *Star Wars*) or "Mystery" (the language of a one-sided apophatic theology). Individuals may, of course, choose their personal ways of imagining and speaking to God if it contributes to their devotion, but for public communal teaching and worship there must be a universally recognized symbolic tradition.

Yet some theologians today argue that in order to match the symbols they find congenial or of service to their favorite cause the traditional symbols of a religion must be radically revised. They fail to see that this may amount to founding a new religion, as Muhammad did by reorienting the direction of prayer from Jerusalem to Mecca. It is no small change, therefore, when the traditional names of God chosen to express the monotheism of Judaism, Christianity, and Islam are altered. This is especially true if the new names more fittingly express an impersonal Deism, or a pantheistic or panentheistic religion of the type of the Emanation Religions in which the Mother Goddess and her creation are monistically fused.[3] If such changes of symbols become necessary to maintain their power, they must be made only after a profound theological analysis of their original archetypal meaning, not merely because superficially they seem merely to reflect the obsolete culture of their origin. The fact that the religion they originally expressed has survived centuries of cultural change is evidence that they have a deep trans-cultural meaning.

These two controversies are mentioned here only to make the point that although the Mythological Religions are today largely marginalized, one who is choosing a world-view and value-system needs to reflect on how important a role myth and metaphor play in any world-view and value-system, even a Humanist one. As I argued in Chapter 2, Humanism may be satisfied with literal scientific language in constructing an objective world-view but at least in its subjective, romantic construction of a value-system it uses the mythical language of literature and the arts. In Chapter 5 I will explain further why gender symbolism has proved necessary to the expression of the Creation Religions and can be manipulated by the members of a religious tradition only at great risk. My point here, however is not to discuss the problems of fundamentalism or inclusive language. Rather it is to call attention to the fact that symbolic language, central to the Mythological Religions, in spite of the marginalization of these religions by modern science, remains of great significance today. We will fail in evaluating the options for a choice of a world-view, if in seeking to appreciate any world-view at its real worth we fail to understand its symbols.

2. Prehistoric Religion

From the beginning of written human history, religion has appeared to be the framework of human life, but we have no way of knowing about prehistoric religion except through hypothetical reconstructions from such scanty artifacts as have survived.[4] The most expressive of these are paintings preserved in caves and a few statues and carvings. Also some information can be gleaned from the manner of human burial and the remains of what appear to have been animal sacrifices.

These artifacts suggest that early humans engaged in behavior usually interpreted today as religious. Our remotest ancestors must have asked themselves ultimate questions about the mystery of life when they fashioned figurines of pregnant women and paintings of herds of reindeer, some pregnant. Surely, they must have wondered what became of the dead when they buried them so carefully. Why would they have offered sacrifices, without at least fearing there were spirits to be propitiated? Their art also suggests they tried to control these vicissitudes of life and death by magic.

Support for our reconstruction of prehistoric religion comes from comparing it with the religious practices of peoples who today still live by simple food-gathering and hunting much as did the ancients. To call these modern peoples "primitives" is misleading, since, of course, they have had just as long a historical development as we ourselves. Nevertheless, the similarity of their economies to those of early peoples makes it somewhat plausible that their religious artifacts and practices provide a clue to interpret the artifacts that survive from the remote past. On the basis of such meager data we can reasonably conclude that from a very early period the human family had developed mythic worldviews and value-systems much like those of peoples who today live by a simple economy and technology.

3. The Pre-Literary Religions

I will use the neutral term "pre-literary" for the religions of modern people whose culture is based on a relatively simple technology and whose beliefs and traditions can only be known orally since they lack a written religious literature. Some use the term "primal religions"[5] when referring, for example, to the religions practiced in a number of Pacific Islands, Australia, New Zealand, the Philippines and Japan, and by certain isolated tribes in Siberia, India, Malaysia, the Andaman Islands, and the natives of sub Saharan Africa, who have kept their own cultures. Today, these pre-literary tribes taken altogether are estimated to include not more than about one hundred million persons out of our world population of 4.5 billion, less than 3% and declining.[6]

The first thing to note about the religions of these groups is that they are *tribal,* intimately fused with the total culture of each group and clearly marked by its geographic situation, economy, and technology. Their religion pervades their whole way of life and is difficult to distinguish from its other features. No tribe that has been studied lacks a religion of its own. This does not mean that the religion of one tribe is impervious to influence from others. Nor does it mean that all individuals in a culture are convinced believers. Paul Radin[7] has shown that there are "village atheists" and doubters even among tribes where social conformity has a high priority. Therefore, it is hardly possible to review even superficially the great variety of such religious systems, but they have many common features which raise serious questions for those who have accepted the Humanist world-view as adequate to universal human experience.

In the nineteenth and early twentieth century many theories of the origin and evolution of religion were developed by anthropologists such as Tylor, Spencer, Frazer, Lang, Schmidt, Lowie, etc. Thus Tylor believed religion began with animism (others said fetishism or totemism), developed into polytheism, and finally into monotheism (with the implication that the next stage would be an advance to scientific agnosticism). Lang and Schmidt, however, brought forward evidence that monotheism came first and degenerated into polytheism. Today anthropologists have generally abandoned such evolutionary schemes for lack of sufficient data to verify them. Yet Schmidt's conclusion from his extensive study of the technologically simplest societies that a belief in a supreme High God is almost a cultural universal, only partially disguised in more developed societies by the mythologies of many gods and spirits, has never been disproved. While he attributed this to a "primitive revelation," as I will show in Chapter 5 it is based on common sense reasoning about experiences universal to humankind.[8]

Most anthropologists today, however, do not assign any single cause for the origin of primal religion. The data rather indicate four generalizations: (1) Religion is a universal feature of human culture. (2) It serves many functions in human life (though, as I have argued, the specifying function is to supply a world-view and value-system). (3) The major religious concepts of the "divine," of the soul, the future life, etc., are widely present at all levels of culture. (4) The distinction between "magic" and "religion" is never very sharp. Fortunately for our inquiry, these pre-literary religions, although they differ vastly in detail, exhibit certain common features. Any one of these, however, may be missing or obscure in the religion of a particular tribe. The first of these generally common features is that while all these people understand and use the concept of natural causality (e.g., fire burns, knives cut, water cleanses, etc.), they also attribute many phenomena to invisible forces which modern science does not recognize.

Observers have argued whether these "forces" are always conceived as personal (*animism*) or as impersonal (*manism*). But all of us use concepts derived from the experience of our own personal actions and apply these by analogy to the behavior of animals and the actions of inanimate objects. Hence, it is not strange that people in cultures not based on modern science should tend to personify all invisible forces; yet, just because such forces are invisible, these people may have only a very vague and thus impersonal concept of them. Consequently, it seems accurate enough to speak of them in general as "spirits," as do many anthropologists, acknowledging that sometimes a "spirit" is only an ill-defined and faceless "force."

Among these spirits are those of dead members of the tribe, the ancestors. A variety of theories about the fate of the dead can all exist together in a single tribal religion without the natives making any attempt to reduce these theories to a consistent, unified account. The dead may be thought to be asleep (yet still existing) in the grave; or they may be shadowy ghosts wandering about in the dark underworld.

On the other hand they may be thought to be alive in some remote region of the earth or in the sky, or to be reincarnated in human or even in animal form. They are often supposed to hover for a time around their former home, watching over the family or tribe before they depart to their ultimate state. Often they are believed to threaten the living in revenge for injuries done them in a former life or for the failure of the survivors to perform their funeral rites properly. Consequently in these religions rituals to honor or placate the dead or to receive their guidance are common. The ancestors are experienced as still very much present and, in tribes with a developed artistic tradition, they are often represented by what the early missionaries thought were "idols."

Common also is belief in many superhuman spirits who make themselves evident in natural objects and events, in rocks and mountains, in rivers, springs, and the ocean, in trees and plants, in all kinds of beasts, birds, and fish. These spirits may be either good or bad, but even the good ones if displeased may prove dangerous. Finally, this spirit world may have a complicated hierarchy of beings, often divided into two main classes of "gods" and "lesser spirits" and each of these classes may have many subdivisions. The technological simplicity of these cultures by no means implies that their picture of the cosmos is also always simple.[9]

We would be mistaken, however, to think of these higher beings as supernatural in the modern sense, because in these cultures "nature" is not conceived in our scientific way as governed by invariable natural laws. People in cultures that are technologically simple are, in a sense, more empirical than we are and hence are less inclined to abstract general laws from the actual irregularity of experience in a scientific way. Therefore, they interpret unusual events not as the effects of the coincidence of many natural causes (i.e., as chance events) but as the purposeful acts of free persons, although these persons are invisible. Thus it becomes a problem to get along with this world of invisible persons just as with the visible members of the tribe.

This process of communication and social adjustment with the spirits is brought about by the symbolic acts that we call "ritual" and "myth," that is, non-verbal and verbal signs that mutually interpret each other. The notion of "magic" has much puzzled anthropologists.[10]

Certainly some of what we call magic is simply crude technology based on an inadequate understanding of natural cause and effect, as in the use of various folk remedies in medicine. But what characterizes most magic is that it seeks to effect certain results by *contagion.* For example, a cannibal acquires the courage of another warrior by eating his flesh, as when a magician seeks to kill an enemy by putting needles in a doll that represents the enemy.

While contagious magic implies some kind of physical causality, sympathetic magic need only imply *symbolic* causality, that is, causality by communication, since one mind works on another by the use of signs. Consequently, the practice of magic is frequently linked somehow with the belief that the magical act summons a spirit to perform the desired task. Thus magic and prayer are not sharply distinct. By ritual and myth or by magic signs and formulas the human person communicates with the world of invisible spirits and shares their superior power over the visible world.

Rituals and myths may be important for any activity of life but especially for the "limit situations" that specify the field of religion as matters of ultimate concern. Hence begetting and birthing, passing from childhood to full membership in a tribe, handing on tribal wisdom, waging war, healing sickness, and mourning death are often ritualized. Because rituals and myths embody this heritage of wisdom, their origin is commonly attributed to a god or a great ancestor or "culture hero" and it is forbidden to alter them even slightly, although inevitably they do undergo development.

The myths commonly refer the affairs of the present to some ideal time ("Once upon a time") when the universe was in order and before it was disturbed by evil.[11] The basic symbols used in tribal myths and rituals exhibit a certain universality (modified by local circumstances) which justifies their being called "archetypal." Nevertheless, this universality of basic symbols need not be attributed (as in the Jungian notion of a "collective unconscious") to innate or genetic factors. It seems sufficiently explained by our common experiences of our human bodies and their needs and of basic family relations from which we learn a vocabulary of symbols common to all humankind.[12]

Rituals and myths are transmitted by the elders in every culture and in part performed by them. Almost all societies also have certain members designated in one way or another to mediate with the spirits, to lead in the performance of the rituals, and to learn, retell, and transmit the myths. Commonly two kinds of these officiants can be distinguished, although the two functions may coincide in the same person. One is the *priest*, who is primarily the custodian of religious traditions, who presides over prescribed rituals, and who is commonly designated in a formal way by heredity or appointment. The other is the *shaman* or *prophet* who communes with the spirits directly and who is generally called to his or her task by extraordinary, often ecstatic experiences.[13] Women may hold either office, but more frequently that of shaman than of priest.

Reports on the relation of these beliefs and practices to "morals" or conformity of the personal behavior of the members of the tribe to accepted standards are often unclear.[14] Observers note that in some of these tribes religion seems to have little to do with morals. But may not this simply mean that among these people, as among us, actual behavior is often inconsistent with moral ideals? In any case, in all these tribes there are standards of behavior whose violation results in sanctions and, as I earlier quoted Joseph Campbell saying, receive support from a tribe's mythology. Some tribes demand very strict and detailed conformity, while others permit wide latitude for individual choice, provided the requirements essential for group membership are observed. Religion always functions to support at least these membership requirements. They are usually inculcated in rites of passage, and their violation is seen not only as insulting to the human community but also as dangerously offensive to the ancestors, spirits, and gods of that community.

Sometimes it is claimed that such tribal standards of behavior are not "moral" or "ethical" but merely irrational "taboos." On examination, however, these taboos are usually found to have at least a symbolic function in support of moral standards.[15] Right moral conduct in the human community is generally thought to be bound up with right cosmic order, so that the violation of one implies the violation of the other. Since, as we have seen, symbolic acts mediate between the human and the superhuman community of spirits it becomes intelligible why it is so essential that the symbolic order not be disturbed, lest the cosmic order also be deranged. A vivid sense of the interconnectedness of everything dominates the thinking of these people who live in close contact with nature.

Some scholars, of whom Durkheim is the outstanding example,[16] have argued that religion is nothing more than a projection of social concerns. Thus the chief god is an idealization of the tribal chief, the court of the gods is a reflection of the court of the chief, the rituals are a projection of court ceremony, etc. Unquestionably one of the functions of religion is to regulate social relations, since it deals with ultimate questions which all members of the community must face, not merely privately as individuals but also as a community sharing a world-view and value-system. It is to be expected, therefore, that there will be a strong interaction between religious and social structures. Nevertheless, to say that the religion of these people is "nothing but" a projection of their social structures is reductionistic. Just as truly one can say that the social structure of a community reflects its religion.

The moral codes of pre-literary people are not as irrational as they may first appear. They embody certain transcultural principles along with adaptations to the local environment. The fact that these cultures are today *marginal* is commonly explained as the result of their technological inferiority that has made them unable to compete with progressive cultures. But others have argued that because of their harmony with nature they are morally superior to peoples whose claim to "advancement" consists mainly in violence, oppression, and technological ravishment of their environment. Thus some ask who were better, the white American pioneers who exterminated the Native Americans, or the Native Americans who for so long had reverently preserved the land in its original splendor. We must weigh these alternative explanations carefully before making any judgment as to which culture is really "fittest to survive."

Yet it must be admitted that the level of insecurity and fear among many of these peoples is very high. They stand helpless before many natural disasters and terrified of the seemingly arbitrary interventions of the spirits. Outside observers of these cultures are often shocked by the widespread dread of witchcraft.[17] Often, also, they note an atmosphere of scrupulosity about proper ritual performance arising from a highly pessimistic view of a hostile world order. Such a view can be paralyzing to human effort and productive of fanaticism and cruelty to the members of a community suspected of the violation of taboos or complicity with evil spirits.

4. The Ancient Urban Religions

With the rise of urban civilization about 6000 BCE writing was developed in Egypt and Mesopotamia, and then in Mediterranean Europe, India and China, and still later and less completely in Central America and Peru. From these literate cultures we have a rich fund of information about religions now extinct. Like the pre-literary, tribal religions already discussed each of these literary religions remained closely related to a single geographically limited culture until in the period centering on 500 BCE some underwent a radical transformation into "world religions." Because they remained localized, each of them had its own unique style, yet they shared many common features.

The most obvious difference between these religions and the preliterary ones is the great elaboration that most of the features of tribal religion underwent in urban conditions. The economic surplus produced by developed agriculture that made the cities possible also made possible and even necessary this greater complexity of religious practices, as it did a greater specialization of social tasks and a rapid development of technologies. Consequently, in these urban centers great temples were erected and a large priestly class was carefully trained to serve them. These priests, concerned to preserve and transmit sacred lore as well as the commercial records sometimes deposited in the temples for safe keeping, were probably the inventors of writing.

In these urban centers every form of art and literature flourished: much, perhaps most, of it religious, to express the multiplication of gods and the elaboration and systematization of mythology. Polytheism was not the creation of urban culture (the West African Yoruba, for example, count at least 400 gods) but it became a characteristic feature of these ancient cities.[18] Nevertheless, belief in a High God, at least in the form of *henotheism* (dominance of one god over the many other gods) was not completely obscured.

Thus in Egyptian mythology there were many gods, vividly represented in sculpture and painting, yet there was speculation about a supreme, creator god, the sun god Re or the god of wisdom Ptah. In the fourteenth century BCE the strange genius Pharaoh Akhenaten even attempted (but without permanent success) to establish a solar *monotheism.*[19] The Supreme Being was usually conceived as a sky god: god of the sun, the moon, of thunder, etc., but along with him the Mother Goddess, identified with the earth, was worshipped under many forms, more prominently where agricultural concerns predominated. Each city state needed its own supreme god and goddess and, as some of these states expanded into empires, these city gods were equated with each other, or added to the pantheon as secondary deities. As might be expected, besides the gods associated with various natural forces, new gods were needed as patrons of various urban crafts, of political interests, civic activities, war and peace.

Certain special features of the major centers of civilization are noteworthy. The oldest cities, those of Mesopotamia, pictured the gods as living at the court of the great sky god and acting as his council.[20] This sky god Anu with the help of the wind god Enlil and the water god Enki or Ea created this world. Later Ea's son Marduk came to be worshiped as the "King of the Gods."[21] Eventually a genealogy of some 50 gods was worked out.

The creation myths of the Mesopotamians reflected the geographical situations of their cities. In the epic *Enuma Elish* Marduk fought the giant sea dragon Tiamat and out of her dead body fashioned the world, just as these people had established their cities by irrigation works and levies against flooding. There were also myths of the golden age before sin and of a great flood which almost destroyed humankind. These peoples, dependent as they were both on seasonal crops and on sea commerce, were careful observers of the heavens and developed the first scientific astronomy. They believed the universe moved through a "great year" of progress and decline in an unending cycle determined by the movements of the stars, so that the future could be predicted by astrology and divination. They worshiped the sun and the moon, and the planet Venus as Ishtar, the great mother goddess. She descended into the underworld to find her lover Dumuzi (Tammuz, sometimes identified with Marduk) so that during the winter of their absence the fertility of the land ceased, to be revived only on their return to the upper world. The *Epic of Gilgamesh* also dramatized the inevitability of death, still the picture of life after death remained vague and shadowy. Yet at Ur, the king received a magnificent burial with all the means to continue his royal life in the underworld.

Worship of the gods was carried on by a learned, hierarchical priesthood according to a festal calendar and in splendid temples raised on artificial mountains. The priestly king entered into a sacred marriage with a priestess representing the mother goddess. He was also believed to be entrusted by the god of the city with a code of laws (for example, the *Code of Hammurabi*) to establish civic justice and peace. Violators of the laws were severely punished to placate the offended gods. We do not know, however, that the priests ever developed a systematic theology to render this complex of beliefs self-consistent.

In Egypt at about the same time a parallel religious view evolved, characterized, however, by several special features.[22] Cult centered on idols fashioned with an artistic subtlety surpassing that of Mesopotamia, many in animal form. Living animals were also worshipped. Remarkable concern was shown for existence after death conceived as a continuation of earthly life either in the underworld or sometimes in the heavens. Therefore, corpses, first of the pharaoh and sacred animals, then in time of lesser mortals, were mummified and preserved in monumental tombs such as the pyramids with their accompanying temple complexes. The pharaoh, thus destined for immortality, was thought to be a son of a god and could only marry within his own family.

One of the important myths was that of Isis (the Nile?) and Osiris (the harvest?), in which the mother goddess sought out her spouse, murdered and emasculated by his brother Seth (the desert?) in order that the fertility of the land might be maintained. The priests attempted to develop consistent theologies, but their mythological system remained, as far as we know, very fragmentary. The Egyptians did not equal the Mesopotamians in the development of codes of law, but their ethics took the form of the kind of wisdom literature familiar to us from the Hebrew Bible.

In Europe, especially in coastal regions, contemporaneously with these great urban civilizations flourished the mysterious megalithic cultures which were not urban but which nevertheless left great monuments such as Stonehenge in England. The builders evidently worshiped the celestial bodies since these monuments are sometimes accurately oriented to the solstices.[23] These cultures were succeeded by the spread of peoples speaking Indo-European languages, the so-called Aryans. These included: the Celts in the west, Slavs in the east, the Greeks and Latins in the south; and then from the north the Germans who overran the Celts. These tribes produced a new family of cultures whose religions had many common features, especially the threefold division of society into the warrior, priestly, and farmer classes, each marked by a special ethos.[24] This threefold class division was reflected in the gods each level of society favored.

Of these Indo-European religions, it suffices here to consider as typical those of the Greeks and Latins which became by far the most influential for the origin of the options which still present themselves to us today. When Greek speaking people invaded their present territories and Ionia (eastern Turkey) they found there already the culture whose source was the island of Crete, which had relations with that of Egypt and where, as far as we can judge, the cult of a mother goddess predominated.[25] The Greeks assimilated elements of this Cretan religion and female goddesses remained prominent in their worship. The patroness of the great culture center Athens was Athena the Virgin, powerful in wisdom and in war. The Indo-European pattern predominated, however, and the major gods were conceived as forming a court on Mt. Olympus under the rule of Zeus, the supreme god of the sky and of thunder, who had overcome the Titanic gods of violence and confusion by establishing an orderly universe. These major gods each had his or her own cult under various titles in different places, but poets such Homer, Hesiod, and Pindar systematized these in a rather consistent total mythology, representing them as descended from common ancestors.

As pictured by the poets and in the remarkably realistic yet idealized art of the Greeks, these Olympian gods were heroic figures symbolizing the great forces of nature and of orderly society, but also very human in their passionate loves and wars. Since the supremacy of Zeus did not seem to produce perfect cosmic unity, many felt that above all the gods stood Fate (Moira), impersonal and implacable determinism. Popular religion was not as harmoniously systematic as the myths of the poets, but often centered on local minor divinities associated with springs, rivers, winds, rocks, trees, animals, the fertility of the fields, etc. To keep all these deities propitious demanded many taboos, rituals, sacrifices, and purifications to be observed.

As E.R. Dodds has shown,[26] Greek religion was often darkly "irrational" and yet in the great civic cults it had the appearance of great beauty, order, and reasonableness. Two special features of Greek religion need special comment. The first is the existence of the "mysteries," special cults requiring a solemn initiation to reveal secret doctrines. One of the chief mysteries was the Eleusinian based on the fertility myth of the rape of Persephone from her mother Demeter by Hades, the god of the underworld, who reluctantly permitted her to return to earth for half of each year. The other chief mystery was the Orphic based on a similar myth of the descent into the realms of the dead by the magician and musician Orpheus in search of his wife Euridice. These mysteries promised initiates future lives of happiness just as vegetation revives after the death of winter. Such assurance was much needed because the Greeks, although they yearned for immortality, generally expected only a shadowy, hopeless existence in the grave. A second notable feature of Greek religion was the great interest in oracles such as the one at Delphi where an ecstatic female prophetess answered questions submitted to her, often by the heads of the city-states.

The religion of the Romans paralleled that of the Greeks, but had a very different style.[27] Its chief god, equivalent to Zeus, was Jupiter and its other deities also matched the major Greek gods. Yet the Romans lacked an extensive narrative mythology and its innumerable lesser gods tended to be mere abstractions standing for mysterious powers or *numina* whose cult was maintained in Rome by a rich calendar of festivals.

Deeply embedded in Roman religion were features derived from an Italian people of non-Indo-European language, the Etruscans, who for a time ruled Rome. The Etruscans emphasized the cult of the dead and the practice of divination that, for the Romans, had to accompany every important event. Its strongly social character marked Roman religion so that it was directed to preserving the family, the state, and the army. As the Roman Empire expanded it assimilated to itself the gods of all the peoples it conquered, and exalted the worship of the Emperor, chief of the army and symbol of the state.

The Indo-European speaking peoples spread not only in Europe but simultaneously into what is now Iran and India. The religion of these self-styled Aryans ("noble people")[28] in their Indian immigration is known to us through the *Vedas* (usually dated after 1500 BCE) transmitted orally for many centuries through a priestly class, the Brahmins. The Aryan threefold class system was retained, but the Brahmins became especially powerful in India, and eventually an inferior fourth class was added, probably to include the native Dravidians. These natives already had a well-developed urban culture in the Indus Valley with certain features such as yoga asceticism and worship of a mother goddess[29] that were gradually assimilated by the Aryans into their own Vedic religion.[30]

The Vedic hymns (*Rig-Veda*) celebrate a pantheon similar to the Greeks but adapted to a very complex ritual system of sacrificial rites necessary to consecrate every function of daily life. The other three Vedas are detailed instructions for the proper performance of these complicated rites. The ethical values promoted by Vedic religion are expressed in the law code of *Manu* and in the great epic poems the *Mahabharata* and the *Ramayana*.[31] These classics provided a gallant warrior ethic for the warrior class, a world renouncing, ascetic ethics for the Brahmins and an ethics of earthly pleasure for the peasants. Thus the Aryan three-class society was reinforced and eventually rigidly fixed as the *caste system*.

Contemporaneous (according to linguistic evidence) with the *Vedas* of the Aryan Indians are the *Gathas* of those Aryans who immigrated into Iran. They are attributed to a Zarathustra (Zoroaster) about whom little is known.[32] Although the *Gathas* know a supremely good god Ahura Mazda they also speak of other gods, such as the sun god Mithra. How these polytheistic religions of the Indo-Europeans came to be reformed in later Hinduism and Zoroastrianism will be discussed in the next chapter.

Further east in Asia, contemporary with the Vedic period, was the non-Indo-European Shang culture of China that we have already examined in Chapter 2.[33] As described there Shang religion was polytheistic, but the personalities of its gods were vague. Its chief god was the sky god Shang Ti, replaced under the Chou dynasty (1100-221 BCE) by T'ien, usually translated as the impersonal "Heaven." The Emperor was also a priest who alone offered sacrifice to Heaven for the people. Many of the popular gods were spirits of fertility of obvious interest to a mainly peasant population concerned for their crops and herds. Divination was vital to the state cult, while for a more personal devotion reverence paid to the ancestors was paramount. Indeed, this ancestor worship was perhaps the most characteristic feature of Chinese religion even as it is today of African religion. Although the ancient Chinese spoke of the High God impersonally as we speak of "Nature," they were very concerned that the social order should be kept in harmony with the order of this Nature. The order of Nature they conceived as a balance between two fundamental opposites: a masculine active principle (*yang*, symbolized by the sun and the circle) and its complementary feminine passive principle (*yin*, symbolized by rain clouds and the square).

The pre-Confucian Chinese ethical system stressed this balance of life, grounded in family loyalty. Its ideals were expressed in the Five Classics that Confucius was to edit as the basis of his reform; the Books of *History*, *Spring and Autumn Annals*, *Divination*, and *Poems*, and the now lost Books of *Music* and *Ceremonies*. To perform these ceremonies was chiefly the duty of a priestly caste at the court of the Emperor or the feudal lords. But there were also, especially in South China, both men and women who assumed the charismatic role of shaman or prophet.

The Japanese islands were originally inhabited in their northern parts by an Asiatic people of pre-literary culture, the Ainu.[34] The present Japanese entered the islands from Asia not earlier than the 600's BCE. Little is known of their history until as late as 600 CE. Certainly, however, their original religion, Shinto, was also of the pre-literary type based on the worship of the spirits of natural forces and reverence for the ancestors. Its fundamental concept was that of the *kami*, a very vague notion of spiritual powers which could be embodied in many different persons and objects.

In the Americas, inhabited after the last ice-age by peoples of Asiatic origin, great cult centers also arose among the Olmecs, Mayas, Aztecs and others in Central America and Mexico and the Incas in Peru, perhaps having some trans-Pacific stimulation but certainly exhibiting strong original features. About the beginning of the Christian era these cultures produced cities with a magnificent architecture of pyramids and temples, served by a carefully trained priesthood which developed perhaps the most systematic mythologies of any known peoples. Common to these American religions was an elaborate correlation between a hierarchical social system and the cosmic order. The tribes of North America and of South America outside Inca territories had simpler cultures than those of Central America and Peru. Yet their religions shared many features of those great cultic centers and in some areas, such as the Mississippi Valley, had important cult centers of their own.[35]

Among the Central Americans time was divided into cyclical world-epochs and events carefully dated by a wonderfully accurate calendar, expressing a strong sense of fatality and determinism. Space was divided into the four quarters of the horizon and the three levels of the underworld, earth, and heaven. Colors were systematically attributed to these divisions of time and space. Social classes, occupations, geographical areas, and tribal affiliations were correlated with these cosmic categories. A hierarchy of the gods of nature and various occupations was elaborated under a supreme creator god (sometimes with a wife). Sacrifice, including human sacrifice, was considered essential to maintain the vitality of gods and men and the stability of the cosmic and social order. Especially among the Aztecs, the cult of war gods flourished with the special object of obtaining human victims for sacrifice. Common to both major centers was the notion that the lives of men and even of the gods depended on the lives of their "doubles" or guardian spirits. Inca religion had a simpler pantheon and put great emphasis on the worship of mummified ancestors or of stones representing them.

5. Mythic Religion vs. Humanism

If we compare these various prehistoric, pre-literary, and ancient urban forms of religion on a world scale, we can note a number of common features. The underlying universality of such beliefs naturally raises the question whether any of these religions can be considered a possible option for modern men and women in preference to the Humanist philosophies of life discussed in Chapter 2. At first sight it seem this is a silly question, since the very fact that these religions (at least in the ancient forms described above) are now dead seems to settle the matter. Since it is characteristic of these religions that they were closely tied to a particular place and culture, it is not possible that a modern person could join a community which no longer exists. I might like to become a citizen of ancient Athens and share in the faith that produced classic art, literature, and wisdom, but I cannot. Yet some marginalized people, Native Americans in the United States for example, are today struggling to restore their native cultures and religious practices. Furthermore we see some nostalgic and not very authentic attempts of Europeans and Americans to revive paganism such as the Druid societies and the Wicca covens of witches.[36]

It seems a more realistic possibility that with our present historical knowledge we might recover the profound insights common to these religions that scientific and technological progress may have distorted and suppressed to the disadvantage of modern life. As we have seen, psychoanalyst Carl Gustav Jung and other students of mythic cultures have envisaged such a retrieval.[37] They have argued that early religions met fundamental human needs no longer satisfied by modern philosophies of life. In our own country students of surviving Native American religion have found in its world-view and value-system, its myths and rituals, deep healing for modern existential anxieties.[38] They have argued that only by the invocation of archetypal symbols in myths and rituals can humanity deal with its ultimate concerns.

First, we can compare Humanist to mythic religion with respect to the chief article of faith of Humanism, namely, confidence in the human power to control the world by scientific technology and remake it creatively according to freely chosen goals and culturally formed values. The mythic religions, on the other hand, rest on the conviction that human happiness depends on living in harmony with a cosmic order which exceeds human control. Not, indeed, that these cultures have denied the human capacity to develop technological control over natural processes. The simplest cultures have developed various arts of survival and the urban civilizations have achieved wonderful technological feats such as the invention of cereal agriculture, irrigation, metallurgy, astronomical observation, accurate calendars, navigation, monumental architecture, and above all writing.

In the mythologies of these cultures great inventions are commonly attributed to "culture heroes" who are inspired and aided by the gods or are themselves demigods. These technologies, moreover, are so mixed with magic and propitiation of the gods and spirits that their efficacy is not attributed principally to human but to superhuman power. Consequently, for these people human control, although real, is subordinated to divine control and must be in harmony with it, if it is to succeed. Certain myths such as that of Prometheus who helped man steal fire from the gods, the Bible story of the Tower of Babel, and the Trickster figure in Native American mythology warn mortals not to try to rival the gods. Hence in these religions sin and its evil consequences, as well as natural disasters, are understood as failures on the part of humans to correspond with a cosmic order controlled by the gods.

Obviously this means that the cosmic order is not the result of impersonal, non-teleological forces as Humanism, with its confident reliance on modern science, supposes. Rather it is the work of intelligent, superhuman persons with whom humans can enter into communication and social relationships. Although sometimes in these mythic cultures the superhuman powers are only very vaguely personified forces (*mana*) overshadowed by an impersonal Fate, yet they are conceived by analogy to human agents rather than to natural forces in the modern scientific sense. Thus these powers *know* what human beings are doing and thinking and they *respond* to human communication. That is why even magical efforts to control these powers depend not so much on cause and effect relationships as on the use of *symbols* whose function is communication.

Therefore the question at issue between the Humanist world-view and the mythic one is whether these "gods" and "spirits" and "powers" really intervene in the world of our experience. Can we communicate with them and seek their aid? Or is science alone able (in principle at least) to give human beings effective control over this world? The Humanist world-view excludes the existence of these superhuman presences and is outraged that religious leaders should foster such illusions. For example the anthropologist James Lett in an article "Science, Anthropology, and Religion"[39] berates many of his colleagues who study religion in its own categories (an *emic* method) rather than in the categories of science (an *etic* method). He forthrightly maintains that there is no way to obtain objective truth except through science although it can only hope to attain probability. He goes on to assert, "[W]e know that no religion is true because we know that all beliefs are either non-falsifiable or falsified. In the interests of scientific integrity, we have an obligation to declare that knowledge."

Thus while the mythic view does not necessarily exclude scientific explanations but accepts them as partial but insufficient explanations of experience, modern science (as Lett and many other Humanists understand it) emphatically rejects the existence of God or a spiritual realm. The Humanist rejects this mythic approach as irrational and sure to doom humanity to neglect the one capacity that raises it above brute existence, the power of intelligence. Living in a world of myth humanity can never fully develop this capacity, and hence will remain largely in ignorance, a victim of disaster and disease, famine and fanaticism. Only in those modern cultures that have rigorously excluded mythic thinking has modern science and technology been able to develop; and it is these cultures that are rapidly coming to rule the globe. The mythological world-view has perished in developed countries and survives only among marginal peoples.

On the contrary those who accept the existence of a spiritual reality other than the material realm that is the limited subject of scientific methods, would find that Lett's assertion begs the question. I will show in Chapter 5 that there are modern philosophers who reject Lett's assertion that science falsifies all claims for the existence of God and a spiritual realm. To the contrary they argue that when modern science is freed of certain prejudices imposed on it by modern philosophers, it actually demonstrates that science would be impossible if it were not for the existence of a spiritual realm. Moreover, as our survey continues, it will be evident that in all world-views, including as we have seen in this chapter that of the Mythological Religions, the question of the Totality of the real is raised. In spite of the great variety of answers to this question, the most common is a vague monotheism. In all world-views a Supreme Being as the origin and ground of all that is, material or spiritual, appears at least in the background. Thus in Mythological Religions there are generally myths related to a High God, male or female, who rules all things. This One may not be of such immediate concern as other spirits, or even receive such explicit worship, but is presupposed as embracing all. Even Humanists like Albert Einstein can say such things as,[40]

> I cannot imagine a God who rewards and punishes the objects of his creation whose purposes are modeled after our own — a God, in short, who is but a reflection of human frailty. Neither can I believe that the individual survives the death of his body, although feeble souls harbor such thoughts through fear or ridiculous egoism. It is enough for me to contemplate the mystery of conscious life perpetuating itself through all eternity, to reflect on the marvelous structure of the universe which we can dimly perceive, and to try humbly to comprehend even an infinitesimal part of the intelligence manifested in nature.

Of course some Humanists also declare themselves open to the possible existence of God, of extraterrestrial intelligences, or of "psychical phenomena" attributed to the survival of human minds after death, and even engage in research on "paranormal phenomena." Nevertheless, they maintain that only if such existence can be verified by science (as it is currently interpreted by such scientists as Lett) should it be accepted as objectively true. Defenders of the mythic world-view, on the other hand, would argue that scientific explanations and tests are by their very nature too limited and reductive to settle such questions. Thus they subordinate the modern scientific method to what they claim is a broader and deeper approach that recognizes that human experience cannot be articulated adequately in literal concepts such as those used by modern science but only in symbols and mythic narratives. They do not contend that scientific explanations of human experience are invalid, but only that they are partial and reductionist.

Again, defenders of the existence of a spiritual realm do not deny that modern scientific technology has given humanity a control over natural forces that religious rituals and magic never provided. They point out, however, that such a technological mastery betters human life only when used under the control of a world-view more profound than science provides. The fact that the scientific world-view has come to dominate modern life to the exclusion of mythic thinking is no proof it has better succeeded in answering the ultimate questions that concern us as human persons. In fact this dominance has given ample proof that the Humanist world-view because of its arrogant materialism can also be ruthlessly destructive of nature and humanity. Modern scientific technology, which might have been used to complement the natural order, is in fact ravaging it, severing the harmonious relation between humanity and nature, and threatening the world with a nuclear holocaust. By divorcing culture from nature it has made us "one-dimensional" neurotics in a social order where hedonism and violence rule the day and night. Have not the worst features of pre-literary and ancient urban cultures been exaggerated under Humanism? The human sacrifices of some ancient religions hardly compare to modern genocide. As for modern rationality, why is it that the Humanist philosophers of our day have concluded that the world and we with it are absurd? Humanism has emptied our world of meaning so that, as Sartre says, "Man is a useless passion."

As I showed in the last chapter, the romantic wing of Humanism has always recognized that "value free" science is incapable of providing the value-system that Humanism must have if it is to be an adequate philosophy of life. Hence Romanticism saw much of value in the mythic cultures. Yet because Humanism remains attached to the notion that only science possesses objective truth, romantics find it impossible to *believe* in the myths they genuinely admire. They are forced to reduce them to manifestations of the unconscious side of human personality. Thus Freud interpreted symbols and myths as a concealment of suppressed biological drives and Jung as manifestations of an inherited Collective Unconscious. They did not explain how such products of human creativity could originate from that level of the human psyche that we share with animals governed by instincts that lack freedom. Today the supposedly scientific theories of Freud and Jung are severely criticized as being as unscientific as the myths they claimed to explain.[41]

To understand the case for mythic thinking better, let us consider a sentence spoken by telephone such as, "Hello, Jill! This is John; I love you." For a physicist such a sentence is a mere sequence of noises explicable as due to a series of movements of the human lungs and vocal organs and transmitted electronically. For the woman answering the phone, they reveal the existence of a unique person opening his interior life to her. A philologist, semiotician, or psychologist who knows both parties can view this as a communicative act whose structure can be objectively studied as a physical reality which is at the same a symbol conveying information other than itself from one thinking, imagining, feeling, willing person to another.[42] The scientist who attempts to reduce thinking, imagining, feeling, willing to currents in the brain and secretions of hormones then has to confront the mind-body problem on whose solution science has made little progress.[43]

Human experience is made up of a sequence of events which have various causal connections, although modern science (contrary to the Enlightenment notion that science rests on absolutely deterministic laws) does not deny a genuine element of chance in the cosmic order. Scientific laws are only generalities, statements of probability that cannot (even given perfect descriptive knowledge of a cross section of the world) absolutely predict the historical sequence of unique future events. This means that in principle actual human experience, which is essentially historical, can never be totally explained by science. Yet the human mind can not only detect certain regularities of nature in this experience, but by a hermeneutic process can interpret even apparently chance sequences of events as *symbols* communicating messages from one thinking subject to another.

Of course such interpretations may err. The paranoiac reads his fears into sounds which are real enough but which appear meaningless to normal people. Nevertheless, normal people are aware of the content of a series of sounds and capable of distinguishing between their own subjective fantasies and the objective sounds. They seldom fail to recognize genuine speech and to interpret it in ways that can be confirmed by others. Recent efforts of Deconstructionism[44] to show that any text means only what the reader makes it mean do not explain why in an ordinary conversation we sometimes understand each other. Sometimes we even understand what deconstructionists are saying!

Those who live in a mythic world recognize natural cause and effect relations, but they also interpret many of these events as *revelatory* of superhuman persons who cannot be directly experienced or heard to speak in ordinary human language. The wind becomes the voice of Someone. The light of the sun with its life-giving or destroying energy becomes a theophany. The huge, resistant bulk of a mountain or a boulder manifests the unyielding presence of a god. An idol, although it was made by human hands, communicates the presence of a superhuman person who has inspired its making and enters into human experience through its symbolic mediation. The mythical stories passed down from generation to generation furnish models by which to interpret the recurring events of the human life cycle.

What, then are we to think of the miracles, prophetic oracles, and the magical and ritual control over natural phenomena that are part of the mythological view of the world? Certainly many religions teach that shamans and prophets and even ordinary persons at certain crises of life can directly communicate with superhuman beings through dreams and trances, often assisted by drugs, music, and ascetical techniques. They also believe that to some persons future events, scientifically unpredictable, are revealed either by visions or trances, or by various methods of divination. Moreover they claim that by magical or ritual acts diseases are miraculously healed and other extraordinary but publicly verifiable, objective effects are produced, and that some persons have innate or charismatic powers to effect such miracles.

Certainly Humanists today cannot find a scientific reason for denying *a priori* the possibility of miraculous events. Some still accept the famous argument of Hume[45] that since miracles are exceptions to natural laws, it is always *more probable* that those reporting them are lying or deceived than that such exceptions have actually occurred. Since historical events are unique and can never exactly repeat themselves, this thesis, rigorously applied, would eliminate history as a valid form of human knowing. Surely we can be certain that President J.F. Kennedy was assassinated and even that there was some probability that he, like any public figure might be, but it is impossible to give a necessary answer to why it actually happened and on a certain date in a certain place.

The skeptical Humanist must claim that either the alleged miraculous events did not actually occur historically, or that if they occurred they can be adequately explained by natural laws and thus lack any special clues to indicate they have a revelatory or communicative character. Certainly, this kind of answer works for many supposedly extraordinary events. For example, the many reports of UFO's[46] often turn out to be mere rumors and if shown to be factual are explicable as ordinary events that have been misinterpreted by the observers. Again many of the claims of "psychics" to predict the future or to perform feats of telepathy, materialization, etc., have been exposed as fraudulent. Perhaps even more telling for Humanist skepticism is the fact that many reports of the miraculous come to us from pre-literary cultures and from the pre-scientific period (e.g., the countless miracles attributed to medieval saints[47]). Even today at Lourdes the number of certified miracles has lessened as more rigorous medical tests have been applied.[48] This seems to show that more critical history would eliminate *all* such marvels. Modern biblical critics, even some who are believers, seem to have given up trying to prove that biblical prophecies have ever been fulfilled and now explain them simply as referring to contemporary events or as prophecies *ex eventu*. Indeed critical historians tend to count reports of the miraculous in a document as *prima facie* evidence against its reliability.

In reply to such arguments, the defender of the mythic worldview can concede that many miracles and prophecies are fraudulent and that believers often tend to multiply them extravagantly, just as there are false scientific theories and others for which the evidence has been exaggerated. Critical examination is always required to screen out the really significant elements in any world-view, those experiences that are both meaningful and verifiable. The real issue is what the *criteria of verification* (or *falsification*) should be.

The Humanist demands of the mythicist that miracles and prophecies be verified *scientifically*. Scientific verification in the strict sense, however, demands objectivity be achieved by controlled and repeatable experiments, or least through repeated observation by neutral, sophisticated observers, so that various kinds of possible errors can be eliminated.[49] As we have already seen, by the very nature of the scientific method that deals with universal laws historical events are never in a strict sense scientifically verifiable since they cannot be predicted by any natural law but only explained as a product both of law and chance.

Critical history rests not on these strictly scientific criteria of verification but on the analysis of documents and corroborative evidence. If there is communication from superhuman beings, it is first of all designed to convey a message to particular human persons according to their own personal conditions.[50] Its public recognition depends not on the ability to verify it by various kinds of public tests but on the *veracity* of the witnesses to whom its truth has been verified in what are perhaps purely personal ways. At most it can be attested by a number of witnesses who confirm each other's testimony.

Moreover, it would seem that superhuman beings, particularly the gods or God, cannot belie their sovereignty over the world by subjecting their communications to the kind of human control involved in human tests of the scientific or human type. It suffices they certify their messages personally to the direct recipient. They commission that witness to speak for them, requiring belief on the part of others because of the credibility of the messenger. The ordinary believer ought not to demand anything more than this sufficient credibility. The fact that this credibility cannot be put to a scientific test does not necessarily remove its certitude. One can argue that we take the word of scientists for the honesty of their experiments, because other scientists can always repeat these experiments, while we cannot do this for witnesses of the miraculous. Nevertheless, in fact, our trust in scientists would suffer from an infinite regress, if at some point we did not accept this witness as final. We who have never seen the planet Pluto cannot reasonably doubt its existence because of the witness of astronomers who have seen it. We do so because we very reasonably trust them here and now, not because other scientists in the future can verify their statements. It is only because we trust them here and now that we believe this future verification is possible. To trust a witness to a miracle is not, therefore, credulous just because we were not present at the event. We may indeed in the future be able to further test the witness's reliability, but that is not necessary to believe him or her here and now.

Finally, the recognition of the truth of any person-to-person communication cannot be reduced simply to objective criteria, but also involves a certain *connaturality*. We know our mother is telling us the truth because through love we share her mind and heart and can recognize her seriousness and sincerity. Similarly the perception of superhuman communication requires a connaturality of life in the recipient. The mystics and prophets and the honest believers may be attuned to recognize divine communication and to distinguish it from what is false.

Therefore it is not surprising that the romantics among the Humanists have themselves brought forward these arguments to show the inadequacy to human experience of a reductively scientistic Humanism. Some urge that the mythological world-view now be respected and supplemented with other forms of human knowledge, intuitive, esthetic, and moral. Many of them have been led by this realization to search for wider and deeper truth in occultism or in exotic religions, although they still cling to the fundamental assumptions of Humanism. Some have actually returned to "paganism," i.e., ancient European Greco-Roman, Celtic, or Germanic mythology. Others have adopted pre-literary religions such as that of the Native Americans or Africans, but the most attractive alternative for many western Humanists has been the Oriental religions. Thus Martin Heidegger, perhaps the most influential of post-modern philosophers, came to believe that the whole history of western thought that culminated in modern science and its technological application in our century was coming to an end. He surmised that, if we are to escape the nihilism of Nietzsche, the future of thought might well be found in the mysticism of the Orient.[51]

To these exotic world-views I will now turn, not in their older mythic phase already described in this chapter, but in their more developed or reformed stage as great world religions. Even in their ancient forms they continue to contribute much to the riches of the Christian world-view for which they laid the foundations and for Humanism in its derivation and reaction to Christianity. Thus in the Renaissance, whose culture Humanists usually much admire, philosophers and artists were able to develop and express in literature and fine art what they called the "Ancient Theology" concealed in Greek and Roman Mythology and revealed in Christianity.[52] Thus in the Sistine Chapel we see how Michelangelo ranks the pagan Sybils with the Jewish Prophets and links them together with nude youths who some say are a Greek way of depicting the world of angelic spirits.

Notes

[1] *Creative Mythology: The Masks of God* (New York: Penguin Books, 1968), pp. 4-5.

[2] Carl Gustav Jung, *The Archetypes of the Collective Unconscious, Collected Works,* vol. 9 (New York: Bollingen Series, Pantheon Books, 1959).

[3] On the romantic and neopagan origins of goddess cults and their relation to occultism and theosophy, see Philip O. Davis, *Goddess Unmasked: The Rise of Neopagan Feminist Spirituality* (Dallas, TX: Spence Publishing, 1998). Also see Manfred Hauke, *God or Goddess?* (San Francisco: Ignatius Press, 1995).

[4] E.E. Evans Pritchard, *Theories of Primitive Religion* (Oxford: Clarendon Press, 1965); Mircea Eliade; *A History of Religious Ideas,* 2 vols. (Chicago: University of Chicago Press, 1978), vol. 1, p. 355; J. Maringer, *The Gods of Prehistoric Man* (New York: Knopf, 1960) and Victor Turner, "Religion in Primitive Cultures," *New Catholic Encyclopedia,* vol. 12, pp. 246-250.

[5] On these see Wilhelm Dupré, *Religion in Primitive Cultures* (The Hague: Mouton, 1975); E.G. James, *Primitive Religion* (London: Thames and Hudson, 1957); Benjamin C. Ray, *African Religions: Symbol, Ritual, and Community* (Englewood Cliffs, NJ: Prentice-Hall, 1976).

[6] Isma'il Ragi al Faruqi and David E. Sopher, *Historical Atlas of the Religions of the World* (New York: Macmillan, 1974), maps pp. xi-xx. See also Chapters 6-8, pp. 45-58.

[7] Paul Radin, *Primitive Man as Philosopher,* enlarged ed. (New York: Dover Publications, 1957), pp. 41-62.

[8] Dupré, *Religion in Primitive Cultures* (note 5 above), pp. 302-308. Wilhelm Schmidt, SVD in his mammoth 12 vol., *Der Ursprung der Gottesidee* (1912-55) gathered an immense amount of evidence for "primitive monotheism." Although Schmidt's "diffusionist"

theories to explain this data are now outmoded, his data exploded any simple view that religion evolved from animism to polytheism to monotheism.

[9] For example the complex system described by R.W. Williamson, *Religions and Cosmic Beliefs in Central Polynesia* (Cambridge: Cambridge University Press, 1933).

[10] On the difference between religion and magic see Dupré (note 5 above), pp. 141-7; 269-71. He concludes that though they are theoretically dialectically opposed, practically the dividing line is fluid. See also Michael F. Brown, "Thinking about Magic" in Stephen D. Glazier, ed., *Anthropology of Religion: A Handbook* (Westport, CT, 1997), pp. 121-38.

[11] On mythic time see J.S. Mbiti's excellent study, *African Religions and Philosophy* (New York: Doubleday, 1970), pp. 15-28 and Mircea Eliade, *Myth and Reality* (New York: Harper and Row, 1963), pp. 58, 108-13.

[12] For an example see Erich Neumann, *The Great Mother: An Analysis of Archetypes* (New York: Pantheon Books, 1955).

[13] See Joan B. Townsend, "Shamanism," in Glazier, ed., *Anthropology of Religion* (Westport, CT, 1997, note 10 above), pp. 429-70.

[14] For attempts to explicitate the value systems of some pre-literate cultures see Richard B. Brandt, *Hopi Ethics* (Chicago: University of Chicago Press, 1954). Also see John Ladd, *The Structure of a Moral Code: A Philosophical Analysis of Ethical Discourse Applied to the Ethics of the Navaho Indians* (Cambridge, MA: Harvard University Press, 1957); and David Little and Sumner B. Twiss, *Comparative Religious Ethics: A New Method* (San Francisco: Harper and Row, 1978).

[15] On the notion of taboo see Niels C. Nielsen Jr., *et al.*, *Religions of the World* (New York: St. Martin's Press, 1983), p. 13 and note.

[16] See Emile Durkheim, *The Elementary Forms of the Religious Life,* trans. by J.W. Swain (New York: Collier Books, 1961).

[17] For examples of this aspect of preliterate religion see E.E. Evans Pritchard, *Witchcraft, Oracles and Magic among the Azande* (Oxford: Clarendon Press, 1937). On a recent visit to Nigeria in talking to Catholic priests and lay catechists who are natives, I found that for them a major pastoral problem is how to reassure their people who though Christian remain deeply fearful of witchcraft and evil spirits.

[18] Ninian Smart, *The Religious Experience of Mankind,* 2nd ed. (New York: Charles Scribner's Sons, 1976), p. 67.

[19] See Eleonore Bille-du-Mot, *The Age of Akhenaten* (London: Evelyn, Adams, and Mackay, 1966). On the relation of Akhenaten's monotheism to that of Israel, see Johannes C. De Moor, *The Rise of Monotheism: The Roots of Israelite Monotheism,* Revised and Enlarged Edition (Leuven: University of Leuven Press, 1997), pp. 53-40.

[20] Henri Frankfort, *Kingship and the Gods* (Chicago: University of Chicago Press, 1969), pp. 215-30, referring to Thorkild Jacobsen, "Primitive Democracy in Ancient Mesopotamia," *Journal of Near Eastern Studies* II (1943), 159-72.

[21] See De Moor, *The Rise of Monotheism,* (note 19 above), pp. 58-64.

[22] On Egyptian religion see C.J. Bleeker, "The Religion of Ancient Egypt" in *Historia Religionum,* 2 vols. (Leiden: Brill, 1969), vol. 1, pp. 401-14.

[23] See Eliade, *History of Religious Ideas* (note 4 above), vol. 1, pp. 114-24 with bibliography.

[24] See Georges Dumezil, *Archaic Roman Religion* (Chicago: University of Chicago Press, 1970).

[25] On Cretan religion see A.W. Persson, *Religion of Greece in Prehistoric Times* (Berkeley: University of California Press, 1950). On Greek religion see W.K.C. Guthries, *The Greeks and Their Gods* (Boston: Beacon Press, 1955).

[26] *The Greeks and the Irrational* (Berkeley: University of California Press, 1951).

[27] See R. Schilling, "The Roman Religion" in Bleeker, *Historia Religionum* (note 22 above), vol. 1, pp. 424-94.

[28] See J.P. Mallory, *In Search of the Indo-Europeans: Language, Archaeology and Myth* (Thames and Hudson: London, 1958) for a discussion of this much debated question.

[29] For a description of yoga techniques see Swami Sivananda Radha, *Kundalini Yoga for the West* (Boulder & London: Shambhala, 1981).

[30] See A. Basham, "Hinduism" in R.C. Zaehner, ed., *The Concise Encyclopedia of Living Faiths* (New York: Hawthorn Books, 1959), pp. 225-60 and Robert D. Baird, "Indian Religious Traditions" in W. Richard Comstock, *et al., Religion and Man: An Introduction* (New York: Harper and Row, 1971), pp. 115-245, with bibliography pp. 245-50. Most of the specialists note that "Hinduism" is not one religion but many; yet there are also many features common to most of these.

[31] See J.A.B. van Buiten, introduction to his translation of *The Bhagavadgita in the Mahabharata* (Chicago: University of Chicago Press, 1981), pp. 14-15.

[32] On Zoroastrianism see R.C. Zaehner, *The Dawn and Twilight of Zoroastrianism* (New York: Putnam, 1961) and Mary Boyce, *Zoroastrians: Their religious beliefs and practices* (London: Routledge, Kegan Paul, 1979); *A History of Zoroastrianism,* 2 vols. (Handbuch der Orientalistik, ed. B. Spuler, Leiden, 1982) and *Textual Sources for the Study of Zoroastrianism* (Totowa, NJ: Barnes and Noble, 1984). I have here followed Boyce's early dating for Zoroaster.

[33] On Chinese religion see bibliography in Chapter 2, note 22.

[34] On Japanese religion see Hajima Nakamura, *Ways of Thinking of Eastern Peoples* (Honolulu: East West Center Press, 1964), pp. 345-587; Joseph M. Kitigawa, *Religion in Japanese History* (New York: Columbia University Press, 1966); and Charles A. Moore, ed., *The Japanese Mind* (Honolulu: East West Center Press, 1967).

[35] See Carl Waldman, *Atlas of the North American Indian,* with maps and illustrations by Molly Braun (New York: Facts on File, Inc., 1985), pp. 57-60.

[36] See Henry Maurier, *The Other Covenant: A Theology of Paganism* (Glen Rock, NJ: Newman Press, 1968) and Starhawk, *Dreaming the Dark: Magic, Sex and Politics* (Boston: Beacon Press, 1982). For a somewhat polemic survey of the current proliferation of pagan cults, see Ralph Rath, *The New Age: A Christian Critique* (South Bend, IN: Greelawn Press, 1990).

[37] See notes 1 and 2 above.

[38] On the religions of the Americas see Ske Hultkrantz, *Belief and Worship in North America* (Syracuse, NY: Syracuse University Press, 1981), pp. 99-116.

[39] In Glazier, *Anthropology of Religion,* note 10 above, pp. 103-20, quote from p. 116.

[40] In an essay in *Living Philosophies* (no editor of this collection is given, New York: Simon and Schuster, 1931), pp. 6-7. His inability to imagine that God rewards and punishes was perhaps connected to his determinism that admitted human free will as subjective only, *ibid.,* p. 3. On other occasions Einstein identified his religion with the pantheism of Spinoza which was also fatalistic—see Paul Arthur Schlipp, ed., *Albert Einstein: Philosophy-Scientist* (Evanston, IL: The Library of Living Philosophers, Inc., 1949), pp. 658-663—and characterized it as a "cosmic religious feeling." Thus for him the Totality is infused with intelligible order accessible to human reason in part, but as Whole only to "feeling" which in a person of German culture probably meant not just emotion but also intuition. How Spinoza and Einstein reconciled determinism with moral responsibility, something they fully recognized in writing and in conduct, is not at all clear.

[41] On the notion of the creativity of the "unconscious mind" see my *Theologies of the Body: Humanist and Christian,* 2nd ed. (Boston: National Catholic Center for Bioethics, 1987), pp. 312-318.

[42] For empathetic insight into Native American ritual see H.B. Alexander, *The World's Rim* (Lincoln, NB: University of Nebraska Press, 1967).

[43] See Roger Penrose, *The Emperor's New Mind: Concerning Computers, Minds, and the Laws of Physics* (New York, Oxford University Press, 1989), who argues that since computers can do nothing but compute and conscious thought is not computation, it is not possible to invent a computer that has consciousness or can think.

[44] For an introduction to this topic see Mark Krupnick, ed., *Displacement: Derrida and After* (Bloomington IN: Indiana University Press, 1983). For basic concepts of modern communication theory and bibliography see John N. Deely, *Introducing Semiotics* (Bloomington, IN: Indiana University Press, 1982). Robin Horton, "African Traditional Thought and Western Science," *Africa,* 37 (Jan. 1967), 50-71 and (Apr.), 155-187 provides a good example of a detailed translation of one world-view into another.

[45] David Hume, *Dialogues Concerning Natural Religion,* ed. by N.K. Smith (Indianapolis: Bobs Merrill, 1964).

[46] Philip J. Klass, *UFO's Explained* (New York: Random House, 1974).

[47] For a discussion of the interpretation of medieval hagiography see Sherry L. Reames, *The Legenda Aurea: A Reexamination of Its Paradoxical History* (Madison, WI: The University of Wisconsin Press, 1985).

[48] For a discussion of basic facts about Lourdes see Patrick Marnham, *Lourdes* (Garden City, NY: Doubleday Image Books, 1982).

[49] See Edward L. Schoen, *Religious Explanation: A Model from the Sciences* (Durham, NC: Duke University, 1985) for a philosophical exploration of the two modes of explanation.

[50] See the game theory discussion in Steven J. Brams, *Superior Beings: If They Exist How Would We Know?* (New York: Springer Verlag, 1983).

[51] See my article, "Truth and Technology," *American Catholic Philosophical Association Proceedings, The Importance of Truth,* 68 (1993), pp. 27-40.

[52] D.P. Walker, *The Ancient Theology: Studies in Christian Platonism from the Fifteenth to the Sixteenth Centuries* (London: Duckworth, 1972).

CHAPTER 4

EMANATION RELIGIONS

1. The Great Reformation

Karl Jaspers, the existentialist philosopher, writes of what he calls the "Axial Period"[1] in human history:

> In the years centering around 500 BC — from 800 to 200 — the spiritual foundations of humanity were laid, simultaneously and independently, in China, India, Persia, Palestine, and Greece. And these are the foundations upon which humanity still subsists today.

During this period the ancient religions of Europe and Asia (but not of Africa and the Americas) underwent a great reformation under a number of remarkable leaders.

In Iran the Aryan polytheism described in the last chapter was reformed by Zoroaster (traditionally dated. c. 660 BCE but perhaps much earlier)[2] as Zoroastrian Dualism. In India it was reformed by the writers of the *Upanishads* (800-400 BCE) as Hinduism (actually many religions), by Mahavira (d. 527 BCE) as Jainism, and by Gautama Siddartha (d. 483 BCE) as Buddhism. In China the nature and ancestor worship of the Shang and Chou dynasties was reformed by Lao Tze (d. c. 517 BCE, if he indeed he was an historical person) as Taoism and by Confucius (d. 479 BCE) as Confucianism. In Israel the great Hebrew prophets from Amos (fl. 720 BCE) and Isaiah (fl. 730 BCE) to "Malachi" (fl. 450 BCE) gave full formulation to the monotheistic worship of Yahweh. In the same epoch in Greece the philosophers, notably Socrates (d. 399 BCE), Plato (d. 348 BCE), Aristotle (d. 322 BCE), and Zeno the Stoic (d. c. 264 BCE) reshaped the old polytheism in a monotheistic direction.

Today the religion of Zoroaster has only about 100,000 adherents (the Parsees) and is significant mainly for its historic influence on Judaism and Christianity. Hence it will be discussed later along with those two surviving religions. The same goes for the religions of Greece that survive only through their notable influence on the development of Judaism, Christianity, and Islam. The reformed religion of China has already been discussed in Chapter 2 as a parallel to the modern Humanist philosophies of life. Therefore, in this chapter I will only discuss the reformed religions of India that have also profoundly affected China, Southeast Asia, and Japan.

In India Jainism is probably as old as Hinduism but today is only a minority religion without wide influence. Though it shares many of the same concepts as the Hindu religions that I am about to discuss in more detail, it differs fundamentally from them in that it is pluralistic, while they are monistic. Thus it teaches that reality consists in an infinity of spiritual beings that have become entrapped in matter and hence in temporal suffering. Salvation is to be achieved by the practice of a rigorous asceticism and nonviolence that alone can free each soul to rise, like a bubble in the ocean, to the top of the universe. There purified souls will remain isolated from each other forever in total spiritual self-sufficiency.[3]

In Indian religion[4] the profound religious developments of the Axial Period seem to have been a reaction to the degeneration in late Vedic times of the traditional sacrificial rituals into mere magic used to control natural forces and of the Vedic gods into mere names for these forces. How could the merely human Brahmins who performed these sacrifices really control the order of the vast cosmos? This could be possible only if within the phenomenal figure of the merely human agent there was an eternal, spiritual soul that was itself divine, a part of, or manifestation of a universal Cosmic Soul.

As this doctrine of Atman spread, the polytheism of the Vedas came to be interpreted by the more enlightened as merely symbolic of the Absolute One. Yet the polytheistic worship of popular religion continued to be tolerated as a stage of religion which, if devoutly lived, would lead to release in some future incarnation. This Absolute One was conceived as super-personal, since any likeness to the phenomenal world, even to the earthly human person, was thought to be utterly inadequate.

Later sacred literature that interprets the Vedas in this sense include the *Brahmanas*, the *Aranyakas*, and the *Upanishads*. Of these commentaries, the latest are the *Upanishads* (about 600-500 BCE and much later) which show the growth of a more speculative religion in which exterior ritual takes second place to interior meditation. This practice of meditation prepared by strenuous asceticism (*yoga*) seems to be the most characteristic feature of Hinduism.[5] Life is divided ideally into four periods: the student, the married man, the recluse living in the forest (usually as a celibate and dedicated to yoga), and finally the enlightened sage. Only the enlightened are released from the endless cycle of reincarnation into this world of suffering. Belief in reincarnation is not peculiar to India; in various forms it occurs in many pre-literary as well as in several ancient urban religions, such as that of the Pythagorean sect in Southern Italy.[6] This doctrine, however, is fundamental to all the main Indian theologies, for which consequently, *salvation is understood as release from rebirth.* This release is achieved by perfect detachment from worldly concerns and total commitment to the goal of enlightenment. According to the *Upanishads* and all forms of orthodox (i.e., based on the Vedas) Hinduism, this serene enlightenment consists in the experience in meditation of the spiritual *self* (*atman*, breath) as independent of the material world and of the same nature as the eternal Absolute Self (*Atman*). Hence whatever causes suffering is perceived to be *maya*, merely phenomenal, incapable of affecting the true Self or forcing rebirth.

Thus the common positive characteristic of the religions of India from the Axial Period on is that they "reformed" the ancient polytheistic religions of their area by emphasizing a supreme unifying principle which can be called the Absolute or the Unconditioned, transcending all empirical reality and all gods and spirits. The negative characteristic is that they deny that this Absolute is the creator *ex nihilo* of the empirical world or the gods by a free act of will as claimed by Judaism, Christianity, and Islam. Instead these religions teach that the gods and the world are necessary manifestations or *emanations* of the Absolute from which they are not essentially distinct.[7]

No brief discussion of these profound Eastern religions can do them justice. Even the distinction just made between religions of creation and of emanation requires qualification. The sacred writings and their commentaries are vast in number, in difficult archaic languages, representing a great range of varied speculations, and composed in literary forms for the most part very different from those to which we Westerners are accustomed. Today the number of Indian experts in this ancient tradition is in decline.[8] Moreover, these texts are generally indifferent to historical data, so that for us who think in historical terms it is hard to position this mass of material in our own perspectives. Nevertheless, these texts have been subject to intense study in the last 150 years by Western scholars. Hence the essential features of these religious options now seem fairly clear, although we must remain open to much more extensive dialogue with those to whom these traditions are native before they can be fully elucidated.

2. Gautama, the Buddha

The central figure of this Eastern religious world is Gautama Siddhartha (563?-484? BCE).[9] His only rivals would be the somewhat older Mahavira (599-527 BCE), the founder of Jainism and the authors of the *Upanishads* (800-400 BCE). The Upanishadic authors remain historically obscure or unknown. Even the oldest of the *Upanishads* in the form we now have them show traces of Buddhist influence.[10] In any case Gautama further developed the tendencies found in these books and his formulations helped to shape later Hinduism.

Critical historical study of the traditional lives of Buddha which were written at least one hundred years after his death have not left us much detail. He was born in a Himalayan hill town, the son of a leader of the Sakya clan, of the warrior rather than the priestly Brahmin caste. As a young man, overcome by a profound sense of the misery of the human condition, he left his wife and son to become a wandering ascetic. After long practice of asceticism, disillusioned with its results, he arrived by a different kind of meditation at Enlightenment and the state of Nirvana that it brings (hence his title, the Buddha or Enlightened One). He then began to preach this way of release throughout northern India, gathering around him a community of disciples vowed to follow this way but also influencing a much wider circle of the laity. At the end of forty years of preaching he died peacefully at the age of 80 after a brief illness.

The fundamental texts in which the teachings of Gautama are preserved are the *Tripitaka* (Three Baskets) that contains (1) the rules of his "monastic" community; (2) dialogues attributed to him and his disciples; (3) doctrinal refinements and solutions of controversies. Some of this material seems to date from as late as 25 BCE, but there is little doubt that it also contains the basic elements of Gautama's authentic teaching. As thus traditionally formulated this teaching begins with the "Four Holy Truths." These are that (1) all human life is marked by suffering; (2) the origin of suffering is desire; (3) release from suffering is to be found only in the cessation (Nirvana) of desire; (4) this cessation can be found by following the path of the Buddha. This way of the Buddha has three aspects: moral living, meditation, and insight or wisdom.

Moral living is summed up in "Eight Precepts," five of them basic: (1) Injure no living thing; (2) Do not steal; (3) Do not be unchaste; (4) Do not lie; (5) Do not indulge in alcohol or drugs. The other three are for more advanced persons and oblige at least on holy days: (6) Fast until midday; (7) Do not dance, sing, or take part in amusements; (8) Do not adorn the body. For monks the rule of chastity means total abstinence from sexual activity, and they are also required to observe two additional rules: (9) Do not accept money; (10) Do not use a soft bed.

The observance of this basic morality and moderate asceticism is the negative requirement of all spiritual progress. Positively this progress is achieved through forms of meditation that ordinarily must be learned under an experienced director who can adapt traditional techniques to the individual. The goal of meditation is to attain to a profound mental concentration in which alone Enlightenment can take place. This Enlightenment is a direct, intuitive understanding of the doctrine or wisdom by which desire and with it all suffering is extinguished in Nirvana.

Another, perhaps later formulation, of this threefold progress is the "Eightfold Path" leading to wisdom, which comprises (1) as regards *knowledge*: (a) right understanding and (b) right thought (regarding the Four Holy Truths); (2) as regards external *deportment:* (a) right speech and (b) right bodily action; (3) as regards *morality*: (a) right moral living, (b) right moral effort, and (c) right motivation; and (4) as regards *meditation*; right concentration. What then is this "wisdom" which is the goal of the Eightfold Path? It is the profound realization that the entire world around us, including our own stream of consciousness, thought, and desire is merely phenomenal and impermanent. This phenomenal world consists of (1) physical objects; (2) our sensations; (3) our imaginations; (4) our acts of will; (5) our thoughts and self-awareness. Since none of these are substantial or permanent, neither our experience nor the individual selves that we suppose are undergoing these experiences are substantial or permanent. Hence none of these are to be desired, not even the self and its desires that also are nothing more than an appearance.

Once an enlightened person becomes aware of this impermanence of all things, including the self, not by faith but by direct intuition, all suffering ceases and nothing remains but the state of Nirvana. This state is indescribable since it is entirely purified of every element of our ordinary experience.[11] Some Buddhist texts speak of it as "nothing" or as "the void," but others speak of it as "bliss." Whether this "bliss" is something positive or simply the cessation of suffering is not clear. Buddha himself seems to have denied that it was annihilation. Certainly, however, it is the cessation of the empirical human person or self, so that nothing remains but an unconditioned Absolute that cannot be characterized in any terms taken from self-consciousness. Buddha, therefore, seems to have refused to attempt to speak of Nirvana in any but negative terms.

Paradoxically Nirvana seems to be the goal of a Buddhist monk's striving and yet it cannot be "desired." Evidently the resolution of this paradox must be in an understanding of what the "desire" from which all suffering originates means. Also it is clear that in such a view the notion of reincarnation loses its primary significance, since there is no permanent individual self that can pass from one body to another. Thus Gautama seems to have accepted the common Indian belief in reincarnation only as a feature of the empirical world of suffering that the enlightened recognize as an illusion.

Thus there is a "Law of Causation" or "Dependent Origination" by which in the phenomenal world one natural process leads determinately to another in an endless cycle of cause and effect. Thus the merits earned or the guilt incurred in one life lead inevitably to one's destiny in the next, until by walking the path of enlightenment this chain is broken. The Buddhist laity, since they have not yet definitively entered on this path, can only hope that by keeping the basic rules of right conduct they may arrive at enlightenment in some future reincarnation. The monks and nuns by taking the vow to enter wholeheartedly into the Buddha's path and living according to all the rules of his community hope to end this present lifetime in Nirvana.

From an early date diverse interpretations of Gautama's teaching were given, producing many speculative schools which developed it in remarkably systematic, philosophical ways. Some controversies concerned details of monastic discipline, but others were metaphysical and epistemological. These theoretical debates did not focus on the nature of Nirvana, since all agreed that it was ineffable, but rather on the nature of the empirical world and the conscious self: In what sense are they real or unreal? If they are not only impermanent but also illusory, how can they cause or undergo suffering? But if they are real, although impermanent, how can we ever totally escape them?

These controversies produced a division within Buddhism between the more speculative Mahayana (Greater Chariot) and what its proponents contemptuously called the Hinayana (Lesser Chariot) which claimed to preserve a simpler, more original form of the Buddha's teaching.[12] In fact these two schools seem to represent two different tendencies which probably were present in Buddhism from its beginning. Both schools revered Gautama yet did not consider him unique, but only one of an endless series of Buddhas who have and will arrive at Nirvana but tarry awhile in our phenomenal world to point us the way to the same cessation of suffering. Zen Buddhism[13] is a Japanese sect of the Mahayana derived from Chinese "Ch'an" that has become especially popular in the West. It was developed in the effort to again focus Buddhism on the individual experience of *satori* (Nirvana) freed of an excessive interest in the classic texts or ritual practices. A Zen Master often assigns a paradoxical expression (*koan*) for the disciple's meditation to awaken him or her to the meaninglessness of phenomenal existence.

Once enlightenment has been attained the Buddhist can continue mundane life with serenity in the understanding of its emptiness. Hinayana is content with Gautama's explicit teaching. Hence it promulgates the ideal of the *arahat* or faithful follower of a Buddha who by this fidelity to his model also attains the goal of Nirvana. The Mahayana, on the other hand, glorifies the *bodhisattva* who having attained Nirvana remains as Gautama did in earthly existence to guide others. This emphasis of the Mahayana on compassion engendered a strong missionary spirit and a tolerance of popular religion, so that in the course of time Mahayana developed a vast mythological system of countless heavens, peopled by innumerable spiritual beings, including the Buddhas of the past and the future. Yet it cannot be called a "mythic" religion, because it teaches that these myths signify nothing other than the ineffable Nirvana.

The notion of a Future Buddha produced a kind of Messianism looking forward to a golden age to come. Thus the concept of the Middle Way as a discipline undertaken under the guidance and after the model of a teacher evolved into reliance on the power of the teacher to deliver the trusting disciple — something like the Christian notion of *grace*. Moreover, this reliance could be placed not only in an earthly teacher but in one of the countless Buddhas in the heavens. Thus a speculative Buddhology developed with the doctrine of the "Three Bodies of the Buddha," namely, the earthly body of Gautama or any one of the temporal Buddhas, the heavenly body of a Buddha in the Lotus Land of Bliss, and finally the transcendent body of Nirvana. The popular piety of the laity thus became trust in a Buddha identified with Nirvana, and the way of salvation might simply be to express this trust by reciting a Divine Name. Such trust, however, need not imply neglect of the moral principles of Buddhism, but only that a way was open to the laity to attain release even if they could not submit to monastic discipline.

In time the principle of *bhakti* or devotion to Nirvana or the ineffable Absolute manifested in our empirical world of suffering as a compassionate Teacher and Savior became the keynote of Buddhism as it became a world religion. This holds not only for its Mahayana form in China and Japan but also for its Hinayana form in Sri Lanka and Southeast Asia. Thus everywhere Buddhism's chief symbol is a serene image of Gautama meditating or teaching that stands for all the infinity of other Buddhas and the Absolute itself.

3. Hinduism

Hinduism is actually a collection of different religions having some traits in common. As these now exist they largely developed out of the tradition of the *Upanishads* and in reaction (yet under the influence of) Buddhism which was, however, itself rooted in the same *tendencies*.[14] The Buddhists did not accept the sacred texts on which the many forms of Hinduism are all based nor the elaborate sacrificial rites or the caste system of the Brahmins as normative, although they were tolerant of the traditional gods and ceremonies and assimilated many of them. In the long run, however, this process of assimilation did not succeed, since Hinduism eventually overcame Buddhism throughout India, except in Sri Lanka. No doubt its characteristic features, especially the caste system which Buddhism did not support, were too much a part of Indian tradition to be replaced by Buddhist universalism.

Yet Hinduism had to reckon with the reforms of Gautama and shifted from the emphasis on the deterministic efficacy of the brahmanical sacrificial rites honoring the many gods to a deeper emphasis on interior, spiritual perfection and the search for deliverance from suffering through union with the Absolute. Hinduism, however, does not accept Gautama's denial of the permanence of the human self (*atman*). Instead it teaches that the goal of moral living, asceticism, and meditation is to discover the self's true nature. Yet, since Hinduism teaches that the true nature of the human self is *identity* with the universal *Atman* or Absolute, is its fundamental outlook really so different from that of Gautama?

Thus the great issue within Hinduism in its controversies with Buddhism, became how to formulate the relation between the many things of this phenomenal world, including individual souls, and the One or Absolute. The most radical answer was given by Shankara (788-820? CE) who with subtle philosophical dialectics argued that all statements about our empirical world of change are inherently contradictory. Consequently, for this system of Non-Dualism (*Advaita Vedanta*)[15] all things are *maya* (appearance) and the only reality is the Absolute.

This doctrine of *maya* does not mean that the things of our human experience are simply illusions. Rather it teaches that to the enlightened mind the plurality and transience of what we experience (including the flow of the self-consciousness of distinct individual selves) is unreal since in an unqualified sense only the Absolute exists. In such a system the notion of *bhakti* or worship is meaningless except for those who have not been perfectly enlightened and who still need to seek the Absolute by such means. Consequently, another great Hindu thinker Ramanuja (eleventh century CE) countered Non-Dualism with another Vedantic system of Qualified Non-Dualism.[16] According to him the individual soul always remains distinct among the plurality of individual entities, but is identical with the Absolute in the same way that the body is identical with the soul that gives it life.

Thus we can say that for the Buddhists and the Vedantists, whether they are pure non-dualists or qualified non-dualists like Ramanuja, the plurality of finite selves and the things of the world are not conceived as *creations* of the One in a strictly monotheistic sense. Instead they are considered as *emanations* from the One with which they remain substantially identical.[17] Nonetheless, to avoid concluding to a pantheism which would simply identify the Absolute with the world or to an acosmism which would deny all reality to the world, these Hindu thinkers often make use of the notion of "play." In an everlasting cycle the world as the free play of the Absolute emanates from it over and over again and is as often destroyed or reabsorbed into the One. Often, therefore, the world is pictured as the wife (*Shakti*) of the Absolute with whom He ever engages in love play. The Absolute, therefore, is eternal, unchanging, while the feminine cosmos is ever changing, undergoing an infinite variety of forms. Hence in Hindu art there is an amazing, phantasmagoric play of forms coming to be and evaporating, all centering on some motionless central figure lost in meditation.

Yet in popular Hinduism these developments increasingly focused on the practice of *bhakti,* devotion to some favorite god.[18] Often it is also believed that there are three supreme gods (the Trimurti): Brahma (the Absolute), Vishnu (the "Creator" in the emanationist sense), and Shiva (the Destroyer). *Bhakti* was not directed toward the ineffable and unimaginable Brahma, but to Vishnu (or Krishna, one of his manifestations) or Shiva (Shankara was himself a devotee of Shiva), or to one of the forms of the Mother Goddess who was the cosmos under its feminine symbol. The Trimurti should not, however, be understood as being anything like the Christian Trinity, since for Hinduism these three names are simply *aspects* of the Absolute, not distinct Divine Persons united in one Godhead.

Today, devotion to the Mother Goddess is perhaps the most popular form of *bhakti* in India. It also gave rise to Tantric Hinduism (and Buddhism) that, along with magical practices, treats sexual activity as a means to mystical union.[19] Westerners are often shocked by the magic and frank eroticism of Tantrism and of much religious art. They are even more shocked by the idea of worshiping a destroying God like Shiva, or a Mother Goddess under her terrifying form as Kali, Goddess of Death.

We need to remember, however, that for Hinduism the world is continually being born and then destroyed so as to emanate again. Therefore, since salvation requires us to transcend this process so as to attain the unchanging Absolute, it is even more reasonable to worship the destructive process which returns the world to the Absolute than the process of emanation which produces a world in which suffering is inevitable.

In this perspective Hinduism, like Buddhism, accepts a wide variety of popular religious practices in honor of many divinities, since all are simply symbols, adapted to the spiritual state of the devotee, pointing to the ultimate Absolute. Each human being may have to pass through countless reincarnations to attain to the enlightenment that finally achieves union with the Absolute either by total identification, as in Non-Dualism, or in a body-soul union as in Qualified Non-Dualism.

The Jainism of Mahavira, already mentioned, shares many of these same features, especially an even more rigorous practice of nonviolence against any form of life. This nonviolence, of course, reflects the logic of reincarnation, since one may someday be reborn as an animal perhaps because of violence to animals. Jainism, however, does not aim at union with the One, but teaches that every soul seeks its own perfection as a self-sufficient monad existing eternally in isolated self-contemplation.[20]

A comparison of Indian religions with those of China prior to the introduction of Buddhism that we discussed in Chapter 2 is enlightening. It is obvious that while Indian religion tends to be other-worldly or transcendental and to focus on spiritual integration or union either through devotion or identification with the Absolute, Chinese religion, dominated by Confucianism, tends to be worldly and seeks to harmonize the social with the cosmic order. Yet the Chinese through the influence of Buddhism and through their own native Taoism as a counterbalance to the formerly official Confucianism also appreciate the transcendental aspect of religion. What the Indian and Chinese traditions have in common is the conviction that behind the multiplicity of the phenomenal world there is an Absolute One which transcends all categories including those derived from human personhood.

This One cannot be called "impersonal" so much as *trans*personal. In China where from an early time only the Emperor could offer official cult to "Heaven," this has resulted in what some writers call "atheism." For the Chinese the universe exists eternally through the balance of Yin and Yang in an endless cycle of change and the Order that maintains its unity in perpetuity is the Absolute. The Indians, on the other hand, see the universe as "play" lacking ultimate significance and hence strive to achieve union by way of enlightenment or devotion to the unchanging Absolute. Thus it might be said that the Indian ideal is *union* with the Absolute, the Chinese ideal is *harmony* with the Absolute.

That these two views may not be so far apart is evidenced by the success of Buddhism in China and the fact that official Confucianism did not find it impossible to assimilate much of the Buddhist metaphysics. The point of conflict always remained whether the contemplative or the active life was to be preferred. But in a faith in a transpersonal Absolute inseparable from the world as either its playful or its natural manifestation India and China seem one.

4. How Absolute is the Absolute?

When the Europeans of the Enlightenment — a very different "enlightenment" than that of Nirvana! — came to know India and China they were fascinated by the richness and ethical rationality of these unfamiliar cultures. They were also repelled by what seemed to them the rank superstition and religiosity of these cultures. They were shocked by the bewildering multiplication of India's temples and images, its countless gods, many of them monstrous or even obscene, its animal sacrifices, its veneration of the cow, the cremation of widows, and the caste system. They were overwhelmed by the vast variety of sects based on obscure and fantastic texts. All these features seemed to mark Hindu religion as even more irrational than the Christianity against which European Enlightenment had reacted. To some, Buddhism seemed a bit more sane than Hinduism, but it was interpreted as nihilistic, pessimistic, and quietist.

To many Humanists it seemed, and today still seems obvious that India can never solve its dire social problems of famine, poverty, illiteracy, and overpopulation except by a radical abandonment of its "mystical" religions for Western rationality, technical progress, and social activism. While a national hero like Gandhi could defend Hinduism, it seems evident that today the educated classes of India are already far on the road to conversion to Humanism as their philosophy of life and now value Hinduism only for its national literature and artistic traditions.[21]

For the reasons given in Chapter 3 the Confucianism of China seemed more reasonable than the religions of India to the men of the Enlightenment, but this too, with the advent of the Republic was repudiated as the basis of national culture. John Dewey, the principal author of the *Humanist Manifesto,* was invited to chart a new course for Chinese education. The present Marxist regime has systematically attacked Confucianism and all traditional religion, although it is now testing a policy of free market economics to compete with the non-Marxist world. The educated elites in China view their traditional religions as a major cause of their country's social injustice and technological and scientific backwardness. In Taiwan, South Korea, and Japan there is religious liberty but these countries exist under the hegemony of the United States whose influence is predominantly Humanist.[22]

Yet from within Humanism since the time of the philosophers Schopenhauer (d. 1860) in Europe and Emerson (d. 1882) in the United States, and increasingly in the twentieth century, there has been extensive study and serious religious interest in Hinduism and Buddhism in the Western World.[23] Although some of this influence involves the acceptance of cult practices, for example in the Hare Krishna Movement, it is to be seen mainly in the adoption of meditation techniques and doctrinal interpretations that are highly philosophical and demythologized or psychologized.

Reciprocally Hindus and Buddhists in their missionary activities or their efforts at religious reforms within their own circles have undoubtedly been influenced by theistic religions and by Western philosophies. Thus in India the important religion of Sikhism founded by Guru Nanak in the 15th century as a doctrinal synthesis of Hindu and Islamic elements teaches a personal monotheism.

What is evident in these efforts at religious synthesis is that many people raised in Humanism, especially Romantic Humanists concerned with values, have begun to ask themselves whether the Humanist reliance on scientific knowledge is adequate to deal with a reality deeper than the measurable phenomena. May it not be that the Kantian denial of the possibility of knowing noumenal reality is due to an unwarranted assumption that the scientific method determines the limits of human knowledge? If such an assumption requires us to rule out the wisdom of the East as irrational illusion is not this an arrogant presumption?

Many Westerners also are experimenting with Yoga and Zen meditation. Some have soon given it up as just another illusion. Some have found it of personal benefit for physical and mental health but nothing more. But some have found in it an enlargement and purification of their understanding of their own lives through deeper insight just as its adepts claim.

The first issue in evaluating the validity of these insights is verification of the doctrine of reincarnation. Reincarnation is certainly one of the principal hypotheses which have been proposed to explain the problem of evil and human suffering in the world and is common to all the Hindu religions, although not shared by Confucianism. It provides a logical explanation of why some human beings are born in good health and fortunate circumstances and others in deprivation. Is this to be attributed to the rewards or punishment of a soul's behavior in a previous life? May virtuous persons who suffer in this life hope for a better lot in the next and ultimately for some release from suffering altogether? Must the wicked fear a more painful next life, yet always have the opportunity in some future life to repent and gain a better future? Can we trust the many reports of persons who claimed to have been able to remember their previous lives?

On further examination, however, the question arises whether this doctrine is really taken literally by the great Indian thinkers. Since according to Buddhism there really is no *permanent* self, it is difficult to see how anything *substantial* can pass from one body to another. Rather, these thinkers seem to say that enlightenment is a release from the burdensome *illusion* and dread of rebirth. In Hinduism of the major Advaita Vedanta sect release is the realization of the timeless *identity* of the individual self with the Absolute Self. Hence it would seem reincarnation is only *maya*, the playful fantasy of the Absolute Mind, rather than a real process. Only in a system of Qualified Non-Dualism like that of Ramanuja is it logically consistent to assert that the individual soul is a continuous, self-identical reality that can really be reborn into a new body. Yet even for Ramanuja this process remains at the level of *maya*, so that the enlightened sage comes to realize that his *atman* or self has been wedded to the Absolute throughout eternity and that its passage from one body to another in time is only apparent. Thus the doctrine of reincarnation that is the common basis of all the religions of India (other than Christianity and Islam) probably should be understood to mean that only to the popular mind does suffering *appear* to be punishment. In fact it is an error to be recognized as such. The enlightened know that suffering belongs to phenomenal, not ultimate reality.

Thus the truly fundamental issue in evaluating these religions is the validity and nature of the *mystical* experiences at which these religions aim. What exactly is the value of Hindu *samadhi* or concentration that at its height overcomes the distinction between the subject and the object, the relative and the Absolute Self? Or what is the value of the Buddhist *Nirvana* in which all desire for relative reality ceases, leaving only the ineffable Absolute? And what is the value of the Taoist *quietude* in which the meditator experiences complete harmony with the cosmic order? It would be a mistake to suppose without proof that the three experiences in question are identical, since they are not achieved by the same means nor described in the same terms.[24] And to claim the reality of any of these experiences by saying that only those who have achieved it can verify this reality by immediate intuition is to ask the seeker "to buy a pig in a poke." Hence the great Eastern sages have attempted to make their claims plausible by careful psychological and cosmological arguments.

These arguments basically pursue the way of "negativity," that is, they attempt to show that the phenomenal world by the very fact that it is pluralistic and ever changing cannot be self-explanatory but must be a manifestation of some Absolute Ground of Being. Yet they insist that this Ground of Being cannot be conceptualized since human concepts are themselves all representative of plural and changing phenomena. Hence these experiences must be achieved by some kind of super rational knowledge in which the duality of knower and known, subject and object is wholly overcome (Shankara); or in which duality while remaining is that of lover and beloved, body and soul (Ramanuja). In either case it is argued that phenomenal reality, including the individual human self, is only a playful manifestation of the Absolute having no substantiality proper to itself.

The Christian philosopher Jacques Maritain[25] has suggested what is perhaps the best explanation of these types of mystical experience, the objective validity of which he grants. He points out that the kind of meditation achieved through yoga techniques as practiced by different forms by all these Indian schools consists basically in quieting the body so as to permit the mind to concentrate on itself. Such concentration proceeds by deliberate negation, so that each level of psychic consciousness is progressively silenced. First meditators ignore external sense distractions as in sensory deprivation experiments. Then they quiet the activity of the imagination and memory. Finally they deliberately suppress conceptualization and ratiocination. This process of negation produces a gradual withdrawal of "psychic energy" from the organic faculties where it is normally exercised while still maintaining an alert waking state. Thus this concentration of psychic energy produces a very much intensified consciousness not of any external object or its mental images, nor of the lower psychic activities, but simply of the spiritual, intellectual activity of *self-awareness with discursive reasoning*. The yogi in prolonged meditation thus becomes intensely aware of himself simply *as self-awareness*. The human mind, however, is normally directed toward particular objects, not to the subject as such, and it cannot conceptualize or objectivize itself precisely in its own subjectivity. Hence this intense self-awareness can only be a *dark* or negative *existential* awareness without positive form or content. It pertains to the intuitive or immediate rather than to the rational or discursive level of intellection. In spite of its negativity it is a genuine, immediate experience of spiritual reality as utterly other than all the material realities of ordinary experience including even the yogi's own body.

The yogi in *samadhi* knows nothing except that as subject he exists in a way utterly different from the way in which the phenomenal world exists either in physical bodies or their mental representations in the senses, imagination, or conceptual reason. Maritain points out that the yogi can understand this in either of two ways. On the one hand, he may realize (as Ramanuja seems to have done) that he is a spiritual being. Yet because his self-awareness is dark he can also acknowledge that he is a finite spirit whose existence implies the existence of a purer infinite Spirit distinct from himself and worthy of his adoration (*bhakti*). Or on the other hand he can *mistakenly* conclude that since his dark experience veils all differentiation of spiritual reality he is identical with the Infinite Spirit and that the whole phenomenal world is insubstantial. Did Buddha and Shankara opt for this second conclusion?

Perhaps this explanation is not the whole truth. Buddhist and Hindu thought is very profound and its experts may very well find Maritain's "explanation" superficial. What his theory does make clear, however, is that the claims of Hindu and Buddhist thought to arrive at an Absolute by an intuitive route can be given rational support, although the question as to the nature of this Absolute may remain debatable.

Hence the fundamental question that has to be raised concerns the nature of the Absolute not simply in itself, since that is supposed to transcend all human expression, but in *relation* to the world and the human self. Much of the controversy within these schools concerns this relation. Buddhism has tended to answer this question by claiming that when the chain of phenomenal causation is broken by the insight that it is illusory then the *samsara* of the world and the human individual simply evaporate and what remains is a Nirvana that is "Nothing," i.e., the unnameable Absolute. The answer of the Advaita Vedanta of Shankara is not very different except that he accepts the relative reality of the world and individual self as *maya* produced by the play of Brahman. The term "play" (*lila*) is intended to avoid the pantheistic notion that the Absolute produces the world by necessity since this would make It dependent on the world. But why is Brahman motivated to any activity at all outside Itself? A theist would say that God creates not for His own sake but the sake of the creatures with which He wishes to share His self-sufficient happiness. Such a solution, however, gives to the creatures a substantial reality that even Ramanuja cannot admit.

Furthermore, many of these thinkers argue that the Absolute is not only the efficient cause (to use the convenient terminology of Aristotle) of the world but also its *material* cause, i.e., the world is a transformation or mode (to use Spinoza's term) of the Absolute itself. Thus Ramanuja, who is so concerned to retain a distinction between the individual *atman* and the Atman, speaks of the relation between them not only as wife (*shakti*) to husband, but as body to soul.[26] Granted these are analogical expressions (do not Christians claim to be now the

Body of Christ?) and are not to be taken literally, the choice of this last analogy for the relation of Creator to Creature is significant.

The difficulties of this emanationism that, in contrast to creationism, considers the production of the world as a self-modification of Brahman were evident to these thinkers. Madhva (d. 1317) brought many arguments against it, including the dilemma that either this modification is real or illusory, but if real (as Madhva held against Shankara) then Brahman would itself have to be liberated from suffering! Nevertheless, at least according to Eric Lott who has studied this question carefully,[27] Madhva does not break with the traditional Indian view that Nature, Time, and Space exist eternally. Hence even for him the Absolute's creative activity is not really *creatio ex nihilo,* but is simply a transformation of primordial matter. Moreover, even if "reluctantly,"[28] he, like Ramanuja, speaks of the world as God's body.

Is it correct, therefore, to say that these emanation religions can be described as teaching "pantheism" (all is God)? Some would hold that it would be better to say that they teach "panentheism" (all is in God). The later term, however, is not very helpful, since theism holds that God is not only transcendent but immanent, i.e., God is not only absolutely distinct from and independent of the world, but also since the world is absolutely dependent on God, "all is in God." The real debate is between a theistic position that says that the world is produced by a free act of God and, though it remains dependent on God, is in no way identified with God and a non-theistic position that somehow identifies God and the world. This latter position may be understood to say that nothing but God really exists, as in the absolute monism of pure Non-Dualism of Shankara in which the world is a dream or the play of God. Or it may that hold that there is within God some kind of distinction but not one that entails some form of identity, as in Ramanuja's Qualified Non-Dualism in which the distinction is that of soul and body. Or it may take the form of Stoicism in which the material world is God animated by the Logos or natural law. It is this latter position that is usually called "pantheism" and hence the term is repudiated by those who hold that the Absolute is a spiritual not a material being. Therefore, rather than use the term "pantheism" I will speak of these Emanation Religions as forms of *monism* (all is One) since what characterizes them is that they deny an absolute distinction between God and Creation. It is misleading, however, to call theism *dualism*, without pointing out that it is not dualistic in the sense that ancient Zoroastrianism or later Manichaeism are said to have been by teaching the existence of a god of Bad and a god of Good. For Judaism, Christianity, and Islam there is only One Supreme and wholly Good Being who has freely created a good world that is no way divine and permitted his free creatures to sin.

We can conclude, therefore, that these Religions of Emanation have a powerful answer, based on a direct experience in concentrated negative meditation of the spirituality of the human person, to Humanists who deny or are agnostic about the reality of a spiritual Ground of Being. Yet they in turn are liable to the charge of monotheists that they deny the reality of the world and human self, which are also known through direct experience. Moreover to monotheists they seem to end in sheer paradoxes about the reality of Nothing or the self-modification of the Unchanging or about a world created by God out of pre-existent matter not created by God. Whether the monotheists' doctrine of creation can resolve such paradoxes requires further examination. Yet what is certain is that Christians can (and already have) learned much about the super-reality of the spiritual realm and the art of entering it through disciplined meditation from this great Eastern wisdom.

Nevertheless, after facing the fundamental difference between the Emanation and Creation traditions, it is of great importance to point out their tendency to converge. This convergence is in the fact that both overcome the polytheism of the Mythological Religions and join (though not perfectly) in *monotheism,* as R.C. Zaehner emphasized in his aptly titled Gifford Lectures, *Concordant Discord.*[29] Though this does not seem to be true of Jainism, which is firmly pluralistic, the religions of India have a distinctly monotheistic tendency. This is apparent in popular religion in the sectarian devotion to Siva or Vishnu as the One God to whom the other gods are entirely subordinate. It is still more evident in Vedanta and other more philosophical and mystical religious schools that treat the gods of polytheism as no more than popular devotions that veil the perfect unity of the supreme Atman or Absolute. As for Buddhism, it teaches that, for the enlightened, all individual realities are empty in an ineffable Nirvana that is certainly undivided since all such Emanation Religions consider the phenomenal world as lacking in permanent reality. Thus, these religions are an *acosmic* (without a universe) type of monotheism in which only One Absolute Reality is really real. Furthermore, they tend to place their emphasis on intuitions derived from meditation rather than on a revelation to which the appropriate response is the submission of faith made credible by reasoning. Thus the yogi invites his disciple to share his inner meditative experiences rather than preaches a revelation supported by argument. In theistic religions, on the other hand, the doctrine is proclaimed in preaching, supported by apologetic argument, and explained by analogical but rational exposition. This does not mean, however, that theistic religions do not also affirm that the believers should achieve personal, spiritual insight through meditation into the doctrines that they have already accepted. Therefore, in both types of religion mysticism is regarded as a goal to be achieved but by somewhat different paths.

It must be emphasized, however, that from the viewpoint of the Creation Religions the monotheistic aspects of the Emanation Religions remain incomplete and unsatisfactory. The One Absolute in the Emanation Religions is not clearly a Creator able freely to produce a universe distinct from its first cause yet sharing in a dependent yet authentic way in the Creator's real existence. On the other hand to Emanationists the Creationist monotheism is really a dualism, since the Creator and Creation remain divided.

Notes

[1] Karl Jaspers, *The Origin and Goal of History* (New Haven, CT: Yale University Press, 1953).

[2] For bibliography on Zoroastrianism see Chapter 3, note 32 and cf. Mary Boyce's dating of Zoroaster before 1000 BCE.

[3] See Carlo della Casa, "Jainism" in Bleeker, *Historia Religionum* (note 2 above), vol. 2., pp. 346-371; and S. Padmanabh, *The Jaina Path of Purification* (Berkeley: University of California Press, 1979).

[4] For bibliography see Chapter 3, note 30.

[5] See references in Chapter 3, note 30 on the yoga techniques.

[6] On transmigration of souls see Eliade, *History of Religious Ideas* (note 3 above), vol. 2, pp. 191-202.

[7] See Sir Mortimer Wheeler, *The Indus Civilization,* 3rd ed. (New York: Cambridge University Press, 1968) and Ainslee T. Embree, ed., *The Hindu Tradition* (Westminster, MD: Random House, 1972), selections from sources in translation. See also Ralph T.H. Griffith, trans., *The Hymns of the Rigveda,* rev. ed. (Livingston, NJ: Orient Book Distributors, 1976) and Robert E. Hume, *The Thirteen Principal Upanishads* (London: H. Milford, Oxford University Press, 1934). See Hans Küng, *Christianity and World Religions: Paths to Dialogue,* with Josef von Ess, Heinrich von Stietencron, Heinz Bechert (Maryknoll, NY: Orbis Books, 1996) for recent discussion of the fundamental differences between Christianity and Islam, Hinduism, and Buddhism. The evaluations in this book do not differ significantly from mine, except for the major difference that Küng does not emphasize the differences on creation vs. emanation as I do.

[8] See William Cenkner, OP, *A Tradition of Teachers: Sankara and the Jagadgurus Today* (Delhi: Motilal Banarsidass, 1983).

[9] Stephan Beyer, trans., *The Buddhist Experience,* selections from sources (Encino, CA: Dickenson Publishing Co., 1974); T.W. Rhys Davids, trans., *Buddhist Sutras* (New York: Dover, 1969). See also E.J. Thomas, *History of Buddhist Thought* (London: Routledge, 1933) and *Life of Buddha as Legend and History* 3rd ed. (London: Routledge, 1949); Richard H. Drummond, *Gautama the Buddha* (Eerdmans: Grand Rapids, MI, 1974). On Zen see: Heinrich Dumolin, SJ, *A History of Zen Buddhism* (New York: Pantheon, 1963); Edward Conze, *Buddhist Thought in India* (London: Allen and Unwin, 1962). See also: T.R.V. Murti, *The Central Philosophy of Buddhism: A Study of the Mahdyamika System* (London: G. Allen, 1955); Frederick J. Streng, *Emptiness: A Study in Religious Meaning* (Nashville: Abingdon, 1967). On Japanese Buddhism see Carmen Blacker, "Religions of Japan," in C.J. Bleeker and G. Widgren, *Historia Religionum* (Leiden: Brill, 1969), vol. 2, pp. 516-549.

[10] Robert E. Hume, *The Thirteen Principal Upanishads* (note 6 above), Introduction, pp. 6-7.

[11] The various interpretations of Nirvana are critically discussed by Helmuth von Glasenapp, *Buddhism: A Non Theistic Religion* (New York: George Braziller, 1966). A recent study by William Herbrechtsmeier, "Buddhism and the Definition of Religion: One More Time," *Journal for the Scientific Study of Religion,* 1993, 32 (1), 1-18 concludes that if the term "religion" implies belief in superhuman beings Buddhism is not a religion since it is essentially a monism.

[12] See Edward Conze, "Mahayana" in R.C. Zaehner, ed., *The Concise Encyclopedia of Living Faiths* (New York: Hawthorn Books, 1959), pp. 296-320.

[13] See Daisetz T. Suzuki, *Zen Buddhism: Selected Writings of D.T. Suzuki,* edited by William Barrett (Garden City, NY: Doubleday, 1966). An expert in Zen, Masao Abe in *A Buddhist, Jewish, Christian Conversation with Masao Abe* (Valley Forge, PA: Trinity Press International, 1995), pp. 252-253, criticizes Wolfhart Pannenberg's discussion of the relation between Nirvana and Samsara (i.e., enlightenment that daily life even as it is lived is empty). Abe says that Mahayana Buddhism has always taught that "Samsara-as-it-is is nirvana," p. 253. But this does not mean that there is "an immediate identity of samsara and nirvana, immanence and transcendence, but a dialectical identity through the negation of negation. In Mahayana Buddhism, true nirvana is not a static state of transcendence but a dynamic movement between samsara so-called and nirvana so-called without attachment to either." He thinks Pannenberg is mistaken in giving primacy to transcendence and asks, "Is it not true that the *ultimate* reality of God in Christianity is oriented more by transcendence than by immanence and thus cannot be called ultimate reality?", p. 253. The implication seems to be that ultimate reality is monistic.

[14] See Kees Bolle, *The Bhagavadgita in the Mahabharata,* text and trans. by J.A.B. van Buitenen (Chicago: University of Chicago Press, 1980). Cf. also A.L. Basham, "Hindu-

ism" in Zaehner, *Concise Encyclopedia* (note 11 above), pp. 225-260; Thomas Hopkins, *The Hindu Religious Tradition* (Encino, CA: Dickenson Publishing Co., 1971). Also R.C. Zaehner, *Hinduism* (New York: Oxford University Press); V.S. Naravane, *Modern Indian Thought* (Bombay: Asia Publishing House, 1964); Troy Wilson Organ, *Hinduism: Its Historical Development* (Woodbury, NY: Barron's Educational Series, 1974); Heinrich Zimmer, *Myths and Symbols in Indian Art and Civilization* (Princeton: Princeton University Press, 1971).

[15] On Advaita Vedanta see T.M.P. Mahadevan, *The Philosophy of Advaita* (Madras: Ganesh, 1957); and Eric Lott, *Vedantic Approaches to God* (Totowa, NJ: Barnes and Noble, 1980).

[16] See John Braistead Carman, *The Theology of Ramanuja* (New Haven: Yale University Press, 1974).

[17] For a penetrating philosophical treatment see the 1980 Gifford Lectures of Frederick Copleston, SJ, *Religion and the One: Philosophies East and West* (New York: Crossroad, 1982).

[18] See W. Richard Comstock, *et al.*, *Religion and Man: An Introduction* (New York: Harper and Row, 1971), pp. 160-179 and Milton Singer, ed., *Krishna: Myths, Rites, and Attitudes* (Honolulu: East West Center, 1966).

[19] Tantric Buddhism is called the Vajrayana tradition. In Tibet it has preserved an extraordinary number of Buddhist texts which are recently receiving much more scholarly attention; cf. Agehananda Bharat, *The Tantric Tradition* (London: Rider and Co., 1965); Lama Anagarika Govinda, *Foundations of Tibetan Mysticism* (London: Rider and Co., 1969).

[20] See Carlo della Casa, "Jainism" in Bleeker, *Historia Religionum* (note 3 above), vol. 2, pp. 346-371; and S. Padmanabh, *The Jaina Path of Purification* (Berkeley: University of California Press, 1979).

[21] See Richard Launoy, *The Speaking Tree: A Study of Indian Culture and Society* (London: Oxford University Press, 1971) and J. Michael Maher, ed., *The Untouchable in Modern India* (Tucson, AZ: University of Arizona Press, 1972).

[22] See references in Chapter 3, note 30.

[23] See Heinrich Dumoulin, SJ, *Buddhism in the Modern World* (New York: Collier Macmillan, 1976) and Emma M. Layman, *Buddhism in America* (Chicago: Nelson Hall, 1976). Cf. R.C. Zaehner, *Our Savage God: The Perverse Use of Eastern Thought* (New York: Sheed and Ward, 1975).

[24] W.T. Stace, *Mysticism and Philosophy* (Philadelphia: Lippincott, 1960) argued that mystical experience is essentially the same in all religions. This was disputed by R.C. Zaehner, *Mysticism, Sacred and Profane. An inquiry into some varieties of praeter-natural experience* (Oxford: Oxford University Press, 1961) and Fritz Staal, *Exploring Mysticism: A Methodological Essay* (Berkeley: University of California Press, 1975).

[25] "The Natural Mystical Experience and the Void," in *Redeeming the Time* (London: Geoffrey Bless: The Centenary Press, 1943), pp. 225-255.

[26] See Carman, *Theology of Ramanuja* (note 16 above), pp. 124-133.

[27] *Vedantic Approaches* (note 15 above), pp. 115-120.

[28] *Ibid.*, p. 118.

[29] *Concordant Discord: The Interdependence of Faiths,* The Gifford Lectures 1967-1969, 1970.

CHAPTER 5

CREATION RELIGIONS

1. What is Creation?

In a broad sense every world-view includes a theory of "creation," but as was explained in the last chapter "creation" has a different meaning in the Mythological Religions or the monistic Emanation Religions than in religions that teach an absolute distinction between the Creator and his Creation. If the world is only an illusion, as the Buddhists and Advaita Vedantists seem to say, then there has to be some explanation for this error. If the world is real, then either it is somehow the cause of its own existence or development, as ancient materialists thought and even today many Humanists suppose, or it has a cause other than itself. In this last case, it is necessary to ask whether that external cause of the world only actualizes some preexisting substance. This was the view of the Indian Madhva and perhaps also of the Greeks Plato and Aristotle. Or is God the total cause of the world's existence even in its substantiality?

This last view is the fundamental contention of Judaism, and of the Christian and Islamic religions derived from Judaism.[1] Often it is said that what characterizes these religions is their theism or their monotheism. As I said at the conclusion of the last chapter, Judaism, Christianity, and Islam are theistic because they teach that God is personal, while the Absolute of Eastern religions is not clearly so. Yet, as we have seen, Mahayana Buddhism and Advaita Hinduism tend to theism, even to monotheism, since they teach devotion to one God of whom the other "gods" are considered mere symbols or epiphanies. What really makes Judaic monotheism unique is its insistence on creation without any pre-existing entity, *creatio ex nihilo*. Thus these theistic religions maintain the substantial reality of the world and of human persons but stress their total dependence on the free will of a personal God who would be eternally the same even if this God had never created the world.[2]

On the contrary, the Emanation Religions deny the reality of a world other than the Supreme Being or consider it to be a merely phenomenal "play."[3] Or they consider the world to be the Supreme Being's body or think of it as somehow preexisting as the matter on which the Supreme Being acts. Or they think of the Supreme Being as causing itself to be along with the world. Whatever their exact conception of this relation of the Absolute and the world of human experience, they accept some form of *monism* in which the Absolute and the world are not fully distinct realities. In contrast to this monism Judaism emphatically asserts that God is absolutely One and yet capable of producing a fully real world unqualifiedly *other* than himself. It is in this sense not monistic but *dualistic* though it firmly maintains that while God necessarily is, the world exists only in total dependence on God's free will.

According to the doctrine of these religions this absolute creationist monotheism was revealed to Moses but had already been known to Abraham and the Hebrew patriarchs. Biblical scholars date the documents in which this doctrine is first evident only about 550 BCE (Deutero-Isaiah, Isaiah 40-55), and attempt to trace its gradual development from polytheism through henotheism (worship of one God as supreme among many gods).[4] It was not given an explicit formulation as *creatio ex nihilo* until the deuterocanonical book 2 Macccabees written in Greek and dating from as late as 124 BCE. In this text an heroic Jewish woman during the persecution by the Greek tyrant Antiochus Epiphanes encourages her youngest son to accept martyrdom like his six brothers before him.

> "I beg you, child, look at the heavens and the earth and see all that is in them, then you will know that God did not make them out of existing things, and in the same way the human race came into existence. Do not be afraid of this executioner, but be wor-

> thy of your brothers and accept death, so that in the time of mercy I may receive you again with them" (2 Mc 7:28-29).

Though historically monotheism seems to have only been gradually formulated and accepted, it was traditionally held that the origin of the Hebrew nation goes back to events associated with Moses that convinced this people of its unique relation to a God whose supremacy over nature and history was absolute. This is a "jealous God" who permits no rival power, a God faithful to his covenant with his chosen people and demanding of them a reciprocal fidelity. In time they came to understand that the purpose of this vocation was that they were to witness this God as the absolute source of all things to all other nations in order that all humanity might come to recognize the One True God. While it is common for every people to think of themselves as "*the* People" and their favorite god as "*the* God," the Jewish monotheist conviction has had unique historical consequences in that it has produced two other great world religions, Christianity and Islam.

Hence, in spite of their small numbers and internal divisions, the Jews remain a vital leaven in world culture. They declare to all, "If God could create us as a people out of our nothingness as slaves in Egypt and Babylon, and recreate us again and again after many Holocausts, this God must be the One who could and has created the whole world out of nothing."

2. The God of Abraham, Isaac, and Jacob

The God of the Jews in wisdom and love freely creates all things out of nothing, not because they add to the Divine Life but for their sake to share his life with them. After all of humanity had rejected God, he mercifully chose Abraham and from his descendants the Jews to witness him to other peoples. When the Bible speak of creatures existing for the "glory" of God it does not mean that God needs the approval or praise of creatures, let alone their flattery. Rather the Bible is saying that the glory of God is the happiness of creatures called to share in divine happiness, to enter into God's life of knowledge and love. This

God is able to reveal the Godhead to human beings in human terms, although humans can never fully understand the divine wisdom, nor can they measure God's love. Hence God is a person, a knowing, loving, and communicating being, though utterly other than the world, totally independent of it, and of infinite power.

The Jews, while maintaining the personhood of God in this sense and sometimes speaking of him in human terms, came to reject every effort to limit him to any human image or conception. The priests inculcated this anti-anthropomorphic, "negative theology" even among the common people by rejecting the use of any image of God in worship, vigorously opposing idolatry, and even refusing to use the sacred name of God in reading the Scriptures aloud. Yet in order that they might understand that their God is a personal God on whom the people might call in prayer it was necessary that even if God could not have an image God must have a name. Hence Tradition held that when Moses saw the burning bush and heard God call him, terrified as he was, to lead the Hebrews out of their slavery in Egypt, Moses asked the Invisible One hidden in the flame,

> "When I go to the Israelites and say to them, 'The God of your fathers has sent me to you,' if they ask me, 'What is his name?' what am I to tell them?" God replied, "'I am who am.'" Then he added, "This is what you shall tell the Israelites: 'I AM sent me to you'" (Ex 3:13-14).

Though the etymology of this name "Yahweh" is debated by scholars it seems to suggest both the transcendent mystery of God beyond human comprehension and also that God is the source of all that is. Thus "I am who I am" can be understood as a refusal to name the Godhead in a genealogical manner as was customary in Hebrew names (e.g., "David son of Jesse, son of Obed, son of Boaz," Lk 3:31-32) and common in pagan mythology. This God has no ancestors! Yet by saying that God is the I AM it also implies that God has no cause {he is not even his own cause, *causa sui*, as Spinoza claimed) but is the Creator, the uncaused cause of all other things who creates *ex nihilo*.[5]

"Yahweh" in Hebrew is undoubtedly a masculine name as demonstrated by the Bible's consistent use of masculine pronouns in its place. Yet as explained in Chapter 3 concerning the usage of metaphors and symbols, it is a great oversimplification to think that the Jews spoke of God as masculine because their culture was patriarchal. They were very well acquainted with the Great Mother Goddess, especially Astarte, and her male lovers, the Baals (1 K 11:5, etc.) and were often tempted to worship her. It was precisely to oppose such a rival worship to that of Yahweh, that the biblical writers insisted that God be named as male yet have no goddess wife, as did the male gods in the fertility religions. As the prophets (cf. Hosea 1-3) are fond of saying, God is not married to a goddess because his only lover is the Chosen People Israel to whom he is covenanted.

The primary meaning of this symbol of Covenant is not to show that males are superior to females as of course the Creator is to the creature. Faithful covenanted love makes partners relate to each other as equals in mutuality and complementarity not as unequals in dominance and subjection. Thus, the prophets (e.g. Hosea 1-3) always picture God as the male and the Chosen People as female not to demonstrate patriarchal superiority but the intimacy and mutuality of their love that demands perfect fidelity. It is entirely appropriate therefore that Israel, a nation bearing many children is metaphorically female, a common symbol in mythology for nations and cities, e.g., Athens was named for the goddess Athena. Hence in the Covenant as in a marriage Yahweh is Israel's husband.

In Chapter 3, I argued that the relation of mother to child is one of Sameness and that of father to child is Otherness. Because these relations are transcultural they are widely symbolized by gender images. Hence monistic Emanation Religions tend to have Goddesses, though these female divinities may have male partners. Creation Religions, on the other hand, name God as Father who is Other than his creation. In Judaism the Chosen People, and for Christianity the Church, is God's unique love and hence is symbolized as female and Mother, but to my knowledge this symbol is not used in Islamic religion.

Although the Jews retained from earlier religion the use of a temple with elaborate sacrificial and even bloody rituals, they kept these practices under rigid restraint. They have been accused of cruelty in offering animal victims and some have mistakenly thought that these sacrifices symbolized their desire for blood vengeance against their enemies. Really what they offered was the *first fruits*, bloody or unbloody, of their crops and their herds, as an acknowledgment that these were gifts of God not simply of their own efforts. The biblical account of how God commanded Abraham to sacrifice his son Isaac and then spared him (Gn 22:1-18) is intended to repudiate human sacrifice, while at the same time acknowledging God as the source of all good.

Ultimately with the destruction of the third Temple in Jerusalem by the Romans in 70 CE, the Jews found they could get along without even the Temple or its sacrifices as they had done temporarily during their Babylonian Exile. They then contented themselves with the purely verbal synagogue services. Thus Judaism adopted an essentially iconoclastic, purely spiritual worship by reciting the Word of the Sacred Scriptures, the *Torah*. Muslims too worship principally by the recitation of the *Qur'an*. At the Protestant Reformation the reformed Christian Churches adopted a similar style of iconoclastic worship, though they retained the sacraments of baptism and the Last Supper.

The Jewish notion of a *covenant* with God was perhaps derived from their Mesopotamian neighbors, but for the Jews this Covenant was an offer on God's part to guide them in a special way to his kingdom of peace and justice. The People's part in this covenant was to be sincerely committed to following the Creator's guidance by the observance of the *Torah* (usually translated "Law," but more exactly "Instruction"). This *Torah* is embodied in the Five Books of Genesis, Exodus, Leviticus, Numbers, and Deuteronomy attributed to Moses. Yet it also includes the *Oral Torah* or Traditions interpreting the Five Books called the Jerusalem and Babylonian *Talmud*. The oldest part of the *Talmud* is the *Mishnah* not recorded in writing until about 200 CE. Modern scholarship sees the Hebrew Scriptures as gradually evolving out of this living oral Tradition and successively edited written documents until they reached their fixed form about the first century BCE. Yet to admit this evolution is not necessarily to deny the Bible's inspiration and unity.[6] For scholarly, believing Jews the Mosaic events that created the People contained virtually the whole development that followed and which remains true to its roots.

The Jews, like all of us with regard to our deepest loyalties, were not always true to their commitment to the Torah and the Covenant, and their own Scriptures record these failures with amazing frankness, attributing the historical sufferings of the people primarily to this infidelity. To arouse his People to repentance God in his mercy and special love for them sent a succession of prophets who warned of the coming punishment of the Exile. They also continued to encourage Israel by a renewal of God's promises, including the affirmation of a Kingdom led by an Anointed King of the dynasty of David that with the Exile had sunk into obscurity.

From these prophecies arose a body of literature reinforcing fidelity to the Torah, but criticizing its merely external, legalistic observance, and demanding a commitment of the heart to God's ways. After the Exile, the Law and the Prophets were supplemented by a considerable body of literature of various forms (the "Writings") that dwell on the theme of God's wisdom in the creation and governance of the world and history. They also transmit in proverbs the results of long human experience (some of it already ancient in Mesopotamia and Egypt) of the ways of practical wisdom in living in the sight of God and rejecting the destructive way of all too human folly. Finally, in the last period before the destruction of Jerusalem, this canon was supplemented by still other writings, some of an apocalyptic nature that announced the approach of God's intervention to establish his Kingdom definitively.[7]

When the Romans destroyed the Temple in 70 CE, the Jews who already after the Exile had been widely dispersed throughout the Mediterranean world (the Diaspora), became a people without a homeland. Nevertheless, the subsequent history of Judaism is not that of a cultural vestige, but a living and developing religion whose influence has constantly increased.[8] Tragically it is also the history of cruel persecutions and expulsions, principally, but by no means exclusively by Christians, culminating in our times in the Nazi Holocaust and the re-establishment of Israel as the Jewish homeland under Zionist leadership.[9]

The obligation to study the Torah has made the Jews a people who greatly value education, scholarship, and science. In recent times, in spite of their religious iconoclasm, they have also become leaders not only in literature and music but also in the fine arts from which their iconoclasm formerly excluded them.

More fundamental, however, has been the religious and moral contribution of the Jews both through their direct influence and their indirect influence through the daughter religions of Christianity and Islam. Besides the dominant and very practical Pharisaic tradition centered on the Torah, there has also been a counter tradition in Judaism expressed in the medieval *Kabbalah* which engages in a speculative and mystical reflection on the Scriptures.[10] Both these tendencies appear in Hassidism, i.e., in movements to foster an intense piety and loving enthusiasm for the service of God. The Kabbalists, basing their speculations on the Genesis account of creation and the mystical visions of the prophets, developed various theories of the inner nature of God. Such tendencies were not merely medieval, since it is probable that Gnosticism had its roots in pre-Christian Jewish developments. Although such theories are not always reconcilable with Jewish orthodoxy, they are not considered outside the range of authentic Judaism that is more insistent on orthopraxis than orthodoxy. In fact only a rather small minority of Jews today are Orthodox; many are Conservatives (in liturgy), or Liberals, and many in Western countries are Humanists.[11]

3. Christianity

At the very time Judaism in the land of Israel was reaching the great crisis that was to end with the Roman destruction of the Temple in Jerusalem, there were many sectarian groups among the Jews seeking to interpret that crisis and predict its outcome.[12] The Sadducean sect was favored by the priests and aristocrats who reluctantly collaborated with the Roman oppressors both because these leaders from long political experience sought compromise rather than confrontation and because of their liking for Hellenistic culture. They accepted as inspired only the Five Books and rejected belief in angels and the resurrection as not clearly attested there.

Strongly opposed to the priests of the Temple was the sect of the Essenes, who withdrew from the Temple services. Some of them founded a celibate community in the desert at Qumran overlooking the Dead Sea. Under someone known to us only as the "Teacher of Righteousness" and his successors they sought to keep themselves pure of heathen contamination while preparing for what they believed to be the inevitable holy war between the Sons of Light and the Sons of Darkness. In this war all the apocalyptic expectations pictured in the literature of the time would be fulfilled and the Messianic Kingdom of God definitively established.

Some Jews, however, were not content to await God's intervention but supported the Zealots who engaged in terrorist activities against the Roman government. This struggle reached its climax in two unsuccessful revolts. The first of these in 66-68 CE was under a Zealot named Eleazar and led to the destruction of Jerusalem in 70 CE. The second was under the supposed Messiah Bar Kochba in 132 CE which ended in total defeat and the banishment of the Jews from Jerusalem, renamed Aelia Capitolina.

Besides these extreme parties were those Jews who viewed the Roman oppression not in terms of collaboration or revolt but in more exclusively spiritual terms. The most influential was the party of the Pharisees or Separatists who sought to extend the laws of ritual purity directly applicable to the priestly service in the Temple to all Jews in order to preserve Jewish identity against pagan influences.[13] They opposed the actions offensive to the Law of the Roman government but did not advocate its violent overthrow. Although they strongly criticized the behavior of the priests, they did not absent themselves from the Temple services but instead urged their reform. They insisted on strict fidelity to the Torah, written and oral, and on its careful study by all male Jews.

After the fall of the Temple it was the Pharisees who maintained the unity of the Jews in their dispersal. They based this on their determination of the canon of the inspired Scriptures (*Tanak*) from which they excluded works not written in Hebrew or Aramaic and the apocalyptic literature except for the remarkable Book of Daniel. In their insistence on ritual purity they gave great emphasis to the unwritten Oral Law in whose light the Scriptures were to be interpreted. Thus the leaders of Israel were no longer the priests, made obsolete by the destruction of the Temple, but rabbis who were learned in the interpretation of the dual Torah, especially its legislation.

In the generation immediately before the fall of the Temple, John the Baptizer of a priestly family led another movement of reform. He lived an ascetic life in the desert near Qumran and was perhaps influenced by their movement. Yet his own preaching had a different purpose. Announcing the imminent advent of the Messiah, John called for a sincere repentance of the people and baptized them in the Jordan to prepare them for that great event. He was beheaded at the command of King Herod Antipas in about 29 CE but his teaching continued to be influential and survives even today in Iraq and Iran in the Mandaean sects that still practice baptism but have also undergone dualistic influences.

Jesus of Nazareth, by occupation a carpenter, but legally of Davidic descent, at about the age of thirty accepted the baptism of John and then began to preach, as John had, the imminence of the Kingdom of God, the Messianic Age.[14] His preaching, however, in striking distinction from John's, was soon marked by wonderful phenomena, especially by what appeared to many to be the "casting out of demons," physical and mental healings, and even revivals from death that gained him a widespread following. These disciples were from the north of Palestine in Galilee where Nazareth is located, a region partly Jewish and partly pagan. They were peasants despised by the largely urban Pharisees for their ignorance of the Law.

Lest his message be distorted by the eagerness of the crowds for miracles, Jesus taught them in parables, short symbolic stories centering on the approach of the Kingdom and the repentance and the moral reform required of those who were to enter it. Thus he attempted to avoid encouraging incendiary political tendencies that could lead to direct confrontation with the authorities.[15] At the same time he gathered about him a select group of Twelve of varied backgrounds who traveled with him on his preaching journeys and to whom he imparted his fuller and more explicit teachings.

Two features of Jesus' teaching marked it off from that of the Pharisees who quickly viewed him with suspicion in spite of the fact that in many respects his teaching seemed in harmony with their own. The first was his insistence on the nearness of the Kingdom. John the Baptizer had been suspect to the Pharisees for the same reason, since they were well aware that such apocalyptic ideas were politically dangerous and encouraged fanaticism such as that of the Essenes and Zealots, while the Pharisees favored moderation and patience. Jesus' preaching of the advent of the Kingdom was even more sensational than was John's. While the Baptizer only predicted the imminent coming of the Messiah, Jesus (without openly making this claim for himself) seems to have claimed that the Kingdom had *already* begun to be present in the authority of his teaching and his acts of casting out demons and healing the sick.[16]

Furthermore, Jesus claimed an intimacy with God that (as it was reported in the primitive Church) permitted him to modify the Law, forgive sins against the Law, and say such things as the following:[17]

> All things have been handed over to me by my Father. No one knows the Son except the Father, and no one knows the Father except the Son and anyone to whom the Son wishes to reveal him (Mt 11:25-27; Lk 10:21-22).

From his teaching and life the early Christians, many still Jewish or identifying themselves with Jewish history, came to believe that:[18]

> In times past, God spoke in partial and various ways to our ancestors through the prophets; in these last days, he spoke to us through a son, whom he made heir of all things and through whom he created the heavens (Heb 2:1-2).

Thus for early Christians who wrote the New Testament Jesus was the Messiah, who fulfilled the prophecies of the Hebrew Scriptures. But more than that, he was the Son of God to whom the creation of the world could be truly attributed. Since for monotheism God is primarily defined as the Creator *ex nihilo,* this claim at once identified the Christian world-view and value-system with that of Judaism and yet stood in seeming contradiction to it.

The Pharisees saw plainly that it was one thing to arouse eschatological expectations as the prophets of old had done, and quite another to claim they were beginning to be fulfilled in the here and now. While some of their party were willing to wait until the truth or falsity of such claims was exposed by events, others felt a responsibility to actively oppose their acceptance by the people.

The second unique feature of Jesus' teaching was his insistence that the Kingdom of God was being opened by his teaching and actions to all human beings, whatever their earthly condition. Not that entrance into the Kingdom made no demands on those who sought to enter. Jesus in fact insisted on an interpretation of the Torah that was morally more demanding than what was general among the Pharisees. For example, he condemned divorce and remarriage and demanded even that his disciples love their enemies. Yet, while maintaining the validity of the ritual laws of the Torah, he disparaged an excessive emphasis on ritual purity. He also taught that the actual beginning of the Kingdom of God on earth implied, as the prophets had foretold, that the Spirit of God was to be poured out on all. Thus it would be possible now for all to meet the strict requirements of entrance to the Kingdom, whatever their past lives or ignorance of the Law.

Jesus demonstrated this teaching by remarkable acts of compassion even to the most despised members of Jewish society, the lepers, the prostitutes, the public sinners, and even the pagans. The Pharisees, of course, did not deny the moral beauty of mercy and compassion, nor the necessity of right intention in the practice of the Law as is evident from many sayings in the rabbinical tradition. They, however, were alarmed at what appeared to them as an excessive, impractical idealism that would endanger the casuistic "fences" that they were so carefully building around the Torah and on which they believed the solidarity of the Jewish nation depended.

If this conflict had been confined to Galilee, it might never have reached a crisis. But Jesus insisted on teaching also in Jerusalem at times when as a pious Jew he went up with his Twelve especially chosen disciples to take part in the great feasts prescribed by the Torah. His appearance (probably in the year 30 CE) in Jerusalem for the Feast of the Passover precipitated a series of events that led to his trial and death sentence by the Roman procurator Pontius Pilate. The exact complicity of the sectarian leaders and Jewish authorities in these events is disputed.[19] Nevertheless, from the Jewish authorities' point of view the death of such a troublemaker who endangered the precarious *status quo* and perhaps even the existence of the nation itself by heretical teaching must have been a relief.

For the considerable number of Jews who had believed in Jesus as the Messiah or at least as prophet his death was a bitter disillusionment. For most Jews, the majority of whom probably were already in the Diaspora, it was all a very remote matter if they ever heard of it at all.

The Roman government condemned Jesus to death by the ultimate cruelty of crucifixion that they often used for subversives. Although even his disciples, after Jesus' burial, believed that this was the end of all their hopes, in a few days they began to claim that he had again appeared to them and to many others alive. They said he had risen from the dead and commanded them to preach his Gospel throughout the world, not merely to the Jews and a few aliens as he had done, but to all the nations.[20]

They also claimed he had promised them the Divine Spirit who would make whatever remained obscure in his teaching clear and empower them to continue his works, including his miracles. This promise they said had been fulfilled on the feast of Pentecost following the Passover when he had died. Moreover, they were convinced that by the power of this Holy Spirit he remained present with them in some invisible manner in the Eucharist or memorial supper of bread and wine.[21] On the night before his anticipated crucifixion he had commanded them to reenact it until he should return to earth to consummate God's Reign.[22] Hence for Christians this memorial of his sacrificial death, the Eucharist (Thanksgiving) replaces the sacrifices of the Temple by fulfilling what they only symbolized, a worthy offering to God of all his gifts including his greatest gift, his Incarnate Word.

These claims, of course, appeared incredible and heretical to most Jews who encountered them. During the crises of the two revolts against the Romans the Jewish Christians refused to participate in the defense of the nation. Perhaps it was this nonviolence of the Jewish Christians that seemed a betrayal of their country that led to their definitive excommunication from the Jewish synagogue, although this had taken place locally in various places from an early period. There is no clear evidence that the Jewish Christians themselves wished to withdraw from the synagogue, since they regarded themselves as loyal to the Jewish Covenant and the teachings of the prophets.

In the meantime the Christian community was spreading outside Israel both among Diaspora Jews and among pagans in accordance with Jesus' insistence on the universality of the Kingdom. The problem of course was how the pagans could be integrated into this community of the "invited" (*ecclesia*) or Church. In the ancient world religion was often intimately united to the nation and state. The Jews, even in the Diaspora, sustained their religious identity first through their relation to the Temple and after its destruction in their hopes for the restoration of their own kingdom. The Christians eventually found a similar kind of support for themselves when the Roman Emperor in 313 adopted Christianity as the state religion. Yet as previously they had managed to exist under the Roman Empire, even after they had become its official religion they continued to see a certain distinction between Church and State. Had not Jesus commanded, "Give to Caesar what is Caesar's, but to God what is God's" (Mk 12:17)? Thus Christianity has remained fundamentally independent of any nationality, unlike the Jews for whom the Holy Land has remained a central concept. For Catholic Christians, though, Rome has a special significance since it is the Bishop of Rome who is recognized among the bishops as the successor of St. Peter, Vicar of Christ as Head of the Church, who with St. Paul was martyred there. Yet even this Petrine office can be located elsewhere, as it was at Avignon, France, from 1309 to 1377.

Orthodox Jews believe that the Torah binds only Jews and that non-Jews may be saved by obeying some less perfect law, such as that given to Noah. They believe also that Jews have a duty to witness the One God to all nations and that with the coming of the Messianic Age all nations will come to recognize him and acknowledge the hegemony of the Jewish nation. While Orthodox Jews accept converts and there have always been provisions for proselytes and friendly "Godfearers" in Jewish law, generally speaking Judaism has not been a missionary religion because for it religious identity is closely associated with identity of descent that might be diluted by proselytism.

The question arose very early whether the Christian Church, a sect as it were of Judaism, must insist that its converts become Jews observing the details of the ritual law as Jesus and his first followers had done. Peter, whom Jesus had named chief of the Twelve, first opened the way to the reception of Gentiles without requiring circumcision.[23] It was Paul of Tarsus, himself a "Hebrew of Hebrew parentage" (Ph 3:5), however, who actively preached the legitimacy of the conversion of the Gentiles without Judaization, but not without considerable struggle with his fellow Jewish Christians. This solution was accepted (with the condition that Gentile converts should at least observe the law of Noah; cf. Gn 9:1-5; Ac 15:24-29) by a meeting of Church leaders in Jerusalem headed by Peter and including James, a relative of Jesus and leader of the Jerusalem community. From that time on the Christian Church took its permanent form as expressed in the documents of the New Testament.[24]

How then is Christianity distinct from Judaism?[25] It has retained the essential foundation of Judaism, its monotheism and creationism. In the New Testament there is never any question but that there is only one God who freely created all things out of nothing. Yet if Jesus was the Divine Son, and the Holy Spirit (whom he promised would descend on his community and as they believed they had experienced at Pentecost) was also Divine, how then could Christians consistently proclaim the monotheism of Abraham and Moses? Muhammad thought they could not.

The obvious way out of this paradox would have been to consider the Son and Spirit as exalted creatures of God, perhaps messenger angels of high rank, as in some Jewish literature Michael and Metatron were described. This solution was accepted by some Christians and when formulated by Arius (d. 336) achieved wide currency, but it was definitively rejected by the Council of Nicaea in 325 as contradictory to the universal practice of the Church of worshiping Jesus as Lord and Savior. As regards the Spirit the same decision was made at the First Council of Constantinople in 381.

That these declarations appeared to involve a metaphysical contradiction was perfectly clear to these Councils, many of whose member bishops were well acquainted with the demands of Greek logic and metaphysics. How is it possible to claim consistently both that there is only one God and that the Son and the Spirit are also God, while at the same time denying that these Three Divine Persons are one identical person? Yet the early Councils believed they could resolve any such paradox without denying the transcendent mystery involved.[26] If they were mistaken in this (an issue to be discussed later), it was not because they ever wavered in their monotheism which remained for them the primary assumption in terms of which their other formulas of faith had to be interpreted. The Jews, however, believed that the Christians had fallen into flat contradiction, and generally explained it as a compromise with the polytheism of the pagans.

4. Islam

The doctrinal struggle over Trinitarian doctrine and its consequences for the understanding of the person of Jesus continued in the Christian Church to the Sixth General Council in 680. In the meantime the new religion of Islam ("submission to the will of the One God") came on the scene as a much more threatening rival to Christianity than Judaism.[27] It originated in the Arabian city of Mecca that had for long been considered a sacred city by the Arabs, particularly because of the Ka'ba, a shrine housing a black stone reputed to have fallen from heaven, located near a sacred well Zamzam.

Mecca was flourishing as a crossroads of trade but was suffering from social disorders for which its primitive polytheism provided no satisfying answers. Jews and Christians were constantly passing through it on business, and local holy men were already speaking of monotheism. What is surprising is that Christians had not found a way to bring the Semitic Arabs into the Church. Perhaps the reason was that the

Church had exhausted so much of its missionary energies on its own internal doctrinal struggles that had resulted in numerous schisms. Hence the Arabs picked up only confused messages which left them feeling marginal and ignored by the Christian Empire.

In this situation leadership emerged from within the Arab sphere, stimulated, however, by secondhand stories from the Jewish and Christian Scriptures. The probably illiterate Muhammad (570-632 CE) had heard these stories on his journeys as a camel-driver for a rich widow whom he subsequently married. He was a man given to long periods of solitary religious meditation during which he, like the prophets of the Hebrew Scriptures, began to receive revelations. At first these greatly frightened him until he came to understand that they were given him by the One God, *Allah* (which means *the* God) with the mission to declare them to all his countrymen and eventually to the world.

These revelations that were written down, probably by dictation, but collected only after the Prophet's death form the *Qur'an* (*Koran*) or "Recitation." This Holy Book is even more central to Islam than the Hebrew Scriptures for Jews or the New Testament for Christians, although it also, like them, requires to be supported by an oral Tradition.[28] This book (a little shorter than the New Testament) is a collection of *sura*'s or separate revelations, each beginning with the formula "In the Name of God, the Merciful, the Compassionate," arranged after the death of the Prophet not according to time of reception or content but of approximate length. The *Qur'an* is believed to be an exact copy of an eternal prototype called the "Well-preserved Tablet" or "The Mother of the Book."

Muhammad seems to have made no claims for himself, except that of being the human channel through whom this revelation was communicated and whose truth he believed to be self-evident to all who would honestly listen, while those who refused to believe were self-condemned to Hell. The truths the *Qur'an* contained had been revealed many times before to previous prophets including Noah, Abraham, Moses, the Hebrew prophets, and Jesus of Nazareth,[29] but had been over and over again rejected by evildoers. The Jewish and Christian Scriptures, however, have transmitted this Tradition only in corrupted form. In the *Qur'an* revelation is once again and finally revealed in its purity. Hence Muhammad, according to the faith of Islam, is only a prophet like those before him, but he is the last and greatest, *the* Prophet.

Muhammad soon gathered around him faithful followers but was violently attacked by others so that in 622 CE he had to take flight (the *Hijra*) from Mecca for Medina where the later *sura*'s were received. These are less concerned with doctrinal questions and more with the proper organization of the community of the faithful. To protect this community Muhammad became an active political and military leader, eventually recovering Mecca and reducing his opponents to powerlessness. After his death his Arab followers achieved political power over the whole of their people and in subsequent years drove on to the conquest of the Near East and eventually much of northern Africa, Spain in the West and Persia and India in the East. Finally, in 1453 they destroyed the Christian Eastern or Byzantine Empire.

Besides these military conquests they undertook successful missionary efforts in Southeast Asia and continue these today in Africa and elsewhere. Except for Spain (whose gradual reconquest was not completed until the fifteenth century), no country that became Islamic has ever ceased to be so, although today Humanism has made deep inroads into Islamic cultures and is provoking the reaction of so-called "Islamic fundamentalism." In spite of Muhammad's acceptance of military conquest as a means of extending Islam, he did not believe in forced conversion.[30] He taught that Jews and Christians, "the People of the Book" (i.e., who had monotheistic Sacred Scriptures, though, he believed, corrupted ones) could be tolerated under certain restrictions. On the contrary people who denied the One God could not be tolerated within the territories controlled by Islam, except on special conditions by treaty and then only temporarily. The *jihad* or holy war (literally the term means "striving") is required by the *Qur'an* not as a means of conversion but of defense of Islam against its enemies and to open the way to missionary activity. Thus Islam is not viewed primarily as a religion distinct from the state, but as a territory governed by laws based on the *Qur'an*.

Although the authority of the *Qur'an* is for Muslims supreme, it is not the only authoritative source for Islam. Much as in Judaism and

Christianity in its pre-Reformation forms, for Muslims Scripture must be interpreted in the light of Tradition. Their Tradition is in the form of sayings (*hadith*) of the Prophet transmitted by a recorded chain of witnesses and the Law (*shari'ah*) supported by an elaborate jurisprudence (*fiqh*) which regulates every aspect of life much as does the rabbinic tradition of the Jews.[31] It has often been said that the power of Islam lies especially in the simplicity and clarity of its monotheism and an equal clarity in its requirements as a way of life governed in all its activities. Of course this raises special difficulties when Islam is confronted with social change.

The most fundamental of the requirements of the Islamic way of life are its "Five Pillars": (1) to witness to the One God and His prophets; (2) to pray five times daily; (3) to fast for the month of Ramadan to honor the *Qur'an* given in that month; (4) to pay the tax to care for the faithful poor; and (5) if possible, at least once to make a pilgrimage to the Ka'ba in Mecca. The significance of this pilgrimage is that Muhammad at first ordered prayer to be directed toward Jerusalem where Abraham had been commanded to sacrifice his son Isma'il (ancestor of the Arabs, not Isaac ancestor of the Jews as the Hebrew Scriptures relate). When, however, most Jews rejected Islam, Muhammad ordered prayers to be directed toward the Ka'ba. The Prophet explained that this well and shrine originally, long before they were polluted by polytheistic errors, were the place where the angel had given water to Hagar and Isma'il and thus fittingly symbolized the original religion of Abraham. Through Isma'il it had been transmitted to the Arabs unadulterated by corruption of the Hebrew Scriptures. By thus re-orientating prayer to the One God to Mecca, Muhammad at a single stroke freed his people and their shrine from polytheism and at the same time made clear the identity of Islam distinct from the religions of Judaism and Christianity associated with Jerusalem. The pilgrims to Mecca also offer (as I have already mentioned) the only sacrifice permitted by the *Qur'an*, a bloody immolation of animals in commemoration of Abraham's sacrifice. This is also performed annually on the Feast of Sacrifices throughout Islam. Islam has no priesthood, however, and, as in Judaism since the destruction of the Temple, its religious leaders are simply teachers or experts on the *Qur'an* and the Tradition.

There are many sects within Islam, since after the decline of the primarily political Caliphate there has been no central religious authority. Its principal division is between the Sunni (the vast majority) and the Shi'ah (dominant in Iran, but present throughout Islamic lands). This schism occurred quite early as a result of a dispute over succession to the Caliphate.[32] The Shi'ah believe that this authority can legitimately be transmitted only to the descendants of Muhammad. This meant, since the Prophet had no male heirs, that the legitimate line passed through the Prophet's saintly son-in-law Ali. Even this legitimate line ended in seven or, according to others, twelve generations. Hence the Shi'ah await the restoration of this line by a miracle in a future leader, the *Mahdi,* and for the present are guided by an invisible teacher (*Imam*) represented visibly by various charismatic leaders.

The legal clarity of Islam has not satisfied all of its followers. Therefore some, occasionally influenced by Christian contacts, have developed on the one hand a systematic, rational theology and on the other an extensive mystical tradition often centered in religious association or brotherhoods, the Sufi. In the Middle Ages theological systems were developed by a number of eminent thinkers.[33] These theologians or philosophers systematized the basic themes of the *Qur'an* by the use of Greek philosophy, principally that of Aristotle and the Neo-Platonists, which they had learned from the Byzantine Christians whom they had conquered. Their own commentaries on these Greek works then became known to the West in Latin translations from the Arabic. Hence these Arabian philosophers are often known by Latinized names such as Avicenna (*Ibn Sina*) and Averroes (*Ibn Rushd*). In the process, however, these Islamic philosophers, unlike the major medieval Jewish and Christian ones, were rejected by their co-religionists as unorthodox and rationalistic.[34] The result has been that Islamic theology today, like post-medieval Judaism, tends to neglect the philosophical aspects of theology and confine itself either to exegesis and application of the *Qur'an,* the Tradition, and the Law or to writings of a spiritual and mystical character.

The mystical Tradition of the Sufi is exceedingly rich and complex and like that of Judaism and Christianity sometimes very ambiguous, and suspected of pantheism.[35] Yet in all its forms it is a search for a spiritual union with the One God by asceticism, prayer, and the service of the poor in complete loyalty to the teachings of the *Qur'an*. One surprising element in the *Qur'an* itself is the role attributed to Jesus and even to his mother Mary whose virginity is declared.[36] Jesus is considered a true prophet in whom the mercy and love of God is manifested in a special way that makes him a model of the mystic. In popular religion in Islam these mystical tendencies take the form, as again in popular Judaism and Christianity, of devotion to the saints, their miraculous powers and their shrines, tendencies often frowned upon by Islamic reformers as dangerous for monotheism.

5. How Is the Creator Known?

We must now consider the exact meaning of monotheism and creationism as it is the common foundation of these three great world religions. Is the existence of a supreme, personal, knowing and freely willing Being, who by a free act is the creator (cause and ground) of all other beings, known only through revelation by such prophets as Moses, Jesus, and Muhammad? Or is the existence of this Being first knowable to all human beings from creation itself?

It is hard to see how one could come to believe in a revelation from God, unless one first had at least some knowledge that God exists. This knowledge would have to come from our human way of knowing. Thus the Scriptures of all three monotheistic religions affirm that the prophets have revealed God, but that anterior to these prophecies He was and is also knowable by all human beings through the evidence of His creation. The role of the prophets was to call humanity to open its eyes to these evidences and to complete this general revelation made to human reason by a deeper and more complete revelation addressed to faith. Whether this general revelation of God is accessible to us by intuition or by a reasoning process is of little concern to the writers of the Scriptures, but they themselves appeal to reasoning at least of a common-sense kind accessible even to the most illiterate and unlearned.[37]

In the Hebrew Scriptures we read that "The heavens declare the glory of God, and the firmament proclaims his handiwork" (Psalm 19:1). This text is only an example of a theme found throughout the Wisdom Tradition. In the New Testament also St. Paul (paraphrasing a passage in the deuterocanonical Book of Wisdom, 12:27-13:1) says,

> For what can be known about God is evident to them [the pagans]; because God made it evident to them. Ever since the creation of the world, his invisible attributes of eternal power and divinity have been able to be understood and perceived in what he has made (Romans 1:19-20).

In the *Qur'an* we also read,

> "The seven heavens and the earth /And all beings therein, /Declare His glory: There is not a thing /But celebrates His praise; /and yet ye understand not /How they declare His glory!" (*Sura* 17:44)

Thus the three monotheistic religions agree that the existence of the visible world makes evident to unprejudiced human observers that its existence and order is not self-explainable but must be the effect of One Creator. This Creator's *power* is seen in the world's existence, his *wisdom* is seen in the order of its natural laws, and his *love* is seen in the generosity with which he shares his gifts with intelligent creatures.

The statistics quoted in Chapter 1 indicate that most people in the United States today whether they are religiously affiliated or not believe in the existence of some kind of God. Though in Europe there are more declared atheists, even there they are only about 10% in any country. We saw in Chapters 2 to 4 that the world religions also all tend to some kind of monotheism, though in very different ways. Even many Humanists acknowledge a deistic God or are agnostic about the question. Real atheism is not very common and frequently when atheistic opinions are analyzed they are not so much an assertion that there is no God, but a denial that God could be the kind of God that others seem to believe in. Often declared atheists, like Karl Marx who was violently opposed to traditional religion as a tool of the capitalists, are actually materialistic pantheists like the Stoics of old, who considered the material universe to be a self-evolving Absolute. In Chapter 3 I have quoted Einstein to much the same effect.

Some philosophers have thought the existence of God is *intuitively* evident and hence requires no reasoned proof. Many other apparently honest people, however, deny that they have any such intuition or religious experience. Moreover if there is such an intuition it remains too vague to be of much help in determining which among the many concepts of God is true. Even if there be such an immediate intuition of God's existence, it must also include the awareness of the created world and at least the self-awareness of the creature that has this intuition. Thus if such an experience is valid, it is also an effect from which an *a posteriori* argument from *effect to cause* may proceed to be convincing to those who do not already have such an intuition or fear that it is illusory. Hence it is important to show the existence of God not merely by a private intuition but in an objective and public manner by a proof from effects known to all human beings.[38]

St. Anselm of Canterbury (d. 1109) proposed a famous *a priori* proof that has fascinated many philosophers, the so-called "ontological proof." It is *a priori* (from cause to effect) because it proceeds from the definition of the nature of God to an effect of this nature, i.e., the property of existence that is caused by this nature, as for example from the definition of 2, as 1 + 1, we can deduce that 2 has the property of being "even." The ontological argument is that since we define God as the Perfect Being and if God did not exist he would not be perfect, therefore he must exist. Aquinas agreed with Anselm that *if* we knew that God is really the most Perfect Being it would logically follow that he necessarily exists. But it is fallacious to assume, before we know God exists, that we can define the term "God" as the Perfect Being by a *real* definition. In fact to define God as the "Perfect Being" before we know he exists is to give him a merely *nominal* definition, i.e., we explain what the word signifies, not whether it exists or is even possible. This is like defining a "square-circle" as a plane figure having four equal sides every point of which sides is equidistant from one point. This is what we mean by a "square-circle" but it also shows that such a thing is impossible. To define "God" as the "Perfect Being" does not prove God's existence is impossible, but it shows us that we do not know whether such a being is possible or not. Only after we have proved in some *a posteriori* way from effect to cause that God exists, can we then prove *a priori* from cause to effect that God's existence is not only possible but necessary. Even in geometry I cannot prove the properties of a circle, before I have first proved that a circle is possible by a theorem that shows that a circle can be constructed.

Reasoned proofs of the existence of God from creation to Creator are found in many theological and philosophical writings reflecting each of these world-views. The classic Christian formulation of such a demonstration of the existence of God from effect (the existence of the material world including ourselves) to the existence of God as its cause was given by St. Thomas Aquinas (d. 1275). Much the same line of argument can be found in both Jewish and Muslim philosophers.

In modern philosophy, however, it has very commonly been assumed that Immanuel Kant (d. 1804), whom in Chapter 2 I identified as the most influential philosopher of Humanism, had disproved the validity of this type of argument. He was, however, apparently unaware of the way in which Aquinas had formulated it. He proposed that it was the "cosmological argument" in the form he knew from Cartesian-Leibnitzian metaphysics. In that form he was able to attack its claim of being an *a posteriori* argument from effect to cause and assert that it was really nothing but a disguised form of Anselm's *a priori* argument, since its premises included the term "God" defined as the Perfect Being. In fact Aquinas in his formulation of the proof had very carefully noted that the term "God" in the premises and in the conclusion stood for "that which all understand to be God" (*hoc omnes intelligunt Deum*). Thus his argument carefully avoids Anselm's error of assuming that we *know* God really to be the Perfect Being before we have proved that he exists. Only in the *Summa Theologiae*, I, q. 4, a. 1, after it has been proven in I, q. 2, a. 3, does he then show that our idea of God is that of a Perfect Being, and that the First Cause really is such.[39] Thus in the Thomistic form arguments for God's existence must be from some observable effect in our world to the existence of the First Cause that we cannot observe. This kind of argument is very common in natural science. For example, our knowledge in current physics of the elementary particles has been acquired by arguing largely from the traces left by their paths through a cloud chamber, not from direct observation that their minute size makes impossible. Similarly the theories of biological evolution or of cosmological evolution from a Big Bang are not based on direct observation of these long past events, but on the effects they have left in our world today.

A more profound attack on the possibility of such a proof of God's existence can be made by denying the *principle of causality* on which it is based.[40] This attack was already made in the late Middle Ages by the Nominalists William of Ockham (d. c. 1350) and Nicholas of Oresme (d. 1382), but has influenced thinking today mainly through the work of the leading Humanist philosopher David Hume (d. 1776). As I explained in Chapter 2, Kant was also to adopt this attack along with his attempt, already discussed, to reduce the argument to that of St. Anselm. Hume argued that when we talk about "cause and effect" all we actually observe is one phenomenon following another. Therefore, Hume contended, all that "the relation of cause and effect" really means is that we become accustomed to experience certain regular patterns in phenomena and so we expect, without knowing why, that they will reoccur.

Thus Hume supposes that by "effect" we mean something that comes *after* its "cause," but for Aquinas this is not its primary meaning. For him an effect is something whose existence depends on the existence of its cause. Moreover that cause must not only exist but must be acting as a cause. Hence properly speaking cause and effect are *simultaneously in act.* Of course we can also speak of effects that exist after their causes have ceased to act, as Hume understood the matter, but this presupposes that when the causation actually took place the effect existed because of its dependence on the cause. For example, I may notice that a room is warm because a fire was going in the fireplace recently but is now extinguished, but this would be the case only if recently the fire was actually *warming* the room. Scientists, therefore, do not determine the cause of natural phenomena merely by observing one event after another, but by determining in various ways that Y can exist only if at some time X existed and was acting to produce Y. Moreover such an explanation is incomplete until the scientist has established *how* X can produce Y, e.g., how a fire can produce energy that warms the room. Even if the universe has always existed in an endless cycle of change, as scientists in Aquinas' time thought probable, his arguments still held because they did not depend on a beginning to the universe in time. Other theories of a universe with no beginning have been developed today, such as Fred Hoyle's "steady-state" universe, or Hawking's universe finite in time but with no beginning, or the theories of those who think Big Crunches follow the Big Bangs endlessly.[41] Yet none of these possible cosmologies are inconsistent with Aquinas' arguments. They would still be valid because the effect to be explained is not the existence of some static entity like the universe as a quantity of matter, but the continuing dynamic actuality of its processes.

As also explained in Chapter 2, Kant has profoundly influenced Humanist thought by his idealism. His idealist epistemology holds to the consistency theory of truth rather than a correspondence theory and hence he understood scientific theories as valid not because they correspond to a reality outside the human mind but because they give a consistent order to phenomenal sense impressions within the human mind. Hence he denied that there can be a valid theoretical knowledge of nonmaterial reality since theories about it are empty of sense data. Yet he still maintained that for practical reasons of morality we ought to act as if we had an immortal spiritual soul and as if there were a God who would reward or punish our behavior. Thus Kant's profound influence on modern Humanist thought has led to the conviction of many today that a rational demonstration of the existence of God or of other spiritual beings is impossible. For example, Hans Küng in his *Does God Exist*?,[42] after rather severely criticizing Kant's system as a whole, accepts Kant's disproof of any theoretical demonstration of God's existence as if it were definitive and universally accepted. And then he proceeds to present his own purely pragmatic argument that, if there is no God, our innate hope that the universe is not absurd would be in vain!

Aquinas' epistemology, on the contrary, rejects idealism and is rooted in Aristotle's conviction that it is possible to construct a natural science based on sense knowledge yet which can discover the intelligible order of the extra-mental world as it really is. Yet both he and

Aristotle are well aware that natural science will always remain imperfect and incomplete. Hence Aquinas is open to the possibility that natural science can discover and demonstrate that God exists as the necessary cause of effects that we observe in our world. That this is actually the case he tries to show by his famous five proofs or *Quinque Viae* based on the proof from *motion* given in Aristotle's *Physics* VIII. This proof Aquinas characterizes as "the most evident" because it argues from the most empirically evident effect, the existence of *change* in the world, or rather from *motion*, since motion is the most obvious and basic kind of change. The other four proofs have independent validity but are evident when seen in the context of the first. Therefore I explain this first proof here for those who have not seen any convincing reasons to accept idealism or the notion that truth is nothing more than mental consistency.

Aquinas' argument is usually presented as it is found in his *Summa Theologiae* I, q. 2, a. 3. This can lead to serious misunderstanding since that version is the summary of a philosophical, not a theological argument, and is treated much more thoroughly in other works. This mistake is compounded when the term "philosophical" is then assumed to mean *metaphysical*. For Aquinas "philosophy" is a much broader term than "metaphysics" and includes what today we call "natural science," and in fact this proof is presented by him in his *Summa Contra Gentiles as* drawn directly from Aristotle's "natural science." Catholic philosophers often do not like to admit this because they know that Aquinas' natural science is now in many respects obsolete. Furthermore, since scientists today often exaggeratedly claim that all their theories are only probable, it would seem that no argument taken from natural science for the existence of God could be certain. To understand the proof, however, as Aquinas meant it, we must not assume that natural science never arrives at certitudes. For entirely sufficient reasons Aquinas was certain the earth is not flat but round and for the same and still more reasons we are still certain it is round. Therefore what Aquinas attempts is first to show that God *exists* by an argument of a purely scientific kind, requiring only the same kind of data that we use today in physics, chemistry, and biology and in ordinary logic.

How does Aquinas prove that an immaterial God exists using

only the data and method of natural science? A full presentation of his argument would require a review of the basic principles of natural science, principles that unfortunately, are often not thoroughly expounded and critically examined in science education today. While the logic of this argument is evidently sound, the premises require to be verified. The proof can be summarized as follows:

> For a body to exist in motion, it must be moved by another actual mover. This actual mover is either:
> (a) itself an existent body that acts only because it too is being moved by another, or
> (b) an existent mover that is not a body.
>
> But an infinite series of movers such as posited in (a) is impossible because they would be only potential not actual movers.
>
> Therefore, since bodies in motion are observed to exist,
> a First Unmoved Mover that is not a body must exist,
> *and such an entity is what is meant in ordinary usage by the word "God."*

The observable effect from which this proof from effect to cause originates is "motion." That things move is empirically evident. That motion is not only the most easily observed kind of change but that it is presupposed by all other kinds of change is also evident. We observe that bodies act on one another only when the distance between them is not infinite, and do so in proportion to their proximity. Hence to initiate any change things must at least come closer so as to act through intermediaries or even come into contact. When Newton theorized that gravity is *actio in distans*, he then had to suppose that this could only be explained by the will of God![43] When modern physics explains one event by another distant event it always supposes that energy passes through an intermediate field, and usually that it is conveyed by waves or particles requiring time to travel.

It is essential to understand exactly what we observe when we see a motion. This must be done by a *phenomenological analysis*, that is, an exact description of a basic experience that is presupposed to any other scientific procedure such as measurement. Since Galileo, scientists have tended to focus on the quantitative measurement of objects so as to be able to fit them into an abstract mathematical model. Later I will show why this is legitimate and necessary for the progress of science, but it also has a down side. Mathematical models can always be constructed to fit observed data but they are still abstractions that only approximate the real physical phenomena. Moreover, they are *static* models, since mathematical objects are fixed and timeless: the numbers 2 and 20 do not change. It is true one can represent the mathematical relations involved in motion; for example, one can represent the path of a moving body and a period of time by lines as if they were spatial dimensions. One can also chart the relations between the position of a body on its path and time elapsed (velocity) and one can represent by a curve the acceleration of motion. Yet all these representations are fixed models that abstract from the fact that a body in motion is never simply located at a point on a line, but that the very essence of motion is that the body is in transit from one part of the line to another. If we are to understand change, and first of all motion as the simplest and most basic type of change, we must describe it not simply by measuring it and diagramming this mathematically, but by noting what is specific to motion in actual experience.

If then we describe a motion as it is a physical reality we find that four correlative aspects must be included in the description. Aristotle and Aquinas called these four aspects four kinds of "cause," but today this is confusing because we use that term to mean only an efficient cause. (1) Something undergoes change and hence is *potential* to a new determination; a billiard ball on this side of the table leaves it and then appears on the other side. This potentiality is what Aristotle in his analysis of motion called the *material cause* of motion, i.e., that which is potential to the act of motion. On the other hand this potentiality is actualized in motion; the ball that was first on part of the table enters another part. This actuality Aristotle called the *formal cause*. From these two observed facts about motion it becomes evident that any movable thing must have *quantity*, that is, must have more than one part. If it were not, since a thing in motion is leaving one part of its path and entering another, it would be either at rest in the first part or in the second. And if this is so, how can it be in motion? But if it is leaving one part and entering another part, it must have at least two parts, and this is what we called "quantity" or "extension." Thus every moving thing is a "body" or something "material" both in the sense that it is potential and in the sense that it is a whole with parts. Note that in this description the term "matter" is much more general than the identification in modern physics of matter with what has inertial and gravitational mass. It includes not only "matter" in this restricted sense, but all the entities known to science that can be measured. Thus modern physics, in spite of its identification of matter and mass, also knows of particles like the photon and neutrino and of "fields" and "space" and "vacuums" that have zero mass. It is just because quantity is the first property of any material thing that natural science is especially interested in measurement and finds mathematical models so helpful.

Motion, however, is not just a measurement, but a real dynamic state of affairs. Since something cannot give itself what it does not have, a thing that does not have this real state of affairs cannot produce it. Hence it must be actualized (set in motion) by another thing, a *mover*. A mover is the "efficient cause" of the motion of the body in motion. Thus there could be no efficient causality if there were no moveable bodies, and a moveable body to be potentially in motion is so because of its material cause and to be actually moving must have the actuality or formal cause of motion.

A motion is said to be "natural" and the subject of study by the natural sciences if it is not man-made or the result of sheer chance but reoccurs regularly. Such a natural motion is given by its efficient cause a predetermined direction even if it never reaches a particular destination. It is this predetermination of a change by its efficient cause that Aristotle called *final* causality or teleology. If motions did not have a direction from their very inception they could not be natural since they would not reoccur. Today scientists often deny that they think in terms of final causality (teleology) because they suppose a final cause implies a conscious purpose on the part of the moving thing, or that a final cause would be some other force in addition to the efficient cause. Yet when a man directs an arrow at a target no one supposes the arrow has any conscious purpose. Nevertheless, it is obvious that its efficient cause (the archer) gave it a motion that had a definite direction. In natural causation the direction is predetermined by some body having a natural force, such as gravity that regularly attracts other massive bodies, or electromagnetism that regularly attracts bodies with the opposite charge and repels bodies with the same charge. The direction given these natural actions is not another kind of efficient force but the direction to the motion given by the efficient force. Yet to omit it from the description of the process is to omit an essential aspect of the event. If natural efficient causes did not give a directional tendency to produce determined effects, science could not recognize efficient causes as causes. Nor would the relatively stable objects that constitute our universe be able to survive. Not only do acorns grow into oaks, but atoms bond to form stable compounds, and elementary particles to form atoms, or our world would be chaos.

The discomfort of modern scientists with teleology is increased by the fact that in mathematical models only material causality and formal causality are adequately represented. This is because mathematics, just as it abstracts from the qualities of things, and considers only their quantities, also abstracts from motion and all kinds of change. The figures of geometry and the numbers of arithmetic are static, timeless objects of thought, not the real, dynamic, changing quantities of real physical objects in which the direction of change is of the essence. It is true that mathematicians can represent the direction of motion by a vector, but this indicates direction along a line that stands for the motion but does not represent its actual transition from potency to act. The mathematician can also represent the velocity of a moving body by plotting the relation between the position of a moving body and the time at which it reaches that position, yet again the diagram showing these variables is *all there at once*, while the physical motion is not. Thus the mathematical models fix motion and its dynamic directedness and disguise final causality.

Thus to have a scientifically adequate description of a moving body we must note that it is changeable because of its material and its formal cause and that it is actually in motion because of its efficient cause and the direction or finality given its motion by that efficient cause. Thus to define a body in free fall, it would be necessary to mention its matter (it is a changeable body potential to motion) and its form (it is a body actually in motion). It would also be necessary to note that it has an efficient cause of its motion (it is a massive body having a natural gravitational force) and its motion has a teleology (finality) or direction toward the more massive body of the earth.

When motion is described accurately, without losing sight of its fourfold character it becomes clear why the major premise of Aquinas' proof, namely, *For a body to exist in motion, it must be moved by another actual mover,* must be true. To be in motion is to be receiving new actuality (to be entering on the first part or some subsequent part of its path), and a potential thing cannot give itself an actuality that it does not yet have. Yet many thinkers beginning with Democritus and then Plato have neglected this truth because they were content with the observation that living things are in a sense self-moving. But this self-movement is not absolute and hence does not contradict the principle that nothing can move itself. A living organism is self-moving but only relatively so, since it has some principal part that moves the other parts and is unmoved with respect to them, but it requires to be moved by activation received from without the system. Thus our brain moves our muscles and our muscles move our limbs and so on, but none of this would happen unless we ate and breathed, taking in energy from the external environment. In fact in every such complex system there is always a principal part or *prime* mover that moves the other parts and is not itself moved by them, but it too has to be constantly supplied with energy to keep it and the whole system going.

In fact there are no perpetual-motion machines. All material systems obey the Second Law of Thermodynamics that any system of moving bodies tends to become more and more random in its motions. Every clock eventually tells the wrong time and finally runs down. Of course for evolution from simpler to more complex systems to occur entropy must decrease, but can do so only *locally* within the total system. This decrease of entropy fortunately has happened on our planet earth with the origin of more complex chemicals and then of life and finally of our extremely complex brain necessary for intelligence. Yet all the time in the universe as a whole entropy continues to increase. This is even more evident in recent physics with its purely statistical laws than it was in an older physics that presupposed absolute determinism. In fact in our universe there is already a major element of chance as is evident in the history of evolution itself.

Thus the self-movement of living things does not contradict the principle that nothing can change itself. But does this hold for inanimate nature? In Aquinas' time, astronomers thought that the motion of the celestial spheres they supposed carried the sun, moon and planets would eventually explain all the motion in the world. It was supposed that though these spheres were independent prime movers, their motions were coordinated by the rotation of the outermost sphere that enclosed the entire universe. The motion of this outer sphere as prime mover, however, was said to be "natural" to it. Since every scientific explanation eventually comes to some fundamental natural forces that explain everything else in nature, but are simply given as natural to the universe in which we find ourselves, it would seem that this is as far as science can go. The ancient astronomy is long ago obsolete. Yet physicists still suppose that eventually they will be able to determine the fundamental natural moving forces that keep the universe going and then somehow explain how these can be reduced to one supreme force that is the cause of the coordination of all independent forces.

At present four natural forces are recognized as probably fundamental: gravity, electromagnetism, and the strong and weak nuclear forces. Furthermore it is theorized that at the Big Bang there was only one such force that caused the continuing expansion of the universe, but which very early in the process divided into the four fundamental forces that now operate. Eventually, however, the small places of increasing complexity such as we observe our earth to be will be washed away in the general process of entropic increase. Finally the universe will end in a state of "entropic doom" in which matter will be so thinly spread and homogenized that nothing will happen regularly by law, but only by chance "quantum fluctuations." It is possible of course that somehow this state of things will then reverse and become a Big Crunch in cycles that go on forever. Yet if it does (and there are good arguments against this possibility) all traces of the universe as it was in the present cycle will be destroyed in the Crunch. Thus there will be no real connections between the universe at one cycle and at another and we can never know anything but our own cycle.

All this is speculation, but it makes clear that according to our present data it is less probable that the universe has always existed and more probable that it had a beginning. Yet Stephen Hawking has invented a mathematical model for a universe that has only lasted a finite time yet had no singular point of time at which it began since in the universe's early development what we now call time had not yet emerged. Aquinas, however, wrote in an age when Christian faith held for a beginning of time but science favored an eternal universe. Hence he was careful to formulate his proof of the existence of God so that it would be valid on either hypothesis, no matter whether the world has always existed or only for a finite time. This is because the effect from which it argues is not simply the history of motion but the fact of motion here and now which cannot be adequately explained by some cause that initiated motion but only by a cause that also keeps motion going.

It is necessary, therefore, to inquire more closely as to what is meant by saying that there are "fundamental forces" that are natural properties of bodies. Ancient astronomy, as I have said, thought that the outermost sphere of the universe had a nature that enabled it to be in perpetual motion. Aristotle recognized that this would be possible only if the spheres moved without friction, since friction would entail an increase of entropy, and thus the universe would run down, while he accepted the astronomers' idea that the universe had always existed.[44] This meant of course that the spheres though material must be of a very different kind of matter than we observe here on earth. Yet even in this very radical hypothesis of a heaven made of matter that was unchangeable except as regards its rotational motion, Aristotle concluded that the natural motion of the outersphere could not violate the principle of "Nothing moves itself." His reasoning was that no finite body can give itself an infinite motion as would be the case if, as Aristotle supposed, the universe is eternal. The truth of this reasoning is evident, since an infinite force in a system would destroy it. The alternative hypothesis, of course, is that the outer sphere was set in motion at a definite time, and in that case it would be obvious that "Nothing can move itself," since an external mover would be necessary to start the sphere moving.

Would the same kind of argument hold for our present picture of the universe in which all motion is reduced to four natural fundamental forces, or in any universe having one or more such forces? The answer is yes, since if the universe has always existed then none of these finite forces or all taken together could keep it going forever. Or, if it had a beginning, for these natural forces to exist and to be actually operating would require a Mover external to the system of the universe. Moreover, as I have already shown, the issue is not just what began the motion, but what ultimately keeps it going here and now.

Some still accept Aristotle's hypothesis that the universe is infinite in time and go further than he did to suppose it is also infinite in size. Hence, they ask why can we not say that the series of movers in the universe is also infinite, so that one need never have to come to some ultimate mover other than the universe itself. Aquinas, however, points out that no matter how many movers there might be in a series of actually moving things, there has to be a first. If there were not, none of the movers in the series would be *actually* moving, but all would be merely potentially moving, able to move, but not actually in motion. Thus Aquinas' proof, which I repeat is only an exact formulation of something that can be understood by common sense, is valid.

I was once asked the question, "If there must be a God because everything has a cause, then what caused God?" Spinoza answered this by saying that God is his own cause (*causa sui*), but as we have seen nothing can cause itself, since nothing can give itself what it does not have. Aquinas, on the contrary, does not say that everything has a cause, but only that whatever is changed is changed by another, but since God is unchanging, the Unmoved Mover, he has no cause. As he said to Moses "I am," not "I come to be."

Yet Newton's Laws of Motion raise a serious problem for Aquinas' proof.[45] The First Law states that "Every body remains in a state of rest or uniform motion in a straight line, unless it is compelled by impressed forces to change this state." Thus it seems that once a body is in motion its motion does not depend on any cause. This seems to contradict the assertion that "Nothing moves itself" since the projectile continues to move long after it has been separated from its mover. It should, however, be noted that Newton himself thought that the very existence of natural laws proved the existence of God.[46] It is clear that his first Law affirms that for a body to begin to move an efficient cause is required. The billiard ball does not move until struck. This is enough to save the principle as it has been stated, but it does leave a question that much bothered Aristotle and the medievals. How can motion as an effect continue after the projectile is set in motion since the distance between it and the mover increases and the mover ceases actually to move? In Newton's term this is answered by saying that no new "force" is required because when the mover set the body in motion it gave it a certain "momentum" or energy equal to its inertial mass x its velocity. This energy is real since Newton's Second Law states that the velocity of motion can be changed by the application of additional force. The Third Law also states that if a moving body strikes another body, there will be an equal action and reaction, i.e., the momentum will be shared.

This is all very straightforward if our concern is to measure the momentum of the body in motion and the proportionate force needed to put it in motion with a certain velocity, but it leaves vague what is meant not just mathematically but physically by the terms "force" and "momentum." It appears that "force" means the action of the mover and by "momentum" is meant not just the motion itself but something added to the body that, so to speak, enables it to keep itself moving. Yet it does not have this momentum of its own nature since it did not have it when at rest but was given it by the mover. The medievals, therefore, who were not like Newton content with measurement but wanted to understand physical causality, said that what had been added to the moving body was not just the motion but an *impetus* alien to the nature of the body itself and capable of keeping it in motion. With Newton they agreed that this impetus would continue to act until partially or wholly destroyed by meeting another resistant body. This impetus added to the moving body was not a substance, but was an active quality like the capacity to exert force that we ascribed to mass, or electric charge. Hence Newton's First Law must be understood not as asserting that a body will continue indefinitely in motion without a mover, but as saying that it continues to be moved not by the original mover but by the impetus or active quality given it by the original mover. In the case of a body moving by reason of some active quality natural to it such as gravity or electric charge, however, the principle "Nothing moves itself" seems to be false. The massive body, when not impeded, will naturally move closer to other massive bodies. The electrically charged body will move toward another body having the opposite charge and be repelled from a body having the same charge. This seems to violate the principle.

Yet it must also be considered that the possession of an active quality capable of causing motion, whether this be imposed on a projectile or, like gravity or electric charge natural to certain bodies, is of itself only a capacity to act. It is not the actual exercise of this capacity. Hence it requires to be activated as, for example, the color of a body is not actually visible until illuminated and remains visible only as long as it is illuminated. It follows that the argument of Aquinas shows that for a complete explanation of actual motion we cannot stop with an imposed impetus nor with the natural forces of bodies. We must still ask how these efficient causes can be *actually* causing the continuation of a motion unless they themselves are caused. They are not unmoved movers, but moved movers. Thus we come to Aquinas' conclusion that every independent series of moved movers and the whole universe as a coordinated system of such series of moved movers cannot actually be producing a motion by moving itself. Hence an Unmoved Mover must be the ultimate cause of this motion and this Unmoved Mover is not part of any of the series nor of the universe as a whole. Since this Mover does not act by being moved by any material body it cannot itself be a material body, since every material body is moved by another mover.

Some have objected that Aquinas' proof, derived as it is from Aristotle, only proves the existence of a Unmoved Mover as the cause of the motion of the universe but not its existence. Hence it does not fulfill the demand of theism for a Creator. It is true that Aristotle, like the proponents of the ancient Mythological and Emanation Religions in general, never seems to come to a clear understanding of the Creator. Aquinas, however, shows that this argument in fact achieves this. The universe accessible to sense observation is constituted from changeable bodies that come into being by change and continue in being in the process of change. Hence the Unmoved Mover in giving them motion causes them to exist, i.e., is their Creator. To suppose that their matter is uncreated and has always existed of itself and that the Unmoved

Mover has merely caused it to move is absurd. Matter is the potentiality of a body to be moved but cannot exist without some actuality (the correlative material and formal cause). The cause of its actuality, therefore, is the cause of its existence, and the actuality of changeable things is produced and maintained as some kind of process of which motion, as we have seen, is the essential condition. Thus the historic arguments by which the foregoing demonstration as formulated by Aquinas has been attacked have not prevailed. Unless, of course, one is ready to accept Newton's reduction of physical reality to mathematical models or Kant's idealism with its denial that science can go beyond mental constructs to the reality of nature.

The other four arguments for God's existence formulated by Aquinas presuppose the effect on which the first is based, namely that the world of our experience is in motion. They, however, are based on other aspects of change than the motion itself. Thus the second argument begins from the observed fact that every change requires an *efficient* cause. This is either the First Uncaused Cause or some caused cause. There cannot be an infinite series of such caused causes unless there is a First Uncaused Cause, since, if there were not, none of the agents in the series would be actually causing. Hence a First Agent must exist and such an Agent cannot be material, since all matter is potential to further actualization. The third argues that changing things are *contingent*, that is, they are not necessarily actual, but depend for their reality on something else, hence there must at last be a *Necessary Being*. Thus the first three ways argue from *efficient causality,* the first from the motion efficiently caused, the second from the efficient cause itself, and the third from the contingency of caused efficient causes that demands a necessary first cause.

The fourth way argues from *formal causality*, that is, from the fact that every change results in some new form or actuality of matter. When we observe that a given perfection of things (for example some degree of energy) exists in different degrees in things, we know that the less perfect must have this perfection not from themselves but from something more perfect. Thus only the most energetic thing can cause less perfect energy in others but not vice versa. Since again there cannot be an infinite series of more and more perfect causes of the lesser perfections of others, there must be a First Most Perfect Cause. The fifth argument is from *final causality* and rests on the fact that the changes that science studies are regular lawlike changes. This means that their efficient causes are predetermined, as we have seen, to produce a definite effect. Since we observe that regular, natural changes have regular natural effects (e.g. seeds grow into plants, chemicals bond with certain other chemicals and not with others), we observe an order of finality in the world. Such an order cannot be infinite but must depend on the existence of a Final Goal on which the unity of the universe depends.

It is this fifth or *teleological* argument that has recently become prominent again in science in the discussion of the so-called Anthropic Cosmological Principle.[47] This Principle states that all that we know today about the universe shows that its structure and natural processes are such that they have ultimately produced intelligent life, although the constant increase of entropy in the universe has made this highly improbable. Human intelligence, however, has as its own goal, to discover the answer to the ultimate question, namely the First Intelligent Cause, the Creator.

These five arguments demonstrate the existence of a First Uncaused Immaterial Prime Mover and Creator, but is this the personal God worshipped by Jews, Christians, and Muslims? Some have argued that it is not. A recent, influential form of this objection is Martin Heidegger's rejection of what he called "onto-theology." He believed that the whole Western tradition of philosophy had been given to a kind of rational, metaphysical *control* of reality that had produced modern technological society, instead of the intuitive openness to reality (Being) transcending human categories characteristic of pre-Socratic thought and Eastern mysticism. He believed that this effort at Western rational control was coming to an end in our times and that the future would see a turn eastward. Hence he denounced the "onto-theology" that would reduce the "Mystery" simply to the supreme degree of some Chain of Being as the classical argument to the Unmoved Mover seems to do. Instead "God" must be thought as an utterly different order of reality than the objects of scientific definition and control. What a theology that was not an onto-theology might be Heidegger never said except to refer to Eastern mysticism.

Heidegger's accusations have some credibility when applied to the post-Kantian intellectual milieu in which he wrote. As we have seen, Kant held that we think only by fitting the phenomenal world into our own mental categories and concluded that since God escapes these categories we cannot know God but can only posit our conception of God as a regulative idea needed for a consistent moral life. Heidegger, however, radically misread the Christian Tradition. Aquinas in introducing the *Summa Theologiae* I, q. 2 intro., says "First we will consider whether God exists, and second, what God is, *or rather what he is not*" thus indicating that God is indeed a Mystery, infinitely exceeding any conceptions we may have of him. Furthermore, Aquinas in I, q. 2, a. 6, ad 3 distinguishes between theology as a rational wisdom based on faith and that wisdom which is the Gift of the Holy Spirit as it gives the believer an intuitive connaturality with God. Thus Christian theology is open to mystery in a way that surpasses reason as it reduces reality to human terms in order to gain a certain control over it. Heidegger's misunderstanding can, at least in part, be explained by the faulty exposition of Aquinas' thought by many Neo-Scholastics. They failed to see that for Aquinas a rational theology has two distinct phases. First natural science proves the *existence* of God by the arguments just discussed. Second this makes possible a metaphysics in which the question of the *nature* of God is explored by a methodology very different from that of natural science but presupposing its demonstration of the existence of immaterial reality. Neo-scholasticism tended to confuse these two steps by treating both as the work of a metaphysics whose foundations remained tenuous. No wonder then that Heidegger thought this metaphysics and its theology was too much enmeshed in natural science understood in the modern over-technological manner.

Before we proceed to the second or metaphysical phase of Aquinas' argument, a second way in which natural science within its own proper scope demonstrates the existence of immaterial reality must be considered. A possible objection to all that has been so far said might be that to talk about an immaterial cause of material reality is empty talk because immaterial reality is too remote from our experience. For Aquinas, however, this is not the case since within the scope of natural science is the study of the human being in its behavior, and this behavior manifests that reality is not restricted to changeable, material reality. This demonstration is parallel, but not the same as the one already given for the Unmoved Mover of the universe and can be summarized as follows:

> Human beings are finite organisms whose prime material mover is the brain.
> But the specific principal operation of human beings is intelligent thought.
> Intelligent thought cannot be the operation of the brain which can only be its instrument.
> *Therefore, the proper unmoved mover of the human body exists as an immaterial formal cause of the body, an intelligence sharing in its finitude and creatureliness.*

Aquinas, following the science of his day, thought that the prime organ of the body is the heart, but today we know it is the brain. Moreover, we know that it is the complexity of this brain that specifically distinguishes human beings from other animals and makes possible their unique behavior. Aristotle and Aquinas had already shown this human specification by the power of true language and the ability to deal with abstract concepts that syntactical language manifests, along with the development of technology and culture beyond the limits of animal instincts. The question, therefore, becomes what today is much discussed by scientists as the unsolved mind-body problem and as the possibility of artificial intelligence.

I do not have space to discuss this issue at length. Aquinas notes that human thought requires that we not only are conscious but that we are self-conscious. This means that we not only know, for clearly animals have sense knowledge, but that we know that we know. This is required if we are to be critical of our own thought, as is exemplified by science. Yet we also require sense knowledge and hence sense organs to obtain the data without which the self-conscious, abstract work of intelligent thinking that processes this data is observed to be impossible. Thus Aquinas insists that in this life human intellectual thought without images in the primary sense organ is impossible, yet such images are instruments to abstract thinking, not the concepts of that thought.

We cannot think the abstract number 10 without an image of ten fingers, etc. or at least the word "ten" derived from such concrete images. Yet our consciousness that we are thinking the abstract 10 of arithmetic and keeping it clear of the irrelevancies found in any images of ten we may have cannot, argues Aquinas, be the operation of a material organ. This is because to be "material" is, as already indicated, to be a body having quantity or extension. This is true of every image other animals and we ourselves can form and hence such consciousness of sensible objects or their images is not specifically human. But the "self-consciousness" of humans, since it involves the abstraction required to arrive at universal essences such as the number 10, cannot be the operation of something that is extended. To be extended is to have at least two parts and those parts, though they can have a common boundary, must not be identical. Since self-consciousness, knowing that I am knowing and abstracting the essential from the irrelevant, requires the identity of the knower and the known, it cannot be the act of an extended, material organ with nonidentical parts.

This becomes clear when we see that the brain and a computer made to imitate it are extended and that for this reason operate only by a complex network of neurons or electrical circuits. These attempt to bring one part of the brain or the computer into communication with the other parts, yet can never bring all the communicated information to identity at a single point. It follows that while the brain can program images that model abstract concepts ever more precisely and a computer can be devised to come closer and closer to what the brain can do, neither can produce self-consciousness and abstract thought. Therefore Aquinas concludes that the human intelligence uses the organ that is the material prime mover of the body as necessary to thought but only instrumentally, while the ultimate unity of the body must be an existing immaterial intelligence. Since, however, this immaterial intelligence cannot naturally operate without the instrument of the body, this argument does not lead to an Unmoved Immaterial Mover with an existence distinct from that of the universe it moves, but to an Unmoved Immaterial Mover that shares the existence of the body without dualism. Aquinas, therefore, avoided the Cartesian dualism that many scientists today suppose is the only alternative to a materialistic identity of the mind with the body. Thus, if we accept Aquinas' arguments, natural science establishes the existence both of an infinite Unmoved Immaterial Mover of the universe far beyond our experience, but also finite, created, human intelligences requiring material embodiment, that are most intimate to our own self-conscious experience. The fact of the immateriality of our souls, therefore, provides us with a fitting analogy by which to understand the mysterious Unmoved Mover of the universe.

This raises a further question for natural science. If besides the uncreated God, there are created intelligences that are embodied, is it possible there are created intelligences that like God, are purely spiritual and without bodies? We have seen that not only the Mythological Religions but all the Traditional Religions claim that such spirits exist and even claim acquaintance with them. Thus Jesus clearly confirmed the existence of angels already recognized by the Hebrew Scriptures and so does Muhammad in the *Qur'an*. Only the world-view of Humanism tends to exclude such beings. Yet the romantic side of Humanism has been open to the question and many speculations on the subject are current today. The more science seems to enlarge the universe, the more people wonder, "Can we be alone in such vast spaces and ages?"

Aquinas, in light of the science of his day, did not think that all the motion in the universe is caused by the outer sphere. Each planet and the sun and moon were in independently moving spheres which were prime movers. The motion of the outer sphere insured the coordination of these relatively independent movers but did not simply subordinate them in a merely instrumental way. He regarded this as a natural science proof of the existence of angels which did not absolutely eliminate the possibility that the Unmoved Mover directly produced the effects attributed to the angels, but made it physically certain, considering the fact that the Creator acts through secondary causes, that they exist. This argument, like that for God, does not rest on the details of ancient astronomy but still applies to the universe as revealed by modern science. As we have seen, present theories do not reduce all the four fundamental forces to one force after the very earliest phase of the Big Bang. More important, as I have argued elsewhere, is the significance for modern science of modern theories of cosmological and biological theories of evolution. As we have seen, evolution to more complex objects runs counter to the entropic decay of the order of the universe and can only be local and temporary, yet it has to occur dramatically and the Anthropic Cosmological Principle suggests that the design of the universe as a whole favors it. Moreover, it is increasingly recognized that the Darwinian theory of natural selection is inadequate as an explanation for the long historical scenario required to produce the extreme complexity of the human brain. Is it really credible that an effect of such complexity could result from a history in which every step was less and less probable? Complex chemicals can be produced from simple materials in a laboratory by ordinary natural processes although they never occur in nature unless a chemist guides the necessary sequence of steps that do not naturally occur except perhaps in organisms. No natural law determines the course of this production though it is brought about by purely natural forces that normally produce nothing much. It is the guiding intelligence of the chemists using these forces that produces the evolution from simple substances to complex. By this analogy, therefore, we can make sense of evolution without introducing any sort of vitalism or *élan vital* or panpsychism into biology, provided we admit that in our universe, just as scientists have embodied immaterial intelligences, so the universe as a whole includes unembodied intelligences. Their presence does not replace natural physical processes but uses them to produce the direction of evolution to the production of the scientists as intelligent bodies.

Note again that for Aquinas it is natural science as he understood it, namely, as a study of changeable being in its dynamism not just mathematical models of changeable being that proves the existence of an Unmoved Immaterial Mover and the immateriality of human intelligence and pure created intelligences. This is not metaphysics since it presupposes this task as accomplished.[48] But at this point natural science reaches its limits since its conception of such realities remains negative (i.e., they are not material). Yet natural science does also establish the positive truth that these immaterial beings are the causes (efficient, formal in the sense of exemplary, and final) of the objects that natural science can explore by its own methodology.

Therefore Aquinas holds that natural science can prove the existence of an Unmoved Mover, that is, of the kind of being meant by the ordinary usage of the word "God." He makes no claim that this gives any more than a very imperfect (although true) understanding of what "God" is. Thus in knowing the existence of someone we still do not know whether he is friend or foe, or, if a friend, what it is that we have in common that makes us friends. Of course, in a common sense, prescientific form these arguments for God's existence are accessible to all of us human beings who ask ourselves, "Why does anything at all exist?" No wonder then that the world religions all tend to monotheism and even most Humanists would not accept polytheism.

To move further to try to form some idea of what this spiritual Reality is like, it is necessary to develop another discipline than physics, namely metaphysics. Metaphysics is said to be the science of "being as such," but if no beings exist that are not changeable, material beings naturally subject to motion, then the science of "being as such" is natural science. Aristotle, and Aquinas following him, concluded that until natural science has proved that "being as such" also includes immaterial beings, no metaphysics would be either possible or necessary. Yet after natural science has established the existence of immaterial beings, metaphysics has a proper subject, namely, Being as it includes both material and immaterial beings and what is *analogically* common to them all. Even then, as Aquinas points out (*pace* Heidegger), this does not make metaphysics an onto-theology. God is not part of the subject matter of metaphysics but its *principle* and hence enters metaphysics as that which explains "being as such" not as that which is explained by "being as such" since it transcends the whole of created being. Of course some philosophers, including Leibnitz from whom Kant derived his notion of metaphysics, have thought that metaphysics is about *possible* beings and hence can begin its study with no more than the *possibility* that Being includes more than material beings. But without a proof that immaterial beings in fact do actually exist, we cannot be sure they are even possible. To talk about "nonmaterial beings" does not prove that we know enough about the concept to be able to assert that it designates a real possibility.

Thus to take the further step of seeking to get some idea however inadequate of the nature of this First Cause, it is necessary to proceed by *analogy* from effects to cause. A cause must in some way however remotely resemble its effect, since a cause cannot give to its effects what it does not itself possess. We get some true notion of a cause from its effect while realizing that the effect may not manifest the whole reality of its cause, any more than we can judge the total genius of Michelangelo from only one of his perhaps minor works.

Such a metaphysical (transcending physical or natural science) analysis of the meaning of the existence of a nonmaterial First Cause leads logically to a deeper understanding not only that God is but also *what* and *who* God is. It follows from the five arguments just given that God exists as a spiritual (immaterial) being. This Supreme Being must necessarily exist, must be perfect in every way, and is the goal to which the whole universe strives as its final cause, or ultimate destiny. God must also be the necessary being, always actual, and free of any potentiality for change. That the First Cause is "unmoved" does not mean, as process philosophers have claimed, that God is static, inert. As Cause of all motion, activity, and change God possesses whatever is positive in motion, activity, and change. He is Pure Act. Since we humans are effects of this First Cause and are persons having a nonmaterial intelligence and free will, we can meaningfully, though only analogically, conclude that the First Cause is in some very real sense a Person that thinks and wills freely. Aristotle concluded that God is "Thought Thinking Itself" from which Aquinas draws the conclusion that God is also Love Itself, since it is thought that makes us free and able to love what we know.

Humanists have always been inclined to deism on the grounds that even if a Creator is required to explain the existence of the universe, the universe as discovered by science is a machine that once constructed runs itself like a clock. For deists revelation, miracles and prophecies are also impossible for God to do, not because he lacks power, but because they think that such "interventions" in the natural order would imply that the natural order of Creation is imperfect. They are right, of course, in supposing that the universe is made to operate on its own laws as a well-designed machine. Nevertheless, as we have seen, even the best designed material machine needs an intelligence to keep it operating, especially if it is designed not just like a clock to do repetitive things, but to evolve to more and more complex activities. Consequently, the Prime Mover's work is not done at creation. He is not just a "watchmaker" but a constant regulator and guide. Surely in our computer age we should realize that mechanisms however well designed require an intelligence to operate without error for very long, and the more complex the mechanism (and today we more and more see how complex the universe is) the more regulation it requires to keep going. Moreover, there is no reason to think of the universe as having an order that is complete. It can be argued that since the human soul is immaterial yet substantially one with the body, the conception of each unique human being requires a direct act of creation by God.

Yet Kant concluded that to petition God in prayer insults him, since he has already willed to provide us with whatever is best for us. Kant, therefore, accepted only the prayer of praise of God, not of petition. Aquinas, on the other hand, argued that just as God works through secondary causes and especially through created persons so that they might share in his work, so God wills that by prayer we can be true secondary causes of what God has willed to do in the world. God is not literally "moved" by our prayers, but he uses our prayers to carry out his gifts to the world. If God is truly personal, certainly he wishes his creatures to know him, to communicate with him, and ask his help.

There is, nevertheless, another line of argument against the possibility of proving God's existence that has had even more universal effect than Kant's epistemological idealism.[49] It is the contention that since, if there is a God, he must be wise, good, and omnipotent, he therefore would have made a good world, while in fact the world is full of terrible evils, physical and moral, to the point of absurdity and blank indifference to human happiness. Therefore there can be no God. I will discuss this fundamental difficulty in the last chapter of this book. Here it suffices to point out the following facts that require serious attention. First, all the world religions and Humanism as well originated in an attempt to solve the problem of evil. Yet it is uncritical for any of these world-views to declare dogmatically that its explanation of evil is the only correct one. It is just on this point that ecumenical dialogue is necessary. Second, the classical theistic proofs of the existence of God do not logically depend on the premise that the world of our experience is perfectly good, nor even that it is more good than evil, but only on the fact of the existence of some good, however minimal. The term "evil" implies the existence of something good in which it exists only as a lack of a perfection normally due to that good thing. No one can have an evil disease who does not first have the good of life. It is the existence of this basic goodness, without which there would be no world at all, that any theistic proof claims to demonstrate.

6. An Alternative Way to the Creator

Modern philosophy, generally Humanist in origin, has nevertheless sometimes sought a rational defense of the existence of a Creator. Yet in doing so, it has to face the problems raised by Descartes and Kant concerning the basis of certitude in knowledge. In Chapter 1 we described how the Enlightenment and Humanism arose out of the disillusionment of the intellectual elite of Europe with the religious wars among Christians that cast doubt on the truth of the Christian revelation. At the same time the rise of modern science seemed to show that the power of human reason is sufficient to solve all human problems. Yet the skeptical climate produced by religious controversies also seemed to cast doubt on the certitude of human reason itself since reason had been so intensely applied without success in solving these controversies. Many intellectuals either turned to revelation in blind faith (*fideism*) or like David Hume, succumbed to skepticism.

Then a way out seemed to be provided by a contemporary of the great pioneer of modern science, Galileo (d. 1642). René Descartes (d. 1650), a sincere Catholic, was influenced by St. Augustine and through him by the ancient Platonic philosophy that grounded human knowledge in ideas innate to the human intelligence, transcending mere sense knowledge. As a mathematician of genius Descartes also loved the clear and distinct ideas that produce the kind of certitude possible in mathematics. Hence he argued: *Cogito ergo sum*; I can at least be certain that I think, since even if to doubt I must also think. Hence from this certitude that I am a thinking *subject* free to question every thought,

I can argue to the certitude of other truths. Furthermore, since I did not create myself with the power to think there must be a Creator who gave me this power. Since there is a Creator who gave me the power to think about an external world, he certainly would not permit me to be deceived about its real existence and governance by the natural laws science discovers.

This Cartesian (from Descartes' name) "turn to the subject" is the basis of most "modern" philosophy, including that of Immanuel Kant whose attempted refutation of the classical proofs of God's existence was discussed in Chapter 2.[50] Through Kant and other thinkers it has greatly influenced Christian theology in both Protestant and Roman Catholic forms. In recent Catholic theology it has had special influence through a revision of the thought of St. Thomas Aquinas called "Transcendental Thomism" precisely, because it replaces St. Thomas' Aristotelian starting point with that of Descartes' Platonism.

For Aquinas like Aristotle all human, rational knowledge begins with our experience of the material world of the senses. Only by the long argument sketched above is it possible to arrive at a critical knowledge of immaterial realities such as the existence of God and the spirituality of our own minds. For Descartes, influenced by Platonic belief in innate ideas, and for Kant who for innate ideas substituted innate categories by which we must order sense data, certitude could not be based on sense knowledge but only on our mental operations.

Early in this century Joseph Marechal, S.J., in his *The Point of Departure of Metaphysics,*[51] while still defending the validity of St. Thomas Aquinas' approach, attempted to dialogue with modern philosophy by approaching the same question of our rational certitude of God's existence from a Cartesian-Kantian point of view. Marechal's Transcendental Thomism has influenced Bernard Lonergan, S.J.[52] and especially Karl Rahner, S.J., leading Catholic thinkers of the Vatican II period, to develop a *fundamental theology* that replaces the older Thomistic *apologetics* which used prophecies and miracles as arguments for the credibility of alleged divine revelation.

Rahner in his work *Spirit in the World*[53] was careful to retain from Thomism the anti-Cartesian view that all purely human knowledge depends on sense-knowledge and also to reject Kant's arguments that a metaphysics of spiritual reality is impossible. Yet he adopted Descartes' and Kant's "turn to the subject." Thus Rahner held that proofs for the existence of God need not, as Aquinas thought, rest on the data of the senses used by natural science. Instead they can be based simply on our self-awareness as knowing subjects who have an innate drive to ask questions and make free choices. Thomists, of course, did not deny that in every act of thought and free choice we know that we are thinking and willing. But they contended that human thought originates not in our thinking about our own thinking but in our knowledge of the material world and of ourselves as material bodies. It is only by a long process of analysis and reasoning, like that sketched in the preceding section of this chapter, that for Aquinas we can come to distinguish spiritual being such as our intelligence and free will from material things such as our brain and its functions. Rahner and the Transcendental Thomists also recognize that our self-knowledge is somehow dependent on our bodily situation in the world and hence is indirect and "unthematic." Yet they hold that our self-consciousness is sufficiently certain to furnish a sound basis for reasoning to the existence of God, prior to any detailed analysis of the material world itself. For those philosophers, therefore, who have made "the turn to the subject" the existence of God is (in one way or another) the background or "horizon" of all certain knowledge about the world and its history.[54]

These Transcendental Thomists argue that since we are certain not only that we are thinking subjects, but subjects that have a dynamic drive to ask questions, we can demonstrate that there must be an answer to our ultimate question, "Is there a God?" If He did not exist, how could we even ask that question? Thomists do not accept Marechal's claim that we know from our originally vague self-awareness that we are subjects innately driven to question until we stand convinced that God is the Absolute Answer. Thomists deny this because a question is meaningless unless it is raised by a problem in our explicit experience. The question, "Whether the First Cause of the World is nonmaterial?", has no meaning until our study of the material world gives us some reason to ask it.

Such a puzzling fact of sensible experience that raises the question of God is that the world of our senses is in the process of change.

Aquinas showed in his *Quinque Viae,* explained above, that this puzzling fact of sensible experience is that the world about us is constantly in a process of change. It is this fact that makes us ask the question about a First Cause of change. This question can only be answered by an *a posteriori* proof from these observed effects to their cause, not by some transcendental *a priori* deduction from our awareness that we are transcendental questioning subjects.

No doubt this is why those Humanist scientists who believe that science has established that the material world has no cause do not any longer ask if there is a God. Also if they believe that a brain or a computer can think, they no longer ask a question about whether we have spiritual souls. The apologetic task is to show that scientists cannot avoid these questions. This is true, however, not primarily because scientists are conscious that they are thinking subjects, but because the material world they are trying to study would be ultimately inexplicable if they do not face this question. Evidence for the systematic avoidance by many scientists today is amply demonstrated in Alan Lightman and Roberta Brawer, *Origins: The Lives and Worlds of Modern Cosmologists*,[55] interviews held with some 27 leading cosmologists. Thus Stephen Weinberg, Nobel Laureate in Physics in 1979 was questioned why he had said in his book *The First Three Minutes* that "the more the universe becomes comprehensible, the more it seems pointless." He at first answered this by saying, "One thing that does seem to help, one of the things that makes life worthwhile, is doing scientific research." When he realized that it was hard to explain why doing scientific research was worthwhile if it led only to comprehension of something that was "pointless," he then added rather confusedly:[56] "For you to say things are pointless, you have to ask, 'Well what point were you looking for?' And that's what needs, I think, to be explained. What kind of point would have been there that might have made it not pointless. That's what I really would have to explain."

Rahner, however, pursuing this "turn to the subject," attempted in his great work in fundamental theology, *Foundations of Christian Faith: An Introduction to the Idea of Christianity*[57] to begin his effort to make this faith credible with the thinking, freely willing subject. With only that data he tried by a "transcendental deduction" to demonstrate what the ideal religion would be that could satisfy the subject's innate drive to question and choose. Hence in the original German the main title of his book was *The Idea of Christianity*, retained only as a subtitle in the English translation. Having thus deductively established the idea of a true religion without reference to scientific or historical data, Rahner then proceeds to "correlate" this with the actual historical data of Roman Catholicism and thus demonstrate its rational credibility as the only religion that could meet this ideal.

This procedure was connected with Rahner's famous notion of "the anonymous Christian" and the "supernatural existential." According to this theory every human subject in actual historical reality has its existence not only in the natural order but also in the order of grace that flows from God's will that all humans be saved. Therefore all humans, whether they have realized it or not, exist in relation to God not only as creatures but through grace. Thus they can be said to be "anonymously Christian." Hence in their experience as thinking, willing subjects there is at work some experience of God as a gracious God who is revealing himself even though in a hidden and unrecognized way. Thus the classical Apologetics addressed to nonbelievers can be replaced by a Fundamental Theology addressed to all human beings by which they can explore their human experience to uncover the work of grace in their inner lives and thus come closer to the Mystery. The influence of this line of argumentation is evident in Vatican II's *The Church in the Modern World* (*Gaudium et Spes*) when it calls the modern world to raise ultimate questions about human destiny.

This is not the place for a detailed critique of Rahner's Fundamental Theology though it is clearly well worth study. I too argued in Chapter 1 that all human beings have to seek a world-view and value-system to answer the fundamental life problems that arise in their experience. Nevertheless, it must be asked whether the Transcendental Thomist approach to the God-question can really stand on its own. Certainly such a subjective approach is attractive to many moderns who seek a personal spirituality. They have been taught that the only objective knowledge comes from modern science and that modern science has no way to affirm a spiritual realm or establish moral values. Thus Rahner, who in his later years admitted he had never given much attention to modern science,[58] found this transcendental approach more helpful, since the very term "transcendental" means a grounding of knowledge in the subject transcending the data of the material world and hence the relevance of science.

The weakness of such an approach to the modern scientific world, however, is also evident and has been pointed out by many critics.[59] A theistic revelation is not credible to those who do not know or at least do not recognize that the existence of God can be demonstrated scientifically from the existence of the world. The attempt of Marechal and Rahner to demonstrate this from the fact that human questioning cannot find an answer unless there is a final and Absolute Truth, to many moderns is far from convincing. It is true that we as thinking beings are questioning beings, but our questions must be aroused by experiences that give us meaningful questions. The modern skeptic can well ask the Transcendental Thomists how they know that there are any meaningful questions that cannot be answered by science in purely materialistic terms. For Aquinas this difficulty is answered, as we have seen, by showing that scientific questioning is always incomplete unless it comes to a First Cause whose existence is proved from its effects known to science. Therefore, Transcendental Thomism presupposes non-transcendental Thomism or some other philosophy that begins with the existence of the material world not the "spirit in the world."

This is not to deny that Rahner's Fundamental Theology provides a subjective support to a more objective apologetics since it can help moderns whose idea of scientific objectivity is too restrictive to acknowledge the reality of the spiritual realm. While it can show that theism and Christianity are fitting correlatives to our historical experience and thus stimulate Humanists and those of other philosophies of life to further investigate theistic and Christian claims, it cannot furnish a satisfactory verification of those claims to the hardheaded Humanist.

Rahner's thought has been helpful in strengthening their faith for those who already believe in a God like that of Christianity, but it cannot do the job of an objective apologetics addressed to atheists, agnostics, deists or pantheists. Yet it may have attraction for those in the Emanation Religions who follow not a rational, discursive approach to the choice of a world-view, but an intuitive one based on self-consciousness heightened by meditation, though as Jacques Maritain showed such a purely natural mysticism has its risks.

Therefore a case for the theistic Creation Religions demands, as a prerequisite to the rational credibility of God's self-revelation, faith that God can first be *objectively* known to human reason as the First Non-Material Cause of the material world. This claim, verifiable by all humanity at least in a common-sense way, has also been defended by profound arguments drawn from natural science and supported by metaphysics. Hence in choosing a world-view and value-system these arguments must be seriously examined and compared to those favoring Humanism or the Mythological and Emanationist Religions.

Notes

[1] The *Encyclopedia Judaica,* 16 vols. (Jerusalem: Keter Publishing House, 1972) is the best reference work. See also Leo Baeck, *The Essence of Judaism* (New York: Schocken, 1961); George Fohrer, *History of Israelite Religion* (Nashville, TN: Abingdon Press, 1972); Robert M. Seltzer, *Jewish People, Jewish Thought* (New York: Macmillan, 1980); Ellis Rifkin, *A Hidden Revolution: The Pharisees' Search for the Kingdom Within* (Nashville, TN: Abingdon Press, 1978).

[2] See Yehezkel Kaufmann, *The Religion of Israel: From Its Beginnings to the Babylonian Exile* (Chicago: University of Chicago Press, 1966); Walther Eichrodt, *Theology of the Old Testament,* 2 vols. (Philadelphia: Westminster Press, 1961, 1967); Gerhard Von Rad, *Old Testament Theology,* 2 vols. (New York: Harper and Row, 1965).

[3] That Hinduism speaks of the world as God's "play" might seem to express agreement with the Creation Religion teaching that the world is a *free* creation of God, but it also suggests that the world is produced for God's sake, for his amusement. On the contrary the Creation Religions hold that God creates freely for the sake of the world, not for any gain on God's part. It is true that the Bible sometime speaks of God's Wisdom "playing before him on the earth" (Pr 8:30) but this is a way of describing the beauty and wonder of the creation, not God's purpose in creating it. The Bible does speak of God acting for the sake of his own "glory," but this "glory of God" is not some gain for God but is God's self-revelation to humanity for its sake. Thus we pray, "Hallowed be thy Name" not to make that Name holy, but that all humanity will come to know God's holiness.

[4] For the development of the concept see Eichrodt and Von Rad in the previous note and Leo Scheffczyk, *Creation and Providence* (New York: Herder and Herder, 1970), pp. 321ff. For a highly speculative effort to trace this development that has the advantage of making use of recent extra-biblical data see Johannes C. De Moor, *The Rise of Monotheism: The Roots of Israelite Monotheism,* revised and enlarged edition (Leuven: University of Leuven Press, 1997), pp. 53-60.

[5] See G.H. Parke-Raylor, *Yahweh: The Divine Name in the Bible* (Waterloo, Ontario, Canada: Wilfrid Laurier University Press, 1975). According to John L. McKenzie in the *New Jerome Biblical Commentary,* ed. by R.E. Brown, J. Fitzmyer, and R.E. Murphy

(Englewood Cliffs, NJ: Prentice-Hall, 1968), p. 1286, the name probably means either "the Creator who causes things to be" or "the One Who Is" but there no evidence that the biblical writers knew its etymology.

[6] On the problems historical criticism of the Talmud involves see Jacob Neusner, *Studying Classical Judaism: A Primer* (Louisville, KY: Westminster/John Knox, 1991).

[7] The Protestant Old Testament is identical with the Jewish canon of Scriptures and thus excludes the 7 deuterocanonical books and portions of Daniel and Esther included in the Eastern Orthodox and Catholic canons. On the history of the difference see James C. Turro and Raymond E. Brown, "Canonicity" in *The Jerome Biblical Commentary,* pp. 515-34.

[8] See Daniel J. Silver and Bernard Martin, *A History of Judaism,* 2 vols. (New York: Basic Books, 1974) and Jacob Katz, *Tradition and Crisis* (New York: Free Press, 1961).

[9] See Hans Joachim Schoeps, *The Jewish Christian Argument* (New York: Holt, Rinehart and Winston, 1963); Edward H. Flannery, *The Anguish of the Jews: Twenty-Three Centuries of Anti-Semitism* (New York: Macmillan, 1965); Samuel Sandmel, *Two Living Traditions* (Detroit: Wayne State University Press, 1972). Also John T. Pawlikowski, *The Challenge of the Holocaust for Christian Theology* (New York: Center for Studies on the Holocaust, Anti-Defamation League of B'nai Brith, 1978); Arthur A. Cohen, *The Tremendum: A Theological Interpretation of the Holocaust* (New York: Crossroad, 1981); Henry James Cargas, *When God and Man Failed: Non-Jewish Views of the Holocaust* (New York: Macmillan, 1981).

[10] See Gershom Scholem, *Major Trends in Jewish Mysticism,* 3rd ed. (New York: Schocken Books, 1954); Elie Wiesel, *Souls on Fire: Portraits and Legends of Hasidic Leaders* (New York: Random House: Vintage Books, 1973).

[11] See Nathan Glazer, *American Judaism* (Chicago: University of Chicago Press, 1957).

[12] See Marcel Simon, *Jewish Sects at the Time of Jesus* (Philadelphia: Fortress Press, 1967). Also Geza Vermes, ed., *The Dead Sea Scrolls in English* (Harmondsworth: Penguin, 1962); F.M. Cross, Jr., *The Ancient Library of Qumran and Modern Biblical Studies,* 2nd rev. ed. (Garden City, NY: Doubleday, 1961); and Helmer Ringgren, *The Faith of Qumran* (Philadelphia: Fortress, 1963).

[13] On the debated question of what the Pharisees actually taught see E.P. Sanders, *Jewish Law From Jesus to the Mishnah: Five Studies* (Philadelphia: Trinity Press International, 1990) in which he attacks the contrary views of Jacob Neusner.

[14] For historical problems, cf. John Meier, *A Marginal Jew: Rethinking the Historical Jesus* 2 vols. (Garden City, NY: Doubleday, 1991, 1994). For more theological interpretations see W.D. Davies, *Sermon on the Mount* (New York, Cambridge University Press, 1966); David Flusser, *Jesus* (New York: Herder and Herder, 1969); Louis Bouyer, *The Eternal Son* (Huntington, IN: OSV Press, 1975). Also see Walter Kaspar, *Jesus the Christ* (New York: Paulist Press, 1976); Jean Galot, *Who is Christ?* (Chicago: Franciscan Herald Press, 1981); and Wolfhart Pannenberg, *Jesus: God and Man,* 2nd ed. (Philadelphia: Westminster Press, 1981).

[15] S.G.F. Brandon, *Jesus and the Zealots* (Manchester: Manchester University Press, 1967) argued Jesus was a Zealot, but was answered by Oscar Cullmann, *Jesus and the Revolutionaries* (New York: Harper and Row, 1970) and Martin Hengel, *Was Jesus a Revolutionist?* (Philadelphia: Fortress Press, 1971).

[16] On what Jesus meant by the "Kingdom of God," see Benedict T. Viviano, OP, *The Kingdom of God in History,* Good News Studies (Wilmington, DE: Michael Glazier, 1988), pp. 13-29.

[17] This text, since it is common to Matthew and Luke and not in Mark, is assigned by the common opinion of scholars to Q and hence is considered a very early tradition. For the minority who hold for the priority of Matthew the same, of course, is true.

[18] Hebrews, though probably not by Paul, is Pauline and by some scholars dates before the

fall of the Temple in 70 CE. It seems (Heb 9:6-10) to presuppose the Temple sacrifices are still standing, cf. Paul Ellingworth, *The Epistle to the Hebrews: A Commentary on the Greek Text* (Grand Rapids, MI: W.B. Eerdmans, 1993). He quotes many authors who favor this date and concludes "All these considerations, separately and even together, fall short of proof; yet the balance of probabilities has led many writers to prefer a date before the fall of Jerusalem. The apparent threat of renewed, possibly more severe persecution may suggest a date not long before AD 70; if Hebrews was written in (or to) Rome, a date not long before 64 is possible. It is difficult to be more precise. It is in any case an open question how far the war which led to the destruction of the temple could have been foreseen, especially by anyone living outside Palestine," p. 33. Recently Marie E. Isaacs, *Sacred Space: An Approach to the Theology of the Epistle to the Hebrews,* JSNT. Supplement Series 73 (Sheffield, England: University of Sheffield Press, 1992), p. 67 concludes that it was either written just before or very soon after the Temple's destruction.

[19] See Raymond Brown, *The Death of the Messiah,* 2 vols. (Garden City, NY: Doubleday, 1994).

[20] On the Resurrection see Pierre Benoit, OP, *The Passion and Resurrection of Jesus Christ* (New York: Herder and Herder, 1969); Edward L. Bode, *The First Easter Morning: The Gospel Accounts of the Women's Visit to the Tomb of Jesus* (Rome: Pontifical Biblical Institute, 1970). Also Reginald H. Fuller, *The Formation of the Resurrection Narratives* (New York: Macmillan, 1971); Xavier Leon-Dufour, *Resurrection and the Message of Easter* (New York: Holt, Rinehart and Winston, 1974); George Eldon Ladd, *I Believe in the Resurrection of Jesus* (Grand Rapids: Eerdmans, 1975). Also Edward Schillebeeckx, *Jesus: An Experiment in Christology* (New York: Seabury, 1979), pp. 399-438; James D.G. Dunn, *Christology in the Making* (Philadelphia: Westminster, 1980) with good bibliography (pp. 354-403). The apologetic work of Gerald O'Collins, SJ, *Jesus Risen* (New York: Paulist Press, 1987) is to be especially recommended.

[21] This tradition is witnessed as early as 52-59 CE in 1 Corinthians 11:20-22 as an already accepted custom going back to Jesus and the Twelve.

[22] On the various theories of New Testament eschatology see the summary of David M. Stanley, SJ and Raymond Brown in *The Jerome Biblical Commentary* (note 5 above), pp. 777-82, and George Eldon Ladd, *The Eschatology of Biblical Realism* (Grand Rapids, Eerdmans, 1974), pp. 142ff.

[23] For this initiative of Peter, too often attributed to Paul alone, see the discussion in Roland Minnerath, *De Jerusalem a Rome: Pierre et l'Unite de l'Église Apostolique,* Theologie Historique #101 (Paris: Beauchesne, 1995), pp. 72-101.

[24] For a recent study on how the Church was organized see Hermann Hauser, *L'Église a l'Age Apostolique: Structure et evolution des ministeres,* Preface by Pierre Grelot, Lectio Divina 164 (Paris: Cerf, 1996).

[25] For the transition from Judaism to Christianity see Martin Hengel, *Judaism and Hellenism,* 2 vols. (London: SCM Press, 1974) and Jean Danielou, *A History of Early Christian Doctrine,* 2 vols. (London: Darton, Longman and Todd, 1964).

[26] See Bernard J. Lonergan, SJ, *The Way to Nicaea* (London: Darton, Longman and Todd, 1976).

[27] David Ede, ed., *Guide to Islam* (Boston: G.K. Hall, 1983) with an excellent annotated bibliography; *Encyclopedia of Islam, New Edition,* ed. by H.A.R. Gibbs and J.H. Kramers (Leiden: E.J. Brill, 1960) and the *Shorter Encyclopedia of Islam* (1953) by the same editors and publisher; W. Montgomery Watt, *Muhammad at Medina* (1955) and *Muhammad at Mecca* (1953) both vols. condensed in *Muhammad Prophet and Statesman* (1961) (Oxford: Clarendon Press); H.A.R. Gibbs, *Mohammedanism* (New York: Oxford University Press, 1950); Faziur Rahman, *Islam* (Garden City, NY: Doubleday Anchor Books, 1968); Dwight, *Islam* (Chicago: Phoenix Books, 1961) and G.H. Jansen, *Militant Islam*

(New York: Harper and Row, 1979); M. Donaldson, *The Shi'ite Religion* (London: Luzac and Co., 1933); G.E. von Grunebaum, *Medieval Islam* (Harper and Row, 1979).

[28] *The Holy Qur'an,* translation and commentary by A. Yusuf Ali (published for the Muslim Students' Association by American Trust Publications, June 1977); E.R. Bell, *Introduction to the Qur'an* (Edinburgh: Edinburgh University Press, 1953).

[29] Geoffrey Parrinder, *Jesus in the Qur'an* (New York: Barnes and Noble, 1965) and Kenneth Cragg, *Jesus and the Muslim* (Boston: George Allen and Unwin, 1985).

[30] See Magid Khadduri, *War and Peace in the Law of Islam* (Baltimore: Johns Hopkins Press, 1955).

[31] See Joseph A. Schacht, *An Introduction to Islamic Law* (Oxford: Clarendon Press, 1964).

[32] Cf. Niels C. Nielsen, Jr., *et al., Religions of the World* (New York: St. Martin's Press), pp. 647-657.

[33] See W. Montgomery Watt, *Islamic Philosophy and Theology,* Islamic Surveys, vol. I (Edinburgh: Edinburgh University Press, 1962).

[34] See Parviz Morewedge, ed., *Islamic Philosophical Theology* (Albany, NY: State University of New York Press, 1979).

[35] A.J. Arberry, *Sufism* (London: George Allen and Unwin, 1950); Margaret Smith, *The Sufi Path of Love* (London: Luzac and Co., 1954); Seyyed Hossein Nasr, *Islamic Spirituality: Foundations,* vol. 19 of *World Spirituality: An Encyclopedic History of the Religious Question* (New York: Crossroad, 1987).

[36] *Qur'an,* III, 35-37; 42-51; IV, 156; XIX, 16-33; XXI, 91; LXVI, 12.

[37] See W.D. Davies, *Paul and Rabbinic Judaism* (Philadelphia: Fortress Press, 1980), pp. 27-29.

[38] See Hans Küng, *Does God Exist? An Answer for Today* (Garden City, NY: Doubleday, 1980); William J. Hill, OP, *Knowing the Unknown God* (New York: Philosophical Library, 1971); Germain Grisez, *Beyond the New Theism* (Notre Dame IN: Notre Dame University Press, 1975).

[39] See Thomas C. O'Brien, *Metaphysics and the Existence of God* (Washington, DC: Thomist Press, 1960) for an excellent study of this question.

[40] On the attack by Hume and Kant on the classical proofs of God's existence see Frederick Copleston, SJ, *A History of Philosophy* (Garden City, NY: Doubleday Image Books, 1960), vol. 5, pp. 63-121, vol. 6, pp. 30-140. Also James Collins, *God in Modern Philosophy* (Chicago: Henry Regnery, 1959) and Grisez, note 38 above. On the history of the scientific view of causality see William A. Wallace, *Causality and Scientific Explanation,* 2 vols. (Ann Arbor, MI: University of Michigan Press, 1974).

[41] On the Big Bang Hypothesis and alternatives see Willem B. Drees, *Beyond the Big Bang: Quantum Cosmologies and God* (La Salle, IL: Open Court, 1990).

[42] See note 38 above.

[43] See John Henry, "'Pray Do Not Ascribe That Notion to Me': God and Newton's Gravity" in James E. Force and Richard H. Popkin, eds., *The Books of Nature and Scripture: Recent Essays on Natural Philosophy, Theology, and Biblical Criticism in the Netherlands of Spinoza's Time and the British Isles of Newton's Time* (Dordrecht/Boston/London: Kluwer Academic Publishers, 1994), pp. 123-148.

[44] Aristotle accepted such an eternal universe because he believed the claims of the Babylonian astronomers that no change in the heavens had been observed by them for thousands of years. It was Galileo's telescopic observation of the sunspots that first falsified this theory. It is often forgotten that this did more to revolutionize science than Galileo's advocacy of Copernican heliocentrism since that was not necessarily in contradiction to such ancient theories.

[45] For discussion of Newton's Laws of Motion in relation to Aquinas' proofs see Vincent E. Smith, *The General Science of Nature* (Milwaukee: Bruce, 1958), pp. 63-69, 373-84.

[46] John Henry, "'Pray Do Not Ascribe That Notion to Me.'...," *op. cit.*, pp. 123-148.
[47] See J.D. Barow and Frank J. Tipler, *The Anthropic Cosmological Principle* (New York: Oxford University Press, 1986, 1996). For discussion see Errol E. Harris, *Cosmos and Anthropos: A Philosophical Interpretation of the Anthropic Cosmological Principle* (Highlands, NJ: Humanities Press International, 1991) and *Cosmos and Theos: Ethical and Theological Implications of the Anthropic Cosmological Principle* (same publisher, 1992).
[48] It can be objected that in Aristotle the discussion of the intelligences that move the spheres is found in *Metaphysics Lambda* not in his physical works and Aquinas does not remark on this fact. I incline to the view that it would have had its proper place in the *De Caelo,* generally thought to be a rather early work written before *Physics VIII* and its final treatment of the argument for the Unmoved Mover summarized in the *Metaphysics.* Hence had Aristotle revised the *De Caelo* I believe he would have included a fuller discussion of the intelligences and movers of the spheres and a more satisfactory discussion of the agent intellect in *De Anima.* In any case Aquinas goes beyond him in both instances, but in accordance with his usual method of "benign interpretation" does not emphasize that he is doing so.
[49] See St. Thomas Aquinas, *Summa Theologiae,* I, q. 2, a. 3, obj. 1 and 26. For a history of the problem see John Bowker, *Problems of Suffering in the Religions of the* World (Cambridge: Cambridge University Press, 1970).
[50] On "the turn to the subject" as it affects theology see Fergus Kerr, OP, *Theology after Wittgenstein* (Oxford: Basil Blackwell, 1986), pp. 3-27.
[51] *Le Point de Depart de la Metaphysique: Leçons sur le Developpement historique et theoretique de probleme de la Connaissance* (Paris: Desclée de Brouwer, 1944, originally published between 1922-26), 5 vols.
[52] See his *Insight: A Study of Human Understanding* (New York: Philosophical Library, 1957). For his account of his own relation to Marechal see his essay, "Insight Revisited," in *A Second Collection,* ed. by W.F.J. Ryan, SJ and B.J. Tyrell, SJ (Philadelphia: The Westminster Press, 1974), pp. 263-278.
[53] Translated by William Dych, SJ (New York: Herder and Herder, 1968).
[54] One might object that this is not true of Kant and his followers. It is true that Kant does not believe that we can *theoretically* know the existence of God or the spiritual human self, since these pertain to the noumenal world not the phenomenal world of our sense experience. Nevertheless, in his system taken as a whole and thus including *practical* knowledge, the existence of the morally responsible self and of God as the standard of right and wrong are indispensable *regulative* ideas that provide unity to our world-view and value-system. What Kant denies is that the existence of God and the self can in any way fall within the scope of Newtonian natural science that alone can give us objective theoretical certitude. The Transcendental Thomists modify Kant on this point by arguing that our self-consciousness is not limited to the phenomenal but as Descartes thought extends to the noumenal knowledge of the self as an existent being.
[55] Cambridge, MA: Harvard University Press, 1990.
[56] Wineberg must be given credit for the fact that he did attempt to clear up this confusion in his interesting book *The Dream of a Final Theory* (New York: Vintage Books, 1993) but not with notable success.
[57] New York: Seabury, 1978.
[58] In "The Experiences of a Catholic Theologian," *Communio,* 11, no. 4 (1984), p. 412, Rahner said, "Certainly, the theologian has ultimately only one thing to say. But this one word would have to be filled with the mysterious essence of all reality. And yet each time I open some work of whatever modern science, I fall as theologian into no slight panic. The greater part of what stands written there I do not know, and usually I am not even in the position to understand more exactly what it is that I could be reading about. And so I

feel as a theologian that I am somehow repudiated. The colorless abstraction and emptiness of my theological concepts frightens me. I say that the world has been created by God. But what is the world about that I know virtually nothing, and as a result the concept of creation also remains unusually empty. I say as a theologian that Jesus is as man also Lord of the whole creation. And then I read that the cosmos stretches for billions of light years, and then I ask myself, terrified, what the statement that I have just said really means. Paul still knew in which sphere of the cosmos he wanted to locate the angels; I do not." It would be misleading, however, to omit reference to articles in which Rahner did touch on scientific questions. For example, in *Theological Investigations* (London, Baltimore and New York: Darton, Longman, and Todd / Helicon / Herder and Herder / Seabury, Crossroad, 1961-1992, 23 vols.) we find such articles as "Theological Reflections on Monogenism," vol. 1, pp. 229-296; "Theology as Engaged in an Interdisciplinary Dialogue with the Sciences," vol. 13, pp. 80-93; "On the Relationship Between Theology and the Contemporary Sciences," vol. 13, pp. 94-104; and "The Body in the Order of Salvation," vol. 17, pp. 71-89. Yet in such articles Rahner takes philosophy as entirely transcendent to natural science.

[59] It is well known that another major theologian of the Vatican II period Hans Urs von Balthasar was a constant critic of Rahner's theology. Their differences are summed up by John O'Donnell, SJ, in his *Hans Urs von Balthasar* (Collegeville, MN: The Liturgical Press, 1992), p. 154: "[T]he differences between Rahner and Balthasar are profound, especially as regards method. Balthasar could never tolerate Rahner's transcendental method, which seemed to him a Procrustean bed in which Christianity had to be reduced in size in order to find a place. Moreover, Balthasar's entire theology is much more oriented to the paschal mystery than is Rahner's and he often argued that Rahner's whole frame of reference lacked the dramatic dimension and thus eclipsed the cross which is the culmination of the interaction of divine and human freedom." From a very different perspective see also Fergus Kerr, OP, *Theology after Wittgenstein,* note 50 above.

THE ECUMENICAL CHOICE

CHAPTER 6

THE DIALOGUE OF THEISM WITH NON-THEISM

1. Is Such Dialogue Possible?

In the last Chapter, I showed how the theistic religions have claimed that not only the atheism, agnosticism, or deism of Humanism but also the pantheism of the Mythological and Emanation Religions are false. The theistic religions base this claim not only on revelation, but also on what they claim is rational proof that the world owes its existence to a Creator who has produced it by an act of free will. In view of this flat contradiction between theism and non-theism is any dialogue between theistic religion and non-theistic philosophies of life possible?[1]

In considering the atheism of some Humanists such as the Marxists who have had worldwide influence in the twentieth century, the first thing to be noted is that Humanism especially distrusts Christianity as the traditional religion of most developed countries. It believes with Marx that "religion is the opiate of the people." It is an exploitative ideology used to pacify the oppressed so as to weaken them in their struggle for liberation. The "theologians of liberation"[2] agree that Marx was right to expose the ideological use of religion as a tool of exploitation. But they argue that this very exposure makes it possible for the world religions to free themselves from this co-option by the oppressors by making a "preferential option for the poor." Liberation theologians claim that this is the way to recover the original meaning of the religion of the great ancient prophets who denounced injustice and announced the intervention of God in support of the aspirations for freedom of the oppressed.

Thus, for example, the religion of the Hebrew Scriptures depicts a liberating God who delivers his people from enslavement and alienation. Similarly Jesus Christ announced the fulfillment of the promises of the prophets in the coming of God's Kingdom and actually inaugurated this Kingdom by rejecting all domination and accepting the marginalized as his brothers and sisters. Muslims also claim that Muhammad brought a message of universal brotherhood, of social justice, and of militant defense of his people against oppression. Thus all these prophets, Jewish, Christian, and Islamic contended that belief in One Creator, God of Justice and Mercy, is the only consistent ground for social justice.

Without such a belief in a liberating God how can the powerless claim the moral authority to denounce the powerful or have any real hope of achieving liberation? Is not Marxism in fact simply a concealed version of the Christian hope for the coming of the Kingdom of God? Marxism's practical failure in Russia, China, and elsewhere to establish real freedom or equality seems proof that without belief in God its atheism is bound to end in a new and even more cruel oppression.

As for the "materialism" proposed by many Humanists as a "scientific" basis for its atheism, this seems at the end of the twentieth century to be little more than an outdated scientific Positivism that has all the weaknesses of Nominalism and Empiricism. Humanism, however, should be given credit for calling attention to the mistake of the theistic religions in accepting a too Platonic, idealistic, other-worldly interpretation of their own Scriptures. They should have given full weight to the earthly, economic aspect of human existence plain enough in the original meaning of the Hebrew Scriptures, the New Testament, and the *Qur'an.* The doctrine of creation when given its full weight in monotheistic theology can easily assimilate the Humanist materialistic insights without falling into Platonic spiritualism. Consequently, monotheists need not take second place to Humanists in their devotion to scientific progress, the advance of technology, and the economic analysis of social forces and social change.

Similarly, theists in dialogue with Humanists can reply to the charges that religion is an obstacle to scientific advancement by arguing as Alfred North Whitehead did[3] that belief in a Creator was historically the rational foundation for the advancement of modern science. Theists can also point out that the growing skepticism, relativism, and irrationalism of Humanist society today threaten to undercut the confidence in human reason on which modern science has been based. If the world is absurd and the moral order is a merely human construct, what hope can we realistically have for the kind of world of which the Humanism of the Enlightenment dreamed?

Once that hope was undermined by agnosticism, the Humanist culture has more and more suffered from confusion and existentialist despair. Humanists today seem to take a rather empty comfort in their sense of intellectual sophistication and moral emancipation in a mad world that they no longer hope to control. Yet theists can be grateful to Humanists because the Enlightenment exposed the obscurantism and fanaticism into which the world religions have often fallen. Humanism's noble vision of human equality has acted as a powerful purgative for theists who through compromise with the violence of the world empires had lost their own original vision of human dignity.

More specifically theists can concede to modern philosophy since Kant that in trying to undermine the classical proofs of God's existence Kantianism has done religion a great service. Kantians have taught us to use a "critical" and hermeneutic method by which to analyze the pluralism and cultural relativism of human thought-systems and the large element of historicity and perspectivity in any philosophical or theological world-view. This has permitted the theistic religions to understand themselves historically and developmentally, and thus be freed from a naive literalism in the understanding of their own faith. Moreover, it has liberated them from fanaticism and opened them to an ecumenical willingness to learn from other philosophies and religions.

These gains, nevertheless, do not require theists to accept a "demythologizing modernism" that requires them to reinterpret their doctrines to the point that they lose their original meaning and become empty jargon to be filled up with the current opinions of a dominant Humanism. In fact the theistic Creation Religions differ markedly from the Mythological Religions and do not require to be "demythologized" for their claims to be critically examined. For its own part, Humanism ultimately rests its claims on an interpretation of the scientific world-picture. Since it has taught the theists that interpretations of empirical fact often represent an imposition of an ideology that is not necessarily derived from these facts, the theists are freed to give their own interpretation of the scientific world-picture. Such an interpretation need not exclude the findings of modern science, since, as was explained in Chapter 5, these findings can be used to argue for theism.

What then of the dialogue between the theists, polytheists, and emanationists?[4] We have seen that the religions of pre-literate people generally include a belief in a supreme High God, and that the polytheistic religions have generally developed in the direction of theism by explaining the gods either as creatures of the One God or as symbols of that God. Consequently, in such cases the issue is not the existence of the One God but of God's relation to the world: is God the Creator in the theistic sense? This today remains the real issue between the highly developed theories of Hinduism or Buddhism and the theistic religions. The former propose an Absolute of whom one can speak only negatively and of which the world and the human spirit are necessary phenomenal manifestations rather than free creations absolutely distinct from their Creator. Obviously we are dealing here with metaphysical questions of great subtlety and with answers to these questions separated by enormous semantic gaps. Thus neither side ought to leap to conclusions about what the other is really saying.

From the theistic side, however, there is no need to reject the negative theology of the Emanation Religions which insists that all language used of the Supreme Reality is analogical and utterly inadequate to its reality. Such a negative method has already been well assimilated into the theistic theologies through the influence of Plotinus (d. 270 CE), whose thought is of much the same type as that of Indian thinkers. It was a method also used by the Jewish mystics of the Kabbalah, by "negative" (*apophatic*) Christian mystics such as St. John of the Cross, and by the Muslim Sufi.[5] The theistic emphasis on the positive (*kataphatic*) aspect of analogy is not contradictory but complementary to such a negative mystical theology.

Hinduism, particularly the Vedanta, as we have seen, seeks to explain the world as the "play" of the One God, as his body, or spouse.

These analogies are acceptable to theists provided they are freed from any literalism that would (a) reduce creation to mere illusion; or (b) make it necessary rather than free. As for Buddhism, the immense variety of its own self-interpretations seems to give room for a similar convergence. If Nirvana is understood as annihilation of the created human self, or if the Absolute is understand as literally nothing, or alternatively as simply the empirical world recognized as identical with the Void (in the manner of some Zen thinkers), then such views are certainly contradictory to theism.[6] But if Buddhist enlightenment is understood as the realization of the utter relativity (or emptiness) of created reality *in relation* to the ineffable Creator, then it is not contradictory to the theistic negative theology.

Polytheism in a literal sense has few defenders today, but there are some who argue that as a symbol it is preferable to theism because it more adequately reflects the pluralism of the cosmos. They think it is also a better model for human society, since they believe that monotheism tends to support authoritarian monarchy or dictatorship.[7] Theists would answer that in fact monotheism is perfectly compatible with a pluralistic conception of the cosmos, since it signifies that the unity and harmony of the cosmos is not intrinsic to it but has its source in the Wholly Other. Hence it effectively opposes the idolatry of looking for this absolute unity in any worldly ruler or organic state. All earthly powers are subject powers and hence divided. In Christian theism the symbol of the *communio sanctorum*, the communion of angels and saints centered in the One Creator, represents this pluralistic aspect of the cosmos.

Thus the *a posteriori* arguments from the creation for the existence of One God are paralleled in some form in all the traditional world religions. Their theoretical refutation has been based chiefly on the Humanist skepticism of Hume and the idealism of Kant, epistemologies that tend to undermine the validity of modern science and thus also the confidence in reason on which Humanism is based. Hence Humanists today to refute theistic claims seem to rely more on pragmatic arguments based on the supposed social conservatism of organized religion. Such arguments will lose much of their force if the three great theistic religions react positively to these criticisms and renew the advocacy of social justice that the liberation theologians have shown is inherent in the traditions of the Creation Religions.

2. Why Must Revelation be Received on Faith?

Those Humanists who are deists acknowledge a Creator but think that this Creator has left its creatures to operate according to innate and even deterministic laws. Yet it seems this Creator has created us as intelligent persons to whom the existence of God is knowable from the creation. Hence if creation can only give us a very inadequate idea of what God is like, it would seem plausible that a wise and good God would desire to make himself better known to his intelligent creatures. Thus it would seem, contrary to deism, that God might wish to reveal himself more fully to these created persons. Moreover, the very existence of so many religious theories about God, even the persistent efforts to disprove these theories, seems to indicate that human beings have a natural desire to know God, if there is a God. The human mind ceaselessly questions the world and human existence and is not content without raising questions about the Ultimate. Can such a profoundly innate desire be in vain?[8] In fact all three of the great Creation Religions claim that God has historically spoken to certain privileged human beings, the prophets, and through them has more fully revealed himself to others, giving guidance to human life.

In the Emanation Religions there are also sages and *avatars* of the Absolute who have somehow come to know the Absolute and out of compassion for humanity seek to communicate this knowledge to all.[9] In these religions, however, the distinction between the seeker and the Absolute is only an illusion to be overcome, or, for the Qualified Non-Dualism of Ramanuja, no more than the distinction between the mind and its body. Therefore, for consistently monist religions revelation can only be an awakening to a truth already unconsciously possessed by the seeker. An *avatar* such as Krishna or Gautama is only a symbolic manifestation of this eternal truth within us. The enlightened sage is only one who, having achieved enlightenment himself, guides others on their way to the same self-knowledge. Thus in these religions revelation cannot be taken literally in the sense of the Creation Religions that teach that the One Personal God speaks to and through human persons infinitely distinct from himself. Revelation therefore requires and empowers the human recipients to respond in faith.

Thus one should not impose on Eastern Emanation Religions the familiar Western categories of "philosophy" (and science) based on human reason and "theology" based on faith in revelation. Chandradhar Sharma in his *Indian Philosophy: A Critical Survey*[10] writes:

> Western Philosophy has remained more or less true to the etymological meaning of "philosophy," in being essentially an intellectual quest for truth. Indian Philosophy has been, however, intensely spiritual and has always emphasized the need of practical realization of truth The word *darshana* means "vision" and also the "instrument of vision." It stands for the direct, immediate and intuitive vision of Reality, the actual perception of Truth, and also includes the means that lead to this realization. "See the Self" (*atma va drastavyah*) is the keynote of all schools of Indian Philosophy. And this is the reason why most of the schools of Indian Philosophy are also religious sects.

Thus to promote successful dialogue between East and West we need to distinguish three types of knowledge: (1) Philosophy in the Western sense is a search for truth by human reason; (2) Enlightenment in the Eastern sense is a direct mystical intuition of Reality attained by meditation; (3) Theology in the theistic sense of Judaism, Christianity, and Islam is knowledge of mysteries beyond both reasoning and intuitive human power that God freely reveals to humanity and enables us to accept in faith. Hence only in the theistic Creation Religions is a "revelation" possible if taken in the strict sense of a communication of God to his creatures of truths that are utterly beyond their power to discover. Scientistic Humanism accepts only the first of these three types of knowledge, although romantic Humanism may accept the second. The Creation Religions accept all three, but with somewhat different emphases, since philosophy has played a rather secondary role in Judaism and latter Islam. Also Creation Religions tend to divide the second, mystical form of knowledge into intuitive knowledge based on human powers (natural mysticism) and that based on revelation (supernatural mysticism). The Emanation Religions, as Sharma is pointing out in the quotation, identify the first type of reasoning knowledge with the second, intuitive knowledge to which latter they give overwhelming importance. They, therefore, have little to say about the third type of revealed knowledge though for the Creation Religions this has the predominance.

In Chapter 1 it was pointed out that the functional definition of "religion" or "philosophy" of life abstracts from these distinctions. In the dialogue between East and West, however, it is essential to see that for the East "philosophy" and "religion" are not clearly distinct. Furthermore, for the East "philosophy-religion," is primarily not either a process of rational argument nor faith in a revelation but an intuitive enlightenment attained by meditation on the true nature of the Self. The Self moreover is not precisely the human self but the Absolute Self from which individual selves are not completely distinguished, or, as with Buddhism, are not themselves real.

Hence the term "faith," commonly used today for all religions, has very different senses for the Creation Religions and the Emanation Religions. For the latter "faith" is trust in some sage who, a disciple believes, has already attained enlightenment, but the disciple must ultimately attain this enlightenment by his or her innate powers. For the Creation Religions, on the contrary, enlightenment is possible only in the next life in the Beatific Vision, while in this life one must walk by faith in a revelation given by God. As the New Testament says, "Faith is the realization of what is hoped for, the evidence of things not seen" (Heb 11:1). Thus for theists even the highest intuitive supernatural mystical experience is only a form of faith. It is centered not on any experience possible in this life but on the Word of God to which the believer must cling in darkness. Thus the Emanation Religions, because of their monism by which God and creatures are ultimately identified are not based on faith in the theist sense, but on personal experience. While both types of religion have "discipleship" in common, for non-theistic religions the disciple trusts the guru only to help him achieve his own enlightenment in this life or in some future incarnation. For theistic religions, on the other hand, in this life disciples trust Moses, Jesus, or Mohammad as messengers of God's revelation that promises the Beatific Vision in the next and final life of heaven but not here on earth. They do admit, however, that even in this life faith can deepen to a mystical intensity that approaches but cannot achieve face to face vision.[11]

There are several serious difficulties about this theistic concept of revelation.[12] One objection that is felt very strongly by thinkers of the Enlightenment is the "particularity" of special revelation. Why would a generous God make himself intimately known only to the insignificant people of Israel, or nomadic Arabs? Why would a caring God neglect the rest of humanity? The Emanation Religions seem superior in that they offer enlightenment equally to all in this life or a future incarnation. Consequently, while deistic Enlightenment thinkers affirmed that God is revealed in a general way to all in nature, they rejected special revelation to individual prophets or a chosen people. Why also did an inclusive God chiefly choose *white male* prophets? Moreover, how can we recognize a true prophet from a madman or a demagogue? Finally, how can we understand God's Word, even if this Supreme Being does speak to us? Is it not rather that we impose our notion of God as the Supreme Being (what the philosopher Martin Heidegger called *onto-theology*) on an ineffable Absolute?

Judaism, Christianity, and Islam all teach that God has revealed himself to all members of the human race but to most by the mediation of a few chosen messengers. They reject the idea that God should have revealed himself directly to every individual or every people because the order of creation shows that God prefers to share his power with his creatures as far as possible. Therefore as in ordinary human life some persons are especially gifted and serve as teachers for others, so God may choose to reveal himself to others *through* prophets. A genuine prophet must not only be enlightened by God about what he or she is to say, but must also be enlightened to know that this message truly comes from God and not from some other alien source nor simply from the prophet's own mental processes. This enlightenment must be an immediate intuition directly caused by God who also makes the prophet objectively certain that it is God's Word. This prophetic certitude is, therefore, superior in mode to the faith of those who believe through him, but by the gift of faith they participate in its certitude. Thus it can be said that both the prophet and the faithful who do not have the gift of prophecy both believe in God on God's word, not simply on their own experiences. Hence it is not at all unreasonable that most of us must receive God's revelation through others not by a personal vision, or that humanity as a whole should receive it through a Chosen People.

Therefore, these theistic religions hold that those who do not share the prophetic illumination can receive the divine message only by believing God's word through belief in the prophet. They cannot distinguish true from false prophets by the *intrinsic* truth of their message (as in non-theistic religions disciples of an enlightened sage come to their own enlightenment) since the divine revelation is given principally to teach truths which are beyond any human power to attain. Yet the true prophet may be discerned by *extrinsic signs* furnished by God, such as the fulfillment of predictions about the future and by other miraculous events which so accompany the revelation as to sufficiently confirm it.[13]

Thus the Jewish prophets such as Elijah (2 K 17-19) are pictured in the Hebrew Scriptures as confirming their prophecies by predictions and miracles. The New Testament reports similar extraordinary acts by Jesus and the Apostles in confirmation of their teaching.[14] While Muhammad did not claim in the *Qur'an* to have worked miracles, he pointed to the *Qur'an* itself as such a miracle. Moreover Muslim Tradition claims both predictions and miracles as confirmations of its truth. Since the eighteenth century, however, there has been widespread skepticism about both the prophetic predictions and the miracles recounted in the Bible. Indeed, the historical-critical method of exegesis often uses the presence of miracles in a narrative as evidence that it is not historical.

3. Is Revelation Verifiable?

In Chapter 3 I discussed objections to the belief in the "supernatural" and the "miraculous" derived chiefly from the eighteenth century philosopher David Hume. Here we need to expand this discussion also to include the principal reasons that Humanists have given against the biblical prophecies and miracles, since this remains a principal point on which Humanism and the traditional religions differ and need to dialogue.

A corollary of the notion that even scientific knowledge can only be probable is the famous theory of Karl Popper. He argued that any theory, no matter how verified as probable in view of known data, may be falsified by new data. Thus scientific advance is based not on the verification of theories but on their *falsification*. Hence it also follows that the mark of a good scientific theory is its *falsifiability*. Yet if, as is evident, probability must always rest on some certitudes, falsifiability and falsification must also rest on some certitudes. It is true that scientific hypotheses are open to modification, but unless science has in fact established some truths that it is unreasonable to doubt, both as to the correctness of the data and their theoretical causal explanation, no scientific advance would be possible. Actually what Popper had in mind was not the falsification of every theory but the openness of true theories to further refinement. The only way that Copernicus could have falsified Ptolemaic geocentrism or Einstein Newton's law of gravity was by accepting that the previous theories had given explanations of some certain data in terms of certain causal laws that new data required to be modified but by no means wholly falsified.

Hence some who uncritically accept Popper's thesis deny that a claim for the truth of a revelation could be falsified and hence conclude that this claim has no truth-value at all. Why is it supposed that no claim for a miracle or the revelation to which it attests can be falsified? One reason is that only science can give us objective truth. That of course is a tenet of Humanism, but it is to be questioned. The other reason is that it is supposed that neither verification nor falsification of such an assertion is possible except through those modes of critical testing used by science or by critical history. This is the question I will now examine.

First, against the claim of theists that there can be special supernatural interventions by God that can be known with certitude through signs such as miracles and prophecies, it is argued that such interventions would be inconsistent with the concept of God as wise Creator. It is also claimed that such divine interventions are scientifically impossible (or at least extremely improbable because inviolable laws govern nature). This argument, very popular in the nineteenth century and lingering on as late as Einstein, supposes that the very existence of scientific research depends on the existence of predictive, deterministic laws of nature. It is well known, however, that the present scientific world-picture no longer depends on the positing of absolute natural laws that rigidly determine all future events.[15] Instead scientists are quite comfortable with concepts of indeterminacy, stochastic regularities, chaos, and compexity, etc. They pretty much agree with older philosophical views that saw terrestrial nature as imperfectly ordered by regularities that can best be expressed by statistical laws that admit of indeterminancy (probability) and chance, so that from the present the future cannot be absolutely predicted. For Aristotle and Thomas Aquinas the natural is what happens *in pluribus,* for the most part. Thus science does not claim even in principle that it can explain all historical events except in a general manner that leaves room for their uniqueness.

Thus the scientific theories of cosmic, biological, and human evolution are not simply a set of universal laws, but a description in the light of such laws of an essentially historical process that at any point might have gone in some other direction. That human intelligence emerged from matter can be explained by looking backward on the sequence of events that actually occurred, but looking forward it could never have been predicted, even if there had been some intelligent creature to predict it. Consequently modern science raises no real difficulty against the doctrine that the Creator determines the course of history so as to include extraordinary events without disrupting the general order of natural law. Nor is this inconsistent with God's creative wisdom, since the order of nature and the order of history are both included in God's choice of what sort of universe God wants to create.

Artists like Mozart or Beethoven were able to play one of their compositions as already scored yet introduce embellishments and improvisational passages at will in an actual performance. These improvisations in no way violated the logical structure of their compositions but rather enhanced it. A creator is free with regards to his creation provided all he produces is in accordance with his artistic aim. Since we do not admire a mechanical regularity in a work of human art, but prefer an element of freedom and spontaneity, why criticize the Divine Creator for similar tastes?

A second argument against the possibility of revelation is that even if God were to intervene in nature, scientists could not distinguish a miraculous from a natural event. It is correct to say, "Don't multiply miracles," since an extraordinary event can be extraordinary only in the context of a much more common ordinary state of affairs. We can, therefore, be reasonably skeptical of those who claim too many miracles. Some would argue from the statistical nature of natural laws just mentioned that since the highly improbable *can* happen sometimes it *will* happen. They also are convinced by the historic success of science in explaining previously mysterious phenomena that it is always possible that in the future science will eventually be able to explain any unusual event by natural processes of which we are at present ignorant.

This type of argument is logically weak, however, because it rests on the groundless assumption that because science can explain a great deal about the world it can and probably will some day explain everything. Certainly one can grant that science has demonstrated that it is a powerful method of explaining many aspects of the world that were formerly given wrong explanations. That is why we can trust that it will in time explain many other things better than we can now. Yet science "explains" by discovering the causes of observed effects, and if the argument for the existence of an immaterial First Cause expounded in Chapter 5 is valid, then all scientific explanations are *in principle* incomplete unless they trace the lines of causation they discover back to this First Cause. There I also argued that while the existence and immateriality of the First Cause must be demonstrated by natural science, once this has been established, further attempts to understand its nature pertain not to science but metaphysics. Thus while it is true that, if we are not to become the victims of illusions and frauds, prophecies and miracles require rational verification, it is not obvious that the scientific mode of verification plays the principal role in this authentication.

Moreover, the fact that natural laws are only probable does not mean that some kinds of events are in fact impossible. The statistical laws in question pertain to a mathematical model not to the real physical world in which we can be confident that certain events will not occur; e.g., heavy weights will not suddenly move up rather than down without the action of some other cause than gravity. Thus it is not reasonable to say that the Resurrection of Jesus, if it took place as the Gospel describes it, will some day be explained by science because its mathematical probability cannot be shown to be zero. Nevertheless, it must be admitted that if events are to be judged miraculous it is often not easy to eliminate the possibility that they are inexplicable coincidences due to chance or that someday science will be able to discover their natural causes. For example, although a physician can usually be very sure that a patient in the last stages of cancer will die, there are reports of very rare cases in which the tumor rather suddenly disappears. How can we be sure then that an alleged cure of even so objectively observable a disease as cancer is a miracle? In such rare cases not only the issue of verification by scientific laws arises, but the verification of unique historical events.

Thus a third argument against miracles as evidence for the truth of revelation is the famous and very influential argument of David Hume, already discussed in Chapter 3. Recall that according to Hume since we can only verify historical accounts by their similarity to events that we can ourselves observe in the present, it will always be more probable that an account of a miracle is a spurious invention than that it is true.

In Chapter 3 I noted that Hume's argument proves too much since it eliminates history all together, since historical events are unique. Science works on the Principle of Uniformity by which natural laws are established by their regularity. Thus scientific methods cannot predict or explain history in any but a most general manner. It is true, of course, that science can pass judgment on the impossibility of certain historical assertions. We can be sure, for example, that it is impossible that President Kennedy died of something other than a bullet, because his wound was such that only a bullet traveling at high speed could have produced it. Yet generally such negative conclusions about historical events are only probable. It is only probable, though highly probable, that the one who fired the bullet was Oswald. While miracles are by definition events contrary to historical probability this does not generally establish that they are impossible, nor even that it is improbable that sometimes such improbable events do occur. Hume does not show that miracles never occur, or can never be verified, but only that we must face the question of how this verification is possible if it does not pertain to either the scientific or historical modes of verification.

A fourth argument is that certain "religious" experiences that we may ourselves have undergone and that are reported by many other people are illusory or misinterpreted. Hence these experiences can always be "explained" as psychological illusions, products of the unconscious, etc. Thus the "miracle of the sun" said to have been witnessed by thousands at Fatima, Portugal in 1917 is often explained as mass suggestion, and the miracles of Lourdes as cures of psychogenic ailments.[16] This argument is reinforced by the observation that miraculous events are usually reported in times and places where the culture is permeated by mythology, magic, and demonology. The witnesses are often naïve persons (children, peasants, women!) or psychologically abnormal (hysteric, schizoid) or are abnormally conditioned by sensory deprivation, fasting, use of drugs, hypnotic music, or by rituals such as favor mass-suggestion. Even at Lourdes, the number of medically certified miracles is small and has been reduced as the standards of diagnosis have risen.[17] Therefore, some would claim, it is probable that with still more rigorous testing all such miracles as those at Lourdes would be eliminated as has been done by studying of the reports of UFO's (unidentified flying objects, "flying saucers") at Roswell.

Also it is argued that historical accounts of wonderworking saints, etc., have often been shown to be legendary and filled with stereotypic marvels. Many such persons have been exposed as frauds or self-deluded. Prophecies are very often not fulfilled, or at least not in an objectively verifiable manner. Reports of unusual and obscure events are notoriously untrustworthy, e.g., the controversies over President Kennedy's assassination. These same difficulties hold for the biblical accounts that critical scholarship has shown to be filled with historical improbabilities, contradictions, and mythic and folkloric motifs. The hunger for the marvelous seems to be a basic human trait apparent in purely fictional literature. It is this hunger which best explains reputed prophecies and miracles as projective illusions of the human imagination, often originating in the unconscious.

These are indeed serious reasons for skepticism about reports of miracles whether in the past or present. Thus a critical attitude expressed by the old adage, "Do not multiply miracles" is entirely justified. That is why the Roman Catholic Church from its long experience of human aberrations tries to protect herself from Humanist accusations of credulity and fraud by a careful process of verification before giving any credence to such claims, especially in the canonization of saints. Yet such a critical attitude is appropriate in all serious matters, including all assertions of scientific and historical truth. It does not invalidate science nor historical scholarship to point out the many mistakes and frauds committed in both fields of learning. What is always required is that assertions be critically examined by the mode of verification proper to a given field. As regards the miraculous, one can very well grant that the great majority of such reports in the past and in the present were mistaken or fraudulent (perhaps this is true in all fields of research), without therefore being forced to deny that miracles may not and have never occurred.

Yet *psychological* explanations of reports of miracles and revelations or indeed of many of the phenomena of human behavior have seldom been tested by empirical studies that meet scientific standards. Psychology deals with extremely complex phenomena, especially if we recognize that the mind-body problem remains a scientific mystery.[18] Today the once renowned theories of Freud and Jung that were for a time the accepted explanations of religious phenomena are now severely criticized. Their explanations of human behavior, whether individual or *en masse* in terms of a psychic "unconscious" or "collective unconscious" seem as mythical as the myths, dreams and miracles they propose to explain.

Hence before miracles and prophecies can be credible they must be subjected to critical verification. Yet, as we have seen, the appropriate mode of verification cannot principally be scientific or historic, nor can it depend simply on a facile psychological reductionism. It is noteworthy that these arguments are not really new but have been raised repeatedly in the history of the theistic religions, although they have taken on special force since the rise of modern science. Yet it must not be supposed that people of the past, even those with Mythological Religions, did not recognize that some supernatural claims are mistaken or fraudulent. People of common sense do not believe every tale or accept every claim even in "primitive" societies.

4. Revelation: Communication Verified by Signs

Therefore the foregoing discussion of the arguments against the rational credibility of a revelation supported by alleged prophecies and miracles shows us that none of them are conclusive. Yet it still has to be asked, "What is the proper mode of verification for the claims of a revelation from God?" If the answer is that it is verified by miraculous and prophetic signs, then the question becomes, "How do we verify that reputed miracles and prophecies are really such?"

To answer these questions we must be precise about what is meant by a "miracle" since today the word is used very loosely to mean any event that arouses *wonder* (etymologically it means just that). But for a theist a miracle is not just an extraordinary event but one that by its uniqueness is perceived as an act of communication from God. A Creator God controls the course of events both as these obey the natural laws studied by scientists and also as they constitute the unique temporal sequence with its elements of chance, coincidence, and freedom studied by historians. In this natural and historical sequence of events God chooses to include events so unusual that they arouse the wonder of the humans who experience them. But because they arouse wonder, they also raise the question of *meaning*, just as when someone speaks to us in a foreign language, or in obscure terms in our own language. Hence the *hermeneutic* (interpretative) problem arises, "Do such wondrous events have meaning and what is that meaning?"

It is true, of course, that to verify or falsify a claim that a miracle has taken place requires us first to ascertain by common sense or, when available, the techniques of critical history, whether the event actually occurred and has been correctly described. Also it is necessary to show that such an event cannot be *completely* explained by some solidly established scientific laws and thus may *possibly* be miraculous. To demand, as have some reputable apologists in the past, that it must be an event that is naturally *impossible* seems impractical in view of the fact that present science refuses to go any further than to say that a given event is highly improbable.

How then can a remarkable, scientifically improbable event ever be reasonably recognized as miraculous? The answer to this question seems to lie in the fact that what is claimed for a miracle is that it is a *comunicative act,* a sensible sign that when rightly interpreted enables the human mind to understand what God is revealing. Deconstructionism has shown how difficult it is to know what is meant by any text or speech-act. Hermeneutics (interpretation) is a very subtle art that has to struggle with the complex ambiguities of any text and its various subtexts. Nevertheless, it is absurd to deny we humans do in fact often successfully communicate with each other. Science, art, and communal life would be impossible if we could not make each other understand at least some things that we say. Homer's *Iliad* was once a series of odd and seemingly unrelated sounds, just as now it is a series of odd and unrelated letters on pages, yet in spite of its antique language and literary form Homer communicates his story to the hearer or reader. Einstein's theory of gravity is a small set of mathematical symbols on a page. Once the meaning of these symbols and the truth they conveyed was recognized by only a handful of scientists, today it is widely understood, taught, and applied successfully.

In understanding any communicative act it must first be placed in its social context. The same saying that in one context is a joke, in another is deadly serious. Thus if God reveals himself it is by using a language intelligible to persons in a certain natural and cultural context. Therefore to attempt to verify prophecies and miracles solely by scientific and critical-historical methods is a category error. If miracles occur it is in such a context that they are perceived as *signs* of God's self-revelation by which we can known that they are meaningful communicative acts. Is it not possible that people in cultures other than our own were or are more sensitive to divine communication than we who are perhaps blinded by scientistic prejudices?

Yet the following objection can be raised. If God wishes to communicate with us, and wishes the revealed message to be clearly discerned, why does God not speak first to scientists in ways they can confirm by their highly developed methods of verification? Why does God not then let them assure the rest of us that such communication has taken place? The Christian answer to this, at least, is that God has preferred to talk with the humble rather than men of earthly power,[19] because it is the claim to autonomy and independence of God, so manifest in modern scientism, which has alienated humanity from God. Thus the scientist is not likely to be a willing listener to divine communication, nor an appropriate spokesman for God.

Yet this answer is not intended to favor irrationalism or depreciate science in its own proper sphere. What it is intended to do is show that the verification of revelation through miracles must be such as to be possible to human reason in every time and culture from the most primitive to the most scientifically advanced. It is unreasonable to think that God is under the necessity of subjecting his revelation to human testing by scientific methods. God reveals himself on his own terms. Although he may condescend to permit scientists to examine such alleged miracles as those of Lourdes in ways that are congenial to them, scientists cannot demand this but ought to accept whatever way God chooses to speak to us. If there is a God who speaks, we are the ones who need God's guidance, while God has no need of passing a scientific test of his power.

Therefore to look critically at the alleged biblical prophecies and miracles the proper mode of verification is to ask the following questions: (1) Is it historically certain through reliable witnesses that an extraordinary event has occurred, one not explainable by the course of nature as this is certainly known by reasonable persons in all times and cultures? (2) In their historical context do these extraordinary events that cannot be explained by natural causes or created intelligence and power communicate a message to reasonable persons of good will?

Today some biblical scholars assert that the biblical miracles were recognizable as such only by those who were already believers. While it is true that God may give a miracle to confirm and deepen the faith of those who already believe, it seems more proper that they should be accessible to those who are willing to believe what it is reasonable to believe. Those who already believe do not require to be convinced, while nonbelievers cannot reasonably believe that it is God who speaks through the prophet or inspired teacher without such signs.

5. God's Intimate Self-Revelation

Theistic religions generally hold that God reveals himself to us in a way that exceeds our own powers, because these powers have been weakened by sin. Thus Judaism credits the prophet Moses with reviving among his people the belief in the One God that had become obscured during their sojourn in idolatrous Egypt. Muslims similarly credit the prophet Muhammad with reviving Abrahamic monotheism among the idolatrous Arabs. Christians, however, while agreeing on the need of revelation to revive a knowledge of God and the moral law, evident from creation but obscured in human minds by sin, also believe that God has revealed his own inner life to humanity. God, theists believe, has done this in a way that even with minds unclouded by sin we could never discover by our own powers.

The strongest objection of Emanation Religions against the Creation Religions is that the latter are *dualists* who so oppose the many to the One, creatures to Creator, that between them no close relation seems possible. On the contrary, the Emanation Religions claim to have discovered the ultimate identity of all reality.

Nevertheless, since the Creation Religions insist that the One Creator is infinite and we creatures finite, we creatures have no natural claim to an *intimate* personal relation with God. Consistent theists, therefore, all believe that if such an intimate relation is ever to be established, it must be by a free action on God's part, by *grace*. Even the Emanation Religions to the extent they converge with monotheism have tended to develop this same concept, as for example the graciousness of Krishna to his *bhakti* devotees, or of the myriad Buddhas such as Maitreya and Amida to those who call on their names.

The ultimate gracious act of the Creator would be to admit the creature into so intimate a relation that it could be described by the metaphor of "seeing God face to face." It would be a perfect union of love and knowledge, of friendship consummated, as Christian theology has traditionally called it, by "the Beatific Vision." In Judaism and Islam, however (except for mystical writers who in these forms of theism remain on the fringes of orthodoxy) heavenly existence is pictured not so much as a face to face vision of God as a life of perfect human happiness secured by God's immediately experienced protection.[20] For orthodox Christian faith, however (if not always for popular Christianity), the Beatific Vision is the essential happiness of heaven and the ultimate meaning of salvation, just as identity or qualified identity with the Absolute is for the Emanation Religions. In this respect it seems Christianity more than Judaism and Islam converges with the Emanation Religions.

While all orthodox Christian theologians agree that the Beatific Vision is a relation which can be achieved only by God's grace, they have argued much over exactly what is gratuitous in God's intimate self-revelation.[21] Some have held that this grace consists simply in the gift of our human nature by the Creator. This gift of existence as human once freely given obliges God in justice also to provide us with a way to satisfy our natural desire as persons endowed with intelligence and free will to attain to that perfect beatitude possible only to those who share intimately in God's life. This weak concept of grace, however, seems incon-sistent with the finitude of the creature since it gives the creature an ab-solute claim to attain infinite Truth and Goodness. Certainly God would not create a finite being capable of infinite happiness. But what proves that God would have to destine us to *perfect* happiness? A finite nature has only a limited perfection; why is an absolute perfection due it?

Consequently, others place the gratuity of grace in the fact that if we are to achieve the union with God that we naturally desire, God must freely help us to achieve this goal. But this fails to explain why God is not bound in strict justice to help us satisfy a desire he has himself planted in our nature. Others, therefore, point out that "pure human nature" is a mere abstraction. Existentially, and historically we only experience human nature as both sinful and graced, incapable of being fully human unless this grace enables us effectively to seek intimate union with God. The Church Fathers never divided human life into a "natural" and a "supernatural" level, but simply taught we are created in God's image and thus can rest only in him.

Yet it can also be objected that the Church Fathers were strongly influenced by other-worldly Platonic dualism and therefore tended in their reading of the Bible to minimize the proper autonomy and value of creation and of human nature. Any theology that fails to give human nature a natural end is easily accused by Humanists of dishonoring human nature. They argue that the so-called "natural desire" for God is an illusion based on imaginary claims to "religious experiences" that many modern people do not seem to experience at all. To say that all human beings are unknowingly "anonymous Christians" is an assertion that those of other faiths find arrogant and a barrier to ecumenical discussion.

Hence, some Thomist theologians, concerned to save the absolute gratuity of grace by defending the distinction between "human nature" and grace as "supernatural," argue that, if there is a natural desire for intimate union with God, it can only be "conditional" and amounts to a "mere non-repugnance." In other words, we would desire the Vision if it were possible, but if it is possible it is so only in the sense that no contradiction has been shown in the concept. The difficulty with this view is that it seems to make God's grace entirely extrinsic to our human nature, added to it as a kind of "second story," without any organic relationship. St. Thomas Aquinas himself, who was especially concerned to free the Fathers' theology from the other-worldly rhetoric of Platonism and to defend the genuine autonomy of creation and of human nature, suggested a more nuanced solution, too often misrepresented.

Aquinas held the following. (1) Since we can know by reason that God exists, our natural *intellectual* desire to ask questions about all reality (Being) leads to questions about the inner nature of God. (2) This desire of the intellect can also elicit a natural desire in the human will for union with God as infinite Truth and Goodness. Nevertheless, since our natural knowledge of God through his effects always remains obscure, we remain free not to pursue these questions. Thus we can occupy ourselves chiefly with matters more within our human competency. (3) Yet from the fact that we have this natural capacity to wonder about God we can show that there is no contradiction in supposing that it is possible for us to be receptive to God's revelation of truths beyond our own capacity to discover them. This can take place: (a) if God freely chooses to reveal them; (b) and if these mysteries are not intrinsically incommunicable to creatures. Note that Aquinas makes no claim about the intrinsic possibility of the Vision because we know nothing of this, but only that our reason shows us no limit to the intrinsic openness of the human intelligence to all truth. We are, as far as we know, *capax Dei*, open to God. Thus without being foolish or presumptuous we can hope for what we can in no way claim by right. Our nature as such only demands a natural, limited, imperfect happiness, but it is open to a perfect happiness as a divine gift freely given in grace. Moreover the existential situation of humanity is one of great suffering. Yet there are evidences in the saints and sages of every religion that some have achieved a mysterious spiritual peace. Consequently we cannot help but wonder if perhaps the world historical drama has a meaning and a goal greater than the limits of human nature.

This position defends the completeness and autonomy of the human realm and its concerns, on which Humanists, as well as Jews and Muslims rightly insist. It maintains that, if a wise God had not chosen to invite humanity to his intimacy, a genuine but merely human fulfillment would still have been open to us. It even now remains an essential although partial and subordinate objective of our lives. On the other hand this position strongly defends the absolute gratuity of grace and (in keeping with the negative theology of Eastern thought) the transcendence of the supernatural realm. Yet, without making any unprovable claims to some kind of a universal "experience of grace," it provides a natural opening to question whether or not God has freely chosen to reveal himself to us beyond any claim of our own. We have the natural capacity and intellectual need to ask this question, the freedom to search for an answer, and we see a serious probability that the answer may be joyfully affirmative.

The great mathematician and apologist Pascal pointed out an interesting fact to a worldly gentleman not interested in ultimate questions but who was well acquainted with gambling logic: that the odds favor the one who takes seriously enough the claims of Christianity to devote some time to their honest examination. If the gentleman does not, and the claims are true, his loss is infinite, but if they are false he only loses a little time and trouble.[22]

6. How Theism Includes the Other World-Views

Thus we can conclude that all the monotheistic Creation Religions claim that God communicates with us through prophets, often humble persons rejected by the humanly wise and powerful. Moreover, these theistic religions hold that God makes the fact of revelation rationally credible through miraculous signs and prophecy-fulfilling historical events. These are objectively knowable (but not necessarily scientifically verifiable) to those to whom they are relevant, who are open minded, and who rely on the ordinary tests of common sense to discern the meaning and reliability of the message.

Therefore the Creation Religions are, above all, religions of the Word of God, of God's self-revelation to humanity in the language of humanity. Today there are hermeneutical deconstructionists who claim that real communication between persons is impossible, because I only hear you saying what I think myself, and vice versa. Of course there is a large measure of truth in this disillusionment. We experience how alone each one of us is. How difficult it is really to communicate with another! And yet we also experience that genuine communication does take place, because it is also true that what I think has largely been learned from others. For the Creation Religions ultimately all that we know has been revealed to our reason or faith by God who alone knows anything independently. His revelation of himself to us takes place through nature and history, and, for Christian monotheism, culminates in an intimate communication by grace, not merely to correct human error but also to elevate human nature to an intimate relation with God in his inner life. This intimate mystical union is analogous to that sought by the Emanation Religions but one which remains eternally "I to Thou," and therefore which does not obliterate the monotheistic distinction between Creator and creature.

Thus in seeking a world-view and value-system there is a great advantage in choosing one of the theistic religions, since these religions more fully develop the monotheism to which the Emanation Religions tend as they rise above the polytheism of the Mythological Religions, but which they fail to reach. A perfect religion ought not only promise salvation from suffering but should lead us to intimate union with God. In this respect both the Emanation and Creation Religions have a great advantage over Humanism for which the mortal human person has temporal autonomy but no clear future. Yet the theistic Creation Religions also have a great advantage over the Emanation Religions. Unlike the latter the Creation Religions do not present this union with God as the absorption of the autonomous human persons into the Absolute, but preserve the unique existence of each as the permanent gift of God. In this respect the Creation Religions preserve that human autonomy that is the supreme value for Humanism, but also promise a real participation in the total and eternal autonomy of God. Moreover, the Creation Religions, by the doctrine of the resurrection, overcome the depreciation of the material body in comparison to the spiritual soul that is a negative feature of the Emanation Religions and with it such gloomy doctrines as the Wheel of Reincarnation and the Eternal Return. Yet in all the theistic religions there have been mystics as great as those that are found in the Emanation Religions. These theistic religions promise that this mystical union can be reached in this life not just by persons who have undergone countless reincarnations, but by any believer in God's revelation who is open in faith to divine grace.

Finally the Creation Religions have value-systems in which the love of God and neighbor is significant in a way that is not possible in Emanation Religions, since for them human persons last only until they are reabsorbed in God. Nor is this possible in Humanism where persons simply return to the earth from whence they came. For the Creation Religions the love for God and neighbor is forever, since all created persons will come to share in the eternity of a Personal God. This is not to deny that the Emanation Religions just as they tend to monotheism so also tend to an ethic of love. Nor is it to deny that their search for a mystical union with God often shames those of the Creation Religions who become forgetful that their ultimate goal also is such a mystical union. Thus ecumenical dialogue between these world-views and value-systems can be fruitful and convergent.

Notes

[1] For a general introduction to this problem see Michael Barns, *Christian Identity and Religious Pluralism: Religions in Conversation* (Nashville, TN: Abingdon Press, 1989) and J.A. DiNoia, OP, *The Diversity of Religions: A Christian Perspective* (Washington, DC: Catholic University of America Press, 1994).

[2] See Edward L. Cleary, *Crisis and Change: The Church in Latin America Today* (Maryknoll, NY: Orbis Books, 1985), pp. 51-103.

[3] In *Science and the Modern World* (New York: Macmillan, 2nd ed., 1926).

[4] R.C. Zaehner, *Concordant Discord* (Oxford: Oxford University Press, 1970) discusses at length the problems of dialogue between theistic and non-theistic religions. See also Harvey D. Egan, SJ, *What Are They Saying About Mysticism* (New York: Paulist Press, 1982).

[5] For a concise introduction to the thought of Plotinus see the article of Philip Merlan, "Plotinus" in *The Encyclopedia of Philosophy,* ed. Paul Edwards (New York: Macmillan, 1967), vol. 6, pp. 351-59. Plotinus' disciple Porphyry says that his master had traveled in (northwest) India.

[6] See Hajime Nakamura, *Ways of Thinking of Eastern Peoples: India-China-Tibet-Japan* (Honolulu: East-West Center Press, 1964) on the "phenomenalism" and "this-worldliness" of Zen, pp. 366-89.

[7] See David Leroy Miller, *The New Polytheism* (New York: Harper and Row, 1974); Judith Ochshorn, *The Female Experience and the Nature of the Divine* (Bloomington, IN: Indiana University Press, 1981); Alain Danielou, *The Gods of India: Hindu Polytheism* (New York: Inner Traditions International, 1985) for sympathetic discussions of polytheism.

[8] There has been much controversy over the argument of St. Thomas Aquinas (*Summa Contra Gentiles* III, c. 50, etc.), for the possibility of the Beatific Vision of God based on a "natural desire" to see God which, because natural, cannot be vain. In my opinion this argument is valid if this desire is taken as a positive tendency of the intellect to know all Being, including the Ground of Being. Yet it proves only that on the part of the human subject the Beatific Vision is not impossible but highly desirable, while on the part of the Vision itself it is not, as far as we know, impossible. See Antoninus Finili, OP, "Natural Desire," *Dominican Studies* vol. 1, Oct. 1948 (Blackfriars Publications: Oxford): 1-61.

[9] See Ninian Smart, *The Religious Experiences of Mankind,* 2nd ed. (New York: Charles Scribner's Sons, 1976), pp. 10-15.

[10] New York: Barnes and Noble, 1962, p. 1.

[11] St. Thomas Aquinas held that Jesus in his humanity possessed the Beatific Vision and hence transcended faith, even in this life and that perhaps this was momentarily true for some prophets or mystics such as Moses. Cf. *Summa Theologiae,* III, q. 10, a. 1.

[12] See Avery Dulles, *Revelation Theology: A History* (New York: Herder and Herder, 1969).

[13] See Louis Mondin, *Signs and Wonders* (New York: Desclée, 1966); Richard Swinburne, *The Concept of Miracle* (New York: Macmillan, St. Martin's Press, 1970); R. Douglas Geivett and Gary R. Habermas, *In Defense of Miracles* (Downers Grove, IL: InterVarsity Press, 1997).

[14] See Reijer Hooykaas, *The Principle of Uniformity in Geology, Biology, and Theology:*

Natural Law and Divine Miracle (Leiden: Brill, 1963); Robert D. Smith, *Comparative Miracles* (St. Louis: B. Herder, 1965); Cohn Brown, *Miracles and the Critical Mind* (Grand Rapids, MI: W.B. Eerdmans, 1984) for various opinions.

[15] See Werner Heisenberg, *The Physicist's Conception of Nature* (London: Hutchinson, 1958) for the twentieth century understanding of the laws of nature.

[16] An effort of this sort is Michael P. Carroll, *The Cult of the Virgin Mary: Psychological Origins* (Princeton, NJ: Princeton University Press, 1986) who attempts to explain Marian apparitions (cf. p. 218) as due to suggestion to people intensely excited by some unusual situation and whose world-view favors such expectations. But such psychological factors are not new discoveries and must have been considered by the serious investigators of the genuineness of these apparitions. See René Laurentin, *Lourdes: Dossier des documents authentique,* 3 vols. (Paris: Lethielleux, 1958), summarized in his *Bernadette of Lourdes* (Minneapolis, MN: Winston Press, 1979).

[17] For details on the Lourdes miracles see Patrick Marnham, *Lourdes: A Modern Pilgrimage* (Garden City, NY: Doubleday/Image, 1980).

[18] On claims for mind-body identity based on artificial intelligence see Roger Penrose, *The Emperor's New Mind: Concerning Computers, Minds, and the Laws of Physics* (New York: Oxford University Press, 1989). For current criticisms of the unscientific character of psychoanalytic theory see *Freud Evaluated: The Completed ARC,* Foreword by Freda Crews (New York: Malcom/Macmillan, 1998).

[19] "At that time Jesus said in reply, 'I give praise to you, Father, Lord of heaven and earth, for although you have hidden these things from the wise and learned you have revealed them to the childlike. Yes, Father, such has been your gracious will'" (Mt 11:25). This saying is thought to be from the earliest stratum of Tradition Q, cf. Lk 10:21; 1 Cor 1:27.

[20] On Jewish views of future life see Rabbi Leonard B. Gewirtz, *Jewish Spirituality: Hope and Redemption* (Hoboken, NJ: KTAV Publishers, 1986), especially pp. 42-49, and *Encyclopedia Judaica,* vol. 15, article, "Soul, Immortality of," pp. 174-82. On Islamic views see Jane Idleman Smith and Yvonne Yazbeck Haddad, *The Islamic Understanding of Death and Resurrection* (Albany: State University of New York Press, 1981). Also cf. Seyyed Hossein Nasr, *Islamic Spirituality: Foundations,* vol. 19 of *World Spirituality: An Encyclopedic History of the Religious Question* (New York: Crossroad, 1987), pp. 378-409.

[21] See note 8 above. Henri de Lubac, SJ, *The Mystery of the Supernatural* (New York: Herder and Herder, 1967) started a controversy by defending the pre-Thomistic Augustinian view according to which human nature is intrinsically oriented to the Beatific Vision although it cannot attain it without grace. Thomists generally argue that this fails to do justice to either nature or grace.

[22] *Pensées,* translated by A.J. Krailsheimer (Harmondsworth: Penguin Books, 1966), 149 (430 Brunschvicq), pp. 76-80. For discussion see Nicholas Rescher, *Pascal's Wager* (Notre Dame, IN: University of Notre Dame Press, 1985).

CHAPTER 7

THE ECUMENICAL CHURCH: SIGN OF GOD'S SELF-COMMUNICATION

1. The Search for a Revelatory Sign

In the last chapter I argued that we must recognize that if God freely chooses to reveal himself to all of us, he may also choose to do so to most of us through chosen prophets just as in nature he causes most of his effects through secondary causes. Since the hearers of the message are not themselves gifted with prophetic insight they are not competent to judge its inner truth. Hence, it seems necessary for God to certify the authenticity of his chosen messengers by outer visible signs so that these hearers might be able to discern true prophets from false.

But in our actual experience are there really such miraculous signs pointing us to a divine self-communication more intimate and complete than that to what creation testifies? Surely we have an obligation to keep our eyes open for the possible presence of such signs. Yet we cannot lay down conditions for God to fulfill if he is to speak to us. To say, "I will believe if you do so and so" is an attitude of control. It can close us off from that attitude of openness and willingness to learn that must be the basic condition on our part to be able to hear God, as it is to hear a human friend. The receiver cannot control a free gift such as friendship, or it would not be free.

To look for such revelatory signs, it seems reasonable to turn at once to the Creation Religions, not because God may not be revealing himself in the other religions (it seems likely he is), but because these other religions do not themselves even claim to be revelatory. Humanism supposes that God, if he exists, is silent. The Emanation Religions do not exclude revelation in the strict sense but do not consider it necessary because for them there is no ultimate distinction between the Absolute and the human spirit. Thus for them "revelation" can only mean the rending of the veil of illusion by the enlightened sage by which he discovers his preexisting identity with the Absolute. But if we acknowledge a creator God in the strict sense of *creatio ex nihilo*, then we creatures can know God only if he reveals himself to us either through creation or through prophecy and miracles attested to our senses and reason by signs.

Thus it is to these Creation Religions we must first look to see if they can point out such signs to justify their claims. Moreover, since Christianity claims to be a specification of Judaism and regards Islam as a simplification of the Judaeo-Christian tradition, it will be convenient to consider the claims of Christianity first, and then to compare these with those of Judaism and Islam.

Within the many versions of Christianity how shall we go about asking whether it constitutes a revelatory sign? The Churches of the Reformation in their apologetic generally argue (as Muslims do for the *Qur'an*) that when the Bible is read in the light of the Holy Spirit it is self-authenticating.[1] Converted Christians can recognize the Word of God in the Bible and when it is preached from the Bible simply by the fact of its power to convert them to repentance and faith.[2] Yet only those seem to be convinced by this argument that assume, as the Reformers did, the credibility of the traditional reverence for the Bible as the Word of God. Those who have never accepted this assumption or who have come to question it because of the countless difficulties raised by modern historical scholarship find the logic of this argument circular. Only when the claim that the Bible is God's Word rests on the guarantee of its authenticity and canonicity by the tradition of a living community, the Church, is this claim credible and able to withstand the attacks of historical criticism. Yet the Church's witness to the Bible's divine inspiration is also circular unless public signs authenticate it.

Consequently the pre-Reformation Church both in the East and West claimed that the Church itself was a sign of God's self-revelation by reason of the "four marks of the Church" mentioned in the Nicene-Constantinopolitan Creed, "I believe in one, holy, catholic, and apostolic Church." The Orthodox Church still claims that its unique possession of these "marks" is sufficient to show that it alone is the true Church of Christ and that its teaching is to be believed on divine faith. Yet the Orthodox also hold that only an ecumenical council of orthodox bishops can definitively declare the faith of the Church. Furthermore, they recognize no such council since the Seventh (Nicaea II) in 787. Does this not raise a serious difficulty in discussing the Orthodox claim to have the marks of the Church now? How can one ascertain these marks in a Church that seems unable to declare the faith in a definitive manner to us today?[3]

The Catholic Church in communion with the Bishop of Rome claims that its recent Second Vatican Council was ecumenical, although only some Orthodox bishops were present and then only as observers. This Council declared as follows.[4]

> This is the sole Church of Christ that in the Creed we profess to be one, holy, catholic and apostolic. This Church, constituted and organized as a society in the present world, subsists in the Catholic Church, that is governed by the successor of Peter and the bishops in communion with him. Nevertheless, many elements of sanctification and of truth are found outside its visible confines. Since these are gifts belonging to the Church of Christ, they are forces impelling toward Catholic unity.

This phrasing was carefully chosen to indicate that the Catholic Church does not deny that Christ's Church also somehow includes the other churches, at least those with valid baptism, and especially the Orthodox Churches whose bishops it continues to recognize.

Vatican II also confirmed the claim explicitly defined at the first Vatican Council (1870) that the Church is a "moral miracle." By this is meant that, in contrast to physical miracles of healing etc.,[5] the Church is a sufficient sign present in the world today. By its presence and activity, therefore, anyone can objectively come to see that the Gospel of Jesus Christ as the Church proclaims it is God's self-revelation. Hence all who are able to recognize the meaning of this sign are morally obliged in honesty to believe the Gospel proclaimed by the Church and follow it in their lives. In other words, the Catholic Church claims that just as Jesus' message because of his character and his deeds should have been believed by his contemporaries, so he remains present today in his Church and manifest to the world.

This tremendous claim is bound to seem to many quite preposterous today at a time when all human institutions, and "organized religion" in particular, are regarded with suspicion. This is no doubt why Vatican II, although it reaffirmed that the Church is a moral miracle, did not emphasize this teaching. It is probably also why Catholic apologists since Vatican II tend to avoid reference to the moral miracle of the Church or even to miraculous signs and prophecies altogether, and to seek a different and more subjective route to faith.[6]

They have even abandoned the term "apologetics" for "fundamental theology." The task of such a foundational theology, therefore, is to uncover in our actual experiences, whether as explicit or implicit Christians, those tendencies that constitute us as persons, self-conscious, free subjects capable of interpersonal relationships. In doing so we become aware of the transcendental conditions that are presupposed by every attempt to make sense out of human experience. In the light of this intuitive understanding of what it is to be existentially human, we can come to recognize that in Jesus Christ and in his Church (historically realized most manifestly in the Roman Catholic Church) all these conditions are fulfilled. It is hoped that this "approach from the subject" ends in a correlation between subjective experience and the interpersonally shared experience of a public community, because the human subject is essentially social and political. In Chapter 5, however, it was shown that the philosophy on which such an apologetics is based suffers from the problems of Kantian idealism.

Such approaches from the subject are certainly designed to appeal to the "modern mind" of the Western intelligentsia and the culture that they influence. If we are to be open to God's revelation we must come to know ourselves better in our subjectivity, since an inauthentic understanding of what it is to be human blocks our openness to any reality transcending ourselves and the biases of our culture. Yet the political and liberation theologians are certainly right in criticizing this approach to faith as too much conditioned by a narrowly academic outlook rooted in Cartesian and Kantian philosophy and reflecting the isolation of intellectuals in our capitalistic, technological society.[7] Instead, liberation theology favors an approach that begins with the experienced need of the oppressed mass of humanity. It then claims for the Gospel and for the Church, as a community of hope and common action, the mission from God to lead the oppressed to realize the Reign of God in justice and peace on earth.

Do either of these two newer approaches (one transcendental and subjective, the other objective and prophetically political) replace the older purely objective one from the Church as a moral miracle, recommended by Vatican I and II? The two newer approaches are at odds in that one finds the signs of authenticity in the correlation of the Church's message and life with the religious experience of its members or prospective members, and the other in the effective prophetic message of the Church for social action. Yet both admit that God can make himself known to us only by some sign that is accessible to us not merely as private but as social, public persons. Thus neither approach can entirely dispense with the Church's public witness that to be credible must somehow be marked with signs of its right to speak for God.

2. Ecumenicity as Miraculous

Vatican II only confirmed the notion of Vatican I of "moral miracle" without explicitly developing the theme. Instead it thematized the notion of ecumenicity, both in the narrow sense of a search for unity among Christians, and in the broader sense of a search for unity among all religions and philosophies of life.[8] In our times when many ways of life confront each other and when the divisions within the Church stand as a major obstacle to an effective witness to the Gospel, the Church has a special need to open herself to honest and charitable dialogue with all other views. To be truly "catholic" or universal the Church must not only defend itself, but must also renounce offensive tactics and become accessible to all, while not ceasing to be faithful to the Gospel the Church was founded to witness.

This requires Catholic theologians to rethink the traditional "four marks" of the Church formulated in the Nicene Creed that the scholastics systematized in terms of the Aristotelian notion of the "four causes": unity (formal), holiness (final), catholicity (material) and apostolicity (efficient).[9] If we rethink these marks in terms of ecumenicity we find them transformed in a very interesting way. A church that seeks to be truly ecumenical is first of all "materially" open and *catholic*, inclusive, not necessarily in formal membership, but in the desire to establish a human community with all. It cannot be content if on its part there is anyone it excludes from this concern.

Second, in its *unity* it does not seek merely to find a *modus vivendi* with others. It goes further to enter "formally" into a developing communication with them, a greater and greater sharing of life and all its benefits, so that this "community" becomes a genuine "co-unity," respectful of the unique gifts of individuals and of their existing communities. It does not desire to obliterate or absorb these into uniformity but to become a genuine *in pluribus unum*.

Third, in its *holiness* it is integrally fulfilling (final causality) in that it seeks to share with a common good that centers in a transcendent, intimate relation with God. Thus it brings to everyone in this community whatever is necessary for their "salvation," i.e., their conquest of the evils and injustices of life and their full sharing in its riches.

Fourth, in its *apostolicity* it is "efficiently" divinely empowered (graced) since it has the vitality to overcome the barriers that in human communities prevent the other three qualities from developing. In these last two respects the ecumenicity of the Church ought to transcend the kind of inclusiveness possible to secular community because it is truly religious, i.e., it touches on those matters that are of ultimate concern as the Creation Religions define these concerns. It is such questions that divide people most profoundly and are most difficult to reconcile, or even to dialogue about. Thus its ecumenicity flows from and synthesizes its correlative four marks of unity, catholicity, holiness, and apostolicity.

But how is this complex ecumenicity evidently miraculous? Certainly not in the sense that a kind of ecumenicity is lacking to secular society that also seeks to build a world community so that human needs will be better satisfied. Moreover a certain ecumenicity is also a trait of other religions such as Buddhism or Islam. Nevertheless, it is evident that in the human condition nothing is more difficult than to overcome the human divisiveness that produces national and class wars, and racial, sexual, and religious discrimination. To overcome these in a fundamental way requires a kind of peacemaking that touches the abyss of the human mind and heart inaccessible even to the techniques of depth psychology. Those who have thought that social or economic revolution will bring human unity find themselves bitterly disillusioned. Reconciliation between human beings requires forgiveness, willingness not to judge, and hope for reconciliation that are impossible without a spiritual transformation of the parties.

If we accept the basic tenet of the Creation Religions that God is the Creator of the universe and immediately of the human spirit in its intelligence and freedom we can only look to him to effect such a spiritual transformation. Therefore if this transformation takes place it is in the fullest sense a "moral miracle." Hence a religious community that manifests ecumenicity in all the mutually conditioning (*causae sunt invicem causae*) traits just mentioned certainly must be a sign of God's self-revelation. Thus we have the criteria by which we can hope to identify such a sign.

3. Catholicity, the Sign of Inclusive Care

The most evident fact that can be verified by visiting any urban Catholic church for Mass on Sunday morning, is its inclusiveness, that is, its openness to a great variety of human beings, of every color, sex, age, and social condition. That this catholicity is an essential feature of Christianity is obvious from what seems to be admitted by almost all scholars as historically true, namely, that Jesus of Nazareth, contrary to the attitude of the religious leaders of his time, taught and acted in a totally inclusive manner.[10] He broke down the barriers that separated human beings and manifested a special and very personal concern for the marginalized women, poor, lepers, prostitutes, the pariahs, the powerless, and ignorant whom he met. With open arms he invited all into his community, and its elite were taught to become themselves the servants of the lowest of the low. Although he announced that his mission was directly to his own people, the Jews, when the occasion presented itself he deliberately broke through this limitation (Mk 7:24-30) and his disciples were empowered to extend his mission to all (Mt 28:19). After the first serious doctrinal struggle in the early Church, St. Paul succeeded in establishing this inclusiveness in a formal and definitive way confirmed by St. Peter (Ac 15:1-29) in what is reckoned as the First Ecumenical Council at Jerusalem.

It is true that denominational divisions have sometimes produced Christian Churches that have been restricted to a single nationality, as in some of the autocephalic Eastern Churches or the State Churches of Germany and England; or to a particular social class such as the Dutch Reformed Church of South Africa. Nevertheless, Christianity as a whole, and the Catholic Church in particular, has always been and remains comprehensive and even aggressively inclusive, consistently working through its missionary activities to cross every national, racial, and cultural barrier. While the Church is not always successful in this catholicity, it is evident that the Church keeps trying to become completely catholic. This concern for inclusiveness that marked Jesus and his immediate followers signifies that if God communicates to us through this Church he is revealing himself as a God who wants to extend his message of salvation through his chosen human messengers to all humankind without exception.

Yet is the Catholic Church really inclusive since it excludes heretics, the excommunicated, those married after divorce, those heterosexually active outside marriage, and active homosexuals?[11] The Church replies that it cannot condone all kinds of behavior, because to do so would nullify its obligation to teach the moral truth that the Church claims to teach in the name of God. Sin is sin not because there is a law, even a divine law, let alone a Church law, that forbids it. It is sin because it harms God's creatures, their relations to one another, and their union with God. Hence the Church would not be a caring community if it failed to protest against the harm of sin and reinforce its protest with sanctions. Its only real sanction is excommunication by which it announces that those who persist in certain scandalous sins have excluded themselves from the sacraments that are the signs of *public* participation in the Church's common life. Yet those excommunicated are not excluded from the Church's care, since it prays for them and, like Jesus, seeks the lost sheep's return (Lk 15:1-7; cf. St. Paul, 2 Cor 2:1-4 urging love for an excommunicated man). The Church is always ready to receive them into full forgiveness and communion when they are willing to return to the Christian life. The Church is obliged to do this by Jesus' own words about the love to be shown even to enemies (Mt 5:43-48) and the prodigal (Lk 15:11-32). Of course today women protest their exclusion from the priesthood, but being a priest does not make one any more a member of the Church than being a layperson. Priesthood is a particular office of service to the members of the Church, but it does not entitle one to receive anything essential to the common good of the Church, namely the means to holiness. These are as open to women as to men and it would seem that women have always been more ready to receive them. As for the exclusion of homosexuals, the real issue is whether this condition is to be judged a normal variety of sexuality, or a difficult problem for the Christian seeking to live in conformity with the purposes for which God created us men and women. The Church does not exclude homosexuals but seeks to help them live in a way that she is convinced will be for their real happiness, rather than to be a facilitator of their denial of their problem. Thus the Church excludes no one from her care; but care, to be genuine, must be based on truth not on making people comfortable.

But do not all the other monotheistic religions teach that God is concerned for all his human creatures? Certainly this can be said for both Judaism and Islam and it proves the authenticity of their witness to the One God.[12] It is essential to the vocation of the Jews that they recall the many prophetic predictions in the Hebrew Scriptures that belief in the God of Abraham will be offered to all humanity in the Messianic Age (e.g., Is 2:23; Mi 4:13; Ps 87, etc.). Since the destruction of the Temple, Judaism in the diaspora has been preoccupied with survival. While it admits converts and at certain times and places has put some energy into gaining such converts, nevertheless throughout its entire history its fundamental stance is that its task is to bear faithful witness to the One God. As such it continues to look toward the Messianic Age in the future when all nations come to recognize God.

Judaism does not see itself as commissioned to carry on an active work of building this universal religious community here and now. Its membership is defined not so much by faith as by heredity. An unbelieving Jew (provided he has not openly rejected his Jewishness) remains a member of the religious community. A convert who has passed through a requisite purification also becomes a Jew in the racial as well as the religious sense.

Moreover, for Orthodox Judaism the distinctions of cultic purity, whose purpose is precisely to stress this exclusiveness of the Chosen People, continues as an essential feature of membership in the religious community. Finally, even for the secular Zionists the future of Judaism is believed to be linked to the "Land" and to Jerusalem. Thus although the Hebrew Scriptures clearly teach the catholicity of God's self-revelation, in Judaism it remains restricted until the Messianic Age. Hence Judaism is not a missionary, but a diaspora religion, giving witness throughout the world. Even if in Israel the Temple were to be rebuilt, as some radicals hope, can it really be imagined that the animal sacrifices prescribed by the Torah would again be revived?

Islam is usually considered a missionary religion, and it certainly is an expansionist religion, whose worldwide spread is comparable to that of Christianity. This expansion stems from Muhammad's claim to be the Seal of the Prophets, the ultimate prophet. Many other prophets had before his time been sent to all the other peoples by God, but in time their message became forgotten or corrupted. In the *Qur'an* the message is given in its absolute and final form, so that no further prophecy is necessary. The *Qur'an* is a message for all and Islam is remarkable for its concept of the universal brotherhood of those who have made their submission (Islam) to the One God. Nevertheless, Islam's conception of mission differs significantly from that of Christianity. Originally and for a long period the Islamic community was predominantly Arab or at least under Arab hegemony. From the *Qur'an* it is not clear that Muhammad thought of himself as more than a prophet for the Arabian Peninsula. Yet the original expansion of Islam began soon after his death to extend to the whole Near East and North Africa. It was conducted by the *jihad* (striving, struggle) based on statements in the *Qur'an*. While *jihad* can mean spiritual struggle (asceticism), it clearly also includes military combat to protect Islam from its enemies and was so carried on by Muhammad himself and is continued as an obligation on all male Muslims.[13]

Although the *Qur'an* forbids forced conversion and commands toleration of the "People of the Book" (Jews and Christians) as long as they do not subvert Islamic law, it also commands continual warfare (unless for temporary truce under treaty) against pagans. The usual procedure has been to offer peace on the condition of conversion, and if this is not accepted then to proceed to war until the others submit to the conditions set by the Muslims. It is true that Islam also spread peacefully into Southeast Asia and is now spreading rapidly in sub-Saharan Africa through the influence of merchants and the religious brotherhoods, but this does not exclude the *jihad* if this becomes necessary, as the rise of militant "Islamic Fundamentalism" demonstrates.

Jesus refused the use of force, even in his own defense (Mt 26:51-54). The Christian Church like Islam has claimed the right to defend herself by force, and has even (contrary to its own teaching) used force to make converts. Yet the Church has been conscious that it is difficult to square this with its Founder's teaching and example of nonviolence. Hence the Church has not dared to rely on it, but has always taught that pacific martyrdom is to be preferred.[14] "Martyrdom" for Islam often means death in battle. As a religion it was founded by a prophet who himself led his forces into combat and set a pattern for forcible expansion of *Dar Islam*, the "realm of submission" to God. Thus for Islam in principle there is no distinction between state and religion as, at least in principle, there has always been for Christianity (Mk 12:17). This principle was maintained even under the "Constantinian Establishment" when the notion of Christendom somewhat paralleled that of *Dar Islam*. The proof of this is that the Pope always maintained his religious superiority to the Emperor even when forced to endure the secular ruler's political dominion.[15]

As for the Emanation Religions, Buddhism has made remarkable missionary efforts in Tibet, China, Korea, Japan and Southeast Asia that parallel and may antedate Christian and Islamic missions.[16] Nevertheless, it is obvious that for Emanation Religions, since they reject any ultimate distinction between God and human persons and teach the transmigration of souls, missionary activity has an essentially different meaning than it has in the Creation Religions.

Although Buddhists found communities of monks, these communities exist only to support the life of each individual monk on his way to Nirvana in which the reality of community disappears. This contrasts sharply with the Christian idea of community, a participation in the community of the One Triune God. The purpose of the Buddhist missions is to expose the errors that produce the world's sufferings in order that the empirical world, including all human persons, may be recognized as "empty." The missions of the Creation Religions, on the other hand, are directed to forming an eternal community of human persons centered in God but never identified with him.

The Christian Church, therefore, can be experienced today among all the human communities of the world as characterized by its active concern for every human person on earth. This is because every person is created in God's image and called to eternal life with him, a call that must be answered not by force but freely. It transcends those limitations of nationality, race, or culture that restrict political, economic, or cultural communities, and it is committed to respect the human freedom of membership in a way that Muslims with their Qur'anic political commitment to extend *Dar Islam* are not.

While this inclusiveness is by no means wholly absent from the other world religions, it is not explicit in their essential teachings and practice. What this fact makes objectively clear is not that the Christian Church is superior to other religious institutions but that there is something specific about the message it seeks to communicate and exemplify. This message is that God reveals himself as the God who extends his care to all humanity without exception in a way that completely respects their freedom as persons, transcending all cultural boundaries. This Church can be experienced today in local Christian communities and globally as universal in this inclusiveness or catholicity of its membership, not always perfectly but essentially.

4. Unity, the Sign of the Church as Community

The specific catholicity of the Christian Church, especially as this subsists in the Roman Catholic Church that more clearly transcends ethnicity or nationalism than do either the Eastern or Protestant Churches, cannot be fully appreciated without also considering the unity that makes it truly a community. Of late some theologians speak of Christianity as the "Jesus movement" in order to minimize its institutional character. But this terminology quite fails to recognize the uniqueness of the Church (*kyriakon*, "the Lord's House") that in the New Testament is called the *ecclesia*, "a community called together," and "the Body of Christ" because of its organic (structured and cooperatively functional) character.

What do we experience when we meet the Catholic Church as community? Its mode of existence is most evident in the act of worshiping God on a Sunday morning. For Christians this is at the Eucharistic liturgy that normally includes reading the Scriptures and preaching. With Protestants frequently the Eucharist is omitted (a few denominations have a purely "spiritual" Eucharist) and the service is reduced to Scripture reading and preaching, while sometimes with Catholics and Orthodox the preaching is omitted. Moreover in the Catholic and Orthodox tradition the liturgical hours consisting in psalmody and Scripture reading are also official forms of worship although not generally attended by the laity.

Although a few sects permit any Christian to preside at the Eucharist, in the great majority of churches the president is an ordained male presbyter (recently in some Protestant churches a woman) who acts in the name of Christ. He presides and preaches with an authority that shares in the authority of the original Twelve chosen by Christ to represent him.[17] Thus the fundamental structure of a local Christian Church is that of an elder commissioned to preside at the Eucharist and to expound the Scriptures according to the living tradition of the community as the representative of Christ, the invisible head of the Church. In the power of Christ he is to call people to faith and repentance, and to declare to them Christ's forgiveness of sins.

The members of the community, the laity (*laos*, "people," of which the presbyter is himself one and in need of the very gifts that he distributes) under his presidency worship as a community. They praise and thank God, praying not only for their individual needs but for the needs of the community (in the Catholic and Orthodox Churches for the needs of even the deceased members), and expressing mutual love and forgiveness in the name of Christ.

In some Protestant Churches each local church is independent (congregational polity), although in practice such churches band together in some kind of conference. Others have a larger structure based on a *presbyterium* or assembly of elders, usually with a presiding elder. Many Protestant Churches and all Catholics and Orthodox have a bishop who is the pastor ("shepherd") of a local church of which the presbyters are assistants presiding over smaller assemblies. In the Orthodox Churches the bishops are united through a patriarch or chief bishop for an autocephalous, national church. For the Catholics the Roman patriarch is the chief bishop and head of all local churches.

What is first of all significant in these institutional arrangements is that for Christians, whatever their differences about the details of church structure, the Church is conceived as a single, worldwide community. This community shares in the Eucharist, the Scriptures, and a tradition by which these Scriptures are authentically interpreted. Except in a few sects, such a Christian community has a leadership of ordained ministers (servants) hierarchically ordered to provide both for the local and the universal Church. Membership in this community is based on the rite of baptism that signifies a unity in faith in Christ. Today as the ecumenical movement[18] toward reunion of the various Churches advances, it becomes more and more clear that this fundamental structure has never been lost, although it has been weakened and confused by various abuses and only partially successful attempts to correct them.

Nor does this unity consist only in the act of worship although it is experienced there ideally. All the major Christian Churches subscribe to the same canon of Scriptures (except for the minor issue of the deuterocanonical books of the Old Testament), to the Nicene Creed and to the value system of the Ten Commandments and the Sermon on the Mount. Recent ecumenical discussions have made evident that the differences between them are probably capable of a hermeneutic solution. The real source of division paradoxically seems to be over the understanding of the very feature that the Gospels indicate as a unifying principle, namely the primacy of St. Peter among the Apostles and its consequences for papal authority. Catholics claim that the authority of this Petrine papal office is justified by the biblical account of the appointment by Jesus of Peter as head of the Twelve (Mt 16:13-20; 15-17, etc.).[19] Even on this matter the issue may be not so much the existence of the authority as the manner in which it has been exercised.[20]

This basic unity of worship, government, and teaching exists in the Christian Church in spite of its catholicity that produces an immense cultural, racial, and social heterogeneity in its membership in a way that is quite different from that of other religions. Thus in the Emanation Religions, except on a very local or sectarian level, there is no unity of worship, but a multiplicity of cults of various gods, each of which constitutes for its worshipers a preferred symbol of the Absolute. The closest parallels to a Christian Church, such as the Tibetan Buddhist hierarchy around the Dalai or Pachen Lamas, the former Taoist hierarchy, the Emperor worship of Japan, or the former official Confucianism of China are all confined to restricted localities and particular cultures supported by the political system.

As to the other two theistic religions, Judaism is united by its devotion to its Scriptures and tradition but lacks all organic structure except an ethnic identity or a local, sectarian community. Its present efforts to find this unity in the support of Israel are more secular than religious. Islam, on the other hand, is certainly united by its adherence to the *Qur'an* and the Holy Shrines and is flawed only by sectarian differences of interpretation analogous to those within Christianity. But its organic structure as a community was originally maintained by the political rather than religious Caliphate. After that decline, it has never been able to find more than a local unity of action.[21]

The most unusual feature of the unity of the Christian Church is that it rests not merely on monotheism, a truth accessible to reason, as do Judaism and Islam, but on mysteries beyond the power of human understanding such as the Trinity and Incarnation that are difficult to believe. This difficulty is evident from the splintering of the Protestant Churches over doctrinal questions leaving them open to liberal conformity to Humanism on the one hand and on the other to obscurantist reactions such as Fundamentalism. But the Orthodox and Catholic Churches have shown a remarkable unity of belief in such mysteries in spite of all the vicissitudes of history and the present pressures of Humanism.

In the Orthodox Churches, however, as we currently experience them, this unity of belief has often been sustained only by a static conservatism that makes very difficult an organic development of doctrine.[22] Without such development these Churches still continue to witness to the first seven ecumenical councils, but find serious problems in presenting the Gospel to the world in a way that takes account of the changes of modern times. On the other hand, the Roman Catholic Church, as demonstrated by Vatican II, unlike the Protestant Churches, has been able to maintain all the doctrines of the undivided Church and yet unlike the Orthodox Churches continue a homogeneous doctrinal development and adaptation to modern times.

So trustful is the Roman Catholic Church of its guidance by the Holy Spirit in these developments that it has declared the infallibility of the Church as a whole (to that the Orthodox but not most Protestants would agree) in its definitive teaching. Furthermore (and to this the Orthodox have not agreed) the Roman Catholic Church maintains this infallibility of the whole Church is expressed by the bishops of the Church in communion with the successor of St. Peter, or by the Pope alone speaking for the whole Church. This makes it possible for this Church to insist that its members accept definite and clearly expressed doctrines, while permitting a considerable range of theological interpretation of these doctrines. This eventually produced a genuine but self-consistent development of doctrine throughout its history.[23]

It is this insistence on centralized doctrinal authority to maintain unity that, as already mentioned, has paradoxically become the crux of division between Catholic, Orthodox, and Protestant Christians. No doubt the Roman Church in its conviction of its responsibility for the unity of the Christian community has sometimes exceeded its authority, infringed on legitimate Christian freedom, and exploited its power in a worldly and tyrannical manner, and this has led to or exacerbated disunity. But such abuses or the impatience of genuine zeal only show how necessary such a central authority is if the divisiveness to which human organizations are liable is to be transcended in the interest of a universal community of faith. The remedy is a better exercise of authority, and legitimate resistance to its abuse, not schism or weakening of authority. Ecumenism must seek ways to regain universal submission to unified authority and its moderate exercise.

On the basis of this doctrinal authority the Catholic Church has been able also to enforce a standard of morality and religious practice among its members who accept its guidance. Experience shows, of course, that among its member there are very many who are only nominally Catholic, and many others who, while they sincerely accept the authority of the Church, are ignorant, confused, or inconsistent in following its direction.[24] Because of its catholicity, the Catholic Church does not expel such members except in certain cases where their opinions or conduct are flagrant and scandalous, but continues to work for their complete conversion. Nevertheless, this unity of doctrine and discipline is constantly striven for and in large measure effective in spite of the constant inroads of Humanism. Therefore it is generally recognized that the Roman Catholic Church is the most widely effective Christian Church, and more unified in its religious efforts than Judaism, Islam, or the oriental religions.

Humanists can object that this unity of doctrine and practice in the Catholic Church has been achieved only at the cost of authoritarianism and dogmatism, while Humanism has achieved a certain unity through free exchange of scientific and cultural opinion. Or they may object that the public consensus that they themselves maintain has a scientific character surpassing that of divided Christianity. To the first it has already been pointed out that the authority exercised by the Church is not with respect to human doctrines where agreement can be reached by reason, but with regard to revealed mysteries that require faith and trust in authority. To the second objection it can be replied that Humanists maintain a surface democratic consensus only by the use of political pressure, propaganda, and actual physical force surpassing that used by the Church in its worst abuses, while today the Church is maintaining this unity without such pressures.

The inclusivity and unity of the Church go very deep since they reflect its central doctrines. God as a Trinity is a divine Community in that the absolute oneness of the Godhead is totally communicated between Three Persons absolutely distinct from each other, yet whose personhood consists precisely in their relations to one another. These Three, moreover, are inclusive of all Being (the Father), Truth (the Son), and Goodness (the Holy Spirit). The doctrine of the Incarnation says that the Father has sent the Son to become a member of the human race, graced with the plenitude of the Holy Spirit through whose power the Son forms the community of the Church as his Mystical Body. Thus the Church manifests the Tri-unity of God. The Eucharist, at the center of the Church, is a sacrament of unity by which all humanity is invited to a single table of love, according to the single law of Christian life, the law of love that sums up the Law and the Prophets.

Thus the unity of the Christian Church, in spite of its divisions, makes it unique as a religion in the world today as to faith, worship, and organic structure, and in the Roman Catholic Church this living community is most clearly manifest. Taking the catholicity of membership as a material principle and the unity of the Church as a formal principle, the Church among all the religions and philosophies of the world today is uniquely vital in its witness to God's self-revelation. Is it not, therefore, a sign that God is speaking to us through this Church? If the Church's witness is false, how has it been able to become such a community of faith, when it is evident from other religions that human power of itself has not been able to bring about such unity except by force?

5. Holiness, the Sign of the Church as Graced

This organic unity and vitality of the Church would be in vain if it failed to achieve the purpose for which it claims to exist: to witness God's self-revelation in his (God's) Reign "on earth as in heaven" (Mt

6:10) that it represents by its communal life. This sharing in God's life is the Christian conception of *holiness*, or wholeness, integral human fulfillment,[25] actualization of the potentialities, personal and social, natural and supernatural with which the Creator has endowed us. Ecumenicity demands that the Church as community aim at enabling every member to reach this goal each according to his or her own unique gifts.

Those who visit most Catholic churches during Mass can experience that no matter how lacking in artistic taste the building or service may be, they are witnessing worship that attempts to unite the bodily, sensuous, worldly aspect of human nature to its spiritual, mystical, other-worldly aspect, revering both. The Catholic emphasis on sacramental worship in which the Word and the sensible Action are united always seeks to express the divine through the human in harmony with the basic belief in the incarnation of God the Son in the truly human Jesus.

Humanists put their faith in human powers and seek to develop human moral character and bring about an earthly society of and for humanity, but the notion that such a life is a participation in the life of God is, of course, quite alien to them. They criticize Christianity for its pessimism, its "contempt for the world" and resultant neglect of social justice. This charge of otherworldliness applies not to the teaching of Jesus, but to the effects of Platonism on Christianity in its missionary adaptation to the culture of the pagan Roman Empire. Yet Platonic dualism and hyper-spiritualism, influential as it was, never penetrated so deeply as to cause the Church to abandon its faith in the essential goodness of the material creation and of human nature, body as well as soul. Otherwise the doctrines of Incarnation and Resurrection would have lost all meaning.[26]

Consequently, the Catholic Church has always fostered a genuine (but not secular) humanism based on the dignity of the human person, created in God's own image.[27] The Church early resisted the radical dualism of the Gnostics and Manichaeans, and then the Platonism of the Origenists. Later it rejected Monophysitism that minimized the humanity of Jesus and Iconoclasm that tended to over-spiritualize worship. At the Reformation it opposed Luther and Calvin's pessimistic interpretation of St. Augustine's Platonizing theology, an interpretation that pictured fallen humanity as deprived of free will and even as totally depraved. Luther also stressed the dualism between the Kingdom of God of inner spiritual life and the sinful Kingdom of the World of secular life, and Calvin minimized sacramental worship in the interest of a more spiritual preaching of the Word.[28]

More optimistically the Catholic Church has always respected human nature even in its fallen state. It strongly defends human reason because it believes that reason, when rightly used, leads to Gospel faith. Hence Catholics tend to favor a *philosophical* theology, while the Orthodox favor a negative theology to which philosophy is of little help, while Protestants tend to view philosophy as a risk to biblical theology.[29] Catholics believe that sin has not destroyed the image of God in humanity, but only deprived it of the grace that it now requires to restore it to full humanness and raise it to a share in the divine life. They also believe that by grace they become able to cooperate with God in the work of their own salvation by works that are truly meritorious. The Reformers, on the contrary, frowned on the notion of cooperation or merit, as nullifying grace and tended to treat the believer as the purely passive recipient of divine favor.

Thus Catholicism is favorable to the full development of the human personality in all its aspects, physical, scientific, artistic, social, political not merely as they are necessary for secular life, but as having genuine spiritual value. At the same time it is realistically aware that the world as it exists due to human sin is a very different place than the Creator intended, so that to be truly human, God's grace is necessary to regain what has been lost. Today the political and liberation theologians are assimilating the social criticism of Humanism so as to assist the Church to rid itself of dualistic influences and to be more effective in its concerns for a just and peaceful social order. Thus Catholicism seeks to be an intensely "humanistic" but not secularistic religion.

On the other hand the Catholic Church also stresses the more contemplative, mystical side of religion, prominent in the Orthodox Church, but in the Protestant Churches often muted by an overly moralistic conception of spiritual life. Of course this balance of the active and contemplative is one of the central problems of all religions. Thus the Emanation Religions aim at a very high level of spirituality and have produced remarkable mystics who seek to be identified with the life of the Absolute, but for them this world is necessarily a world of suffering that can be overcome only by escaping it. Consequently, they proffer little hope for the reform of the social order. It is the Creation Religions that seek both mystical union with God in eternal life and the restoration of God's good creation from its devastation by human sin.

In both Judaism and Islam the sense of God's Reign is strong, and both hope to establish his law on earth (the Torah for the Jews and the *shar'iah* of the Muslims). Yet while they teach brotherhood and mercy for the members of their own community, they do not center on the love of enemies and the power of forgiveness, as Jesus commanded his community to do. In fact for this very reason they sometimes blame Christians for a too weak sense of justice. Moreover, within their orthodox forms both Judaism and Islam find little place for mysticism, although in both religions well developed systems grew up outside strict orthodoxy. Thus the mysticism of the *Kabbalah* and of the Hassidim in Judaism and of the Sufi in Islam stands in an uncomfortable and even antagonistic relation with orthodoxy.[30]

This same tension between mysticism and orthodoxy has also sometimes been felt in Christianity and has given rise to "enthusiastic" heresies and sects. Yet the Catholic and Orthodox Churches have been able not only to recognize but also actively to promote the contemplative religious Orders. There have been such mystics as St. Gregory of Nyssa and St. Maximus the Confessor in the East and St. Teresa of Avila and St. John of the Cross in the West (the last two officially "Doctors of the Church"). So far the Catholic Church has managed to accommodate the Charismatic Movement, frequently a source of schism in Protestant Churches in that Protestant mystics have usually been sectarians.[31]

The ability of Catholicism to combine contemplation and social activism is especially manifest in contemplative Orders of men and women.[32] The contemplative Orders maintain the asceticism and total devotion to prayer that marks the monasticism of the Eastern Churches. Yet, in the active Orders devoted to the care of the sick and poor, to education even of the poor, and to the missions, the social activism characteristic of some forms of Protestantism (especially Calvinism) is also retained. These Orders, both types of which were flourishing during the first half of this century and, although now passing through a period of decline in numbers in the face of mounting secular pressures, are still vigorous and taking on new forms. They have continued to produce countless men and women with a reputation of sanctity.

The diocesan clergy, although their role is active rather than contemplative, continue to carry on a life of dedicated service, and practice much of the spirituality of religious, including celibacy.[33] The occasional scandals of clerical sexual misconduct and abuse, although shocking, do not exceed those of most professionals whose dealing with a great variety of persons often opens the way to temptation.[34] The bishops of the Church today are for the most part free of the secular involvements that at the time of the Reformation led them to neglect their pastoral office, and increasingly live a life of simplicity and dedicated service free of political entanglement.

Of course it is very true that the state of religious and priestly life today is far from ideal. Since Vatican II, as at the time of the Reformation and again of the Enlightenment, large numbers of religious and clergy have been dispensed or simply withdrawn from their commitments and married,[35] and among those remaining there is widespread criticism of mandatory celibacy for priests. Scandals concerning concubinage, homosexuality, and even child abuse as well as alcoholism and drug dependency appear in the press and are rumored to be numerous. Other scandals concerning the management of the finances of the Church, dissensions and neglect or abuse of pastoral authority also surface. Since Vatican II, even the Catholic press is busy exposing these all too human failings and it seems realistic to say that not much remains hidden for long.

On the basis of such available information it is also evident that on the whole Catholic religious Orders and diocesan clergy exhibit a very high level of dedication to their calling under rather severe pressures and trials. Strangers approaching these representatives of the Church can be reasonably confident that they are meeting a person of sincere faith, constant prayer, and self-sacrificing concern to be of help in matters both spiritual and corporeal. Moreover, the quality of life of these Church leaders is profoundly shaped by ideals that combine the contemplative and pastoral.[36]

What is said of Catholic religious and clergy applies to those of the other Christian Churches but with one obvious difference.[37] The Churches of the Reformation ceased to require the life of celibacy practiced by Jesus himself and St. Paul and recommended by them to those especially dedicated to the promotion of the Reign of God. The Orthodox Churches from the seventh century had already ceased to insist on it for priests, while retaining it for monks and for bishops. The Catholic Church, however, not without many struggles, has retained it in the religious Orders and as a condition for ordination to the priesthood. The Church believes that even the active pastoral ministry ought to be rooted in the kind of commitment to the search for union with God through asceticism and contemplative prayer that characterized the early Church.

The solemn canonization of saints that continues to take place in the Catholic Church in large numbers is an indication of the high value the Church places on personal holiness.[38] The Orthodox Churches also canonize saints but not frequently. The Protestant Churches certainly have produced members of true holiness but have never subjected them to this kind of objective evaluation. The Roman Church undertakes a prolonged and careful process to ascertain that the candidate died for the Christian faith, or, if not a martyr, exhibited a fidelity to the Gospel, a balance of all the virtues, and above all an extraordinary love of God and neighbor. These qualities must be attested by their lives, writings, and the miracles worked through their intercession. These miracles are examined carefully often with the aid of medical experts.

While these processes are often criticized, there is no reason to doubt that in general they are thorough and objective, since the Vatican is anxious not to promote someone whose shortcomings might be exposed to ridicule.[39] The chief criticism has been that few lay persons are canonized, yet many cases are presented by religious Orders wishing to promote the sanctity of their founder or their own members. It is also alleged that success in the process depends to a degree on the willingness of a religious Order to undertake the considerable expense of the prolonged investigation. If these practical difficulties could be overcome no doubt many married persons would be canonized, since examples of sanctity in ordinary lives are well known.

The use of miracles in canonization brings us to a consideration of the continued existence of miraculous and prophetic signs in the Church, such as those recorded in the New Testament.[40] An argument used by Catholics against the Protestant Reformers was that their teaching was not confirmed by such signs. They replied that such signs ceased with the early Church because the Bible is a sufficient sign. Until the Reformation, however, the Church both East and West took for granted that while such signs might not occur so frequently and dramatically as in the New Testament Church they always would continue.

The Catholic Church has officially examined not only the miracles required in canonization but also those that sometimes are alleged to continue to take place at Lourdes, Fatima, and many other shrines.[41] The judgment on such events is likely to depend of course on one's worldview, as we saw in Chapter 6. Scientific corroboration can go no further than to attest the sudden recovery from pathology physiologically inexplicable in the present state of medical knowledge, or to determine that witnesses are not suffering from ascertainable illusions. But, according to the communication theory described in Chapter 6, such events can only be understood as signs of God's self-revelation. The significance of the evidence can, of course, be resisted by Humanists by an act of faith in a scientism that by its hermeneutic rejects any real possibility of the miraculous.

It should be noted that the Catholic Church does not encourage an excessive interest in the miraculous nor in private revelations. Its experience has been that such an interest leads to an "enthusiasm" that sees miracles everywhere and that tends to alienation from the institutional Church and its authoritative teaching. At the beginning of our century the Pentecostal or Charismatic movement arose in the Protestant Churches and spread to the Catholic and Orthodox Churches.[42] The charismatics, whose prayer is marked by "a baptism in the spirit" and "speaking with tongues," report frequent miraculous physical and psychological healings, and deliverances from demonic possession. These often seem to parallel the phenomena reported in the Acts of the Apostles and throughout Church history, especially in the lives of the saints. In these phenomena it is difficult to separate spiritual, psychological, and physical factors, and the Churches have not subjected them to careful objective examination. The Catholic bishops have been content to permit charismatic gatherings under pastoral supervision because this movement seems to have stimulated prayer and participation in the more formal activities of the Church.

The Charismatic movement has many critics. It has little appeal to those who are disturbed by its emotionality and lack of conformity to traditional liturgical forms. Nor does it appeal to others who see it as naively anti-intellectual, or to social activists to whom it seems too introspective and too little concerned with the social work of the Church. The charismatics themselves point to their successful support of family life, their success in founding base communities, and their engagement in many charitable activities. There seems no question that this movement in the Catholic Church has succeeded in deepening the contemplative dimensions of spirituality in lay groups and has provided new leadership among the laity of people living very holy lives.

A notable aspect of spiritual life in the Catholic Church is that it does not remain merely pietistic, as the charismatic groups tend to be, but produces a high level of intellectual life that remains orthodox.[43] In our times philosophers like Jacques Maritain, Etienne Gilson, Gabriel Marcel, and theologians like Teilhard de Chardin, Karl Rahner, Yves Congar, Hans Urs von Balthasar, St. Edith Stein are scholars of the highest intellectual achievement, thoroughly abreast of modern thought yet men and women of deep spirituality and prayer. This is true also of the Church leaders occupied with pastoral administration. The popes of the twentieth century have been men of remarkable holiness, not only St. Pius X but also John XXIII, not to overlook the remarkable Pius XII, Paul VI, and John Paul II. The deep spirituality of these popes is widely recognized, even when some of their decisions are criticized.[44]

The holiness of the Church belongs not just to an elite but to the ordinary people who participate actively in its life and mission.[45] Such participation means first of all fidelity to marriage and responsibility to children. The dominant Humanism of our time has not been very successful in supporting such fidelity and responsibility as is evident from the statistics on the growing number of single parent homes. Moreover, before the marked decline in the use of the Sacrament of Reconciliation after Vatican II, fidelity to the biblical commandments was maintained for the average "practicing" Catholic by frequent confession. It was well understood that after serious sin the Catholic would go to confession with a sincere purpose of amendment and restitution before again receiving Holy Communion. Admittedly one of the negative side effects of Vatican II was the unintended relaxation of this discipline (as happened more than once in the past) but the pastors of the Church are determined to revive it. The center of Catholic life, even more in this century than in the past, is the Eucharist which provides not only earnest contemplative prayer in union with Jesus, but also instruction on living the Gospel in daily life. Here too recently there has been some relaxation in Mass attendance, but with the reform of the liturgy in the vernacular also a greater participation by the people. The other sacraments too have been liturgically reformed so as to be received with greater understanding.

Perhaps the most evident difference between Protestantism and the older Orthodox and Catholics is the muting of the sacramental principles and its replacement by emphasis on the Word rather than the sacraments.[46] Insofar as this was a reaction to the late medieval neglect of the Word this was healthy and Vatican II has responded by reasserting the importance of the Bible and of preaching in worship. But since Christianity is a religion of incarnation the sacramental principle is essential to its life. It must appeal not only to the intellect by the Word, but to the whole human person through symbols that make their appeal to the five senses. The Orthodox Churches have survived and maintained a degree of unity principally through their liturgical, sacramental life. The Catholic Church is equally sacramental, but has also undertaken repeated revivals of preaching (the Protestant Reformation can be understood as one such revival that tragically widened into schism). Its sacramentalism is balanced by its concern for instruction based on a developing theology.

Thus in the Catholic Church holiness can penetrate both the elite to whom the Word more appeals and to the people for whom the tangible symbols are more effective. We saw that in India it is said that what the sage knows by ineffable mystical experience is made available to the people through myth, ritual, and "idols." This, of course, remains a Protestant suspicion of Catholicism, namely that it is a syncretistic form of Christianity that has absorbed pagan practices in its use of icons and statues and its veneration of the saints, especially in its Mariolatry.[47]

The Catholic and Orthodox answer to such accusations is that they do not accept the idea that the people can be fed with myths and only the wise can receive the real truth. The Church must attempt to instruct even the simplest Christian in the creed and the commandments that are identical with the fundamental principles of theology no matter how profound. One faith is open to all. But this faith has diverse expressions as Jesus himself showed by teaching the crowds in parables whose profound meaning he explained in more literal language to the Twelve (Mk 4:11). Consequently the Church as a comprehensive religion sent not to a mystical elite, but especially to the poor must use every available form of human communication to make this message understandable. It is no accident, therefore, that the Orthodox and Catholic Churches are notable for their sponsorship of the beautiful. The beautiful has a natural relation to the holy, since "the splendor of Truth" and of holiness is the very glory of God.[48]

The relation between the goal of integral human fulfillment and ecumenicity is, therefore, that no human community can be open to the union of all humanity at its deepest and most intimate level unless it can unite all the elements of human existence. It must unite the bodily and spiritual, the natural and the supernatural, this world and the eternal world, the active and the contemplative, the mundane and the transcendent, and thus answer all humanity's ultimate concerns. Surely a religion that can do all this can only be the work of God, who alone can restore humanity to the integrity he intended for it, and lead it on to union with the Trinity. We see how all religions aim at something like this wholeness, but how difficult it is to achieve! If the Christian Church, especially as it is said to subsist in the Catholic Church, does in fact essentially achieve this wholeness, then it is a moral miracle, a revelatory sign of God's communication with us.

6. The Gap between the Gospel and Popular Christianity

The chief objection to recognizing this sign in the Catholic Church is the great gap between its official teaching of the Gospel and the actual life of its people, a gap that we experience every time we meet Catholics in daily life. It must be frankly acknowledged that there is, and has been throughout history, a great gap between what exists now, as in the past, between the holiness of the Church as it is found in its teaching and in the lives of its saints and the practice of popular Catholicism.[49] Popular Catholicism often is centered on devotion to particular "powerful" saints, to relics and shrines, and to special devotional practices such as candle lighting, holy water sprinkling, the wearing of medals and scapulars, the recitation of prayers a certain number of times, etc. The people's devotion to Mary as Mother seems to supplant faith in Christ and to take on the character of the worship of the Mother Goddess so widespread in polytheistic religions. Actual knowledge of Catholic doctrine is often very confused. Morality is conceived legalistically as a series of imposed rules or irrational taboos. The clergy is either disregarded in such popular religion or regarded simply as the performers of certain magical rites, etc.

Thus in the Church in Latin America observers often see a kind of popular religion that is fervent in its practice of devotions but that under a thin veil of Christian symbolism seems really to be the religion of the pagan ancestors. On the other hand, in Europe and North America the mass of Catholics seem little affected by the moral teachings of the Church. They seem to identify themselves as Catholics mainly as a matter of family and national tradition or legalistic scruples while in fact conforming to the world-view and secular values of Humanism.[50]

In the Orthodox Churches the situation seems much the same. In the Protestant Churches a different type of piety is evident but it also takes on fundamentalist or Pentecostal forms that are often anti-intellectual and extreme and spawns cults of a truly bizarre character. Protestantism, however, because of its diversity, tends to allow such popular movements to split off and form new denominations; thus leaving the "mainline" Churches middle-class and respectable, but lacking in much vitality.[51]

There are Catholics who think that the Church today should raise its standards and vigorously eliminate all this popular religiosity as spurious. Parents should not be allowed to have their children baptized unless they themselves are exemplary Catholics, and adults who are not good Catholics should not be counted as members of the Church at all. Nevertheless, the Catholic Church understands itself as the Church of the poor, even more characteristically than of the rich and educated. Consequently, its pastoral policy is to preach the doctrine of Christ, "Be you perfect as your heavenly Father is perfect," while patiently tolerating a low level of understanding and practice among its members with the hope that gradually the Gospel may penetrate their lives more authentically. The fact that the Church's success has until now been incomplete is part of the drama of world history, since there are many social, political, and economic forces working against what the Church is trying to do.

7. Conclusion

We have looked at the Christian Church, and especially at the Catholic Church that stands at its center as the most evident example of its catholicity, community, and holiness that make it unique among the world's religious institutions. No other world religion has developed a truly comparable institution. The Church's very evident shortcomings in achieving its own ideal make clear how many forces there are at work to make it no different from any other human institution political, cultural, or religious. Yet in spite of these it stands out as unique in human experience.

The Christian Church claims to speak in the name of the God of Judaism and Islam and to give that God a personal name and face in history as the Religions of Emanation do not even claim to be able to do, and that preliterate religions only attempt in myth. The Catholic Church's very existence is as a mother reaching out to all kinds of human beings (*catholicity*). The Church strives to bring its members together in a single community based not on human power but on faith (*unity*) and to transform them individually and as community into the image of God (*holiness*). As to the fourth mark of the Church, its *apostolicity,* this relates to the Church's historic development and will be discussed in the next chapter.

In this historical development the Church has reached its third millennium of Christianity but has not yet converted the whole world to the Gospel as Jesus commanded and therefore Pope John Paul II has called its members to repentance and renewal. Yet today the Church continues to strive to bring the Good News to a hopeless world that at the beginning of the third millennium is often on the edge of despair. This courageous hope along with its incomplete but vast achievements presents this Church to those choosing a world-view and value-system as a moral miracle, a sign that gives warrant to its claim that in the Church God is speaking to all humanity and calling all to listen and respond.

Notes

[1] On the claim that the *Qur'an* is miraculous because of its literary qualities and wealth of historical information and religious ideas that are impossible to explain considering Muhammad's lack of education; see Robert D. Smith, *Comparative Miracles* (St. Louis: B. Herder, 1965), pp. 106-64.

[2] On the Protestant view of the Bible as self-authenticating under the light of the Holy Spirit see Robert Preus, *The Inspiration of Scripture* (Edinburgh: Oliver and Boyd, 1957); for Lutheran tradition and for the Reformed see William Niesel, *The Theology of Calvin* (Philadelphia: Westminster, 1956), pp. 30-39.

[3] See Timothy Ware (Bishop Kallistos of Diokleia), *The Orthodox Church* (Harmondsworth: Penguin Books, 1964), pp. 26-50 and 203-15. He insists himself that tradition ought to be "creative" not mere repetition.

[4] *Dogmatic Constitution on the Church (Lumen Gentium)* n. 8, *Vatican II: The Conciliar and Post Conciliar Documents,* Austin Flannery, OP, ed. (Collegeville, MN: Liturgical Press, 1975), p. 357. Controversy has arisen over the term "subsists." I believe it was chosen to assert that Christ's Church already exists essentially in the Roman Catholic communion, without attempting to define exactly how this is to be reconciled with the fact that all baptized persons are also members of this one Church (see n. 3). The answer differs for different churches and is precisely what has to be determined in dialogue, not presumed or predefined. It clearly does not mean that the Church of Christ exists only in the totality of all Christian churches; cf. *Lumen Gentium,* nn. 15-16. The *Catechism of the Catholic Church* (Rome: Libreria Editrice Vaticana, 1994) explains these "marks" (#811-70) in detail. It says, "Only faith can recognize that the church possesses these properties from its divine source. But their historical manifestations are signs that also speak clearly to human reason," and quotes Vatican I, *Dei Filius* 3, DS 3013.

[5] Cf. Vatican I, Session III, *Constitutio de fide catholica,* cap. 3 (Denziger/Schoenmetzer, nn. 301-14). Vatican II uses different language. Yet *The Dogmatic Constitution on the Church (Lumen Gentium),* Chapter 1, in *Vatican Council II: The Conciliar and Post-Conciliar Documents,* ed. by Austin Flannery, OP (Collegeville, MN: Liturgical Press, 1975, vol. 1) continues to speak of the Church as a "sign to the nations," but avoids seeming to substitute the Church for Christ. On this point see René Latourelle, *Christ and the Church: Signs of Salvation* (Staten Island, NY: Alba House, 1972), pp. 15-17, 105-32.

[6] See Gerald O'Collins, *Fundamental Theology* (New York: Paulist Press, 1981), pp. 130-60 and Francis Schuessler Fiorenza, *Foundational Theology* (New York: Crossroad, 1984), especially pp. 256-59.

[7] See Gustavo Gutierrez, *A Theology of Liberation* (Maryknoll, NY: Orbis Books, 1973) for the standard statement of this approach to faith, and for a fuller discussion see Thomas L. Schubeck, SJ, *Liberation Ethics: Sources, Models, and Norms* (Minneapolis, MN: Fortress Press, 1993).

[8] Vatican II, *Decree on Ecumenism (Unitatis redintegratio)* uses "ecumenism" in the sense of "concern for the reunion of all Christians" (see note 4 above, n. 1, p. 452). But since the *Declaration on the Relation of the Church to Non-Christian Religions (Nostra aetate) ibid.,* pp. 738-749, commends the search for religious fellowship with all those of good will, this term is often used in this broader sense, as it is also used in this book.

[9] The "four notes" or "marks" of the Church are derived from the Creed of the Council of Constantinople I (381). On its use see the article of Gustave Thils, "Marks of the Church (properties)," *New Catholic Encyclopedia,* 7: 535-41, based on his book, *Les notes de l'Église dans l'Apologetíque depuis la Réforme* (Gembloux: Duculot, 1937). In Chapter 5, section 5 above the Aristotelian "four causes" are explained and shown to be necessary to describing and explaining any changing reality. Hence it is not odd that the marks of the Church are also four since in these respects it stands out as "in the world" of changing realities to save it but as also "not of the world."

[10] See Albert Nolan, *Jesus Before Christianity* (Maryknoll, NY: Orbis Books, 1978) and Hugo Echegaray, *The Practice of Jesus* (Orbis Books, 1984).

[11] The Biblical warrant for excommunication from Christian community is the teaching attributed to Jesus, Mt 18:15-18 and the practice of St. Paul, 1 Cor 5:1-6:11 besides other texts in the later works of the New Testament that show its practice by the early Church.

[12] See Emil L. Fackenheim, *God's Presence in History* (New York: New York University Press, 1970), pp. 67-98 and Dennis Prager and Joseph Telushkin, *Why the Jew?* (New York: Simon and Schuster, 1983) who argue that the only ultimate solution to anti-Semitism is for Jews to educate the world to the Jewish values of universal human brotherhood under God.

[13] See Malis Ruthven, *Islam in the World* (New York: Oxford University Press, 1984).

[14] See F.H. Russell, *The Just War in the Middle Ages* (Cambridge: Cambridge University Press, 1975) for the theological discussions. The Church's use of force was either apologized for as purely defensive or mistakenly based on the text of the parable in which a master (who seems to stand for God) orders his servants, "Go out into the highways and force them" to come into his banquet (Lk 14:23). But according to a modern exegete on this text, "It means only that the poor and others will understandingly resist in their modesty such an invitation, until they are gently taken and led into the house." Joseph A. Fitzmyer, *Gospel According to Luke (XXXIV)* Anchor Bible (Garden City, NY: Doubleday, 1985), p. 1057.

[15] On the concept *Dar Islam* see Magid Khadduri, *War and Peace in the Law of Islam* (Oxford: Clarendon Press, 1964).

[16] See Chapter 4, note 9.

[17] See André Lemaire, *Ministry in the Church* (London: SPCK, 1977) on the biblical data. The best book, by Pierre Grelot, *Église et ministères: Pour un dialogue critíque avec*

Edward Schillebeeckx (Paris: Cerf, 1983) unfortunately has not been translated. Grelot shows that ministry in the early Church always required apostolic authorization, not merely a charism and ratification by the community.

[18] On the history of the ecumenical movement see Bernard Lambert, *Ecumenism* (New York: Herder and Herder, 1966) and Paul M. Minus, Jr., *The Catholic Rediscovery of Protestantism* (New York: Paulist Press, 1976).

[19] See J.M.R. Tillard, *The Bishop of Rome: An Inquiry into the Role of Peter in the Modern Church* (Wilmington, DE: Michael Glazier, 1983).

[20] See Peter J. McCord, ed., *A Pope for All Christians?* (New York: Paulist, 1976).

[21] See Joseph L. Blau, *Modern Varieties of Judaism* (New York: Columbia University Press, 1966) and J.H. Jansen, *Militant Islam* (New York: Harper and Row, 1979) on the condition of unity in Judaism and Islam.

[22] See M.J. Guillon, *The Spirit of Eastern Orthodoxy* (Glen Rock, NJ: Paulist Press, Deus/Century Books, 1964) pp. 87-96 and George A. Maloney, *A History of Orthodox Theology Since 1453* (Belmont, MA: Nordland, 1976); John Meyendorff, *Catholicity and the Church* (Crestwood, NY: St. Vladimir's Seminary Press, 1983).

[23] For a good description of Roman Catholic Church structures see John L. McKenzie, *The Roman Catholic Church* (London: Werdenfield and Nicolson, 1969). On infallibility see Germain Grisez *et al., The Way of the Lord Jesus* (Chicago: Franciscan Herald Press, 1983), vol. I, chapter 35, p. 831 ff. See also (with some reservations) Francis A. Sullivan, SJ, *Magisterium: Teaching Authority in the Catholic Church* (Ramsey, NJ: Paulist Press, 1984). Also see John J. Kirvan, *The Infallibility Debate* (New York: Paulist Press, 1971); Peter F. Chirico, *Infallibility: The Crossroads of Doctrine,* rev. ed. (Wilmington, DE: Michael Glazier, 1983).

[24] See George Gallup, Jr. and Jim Catelli, *The American Catholic People: Their Beliefs, Practices, and Values* (Garden City, NY: Doubleday, 1987).

[25] See Robert D. Smith, *The Holiness of the Church* (Westminster, MD: Newman Press, 1961). On the concept of "integral human fulfillment" see Germain Grisez (note 23 above), pp. 459 ff.

[26] See my *Theologies of the Body: Humanist and Christian*, 2nd ed. (National Catholic Bioethics Center, Boston, 1997), pp. 103-47.

[27] See Jacques Maritain, *Integral Humanism* (New York: Scribner's, 1968) and H. Richard Niebuhr, *Christ and Culture* (New York: Harper, 1951).

[28] For good expositions of the anthropology of the two great Reformers see Paul Althaus, *The Theology of Martin Luther* (Philadelphia: Fortress Press, 1966) and T.F. Torrance, *Calvin's Doctrine of Man,* rev. ed. (Grand Rapids, MI: Eerdmans, 1957). They did not deny that in some sense the image of God remains in man after sin.

[29] The Reformers sought a thoroughly biblical theology and distrusted fallen human reason. Luther rejected scholastic philosophy, but Calvin insisted on the rationality of faith. Seventeenth century Lutherans and Calvinists developed a "scholasticism" of their own and in the eighteenth began to be deeply influenced by Kantian philosophy. Yet American Protestant seminaries do not emphasize philosophical studies. For the present problems for Protestants see Frederick Sontag, *The Future of Theology: A Philosophical Basis for Contemporary Protestant Thought* (Philadelphia: Westminster, 1969).

[30] See Gerschom Scholem, *Major Trends in Jewish Mysticism* (New York: Schocken, 1941) and Chapter 5, note 10.

[31] See Louis Bouyer, F. Vandenbroucke, and J. Leclercq, *A History of Christian Spirituality,* 3 vols. (New York: Desclee, 1969) and Bernard McGinn and John Meyendorff, *Christian Spirituality: Origins to the Twelfth Century,* Vol. 16 of *World Spirituality: An Encylopedic History of the Religious Quest* (New York: Crossroad, 1985).

[32] Jean Canu, *Religious Orders of Men*, in *Twentieth Century Encyclopedia of Catholicism,*

vol. 85 (New York: Hawthorn, 1960); on religious women consult the articles on particular congregations in *New Catholic Encyclopedia.*

[33] For an extensive attempt to study the condition of the United States Catholic clergy see *The Catholic Priest in the United States,* Committee on Priestly Life and Ministry of the National Conference of Catholic Bishops, 4 vols. (Collegeville, MN: St. John's University Press, 1971) with the critique of Andrew M. Greeley, *Priests in the United States: Reflections on a Survey* (Garden City, NY: Doubleday, 1972).

[34] A.W. Richard Sipe, *A Secret World: Sexuality and the Search for Celibacy,* Foreword by Robert Coles, M.D. (New York: Brunner/Mazel, 1990) gives a rather pessimistic view on the failures of clerical celibacy based on his clinical practice not on a general survey. See the critique by another psychiatrist James J. Gill, SJ in his review, *Commonweal* 118 (Feb. 8, 1991): 108-10 and Vernon Satler, "An Agenda to Reject Celibacy," *Homiletic and Pastoral Review* 91 (June 1991): 72-77.

[35] On the ups and downs of religious vocations see Raymond Hostie, SJ, *The Life and Death of Religious Orders* (Washington, DC: CARA, 1983). The history of priestly vocations is largely parallel.

[36] See Walter Nigg, *Warriors of God: The Great Religious Orders and their Founders* (New York: Alfred A. Knopf, 1959); Gustav Martelet, *The Church, Holiness and Religious Life* (St. Mary's, KS: Review for Religious, 1960). Also see Gerald A. Arbuckle, *Strategies for Growth in Religious Life* (Staten Island, NY: Alba House, 1986); and Robert J. Daly, SJ, *Religious Life in the United States Church* (Ramsey, NJ: Paulist Press, 1984).

[37] See William McKinney and Wade C. Roof, *American Mainline Religions* (New Brunswick, NJ: Rutgers University Press, 1987) for a survey of the present situation and Martin E. Marty, *Modern American Religion,* vol. 1 (Chicago: University of Chicago Press, 1986) for historical background.

[38] See Richard Kieckhefer and George D. Bond, *Sainthood: Its Manifestations in World Religions* (Chicago: University of Chicago Press, 1988); Jacques Drouillet, *What is a Saint?* in *Twentieth Century Encyclopedia of Catholicism,* vol. 46 (New York: Hawthorn, 1958) and P. Molinari, "Canonization" in *New Catholic Encyclopedia* 3: pp. 55-59.

[39] The press has recently seen controversies over certain of these canonizations (extraordinarily frequent under John Paul II), but the issues are debatable. Thus complaints about the beatification of Josemaria Escriva, founder of Opus Dei and the canonization of St. Maria Goretti rest on questionable grounds and that about St. Edith Stein on understandable Jewish discomfort about the conversion of a Jew to Catholicism. While it has been commonly held that solemn canonization involves papal infallibility as regards a dogmatic fact, others question that this applies to every individual case rather than to the Church's general recognition of sanctity.

[40] See Louis Mondin, *Signs and Wonders* (New York: Desclee, 1966); Robert D. Smith, *Comparative Miracles* (note 1 above); René Laurentin, *Catholic Pentecostalism* (Garden City, NY: Doubleday, 1977), pp. 100-31.

[41] See references Chapter 6, notes 14, 16, and 17.

[42] On Protestants see John T. Nichol, *Pentecostalism* (New York: Harper and Row, 1966); Vinson Synan, *The Holiness Pentecostal Movement in the United States* (Grand Rapids, MI: Eerdmans, 1971) and David Martin and Peter Mullen, eds., *Strange Gifts: A Guide to the Charismatic Renewal* (Oxford: Blackwell, 1984). On Catholics see Ronald A. Knox, *Enthusiasm* (New York: Oxford University Press, 1961); E.D. O'Connor, *The Pentecostal Movement in the Catholic Church,* (Notre Dame, IN: Ave Maria Press, 1971); Joseph H. Fichter, *The Catholic Cult of the Paraclete* (New York: Sheed and Ward, 1975). Also see Kilian McDonnell, *The Holy Spirit and Power: The Catholic Charismatic Movement* (Garden City, NY: Doubleday, 1975) with bibliography, pp. 204-22; and James F. Breckenridge, *The Theological Self-Understanding of the Charismatic Movement* (Washington, DC: University Press of America, 1980).

[43] On intellectual life in the Catholic Church in this century see Kenneth Scott Latourette, *Christianity in a Revolutionary Age* (New York: Harper's and Brothers, 1961), vol. 4, Chapter VI, pp. 105-27.

[44] See Eamon Duffy, *Saints and Sinners: A History of the Popes* (New Haven, CT: Yale University Press, 1997), Carlo Falconi, *The Popes in the Twentieth Century from Pius X to John XXIII* (Boston: Little, Brown, 1967) and Nicholas Cheetham, *Keepers of the Keys: A History of the Popes from Saint Peter to John Paul II* (New York: Charles Scribner's Sons, 1983).

[45] See Yves Congar, *Lay People in the Church* (Westminster, MD: Newman Press, 1957) for discussion of the notion of "laity."

[46] See my *Theologies of the Body:* note 26 above, pp. 172-80.

[47] On Marian devotion see Yves Congar, *Christ, Our Lady, and the Church: A Study in Irenic Theology* (Westminster, MD: Newman Press, 1957) and René Laurentin, *Queen of Heaven: A Short Treatise on Marian Theology* (London: Burns, Oates and Washbourne, 1956).

[48] Hans Urs von Balthasar, *The Glory of the Lord: A Theological Aesthetics,* ed. by Joseph Fessio, SJ and John Riches, 7 vols. (San Francisco: Ignatius Press, 1995-7).

[49] P.H. Vrijhof and J. Waardenburg, eds., *Official and Popular Religion* (The Hague: Mouton, 1979). For examples see study of Rosalind B. Brooke and Christopher Brooke, *Popular Religion in the Middle Ages* (London: Thomas and Hudson, 1984) and Peter W. Williams, *Popular Religion in America* (Englewood Cliffs, NJ: Prentice-Hall, 1980).

[50] See reference in Chapter 1, note 8.

[51] On the general condition of the Christian Churches see *Christianity in Today's World: An Eerdman's Handbook* (Grand Rapids, MI: William B. Eerdmans, 1985). For problems confronting Protestantism see Donald O. Bloech, *The Future of Evangelical Christianity* (Garden City, NY: Doubleday, 1983). On the Orthodox see Fotias K. Litsas, ed., *A Companion to the Greek Orthodox Church* (Department of Communications, Greek Orthodox Archdiocese of North and South America, 1984) and Demetrios J. Constantelos, *Understanding the Greek Orthodox Church* (New York: Seabury, 1982).

CHAPTER 8

JESUS CHRIST: GOD'S SELF-COMMUNICATION IN HISTORY

1. Apostolicity, the Sign of Historical Continuity

In the foregoing chapter we considered the claim of the Christian Church to be the trustworthy sign that God is revealing himself to us publicly and personally today. The only realities directly accessible to any of us are the actual events of our own today, the "signs of the times." Although the deeper meaning of these events is often hidden to us because of our lack of perspective, at least we do not have to reconstruct them in the same piecemeal fashion as is necessary when we try to recover the far past. The past cannot be reconstructed without beginning from the present. Moreover, our culture today characteristically considers the past to mean little, even as a warning, for our present. Unless something is "new and improved" as the detergent advertisements say, we judge it to be obsolescent or obsolete and therefore useless. Therefore, this Chapter 8 will center on the life of Jesus whom the Church today claims as its founder. In Chapter 9 I will discuss the question whether in fact the present Church can claim to be essentially the same as the one that Jesus founded.

In choosing a world-view and value-system the appeal to history cannot be refused. The meaning of present events escapes us unless we place them in their temporal context. Time tested truths alone are ultimately reliable. Today the theory of evolution has made us aware that the world cannot be explained merely by the natural laws that account for cyclical events that repeat themselves. The origin and development of the universe, the solar system, life on our planet, the diversity of living things, our own species, and the origin of human cultures, cannot simply be reduced to recurrent patterns.

These organized systems that form our world are the product of unique events resulting not from the concurrence of many law-governed processes but concurrences that are not themselves law-governed. At every point of the evolutionary tree, things might have branched off in a different direction than they actually did. Only by looking back at what has happened can we explain these events as concurrences. Thus the modern picture of the world does not see the laws of nature as ultimate, but rather the ultimate reality is history.[1]

Therefore, we must not look for God's word to us merely in the events of our own time but in those events as they sum up a long historical development. Pre-literate Mythological Religions or the Emanation Religions are largely indifferent to the distinction between myth and history. Even when (as for Confucianism but not for Hinduism and Buddhism) there is a serious interest in history, it is conceived as cyclical and reduced to "the eternal return."

Characteristically the monotheistic Creation Religions recognize the fundamental importance of history and conceive it as a linear unfolding of a divine plan whose goal is beyond history to the Last Judgment and consummation of all things in a heavenly or infernal eternity. These religions exclude cyclical reincarnation and any guarantee that all souls will inevitably return to the One. History remains a drama whose general outcome, the triumph of God, is assured, but whose denouement for the free individual is still to be decided. Some historians believe that the first religion to clearly enunciate this dramatic character of history was Zoroastrianism, now almost defunct but whose insight was taken over by Judaism and is basic to Christianity and Islam.

These Creation Religions, however, have been sometimes tempted to negate their own insight into the significance of history by succumbing to a Stoic fatalism by which human cooperation has nothing to do with the outcome of history that depends solely on the sovereign will of God. Thus Islam is often accused (perhaps unjustly) of favoring fatalism, and in the Churches of the Reformation the theology of Calvin was criticized for the same tendency. On the other hand, Catholicism, though it admits it is difficult to find a satisfactory theology of the mystery of election and predestination, has always maintained that the sovereignty of God does not exclude human cooperation. Grace makes the human will and its activity free to do good freely, while the human will by its very constitution is the sufficient explanation of sinful activity.[2]

2. Historicity and Ecumenicity

In the last chapter it was shown that the ecumenicity that Vatican II claimed for the Church and that demands serious probing as a possible sign of God's self-revelation through the Church has three aspects. It is ecumenical in its material inclusivity (*catholicity*), formal community (*unity*), and final integral human fulfillment (*holiness*) and these mutually qualify each other. It remains now to consider the fourth or *efficient* aspect of this ecumenicity, namely the Church's historicity in the sense of a genuine continuity that manifests the power of God acting through all the vicissitudes of historical change. It must remain faithful throughout its history to the mission given by Jesus Christ to his apostles when he said to them at the Ascension,

> "All power in heaven and earth has been given to me. Go, therefore, and make disciples of all nations, baptizing them in the name of the Father, and of the Son, and of the Holy Spirit, teaching them to observe all that I have commanded you. And behold, I am with you always, until the end of the age" (Mt 28:18-20).

If the Church is a revelatory sign it must also give evidence that its common life transcends and embraces time. Human institutions rise and fall, but the designs of God must encompass these fluctuations in a single plan and empower them by the action of his grace.

The aspect of the Christian Church that makes it a historical reality is traditionally called its *apostolicity*. Apostolicity is the claim that this Catholic Church in communion with the Bishop of Rome is the same Church founded by Christ on the Twelve he chose as his leading disciples and witnesses of his resurrection.[3] A parallel is to be found in Judaism in the claim to be the Chosen People of the covenant with Moses and in Islam in the effort to trace traditions back to the "Companions of the Prophet." The two cases, however, differ in this that for Judaism the timeless Torah and for Islam the timeless *Qur'an* are respectively the bases of Judaism and Islam. Protestant Christianity tends in the same direction, making the Bible the foundation of the true Church, so that the intervening history between the Church of the New Testament and the Judgment is blank. Thus the present Church itself becomes of little religious significance except as a record of the corrupting of the Gospel and its recovery by the Reformers.

Nevertheless, modern biblical scholarship, in which Protestants have been the leaders, has made it plain that the Bible can not be properly understood in this timeless manner but must be placed in the context of the history of the People of God.[4] As for Islam, it is difficult to see how it can assimilate modern knowledge without coming to terms with its own pre- and post-history.[5] The lack of a full appreciation of history on the part of the Emanation Religions places them in a similar dilemma when confronted by Humanism.

Moreover, the continuity of the Church in the New Testament must also be broadened to include "salvation history," i.e., the preparation for Christ's coming in the Old Testament. The notion of salvation history (*Heilsgeschichte*) has been subject to much controversy. Some scholars object to reading the Old Testament from the perspective of the New. Others object that the Bible is not "history" in the modern sense of a critical, documented, continuous and causal account. Still others query how the Jews' own account of their national history is to be related to the secular history of the whole world.

Certainly the Bible is written from a religious perspective for a religious purpose. Furthermore, it is a history of one particular people, the Jews. Consequently, it is extremely selective and written according to ancient literary models not ours. Nevertheless, while making no claim to relate the whole of history (no book can do that), it does claim to relate certain events that give the key to understanding the ultimate significance of all the rest of history. On the one hand the Bible gives a religious interpretation to the history of the Jewish people as an analogy or paradigm of the very different histories of other nations. Every people has somehow been saved by God from its follies or it would not exist! On the other hand, it speaks of unique events, such as the self-revelation of the monotheistic Creator to Moses, the Incarnation of the Divine Son in Jesus, and the empowerment of the Church by the Holy Spirit that have universal meaning for all humanity.

Biblical scholarship, however, has also raised a fundamental problem for historical understanding of Christianity, namely, "the quest for the historical Jesus."[6] Since our testimony to the history of the founder of Christianity as in most other religions (including Islam) rests almost exclusively on the documents that form the canon of the early Church's faith, how can we separate the "Jesus of history" from the "Christ of faith"? Do we even know that Jesus intended to found a Church since he announced the approach of the Reign of God in the End Time? Or did the Jesus Movement settle down some time after his death into an organized Church through influences that were really inconsistent with his teachings?

Two possible ways to approach this problem are available. The first, taken by many Protestants because of their primary reliance on the Bible and their distrust of possibly corrupted Church Tradition, is to try by critical historical methods to separate fact from theological interpretation and legend from history in the New Testament. In this way it is supposed one can arrive at the original historical data, at "what really happened" free of the interpretations and embellishments of the storyteller. Some have even hoped to ascertain by purely historical methods the *ipsissima verba Jesu*, the very words of Jesus himself.[7]

Two serious difficulties warn us against this approach. First, the historical critical method is necessarily minimizing because it rejects all traditions that might be the products of the community's faith. These are thought to be historically suspect. Hence only such as were probably embarrassing to believers or at least such as they would have had no interest to invent them can be accepted as trustworthy. Second, given the relative paucity of these data, such efforts tend to be very speculative and to rest on many levels of questionable assumptions. For example, the fundamental problem of the dating of the Gospels depends on a solution to the so-called "Synoptic Problem" concerning the literary interdependence of the Gospels and of the traditions that lie behind them. The most widely accepted solution, the "Two Document Hypothesis," however, is still open to many serious criticisms.[8]

Consequently, for our purposes a second approach, while not neglecting the valid contributions of the first approach, is more realistic. In the previous chapter I argued that the Christian Church (subsisting most clearly in the Roman Catholic Church) can be experienced in our world today as reasonably trustworthy. Thus we can place *prima facie* confidence in her tradition about her founder and her origin, provided that these traditions are not contrary to certainly established historical facts. Nor is this argument circular since it is grounded in consideration of the Church as she is here and now accessible to contemporary experience. All history has to be known from its effects today, yet it in turn can cast real light on what we now experience. Hence our present experience of the Church is independent of its remote history, although its history can help to explain and confirm what we already know of its present reality.

Hence the burden of proof shifts, so that the Tradition of the Church is taken as genuinely historical provided that it cannot be proved to be merely legendary. In fact in writing secular history this is the method followed by most historians. They generally assume that official documents are reliable unless they give evidence of being untrustworthy, rather than the other way around. To demand evidence that every document is genuine leads to an infinite regress, since the only such evidence that is possible is another document that in its turn may also be suspect. The reason that New Testament historians have been driven into their minimalist stance has been their efforts to meet the systematic skepticism of Humanists about all religious claims as intrinsically unreliable. If on the other hand we accept that there is a God who rules history and probably wishes to reveal himself to us, we will view claims of such revelation with open yet not credulous minds.[9]

3. Historical Credibility of the Church's Tradition

Are the New Testament accounts of Jesus' life, teaching, and foundation of the Church, historically credible? The first issue is the question of the New Testament canon and the lack of other documents confirmatory of the biblical accounts.[10] How did the books that we call the New Testament get selected and why have others been excluded? The process of settling on a recognized list of inspired books of the Bible took a long time. The early Church for the Old Testament generally accepted the canon of the Septuagint or Greek translation used by diaspora Jews but not without question regarding certain books. The traditional Jewish canon with a shorter list of books was not definitely closed by rabbinical opinion until early in the 2nd century CE. Throughout the following centuries some Christian scholars, such as St. Jerome, puzzled over the difference between this shorter Jewish canon and the longer one traditional to the Church. At the time of the Reformation the Protestant theologians, influenced by the concern of Renaissance humanists to return to "original" texts in their original language, claimed that the longer canon reflected the corruptions of which they accused the Roman Catholics and decided to accept the Jewish canon. For this decision modern Protestant as well as Catholic scholarship finds no decisive historical warrant. Because of this action of the Reformers the Catholic Church at the Council of Trent (1546) finally decided for the traditional longer canon, that includes seven books and some brief passages that Protestants call the "apocrypha" but that are more neutrally called "deuterocanonical." Actually the only major theological question this affects is the favorable reference to prayers for the dead in 2 Mc 12:48 that Catholics cite to justify this practice that is not generally admitted by Protestants. The Orthodox Churches seem never to have officially settled the problem, some theologians accepting not only the longer canon but even such works as 2 Esdras and 3 Maccabees, others opting for the shorter canon of the Jews. What is clear from these historic facts is that the formation of the Old Testament canon was a long historic process that can be justified only on the grounds of the Tradition of the Church as an authoritative judge of what is and is not inspired.

As regards the New Testament canon, fortunately for ecumenism there is no disagreement among Protestants, Orthodox, and Catholics, although some sects have added others books as inspired such as the *Book of Mormon* or the writings of Mary Baker Eddy. Yet a mass of ancient material both of the time before Christianity and afterwards also survives that the churches regard as apocryphal because rejected by early Church councils. Was this exclusion justified? The New Testament apocrypha are relatively late in date (with a few possible exceptions), depend on the canonical books, have features common to legendary writings, or are marked by tendencies considered by the early Church as heretical. Thus it is not likely, on the basis of the usual assumptions of historical criticism, that these apocryphal works (other than the writings of the orthodox documents usually collected under the title of "Apostolic Fathers") contain reliable historical data not found in the canonical books. The possible exception would be that some of the sayings of Jesus that they report might be authentic or even closer to the *ipsissima verba* than the New Testament versions.

Recently considerable light has been shed on the historical context of early Christianity by the discovery of the Jewish sectarian Qumran or Dead Sea Scrolls literature, of the Egyptian Gnostic documents, and of the fragment of the so-called *Secret Gospel of Mark*, etc. As interesting as these are to scholars they have not in any important respect altered the picture given by the canonical New Testament. Thus there is no serious reason to doubt that in the New Testament canon we have the most historically reliable documents of this period.

It would be helpful to historians of course if they had documents showing what the opponents of Jesus, particularly the Pharisees, thought of him.[11] From the biographies of other religious leaders we know how different can be the account of an admirer from that of an enemy. From the Pharisaic side nothing is left to us but some accounts in the Talmud, the date of which cannot be exactly fixed. These admit that Jesus existed, that he had a reputation as a wonder worker, but they also claim that he was only half Jewish, the bastard son of a Roman soldier named Panthera. This last item seems nothing more than an attempt to counter the Christian claim that Jesus was born of a virgin (Panthera seems a corruption of the Greek *parthenos*, virgin), that if it has any significance, corroborates the existence of this Tradition.

Yet this paucity of documentation is not odd. For example, we have little data to tell us what contemporaries of Muhammad other than his disciples may have thought of him.[12] A religious movement treasures its traditions, but its opponents may have little reason for recording much about a movement that they regard as a mere fad, better forgotten. Only after a religious movement survives and grows do others wake up to its threat and begin to write against it.

The second question is whether the New Testament documents are close enough to the time of Jesus and the origin of the Church to be credible witnesses.[13] Or is the situation similar to that of the life of the historic Buddha Gautama Siddhartha that depends on documents written in the Indian Tradition where history is little regarded and originating perhaps a couple of hundred years after his death when oral Tradition becomes highly tenuous? It has been pointed out, for example, that few of us have much knowledge about our ancestors further back than our grandparents whom alone we may have personally known. Of course institutions have somewhat longer memories than individuals, but even they often lose sight of their origins.

At the beginning of serious critical historical study of the New Testament, there were many who held that the New Testament documents were to be dated as late as the second century. Today hardly anyone dates them (with the possible exception of 2 Peter) later than 100 CE, that is, within one or two generations from the time of Jesus who died probably in 30 CE. The certainly authentic epistles of St. Paul date from between 50 and 65 CE, within the lifetime of witnesses of Jesus' own generation. The Synoptic Gospels are usually dated not later than 90, still within the lives of some persons contemporary to the events.[14] The variety and relative independence of these documents and the general consistency of the picture they give of Jesus' life and teaching and of Church origins corroborate their credibility.

The tendency of critical scholarship is to emphasize the difference of traditions and the apparent contradictions between them. This kind of research, however, has been carried on now for almost 200 years by a variety of scholars of all Christian denominations and of unbelievers. Yet it has not turned up unresolvable contradictions or other data that would destroy the basic reliability of these documents. Although some of the writings may be pseudonymous (attributed by the writer to a more authoritative personage), this was an accepted rhetorical device of ancient literature. Scholars have also shown that the New Testament writers have different "theologies," that is, theological interpretations of the events, but this has not undermined either their honesty or their fidelity to the living traditions of the Christian community. One of the most recent attempts to call this New Testament evidence into serious question has been the work of the Jesus Seminar centered in Claremont Theological Seminary. Its radical conclusions have, however, been thoroughly criticized by other scholars as methodologically unsound and have failed to gain credence among most scholars.[15]

4. Did Jesus Rise from Death?

A third question is whether a credible picture of Jesus emerges from these New Testament documents. In exploring the New Testament evidence about who Jesus was, what he did and taught, we need not enter into the question of the different theologies that it contains. Rather, our approach can be that of "canon criticism"[16] which takes into account the canonical Tradition of the Church that considers the different perspective found in the biblical books to be essentially complementary. Hence canon criticism treats the Bible taken not as a mere collection of materials but as the work of God as the one principal Author working through a variety of human authors. Thus it attempts a unified, albeit complex synthesis of the message of the Scriptures as a whole. This follows an old saying, "The Bible is its own best interpreter." This collection of books was written and accepted as divinely inspired within an historic community that has preserved and interpreted it. Therefore the appropriate hermeneutical principle to be used in reading the Bible, as in reading any supposedly unified work, must be to interpret the parts in the light of the whole and the whole in the light of the parts.

Protestants, however, have sometimes in the past taken this dictum to mean that the Bible can be understood by individuals apart from the Tradition of the community of faith. Today however Protestant scholars as a result of the study of the history of how the Bible was written have come to see that the faith Tradition of the Christian community is the appropriate context in which the Bible must be read if it is to make canonical sense. This is also why in the Catholic Church the Council of Trent insisted that Christian faith rests not on "the Bible alone" (*sola scriptura*) but on the "Bible and Tradition." Vatican II confirmed this but made clear that Bible and Tradition are not separate sources of faith. The Bible arose from the believing community's sacred Tradition, was collected as the Word of God within that Tradition, and its integrity and inspiration is guaranteed only by that Tradition. The excessively literal hermeneutics of some Protestants, therefore, is not supported by this Tradition that has always recognized that the inspired Word of God takes many literary forms in the Bible, historical, poetic, homiletic, legal, representing culturally different modes of communication. Hence Vatican II defended the *inerrancy* of the Scriptures as regards the "religious message" that the Holy Spirit has wished to convey for humanity's salvation while not excluding errors in other matters, scientific, historic, etc., that are irrelevant to the truth of that divine message that is without error. Nevertheless, this religious message of Scripture includes the assertion that certain things really happened, for example, that Jesus was really crucified. If this assertion is not to be understood historically the Bible is nonsense and the Christian faith is false and cannot be a reasonable choice for anyone's world-view and value-system.

Yet to ask such questions about whether something is an historical fact, it is necessary to be clear as to what we intend by the word "historical".[17] In a hermeneutics influenced by philosophical idealism, a fact is not a fact unless it is a fact for us, that is, unless we perceive it as a fact. At the extreme this means that it must not only be known but must be known as significant or meaningful, that is, it must fit into my "world," the world as I conceive it. Consequently, from this idealistic point of view it is not possible to distinguish between a historical fact as independent of and as dependent on human knowledge. Hence the crucifixion or resurrection of Jesus cannot be "historical," if it cannot be solidly established by the methods of historical criticism that requires it to be consistent with the modern world-view for which such things seem impossible. Therefore, it can only be a truth of faith not of history; that is, it fits into the subjective Christian world-view, but not into any account of critical, objective history that abstracts from faith. Unfortunately some Catholic writers accept this idealistic approach and misquote St. Thomas Aquinas in its favor. But Aquinas clearly teaches[18] that witnesses knew the fact of Jesus' resurrection just as they knew his crucifixion by ordinary human knowledge based on sense observation. Faith indeed was required to understand the full significance of this fact, but it was first known by the senses and by reason. Actually according to the Bible the Twelve did not at first believe, but were convinced by the evidence of their senses (Lk 24:11; 36-43).

We must leave such problems to idealist philosophers and here be content with a realistic point of view. For realists two different questions must be asked: (l) "Was the resurrection a historical fact?" and "How do we know that it is such a fact?" granting that we cannot answer the first without also answering the second. Perhaps the best way to begin is by reformulating these two questions as follows: "Did the early Church claim that the resurrection was a historical fact independent of the way it was known and of the faith of the witnesses?" If the answer to this question is "Yes" then we must ask, "Can we verify this claim?"

The New Testament writers undoubtedly lived in a cultural world very different from our own where there was much less effort to distinguish the various different types of knowledge such as "myth," "tradition," and "history" from one another. But their writings give plain evidence they knew the difference between historical events and fictional accounts meant to convey a theological or moral truth. Sometimes in reading the Bible we are not sure whether a particular narrative is meant to be history or a parable. For example, the question can be raised whether the resurrection of Lazarus is a theological construction resting only on the fact that Jesus sometimes raised the dead.[19] Yet such an interpretation cannot be reasonably applied to the stories of Jesus' own resurrection. The narrators write in an explicitly apologetic mode; that is, they claim the resurrection really happened and attempt to buttress this claim by citing evidence that they mean what they say and are telling the literal truth.

Thus St. Paul (1 Cor 15:3-19) lists the many persons who had seen the risen Lord, then cites his own experience, and finally asserts that if this did not really happen, then the Christian faith is without foundation. Similarly the Synoptics are concerned about the empty tomb precisely as evidence of a historic fact, and all the Gospels insist that the apparitions of Jesus were not those of a ghost, but of a bodily tangible man who was even able to eat. Of course, one might say that these details were given simply to make the fiction more lifelike, as in Defoe's novel *Robinson Crusoe*, but it would be absurd to think that the New Testament writers in such solemn assertions were merely striving for the reputation of skillful storytellers. Their purpose plainly is to convince the reader of the historical factuality of the event and to distinguish the historicity and certitude of this particular fact from other narratives of a more ambiguous character.

But can we verify their claim? I emphasize once again that if the last chapter established the sign value of the Church as it exists today, then the problem is not to establish the truth of its witness to history, but to consider whether the objections raised against its witness are valid. These objections reduce to the fact that our earliest direct witness in the New Testament is St. Paul who speaks simply of his vision on the road to Damascus concerning which he gives no details, while the author of Mark (without the "long ending," 16:9-20, not in the earliest MSS), generally considered to be the earliest Gospel, does not describe any actual appearances of the risen Christ. The other Gospels give accounts of the empty tomb and the appearances to the mourning women and the Twelve, but are not entirely consistent with each other on the details. Moreover, Matthew adds what seem to be legendary apologetic details such as the rolling back of the stone by an angel, unsupported in the other narratives, and all the Gospels place the announcement of the resurrection in the mouth of angels, sometimes in the Scriptures simply a literary device. May not this resurrection tradition have begun with some kernel of historical fact and then been gradually elaborated in its transmission? In Mark it is only described in the long ending. In Luke it is more elaborated than in Matthew and in John still more. Thus it would seem that from some ill defined religious experience of the Twelve an elaborate apologetic legend was gradually created by the Church.

In evaluating this kind of interpretation of texts it must first be conceded there has been some kind of a historical development in the narratives and an increasing rhetorical concern to strengthen the claim of resurrection with apologetically effective details. It must also be conceded that there are discrepancies in the details of the accounts which if they occurred in the testimony of a witness under cross examination might well make the jury question his veracity (cf. Dn 13:51-59). Finally it must be granted that St. Paul's witness has a unique character.

Edward Schillebeeckx in his learned book *Jesus: An Experiment in Christology*[20] deals with all these difficulties at length and concludes that we cannot now determine how the early Church knew the resurrection. Did they know it from apparitions, from the empty tomb, or in some other way? In any case they did not doubt they believed they had "seen" the Lord alive and this certainty, Schillebeeckx argues, suffices for both theology and apologetics. I respect Schillebeeckx' patience in dealing with current critical problems. Since, however, many of these difficulties of the critics rest on their own highly speculative dating and reconstruction of the sources of the New Testament, it is better to ask if the principal difficulties that I have already listed are truly serious. Unless they are, it is unnecessary to enter as Schillebeeckx attempts into the maze of exegetical conjecture.

St. Paul in relating his own special experience of the Risen Lord prefaces it (1 Cor 15:1-7) with the witness of the Twelve and "five hundred of the brethren." Would their witness or his own experience have been very convincing to himself or his hearers if it were known that the tomb in Jerusalem was not empty? St. Paul had a unique vocation that needed to be strengthened by a unique experience. We do not really know the date of Mark nor the origin of its "long ending"[21] and in any case it is clear that the author assumes that the resurrection took place even if he does not describe it. His failure to describe it seems adequately explained by his special theology and literary design that assumes the known fact of the resurrection and seeks to show how ill prepared the apostles found themselves in the face of this astonishing fact that finally demanded their reluctant faith.

The differences between the Gospels are of the sort common in all independent historical accounts and do not nullify their agreement on essential points. Historical documents, unfortunately, cannot be cross-examined for further statements as we can do with a witness before a jury. Yet we cannot reject their evidence because of inevitable discrepancies unless these discrepancies are irreconcilable. Exegetes do not like to "harmonize" discrepant accounts in the Scripture lest they lose sight of the unique viewpoint, purpose, and information of each writer. Nevertheless, in evaluating the historicity of an event related by more than one writer it is necessary to ask whether their accounts are contradictory or susceptible of reconciliation. While we cannot be sure which reconciliation of the resurrection accounts is the best, they certainly are not so discrepant as to be contradictory.[22]

Finally, we should be open to the possibility of some literary elaboration and dramatization of the various accounts to make them conform to the conventional literary patterns of the Old Testament. If the great miracle of the resurrection was a fact, why be skeptical that it was accompanied by other miraculous phenomena? Many mystics throughout Christian history have experienced apparitions of angels. Of course the different theological interests and audiences of the evangelists also condition the accounts.

Each of the points just made deserves extensive discussion, and I do not present them in this summary fashion as adequate answers to the difficulties raised. Yet they should suffice to show that the kinds of difficulties raised by historical criticism against the historicity of the resurrection narratives is far from conclusive. These narratives exhibit, as does much in any historical account, vague areas where the inevitable limitations of our data prevent us from achieving a clear answer, but they do not prove the impossibility of the principal claim, nor even deprive it of high probability. Thus, as the distinguished Protestant theologian Pannenburg has argued,[23] after the most exhaustive critical analysis extending over two centuries of biblical scholarship, much of it ideologically hostile, we are left with the one fundamental fact. This is the certainty that the early Church was firmly convinced that it was a historical fact that Jesus had risen from the dead. This conviction rested on a multitude of witnesses they thought credible who claimed that the tomb was empty and that they had seen, heard, and felt the very same Jesus they had known before the resurrection, although no longer living our mortal life. The claim is clear, the verification depends on the reliability of the witnesses, and only the Church could test that reliability, while today we must test the reliability of the Church in its Tradition by our present and historical knowledge of her character.

It has become a cliché in current theological writing to say, "Of course the resurrection was not the reanimation of a corpse!" It seems to me that the New Testament witnesses would have found that assertion odd. It is true that the biblical witnesses make the point — they even stress it — that the risen Lord was somehow different than he had been in this life. Mary Magdalen and the disciples at Emmaus at first do not recognize him. In the presence of the Twelve he appears in a closed room and disappears in a miraculous manner. In fact all his appearances and disappearances are sudden and mysterious.

Nevertheless, the narratives also stress that the witnesses were able to identify the same Jesus they had formerly known with certainty by his voice, manner, and especially by his wounds. Although St. Paul tells us (1 Cor 15:35 ff.) that the resurrected body is "spiritual" this does not mean immaterial but deathless, free of the weaknesses that for Paul are characteristic of "the flesh." The question of the exact character of the risen body is a matter for speculative theology.[24] The New Testament writers do not speculate, they simply assert that the Risen Lord was the same Jesus soul and body that they had known in life.

5. Jesus as God's Self-Revelation

Convinced that Jesus had really risen from the dead as the central event of history, the early Christians reflected on all that they had known of him before he had been laid in the now empty tomb, already the site of their pilgrimages. They remembered that before his death he had promised them that after his return to his Father he would send them "another Paraclete" (perhaps best translated as "Encourager"), that is, someone in his place to "teach them all truth."[25]

They experienced this help of the Paraclete or Holy Spirit in their courage under persecution and in martyrdom and in the power of their preaching to convert sinners. They also experienced it in the gifts of prophecy, healing, and prayer that occurred in the Community and that assured them of the true meaning of Jesus' life, death, and resurrection. Thus Jesus was seen as standing in direct relation to the creator and savior God of the Old Testament whom he had always addressed intimately as "Abba," Father. He taught his disciples to do the same in the *Our Father*. He was also seen in direct relation to the Holy Spirit who had empowered the prophets and charismatic leaders of the Old Testament in their teaching, martyrdom, and miracles. How the Father, Son, and Holy Spirit were related in view of the fidelity of Jesus to Jewish monotheism was a deep problem for Christians that required working out, but they constantly invoked the Three together in prayer and soon began to baptize new members in their name. Apparently they found confirmation for this in an experience of Jesus himself. When he was baptized in the Jordan by John the Baptist (Mt 3:16-17 and parallels) he saw the Father sending the Holy Spirit in the form of a dove (probably the dove of peace after the flood, Gn 8:11) upon him to strengthen him for his mission.

During Jesus' life he had asked the Twelve, "Who do you say that I am?" (Mk 8:28-29). Peter as head and spokesman of the Twelve answered, "You are the Messiah, the Son of the Living God!" To that Jesus in turn replied,

> "Blessed are you, Simon son of Jonah! For flesh and blood has not revealed this to you, but my heavenly Father. And so I say to you, you are Peter [Rock], and upon this rock I will build my church, and the gates of the netherworld shall not prevail against it. I will give you the keys to the kingdom of heaven; and whatever you bind on earth shall be bound in heaven; and whatever you loose on earth shall be loosed in heaven." Then he strictly ordered his disciples to tell no one that he was the Messiah (Mt 16:16-20).

This account in the more Jewish Matthew, given in much shorter form in Mark and Luke, has the literary flavor of the Jewish-Christian churches and is commonly admitted by scholars to be an authentic tradition. It indicates an early concern of the churches for church unity under the Petrine tradition of those churches.[26] In these traditions Jesus was reverenced as the Messiah or anointed king of the house of David whom the prophets had promised would restore Israel and establish the Kingdom of God on earth. This Kingdom was the reign of God's peace and justice that he had intended in creating humankind but that had been corrupted by human sin. And in that Kingdom all peoples would share through the ministry of Israel.

Both the biblical and extra-biblical literature show us that this expectation of the Messiah was intense in Jesus' time. It seemed that many of the biblical predictions were being fulfilled in the crisis of the Jewish nation under Roman tyranny. Yet the notions in circulation of what the role of the Messiah was to be in this crisis were highly varied. Scholars have doubted that Jesus himself ever claimed to be the Messiah.[27] But they do not doubt that his preaching centered on the theme that the Kingdom of God was about to be realized on earth. It would seem that he did not want to make any public claim to be head of this Kingdom lest it encourage mistaken ideas among the people, many of whom imagined the Messiah as a military leader who would lead a revolt against the Roman oppressor.

Nevertheless, the Gospels, in this key passage (the structural turning point of Mark's Gospel) represent him as privately accepting this natural conclusion of his immediate followers. The evangelists also say that Pilate interrogated Jesus on this point at his trial and that he did not deny it, but made clear (Jn 18:36) that the title "Messiah" need not be understood in a political sense. Jesus rejected the program of the Zealots who sought to achieve the Kingdom by force.

From the evidence of the New Testament there can be no doubt that Jesus' teaching and actions were marked by an advocacy of nonviolence.[28] Yet it cannot be proved that he rejected the teaching of the Hebrew Scriptures on the duty of public authority to use force to maintain human rights by police action or even war. Certainly St. Paul (Rm

13:4) and St. Peter (or the author of 1 Peter 2:13-14) did not interpret Jesus as a pacifist in this strict sense. But it is clear that Jesus taught that the Kingdom of God cannot be brought about by force but requires patient suffering even to death for truth on the part of those who hope to enter it. It was for this reason that he did not attempt to defend himself against those who tried to silence him, but continued to preach even when this meant his crucifixion. While force may serve some good public purpose, primary reliance on force is destructive. When arrested he said to Peter, "Put back your sword where it belongs. Those who use the sword are sooner or later destroyed by it" (Mt 26:52).

This Christian nonviolence is not clearly supported by the Hebrew Scriptures and is far from the spirit of Islam whose founder was a courageous military leader. It has its closest parallel in Buddhism (and Jainism). Christian and Buddhist nonviolence, nevertheless, have very different meanings. Buddhism forbids violence against all living things, because they may be reincarnations of souls, and the motive for this abstention is ascetical, namely, to overcome the passion of anger since all passion hinders that perfect spiritual detachment that is the goal of Buddhism.[29] Christians, on the other hand, while they should reverence all life (and here the Buddhists have much to teach the West) and also seek detachment from disordered anger (but not from righteous anger), are motivated to nonviolence not primarily for ascetical reasons but primarily out of love for human persons who will not be reincarnated but resurrected to eternal life, while for Buddhists the human person is only phenomenal. Jesus taught the love of enemies (Mt 5:43-48). We must forgive their offenses seventy times seven times and positively strive for their redemption, thus imitating God's love for us, so beautifully exemplified in the Parables of the Lost Sheep and of the Two Sons (Lk 15:1-32).

What then was Jesus' conception of God? Jesus did not abandon anything of the fully developed conception of God in the Hebrew Scriptures as the all-powerful Creator, careful of his creation, who inexorably wills that just laws should be fully implemented to bring that creation to its perfection. Justice will be done! But Jesus developed something that is only imperfectly glimpsed by the Hebrew prophets. God is not only the Just One or the Lover of Israel, but he is Love universal (1 Jn 4:8), and therefore a God of unlimited mercy even to those who have chosen to be his enemies.

Because God is Love and true love is self-giving, God wills to give himself to every creature according to each creature's capacity to return love. As God has created that capacity, he also expands it by the work of his Holy Spirit. Thus it becomes possible for created persons to love God as God loves them in true mutuality and reciprocity, to become children and friends of God, and, therefore, in a sense equal to God while still remaining created persons distinct from but totally dependent on their Creator.

Jesus spoke to God intimately as "Abba," "Dear Father." While the Hebrew Scriptures occasionally use "Father" of God, before Jesus it was never the common manner of Jewish prayer.[30] Feminists are mistaken in seeing "Abba" as a reflection of "patriarchalism." Just the contrary is true, because Jesus chose "Abba" to show that the Almighty Creator can be approached as one who never insists on his rightful "dominion." Instead, God, like the father in the Parable of the Two Sons, is utterly non-discriminatory and respectful of the freedom of his children, ever ready to forgive their faults without reproach, in fact, to be their servant rather than their master.

It is no accident, therefore, that Jesus found in certain prophecies of the Hebrew Scriptures the conception of the "Suffering Servant" symbolic of Israel in its fidelity and witness to God under persecution, the best expression of his own role. For him it seems to have been more significant than the title of Messiah as commonly understood.[31] To be truly the King and Savior anointed by the Spirit of God is to be like the God who is Love, who rules by caring and serving. Hence Jesus instructed his apostles with whom he shared his messianic authority that,

> "You know that those who are regarded as rulers over the Gentiles lord it over them, and their great ones make their authority over them felt. But it shall not be so among you. Rather, whoever wishes to be great among you will be your servant; whoever wishes to be first among you will be the slave of all. For the Son of Man did not come to be served but to serve and to give his life as a ransom for many" (Mk 10:42 45).

Only by an anachronistic distortion can this saying of Jesus be understood as an advocacy of "democracy" or "anarchy," as if authority and obedience are to be ruled out because for Jesus all human persons are "equal." Jesus' meaning is that though God as Creator is infinitely unequal to his creatures, he uses his authority for love and only for love. Hence those who share God's authority in the order of society and of the Church are to do the same. It was for this Jesus gave his own authority of service to the Twelve under Peter's headship.

The humility so characteristic of Jesus, as in his washing the feet of the Twelve (Jn 13:1-17), is not a masochistic abasement or denial of his superiority that he also frankly declares. It is simply a refusal to allow his superiority to be a barrier to his love and service of the most inferior. In the other great religious leaders we find something of the same simplicity that has no concern to assert its own dignity or to "stand on ceremony" when such concern would interfere with their respective missions. Yet reading their biographies even in hagiographic form we do not find the portrayal of any such humility as that of Jesus, because none of them laid the primary stress that he did on understanding God as Love even for enemies.

From Jesus' understanding of God as Love flows what even the most skeptical of critics today admit must have been a historical fact about him. It is the remembrance behind all the traditions of the New Testament and integral to the main facts of his life, yet so surprising in its historical context, that Jesus was "the friend of sinners." Clearly he shared table fellowship with the outcasts of society, associated with lepers, with prostitutes, with the hated quisling tax collectors and publicans, with women so little regarded by others, with unclean foreigners. He did so not because he was a bohemian, but because he found in them a potentiality for lovable *goodness* that others did not see. Moreover, his love was creative, because it wakened in these marginalized non-persons a response of genuine love, repentance, and renewed sense of their own worth. The only real anger that Jesus exhibits in the Gospels (and it is a fierce anger) is with the moneychangers who desecrate the Temple and with the scribes and Pharisees who have contempt for "the little ones" whose widows and orphans they cheat.

The Reign (Kingdom) of God that is the central theme of Jesus' teaching is understood by him as the fulfillment of what the prophets foretold, the restoration of the order in society intended by God in the creation. In this order there will be first of all perfect fidelity between man and wife in marriage and they will give wise and loving care to their children. Natural resources will be rightly used so that the earth will be like a cultivated garden producing enough for all and its fruits will be distributed justly so none will be poor. The social order will be one of peaceful cooperation under an orderly government that serves rather than dominates and that extends to the whole human race united by one law of love.

The energies of humanity, however, will not be confined to merely human affairs. The love that motivates all creatures will first of all be a love of God as loving "Abba," inspired by the Holy Spirit of Wisdom that will open human minds to all the wonders of God's creation and of God's own life. Out of this love the human community of faith can live a life of praise and thanksgiving. This intimate contemplation of God will insure that death itself will be overcome so that the friendship with God can continue in the eternal life of human persons, souls and bodies.

This Kingdom of God is open to all. Yet only those who allow themselves to be opened by and to the power of God, so that they can live according to the Kingdom's way of life and love, can enter it. Jesus insisted that this Reign should be awaited with eager expectancy since the time of its fulfillment was a secret of the Father not given to the Son to announce. Yet the Reign has definitively begun to be realized in Jesus and his community and this community must endure bitter opposition from the powers of darkness and from those human persons unwilling to open themselves to its Good News for fear of losing their selfish autonomy. Consequently, the community of those who believe in Jesus and his Gospel, like the faithful "remnant" of the Hebrew Scriptures, will be called to witness to this Good News throughout the world. They must continue to proclaim this Gospel until the Kingdom is achieved on earth as it is in heaven when the powers of darkness, death, and sin against self, neighbor and God are finally overcome. Each individual will be judged on whether each has recognized Jesus in the poor and suffering or neglected him, that is, by the great criterion of genuine and effective love.

Notes

[1] See R.G. Collingwood, *The Idea of History* (Oxford: Clarendon Press, 1962); Mircea Eliade, *Cosmos and History: The Myth of the Eternal Return* (New York: Harper and Row, Harper Torchbooks, 1959); Claude Tresmontant, *A Study of Hebrew Thought* (New York: Desclée, 1960).

[2] Harry McSorley, *Luther Right or Wrong?: An Ecumenical Theological Study of Luther's Major Work: 'The Bondage of the Will'* (New York: Newman Press, 1968).

[3] René Latourelle, *Christ and the Church: Signs of Salvation* (Staten Island, NY: Alba House, 1972), pp. 163-210 speaks of this mark of the Church as "temporality" and shows it is the same as the "stability" referred to by Vatican I. On apostolic succession see International Theological Commission, "Apostolic Succession: A Clarification," *Origins* 4 (19 Sept., 1974): 193-200.

[4] See Avery Dulles, *Revelation and the Quest for Unity* (Washington/Cleveland: Corpus, 1968), pp. 69-74.

[5] On the application of the historical critical method to the *Qur'an* see Toby Lester, "What is the Koran?" *The Atlantic Monthly,* Jan. 1999, pp. 43-57.

[6] See Gustaf Aulen, *Jesus in Contemporary Historical Research* (Philadelphia: Fortress, 1976) and references in Chapter 5, note 14. See also Marcus J. Borg, *Jesus in Contemporary Scholarship* (Harrisburg, PA: Trinity International, 1996). Walter P. Weaver has begun a three-volume series with *The Historical Jesus in the Twentieth Century: 1900-1950* (*Ibid.,* 1999).

[7] See Joachim Jeremias, *The Problem of the Historical Jesus* (Philadelphia: Fortress Press, 1964) for a noted exegete who follows this methodology with some success.

[8] For criticism of the Two-Document Hypothesis see Hans Herbert Stoldt, *History and Criticism of the Marcan Hypothesis* (Macon, GA: Mercer University Press, 1980). For its defense by a Catholic see Joseph A. Fitzmyer, SJ, "The Priority of Mark and the *'Q'* Source in Luke," in his *To Advance the Gospel* (New York: Crossroad, 1981), pp. 3-40.

[9] The debate cuts across Catholic and Protestant lines. For a defense by a Catholic scholar see Raymond H. Brown, *The Critical Meaning of the Bible* (New York: Paulist Press, 1981) and an attack by a Protestant scholar see Gerhard Maier, *The End of the Historical-Critical Method* (St. Louis: Concordia Publishing House, 1977). On newer methods see Jack Dean Kingsbury, ed., *Gospel Interpretation: Narrative Critical and Social-Scientific Approaches* (Harrisburg, PA: Trinity Press International, 1997). See also the evaluation of the various exegetical methods by the Pontifical Biblical Commission (with a Foreword of recommendation by Cardinal Joseph Ratzinger), "The Interpretation of the Bible in the Church," *Origins,* 23, n. 29 (Jan. 6, 1994): 499-524.

[10] See references in Chapter 5, note 7.

[11] The extra-biblical data is summed up by Walter Kasper, *Jesus the Christ* (New York: Paulist Press, 1976), pp. 65-71, and John P. Meier, *The Roots of the Problem and the Person,* vol. I of *A Marginal Jew: Rethinking the Historical Jesus* (New York: Doubleday, 1991).

[12] For Muhammad's life see Chapter 5, note 27.

[13] For standard dating of biblical books see charts in *The Jerome Biblical Commentary,* R.E. Brown, J.A. Fitzmyer, and R.E. Murphy, eds. (Englewood Cliffs, NJ: Prentice-Hall, 1968), Old Testament p. 519; New Testament, p. 526.

[14] John A.T. Robinson, though otherwise not a conservative scholar, in his *Redating the New Testament* (Philadelphia: Westminster, 1976), argued forcefully that the Synoptics were all written before the fall of the Temple in 70 CE. The common tendencies to date them later because they report Jesus' prophecy of that tragic event obviously depend on whether one believes true prophecy is possible. But Robinson points out that in fact these prophecies are couched in general Old Testament language that would surely have been more specific if reported by someone writing after their fulfillment.

[15] For a vigorous critique see Luke Timothy Johnson, *The Real Jesus: The Misguided Quest for the Historical Jesus and the Truth of the Traditional Gospels* (San Francisco: Harper/Collins, 1996).

[16] See Bevard S. Childs, *Introduction to the Old Testament as Scripture* (Philadelphia: Fortress Press, 1979), pp.71-83, on the notion of canon criticism. See also the Pontifical Biblical Commission, note 9 above.

[17] The term "historical" is used to mean (a) what actually happened; (b) what we can prove by critical methods certainly or probably happened (*historisch*); (c) what we know happened as it is meaningful for us (*geschichlich*). See Gerald O'Collins, "Is the Resurrection an 'Historical Event'," *Heythrop Journal* (1967): 381-387.

[18] *Summa Theologiae,* III, q. 55.

[19] On the historicity of the resurrection of Lazarus see Raymond E. Brown, *The Gospel of John,* Anchor Bible (New York: Doubleday, 1966), vol. 2, p. 8.

[20] Edward Schillebeeckx, *Jesus: An Experiment in Christology* (New York: Seabury, 1979).

[21] Most scholars agree that Mk 16:9-20 because of its absence from many early MSS, its awkward joining to what precedes it, and its style and vocabulary is a late addition to the Gospel. Yet in a very precise study William R. Farmer, *The Last Twelve Verses of Mark* (Cambridge: Cambridge University Press, 1974) showed that these arguments are by no means conclusive. According to him this "addition" is absent only in one group of MSS, perhaps to avoid the mention of "snake-handling" (Mk 16:18) that has often occasioned foolish behavior by enthusiasts. Moreover, Farmer shows that the vocabulary of Mk 16:9-20 is in fact not significantly different from that of the rest of the Gospel. Farmer also rejects the generally accepted priority of Mark. See his recent, *The Gospel of Jesus: The Pastoral Relevance of the Synoptic Problem* (Louisville, KY: Westminster/John Knox Press, 1994), pp. 15-40.

[22] In fact the serious discrepancies among the Gospel accounts of the resurrection disappear if only two suppositions that do not destroy their historical reliability are made. (1) For the sake of brevity and clarity Matthew and Mark omit the incident of Mary Magdalen's bringing Peter and John to the tomb *before* the angelic apparition. Also Matthew is concerned to answer the rumors spread by the guards that the Twelve had stolen the body since its Jewish Christian audience may have been acquainted with these rumors. (2) While Luke (but not in all MSS) relates the Magdalen intervention, John, following his usual tendency to dramatize, not only relates it in detail but centers it exclusively on her, omitting the fact that the other women also saw the Risen Christ.

[23] Wolfhart Pannenburg, *Jesus: God and Man* (Philadelphia: Westminster, 1968), pp. 88-105.

[24] On the "spiritual" nature of the resurrection body see my *Theologies of the Body: Humanist and Christian*, 2nd ed. (Boston: National Catholic Center for Bioethics, 1997), pp. 585-604.

[25] See George Montague, *The Holy Spirit: Growth of a Biblical Tradition* (New York: Paulist Press, 1976) and Yves Congar, *I Believe in the Holy Spirit,* 3 vols. (New York: Seabury, 1983).

[26] See *Peter in the New Testament: A Collaborative Assessment by Protestant and Roman Catholic Scholars,* ed. by R.E. Brown, K.P. Donfried, and J. Reumann (Minneapolis: Augsburg Publishing House, 1973) with bibliography, pp. 169-78.

[27] For a defense of Jesus' Messiahship see Sigmund Mowinckel, *He That Cometh* (Nashville, TN: Abingdon Press, 1954), and for his self-consciousness see Jean Galot, *Who is Christ?* (Chicago: Franciscan Herald Press, 1981), pp. 319-75.

[28] See Chapter 5, notes 14 and 15 for references.

[29] See H. Saddhatissa, *Buddhist Ethics* (New York: George Braziller, 1970). The first of the Five Precepts forbids killing insects and all higher forms of life, pp.87-93.

[30] See Schillebeeckx, *Jesus* (note 20 above), pp. 256-57.

[31] See Leopold Sabourin, *The Names and Titles of Jesus* (New York: Macmillan, 1967), pp. 150-60).

CHAPTER 9

THE HISTORICAL CHRISTIAN COMMUNITY

1. The Organization of the Christian Community

If Christianity is to be chosen as one's world-view and value-system it is required that the historicity of the Church as an ecumenical and revelatory sign be established. This means that the Church as we today can experience it has remained essentially identical with the earliest Christian community centered in Jesus, yet that this identity be dynamically developing. The living Lord must remain alive in the Church so that in the Church we experience he is accessible to us as God's self-revelation. Otherwise the Church lacks the mark of *apostolicity* that I argued in Chapter 7 and 8 to be one of the marks by which it is a moral miracle signifying that it speaks with authority from God.

Hence, I must ask what is the continuity between the Church and Jesus or Jesus and the Church? Did Jesus establish an institutional Church or was he simply the influential teacher and model of a way of life, a "movement"?[1] Today many people are repelled by the idea of "organized religion" that seems contradictory to the very notion of spiritual liberation. The many tyrannies of our time have made us also suspicious of authoritarian institutions. Certainly Jesus was well aware of the dangers of human authority with its drive to domination. Yet he also recognized its value for any cooperating community and sought to remedy these dangers that proceed not from the nature of authority as such but from the sinful abuse of authority. This he did effectively by teaching and exemplifying in his own leadership how authority can and should be loving service.

One of the most solid historical facts about the early Christian community is that its form of worship was the table-fellowship of the Eucharist. St. Paul and the Synoptics all attribute the institution of the Eucharist to Jesus himself on the night before his arrest and crucifixion — the Last or Lord's Supper held in the season of the Jewish Passover Meal. While each of the Gospels describes or refers to this event in a different way, they agree substantially with the earliest account found in Paul's First Letter to the Corinthians (11:23-26):

> For I received from the Lord what I also handed on to you, namely that the Lord Jesus, on the night he was handed over, took bread, and, after he had given thanks, broke it and said, "This is my body that is for you. Do this in remembrance of me." In the same way, also the cup, after supper, saying, "This cup is the new covenant in my blood. Do this, as often as you drink it, in remembrance of me." For as often as you eat this bread and drink the cup, you proclaim the death of the Lord until he comes.

According to the Gospel accounts and St. Paul's preaching Jesus intended the Eucharist symbolizing his death on the Cross as a sacrificial act on behalf of all sinful humanity and in obedience to his Father.[2] For the Bible, the essence of priesthood is to be called by God to act as the leader or mediator of a community in its supreme act of worshiping God, namely, the offering of a worthy sacrifice. Moreover the essence of sacrifice is the sacramental gift of self to God as Creator, that is, a gift of self that is given external and public expression. In the Hebrew Scriptures, sacrifice took the form of offering the blood or life-principle of a clean and perfect animal. The Jews did not offer an animal for its own value but as a representation of the life of human beings for which the animals were substitutes. As the *Epistle to the Hebrews* shows, by at least 70 CE[3] the early Church already understood Jesus' death on the Cross as the realization of what these animal sacrifices merely symbolized. On the Cross Jesus offered himself totally to God in obedience to his mission to declare the Gospel, thus exposing the evil of sin and revealing God's love even for his enemies. The Last Supper was a sacramental anticipation of this unique offering. In commissioning the Twelve to repeat this sacrament, Jesus certainly did not order them to repeat the offering on the Cross, because on Calvary this offering was completed once for all. His purpose was to enable Christians everywhere and in all ages to join their own self-offering with that of Jesus in a sacramental manner, that is, in a symbol that actually effects what it symbolizes. As Paul indicates in the text quoted, what this Eucharistic Sacrifice effects is a renewal of the believers' covenant with God, an intimate relation of mutual love between God and the Christian community and among its members. The Epistle to the Hebrews argues that since Jesus performed this supreme priestly act he was not only a priest but the "High Priest." The Jewish priesthood thus came to be seen as merely a foreshadowing of Jesus' priesthood and any subsequent ministry in the Church could therefore derive its authority only as a sign and instrument of Jesus' own.

The New Testament (with the exception of Hebrews just referred to) uses *presbyter* (elder) for the leaders of a local community and avoids the term "priest" for anyone except the priests of the Old Law. This can be explained by the fact that it was important in the first days of the Church not to confuse its new priesthood with that of the hereditary Jewish priesthood with its bloody temple sacrifices. This priesthood had for Christians been rendered obsolete by the sacrifice of the Cross as is argued in the Epistle to the Hebrews that may be dated about 70 CE. Once the Church was no longer predominantly Jewish this avoidance of the term became unnecessary, and the patristic Church never hesitated to parallel the new Christian priesthood with the old Jewish one and to adopt something of the older terminology and liturgical forms.

All our evidence, often exasperatingly incomplete, shows that the Church always conceived the presidency over the Eucharist to be proper only to presbyters authorized to preside over the Christian community. Since the first Christian communities met in "house churches," i.e., larger houses belonging to some more wealthy and prominent converts, it seems probable that these householders were the first leaders of such communities. The terminological distinction between *presbyter* (elder) and *bishop* (overseer) was not made at first, since the bishop was himself also an elder and his primacy in the presbyterium only gradually emerged in definitive form.[4] Yet already by the time of the

Pastoral Epistles of the New Testament the episcopal primacy was established in Pauline Churches.[5] Furthermore bishops and with them the presbyters, were recognized as having leadership, including that of presiding at the Eucharist only because they could claim apostolic authority from Jesus through the Twelve or St. Paul.[6] In about 107 CE St. Ignatius, Bishop of Antioch explained this ecclesial hierarchy as modeled on the relation of Christ to the Twelve Apostles.[7] Yet it also seems that in some places men who at the risk of their lives had been "confessors" of the faith and also itinerant "prophets" were also allowed to "offer thanks."[8] Whether this means, however, that confessors or prophets who were not themselves presbyters actually substituted for a presbyter as president of the Eucharist is by no means clear. It could mean no more than that they were honored by being permitted to add their thanksgiving prayers to those of the presiding presbyter. Certainly by the time of Ignatius when our information is fuller and less ambiguous no mention is made of such a custom. In third rank among the Church leaders according to Ignatius, were the "deacons" whose special duty was to care for the poor. Though it was from their ranks that bishops were often chosen, deacons are never mentioned as presiding at the Eucharist.[9]

Current scholarship today commonly claims that the apostolic Church included a variety of forms of Church government, ranging from a loose charismatic organization in Corinth to a monarchical episcopate in Jerusalem.[10] Since in a large city such as Rome there must have been several such communities, it perhaps took some time before one of these house leaders began to be recognized as bishop of the whole city. Thus, it is possible, as claimed, that monarchical episcopacy (monepiscopy) developed gradually. It is noted that the famous letter called the *First Epistle of Clement to the Corinthians* was sent not in the name of a bishop of Rome but simply in the name of "the Church of God that sojourns at Rome."[11]

Yet the epistles of St. Ignatius, Bishop of Antioch (martyred before 117) and probably appointed by Peter or Paul, shows that in his time in many of the Pauline Churches of Asia Minor there was a threefold hierarchy of bishop, presbyters, and deacons. St. Irenaeus of Lyons gives a list of the bishops of Rome of which Clement is the fourth.

Irenaeus must have been well informed of the Roman Tradition. He had been a disciple of St. Polycarp, Bishop of Smyrna, whom in 177 he met in Rome and to whom one of the letters of St. Ignatius of Antioch is addressed. Polycarp had as a youth known the Apostle John. Thus the "various forms" of Church government posited by current scholarship (probably for ecumenical reasons) could not have lasted long, if indeed they ever existed. Nor is it odd that the Church very early on accepted a single form of Church structure. As the reference to Ignatius of Antioch indicates, the Gospels provide the obvious model for Church organization in the leadership of Jesus and the Twelve, assisted for charitable works by other ministers who are not priests. Yet even if the currently popular reconstruction of the early Church as experimenting with several polities should prove correct, the fundamental fact is that the threefold hierarchy of offices was very early established in both the Eastern and Western Church. Moreover it was and is held by Orthodox and Catholics to be warranted by apostolic tradition.[12] The later view of the Protestant Reformers that it is of purely human origin is not consistent with this Tradition.

With this basic organization of local churches each under a bishop and his presbyterate, assisted by deacons (from whom the bishops were often chosen), the Catholic Church spread through the Roman Empire and beyond its boundaries. Church teaching gradually developed as it faced the opposition of pagans and diversities of opinion within the community itself. These diversities were resolved by clearer formulations of doctrine worked out by outstanding bishops or convocations of bishops. Quite early, certain important cities whose churches claimed apostolic origin, namely Jerusalem, Antioch, Alexandria, and Rome were recognized as especially important and eventually also with them Constantinople when it became the "Second Rome."

Of these "patriarchs" the Bishop of Rome early claimed the primacy because Peter and Paul had been martyred there, and by that fact the right to exercise the role of leadership of the bishops that the Gospels showed had been given by Jesus to Peter over the Twelve. We have already seen that perhaps as early as 70 CE, and no later than 98 CE[13] (see the *First Epistle of Clement to the Corinthians* perhaps as early as 70 CE), the Church of Rome exercises a pastoral concern for another distant Church. Moreover it supports its right to intervene by recalling the memories of Sts. Peter and Paul martyred in Rome. Also in 177 St. Irenaeus of Lyons met his old teacher St. Polycarp in Rome to attempt to persuade St. Eleutherius, clearly recognized as Bishop of Rome, to be moderate in his suppression of the charismatic Montanist heresy. The next Bishop of Rome, Victor I (c. 189 to c. 198) attempted to settle the controversy over the date of Easter for the Churches of Asia and explicitly invoked his right to do so as the successor of St. Peter. From then on Victor's successors continued to make this claim that was generally recognized by the early Church Councils as based on Scripture and Tradition.

After relating this data, however, I want to emphasize that what is important for my argument concerning the *apostolicity* of the Church is not to prove with certitude any particular reconstruction of the historical development of its hierarchical structure. Given the fragmentary character of the available data on the first century of the Church's history such certitude cannot be expected. What is important for my argument is only to show that from a critical point of view the conviction of the Church of the Patristic Period that it was substantially identical with the Church of the Apostles must be taken seriously. Thus, there is no proof that the Church became essentially corrupted, as Protestants and others do when they speak with deprecation of the evidences of "early Catholicism" (*Frühkatholicismus*) even in the Gospel according to St. Matthew. Thus the present claim that the Roman Catholic Church exhibits the mark of catholicity is not historically contradicted but is given significantly probable support from what evidence we have of its first hundred years. To arrive at certitude on this question of catholicity requires the concurrent probabilities of its history taken as a whole and does not rest merely on that obscure period when it was still largely underground because of persecution.

The efforts of the Bishop of Rome and other bishops at maintaining unity of doctrine and government, however, did not always succeed perfectly.[14] Various tendencies, some probably present from the very earliest times within the Christian community, grew and had to be reconciled or suppressed, and when this failed, ended in schisms from the Great Church. Some of these concerned morals and ways of worship, others questions of doctrine. Generally they can be well explained as tendencies to reconcile, sometimes by genuine synthesis, sometimes by mere eclecticism, sometimes by deplorable compromise, the unique features of Jesus' teaching with the philosophical views current in Hellenistic culture as the Church struggled to incarnate the Gospel in this culture.

There were Judaizing tendencies that clung to the Mosaic Law and explained Jesus simply as a prophet. There were anti-Jewish tendencies like that of Marcion (fl. c. 144) and, though it originated within Judaism, also Gnosticism (second century). There were enthusiastic, charismatic movements like the Montanists (second century), and moralistic influences such as that of Stoic philosophy. Most important were the Platonizing tendencies that provided an elevated view of spirituality but introduced dualism into Christian anthropology and led even the great Origen (d. c. 254) to revive the theory of reincarnation.

At the end of the persecution of Christians by the Roman government with Constantine's Edict of Toleration in 311 the Church was growing throughout the Empire. The ideal of martyrdom in imitation of the Crucified dominated the spirituality of this period and gave it tested courage. But it also had some serious negative consequences, such as the moral rigorism of Tertullian (d. c. 230).

2. Incarnation and Trinity

Much more serious were the heresies arising from Platonizing circles, such as that of Arius (d. 336) who taught that the Son is only the first of creatures in a descending hierarchy of emanations from the One. With his heresy began the long series of struggles over Christology and the doctrine of the Trinity that troubled the Church from the Council of Nicaea in 325 that defined the divinity of Christ to the Second Council of Nicaea in 787.

The chief work of these Councils was to establish the doctrines of the Trinity and Incarnation that are contained in the New Testament but not so explicitly formulated as to be immune to many controversies. The teachings of these first seven Ecumenical Councils are still today accepted by the Orthodox, Catholic and most Protestant Churches. Yet they resulted in many schisms, especially in the East, such as those of the Nestorians and the Monophysites who for various reasons could not accept the formulae in which these Councils attempted to state the traditional Christian faith. Today historians tend to attribute these more to misunderstandings and political factors than to real heresy.

What was the developed understanding of the central doctrines of the Church formulated by the first seven Councils and approved by the Roman bishops as the court of final appeal in doctrinal controversies?[15] First of all the Church bore witness that Jesus was truly a human being as we are, except for sin. He was put to death in witness to the Gospel that he had taught and lived, but rose from the dead to immortal life with God.

Second, the Ecumenical Councils taught that in preaching that the Kingdom of God had begun on earth in his own person, life and teaching, Jesus had revealed that his relation to God was that of Son to Father. By this was to be understood that the Son from all eternity had shared the life of God in its plenitude and activity including the creation of the world. Yet this Divine Son in Jesus Christ had taken created human nature to himself (become "incarnate") in order to reveal the Father to humanity. By his incarnation and his sacrificial life this Incarnate Son of God has enabled us who share his humanity to return to that friendship with God. It was for this community with God that we were created before we sinned by freely choosing to go our own foolish and destructive way.

Third, it was understood that Jesus before leaving this world had made a promise (that was in fact fulfilled at Pentecost) to send on his Church the invisible guidance and empowerment of the Spirit of God. This Holy Spirit was also the Spirit of Christ who shares equally with him in the eternal plenitude of God the Father's life.

Fourth, the Councils taught that when the Church, guided by the Holy Spirit, has completed its mission to preach the Good News to all the world for anyone freely to accept or reject it, God's Kingdom will be consummated. All those who accept God's grace will be received in this eternal fellowship. No one will be excluded from it except those who have knowingly and deliberately refused it. Then at last history will yield to eternal life in God's Kingdom.

The practical consequence of these Incarnational and Trinitarian doctrines was that all those who accepted the Good News were obliged to repent, seek the forgiveness of God, and unite themselves to the Church as witnesses of the Kingdom through baptism. Baptism committed them also to a life modeled on that of Jesus, rooted in faith and hope in him and in the love of God and neighbor. This Christian life would achieve its power and fullness in prayer, especially in the Eucharist. Such a life of love would aim at the overcoming of all the evils committed by the fallen angels and humankind desirous of their own autonomy that had distorted God's good creation.

Many had difficulty accepting this teaching for both doctrinal and moral reasons. The Jews, and later the Muslims, thought it denied monotheism and the separation between Creator and creature, because it claimed divinity for Jesus. The philosophically sophisticated pagans thought it was metaphysically contradictory in not subordinating the Son and Holy Spirit to God and materialistic in its defense of a permanent Incarnation and resurrection of the body. The modern world finds these Church doctrines mythical because they involve mysteries or paradoxes irresolvable by human reason and beyond empirical verification.

To such objections Christians reply there is nothing odd in the notion that the nature of God is mysterious beyond human comprehension provided that nothing is said of God that is contradictory and absurd. It certainly would be absurd to say that the One God is Three Gods, or that Three Gods are One God. Equally absurd would be to say that the Son is physically begotten by a God who is pure Spirit. But the Councils made clear that none of these absurdities are stated or implied in Scripture. All terms applied to God must be understood *analogically*. They are derived from our ordinary human experience but used of God in a way which enables us to get some idea but not necessarily an adequate one of a cause from its effect, the artist from his work, because God is the cause of all the things of our experience.

Thus, the Councils understood the biblical account of Jesus to mean that he has revealed to us that while there is only One God, yet within that One God there are relations of communication, of total giving. These relations are analogous to those that exist between human persons who share their spiritual life of knowledge and love. Even within each individual person, as St. Augustine saw, there is an interior communication of knowledge and love.[16]

Since every analogy implies both a similarity and a difference, there is an infinite difference between the Divine Community and any human community. Human persons can share knowledge and love in common but only imperfectly. Much else in their individual existences they cannot share. In the Divine Community, however, whose spiritual being is pure thought and love, there is total sharing, so that their Divinity is absolutely common to all Three. This Divinity is not common in the way human nature is common to three human persons. It is more like the way that one and the same truth is shared by several persons, or as several persons share in a single free purpose. Thus there are Three Divine Persons but not Three Gods. There is One God only.

On the other hand, to look at it another way, God is God the Father who totally communicates his divinity with his Son and Spirit. They have nothing of their own, but receive the Father's Divinity as their very own life in absolute union with him. They are distinct from him only in that they receive the divine life that he gives but does not receive. The Spirit is distinct from the Son only because the Spirit receives his life from the Father through the Son who contributes nothing but what he too has received from the Father who is the Principle and Fount of divine life. While the theologians of the Greek and Latin Churches have expressed this somewhat differently, the East emphasizing that the Father is the principle of divine unity (*monarchy*), the West that this unity consists in the common Godhead itself. The controversy over the *filioque* — the statement added by the Latins to the Creed that says that the Holy Spirit "proceeds from the Father *and the Son*" — seems only a misunderstanding. The Latins understand this as meaning "through the Son" as the Greek Fathers often express it also. They do not understand it to mean that the Son is a second principle of divinity in God, as the Greeks suppose was meant and to which they rightly object.[17]

The Ecumenical Councils also held that it would be absurd to say that Jesus is a man who became God. Or to say that he is a God who became a man and thereby ceased to be God. God is not subject to the incompleteness that all change implies. But the doctrine of the Incarnation does not imply any change in God. It teaches that the Son of God, Second Person of the Trinity, who with the other two Divine Persons created the world, freely chose to create for himself a human nature. He has so related this human nature to his Divine Person as to make himself personally present to us in our world in a way that we can know and understand. Thus when the Twelve met Jesus they knew they were meeting one who was as human as themselves. Yet in time they discovered that this someone as Person had existed for all eternity in the Trinity and thus would be able to lead them into community with the Father by the power of his Holy Spirit.

3. The Constantinian Establishment

As long as the Church was under persecution by the Roman government it found it not too difficult to maintain its identity and the integrity of its traditions, though difficulties arose from the rigorist tendencies of some of its members. The practice of excommunication (exclusion from the Eucharist) and severe public penance for apostasy, idolatry, murder, and adultery were sufficient to maintain discipline. The Roman Church, however, in spite of the bitter opposition of the rigorists, was compelled to moderate these severities in the name of Christian mercy and compassion.

Once the Church was recognized as legal by imperial support and paganism had been legally outlawed and then gradually (but perhaps only superficially) overcome, the Church was faced with the problem of the influx of new members. These new recruits were often neither truly converted nor well instructed. The Church was subject to interference by the government in teaching and discipline and was tempted to rely too much on secular support even to the point of encouraging the State to use force to further the Church's purposes. Yet on the positive side this establishment of the Church by the State also gave the Church full access to the wonderful classical culture developed by the Greeks and Romans. This made possible the amazingly creative period of the Cappadocian Church Fathers in the East and of Hilary, Ambrose, Augustine, and Jerome in the West. The Church for the first time could claim that the Gospel, so Hebraic in its original form, is capable of embracing and bringing to fulfillment all that is noble and true in every human culture. In a Gregory of Nyssa or an Augustine the deepest Christianity is expressed in the richest forms of ancient culture that in their Christian versions seem to find even fuller realization than in the classical originals.

This fulfillment, nevertheless, was only a prelude to a great and long period of trial, understood by the Church as the Gospel way of the Cross permitted by God to test and purify the works of Christians. This trial was the invasion of the Empire by barbaric Germanic tribes from the north, the Mongolian hordes from inner Asia, the Persians from the east, and then Islam from the south. From a Christian perspective Islam can be seen as the punishment of God on the Church for its internal doctrinal squabbles, especially the Nestorian and Monophysite heresies, that led it to neglect preaching the Gospel to the Arabs at a time when they were eager to escape their ancient polytheism. Therefore, Muhammad, influenced by Judaism and Christianity but poorly informed as to the full Gospel, succeeded in bringing faith in One God to his people. In this view, Islam, like Arianism, is a simplified version of Christianity. Both understandably appealed to peoples on the margin of the Roman Empire looking for a monotheism akin to Judaism but not ready for the Christian mystery of the Incarnation. Thus, the Church was for a long time surrounded on north and south by what amounted to hostile heresies and blocked from missionary activity in India and the Far East. Yet, this challenge eventually drove the Church northward and westward to Christianize Europe beyond the bounds of the old Empire and ultimately the New World.

It is customary to separate the Middle Ages and the Renaissance from each other and view the Renaissance as a reversion to paganism. It is helpful to see both as phases of one great movement by the Church. First the Church strove to incorporate the northern barbarians of Europe into patristic Christianity in the "Dark Ages." Then it strove to recover for this patristic synthesis the full riches of classical culture, first in the High Middle Ages its philosophical and scientific riches and in the Renaissance its literary and artistic heritage. The result was that by 1500 Europe, east and west, north and south, was a "Christendom" that had absorbed and surpassed all the culture of the ancients and was now open to the possibility of extending the Gospel world-wide.

Although the Church had lost North Africa and the Byzantine East to Islam, it had held its own against the Muslims in the west and through Spain absorbed much of the Arabian cultural achievements. Moreover, it had given to Christianity a systematic theology, no longer of the pulpit as in the patristic age, but of the universities that it had created. This academic theology had a scientific rigor and a breadth of view capable of accepting and assimilating truth wherever it was to be found. Finally, it had laid the basis for the remarkable development of modern science and technological control that was to emerge from the universities into the academies in the seventeenth century.

Nevertheless, by 1500 the Church was suffering from profound ills incurred in the very process of these successes. First of all, the alienation of the Eastern Church from the papacy that had slowly developed from the Seventh Council (787) had finally become apparently irreconcilable. The failed attempt at reunion at the Council of Florence in 1445 and the subsequent fall of the Byzantines to Islam had tragic results. The Eastern Church, that had achieved the Christianization of the Slavs, has ever since remained in separation from the Western Church and under almost continuous persecution, except for pre-revolutionary Russia.

This terrible blow to the unity of the Church had been prepared by the failure of the Crusades that from 1095 to 1291 aimed at freeing the Eastern Church and especially the Holy Land from Islam. In their intent the Crusades were defensive wars and as such might have been justified. Hence they were often encouraged even by saints and were thought to have the advantage that by a common cause they diverted the Christian nations from fighting each other. Yet they degenerated into unsuccessful wars of conquest and did more than anything else to render chronic the split between the Orthodox and the Catholics. The failure of this great movement can be ascribed to the divisions within the Christian forces and to the Church's own reliance on this use of force more than on a serious effort to evangelize the Muslims urged by St. Francis of Assisi (d. 1226).

The same futile reliance on force rather than on evangelization is apparent in the Church's turning to the State to suppress heresy. This led to her own establishment of the Inquisition in order to keep the control of judgments on doctrinal matters in her own hands, while demanding that the secular arm enforce these judgments. Typical of this corruption was the way in which the Order of Preachers founded by St. Dominic (d. 1221) to overcome heresy by proclaiming the Gospel was soon coopted to carry on the Inquisition. The real answer to heresy, as Dominic and Francis saw it, was preaching, the active evangelization of the common people. This was an enormous task, since the mass of medieval Europeans, especially the former barbarians, were illiterate, half pagan in their way of life, and poorly instructed in even the fundamentals of the Christian faith. These difficulties were augmented by the oppression of the poor by feudal lords, or their urbanization in the newly growing cities, and then by the rise of a greedy capitalism. When we speak of the Middle Ages as the "Ages of Faith" we must remember that the popular religion of the time was very far from that of the fervent communities of the early Church although they too suffered from many defects.

The third evil was the politicization of Church authority and the rise of nationalism. The Constantinian Establishment was a cooperation between Emperor and Pope, although in fact the popes had to struggle hard to maintain a relative independence for the Church. In the Byzantine Empire, as the Eastern Church loosened its ties with the Roman See, Caesaro-papism became endemic. In the West the popes succeeded in their struggle, but only at the cost of themselves taking on many of the political methods of the secular government, a development leading finally to Renaissance popes like Alexander VI who were mere politicians rather than pastors. The Emperor himself soon found himself confronted by the rise of national states and centralized monarchies, especially France. The result was the domination of the papacy by the French Kings and then the Great Western Schism (1378-1417) during which at first two and then three popes divided the allegiance of the Church among them. By an enormous effort the Church overcame this schism, but was unable before 1500 to recover its own normal functioning, because many of the bishoprics had become financial and political commodities exploited by absentee bishops.

The fourth evil was the breaking up of the medieval intellectual synthesis. This synthesis (that included a very lively pluralism) had centered in the medieval universities. In time these universities suffered from the usual occupational ills of academic institutions. Theology became more and more separated from its vital relation to the life of the Church and took on the desiccated, logicizing form of Nominalism. This led both to rationalism and to fideism, and in moral questions adopted a voluntaristic, legalistic stance modeled after the political positivism developed to justify the absolutism of the new national monarchies. When such a nominalistic and legalist theology began to influence the popular religion already described, the result was a superstitious performance of "good works" understood as ritual observances reminiscent of the Pharisaism denounced by Jesus. The rise of a literate laity in Italy in the 1400's and the turn toward the more appealing literary and artistic interests of the Renaissance gave rise to a reaction against university theology and its Aristotelian methodological rigor. Instead the trend was to a more imaginative, but often fantastic, Neo-Platonism with an increased interest in astrology and alchemy.

None of these evils were absolutely new to the Church. They can be roughly paralleled in the New Testament Church itself and they are still with us in other forms today. But in 1500 they had coalesced to produce a European Church culturally very rich and dynamic but no longer under the control of a respected pope or a pastorally active episcopate. Underlying these developments also was the beginning of modern finance capitalism and the replacement of the medieval warrior aristocracy by an oligarchy of commercial wealth.

The Reformation of the Church "in head and members" urged by many saints such as St. Catherine of Siena and ineffectively commanded by several Councils was, therefore, most necessary for the survival of the Church. Tragically, however, it produced a schism that removed much of northern Europe from communion with Rome and provoked a series of religious wars of largely nationalistic character. The Catholic

Reformation continued, through the Council of Trent, to correct many of these evils within the Catholic Church. Moreover, the discovery of the New World and of the Pacific route to Asia gave it the opportunity for an enormous missionary expansion to the west. Yet in the East the collapse of the Byzantine Empire before Islam seemed (after Council of Florence 1445) to deepen the separation from the Orthodox Churches.

The Protestant Reformation in its fourfold split into Lutheranism, Anglicanism, Calvinism, and the Ana-Baptist or Radical Reformation, after losing hope for reintegration into the Catholic Church on its own terms attempted to return to what they believed to be the model of the New Testament Church. These Protestant Churches in their struggle to return to Christian sources attempted to retain as much of the cultural Humanism of the Catholic Church as they could because the Reformers were strongly influenced by Renaissance Humanism. Yet they also found so much of this heritage inextricably linked with the history of what they considered non-biblical developments that they found it necessary to be very selective to avoid "idolatry" and "Pelagianism" (dependence on "good works") in this tradition. Hence these churches tended to become national churches that in becoming "established" often lost much of their religious depth, hardened into state enforced "orthodoxy," and needed constantly to be renewed by pietistic movements that often became sectarian.[19]

The Calvinist Reformed Church was the most dynamic wing of the Reformation, supporting the rise of modern science in the 1600's and of more democratic political institutions and capitalist economics. Calvinists saw these tasks as the proper pursuit of the Christian laity's vocation to witness their faith to the world and to bring about a Christian Republic. Such ideas were also present in the Catholic Reformation, but they did not take the central importance they had in the Reformed Churches.

The Lutheran Church, on the other hand, tended to a kind of conservatism and passive acceptance of government control. After a period of "Lutheran scholasticism" or "Orthodoxy," however, it underwent important changes first under the influence of pietistic anti-intellectual movements and then of the rationalistic Enlightenment and the philosophy of Immanuel Kant. These latter influences made the

Lutheran Churches of Germany the center of a new "critical" approach to the Bible and led to the development of Liberal Protestantism that reduced Christianity to a moral idealism. From the Calvinist side this liberalization was joined by a gradual rationalization of doctrine also under Enlightenment influences, resulting finally in Unitarianism and Deism, i.e., a purely natural, moralistic religion.

After the two hundred years (1500-1700) of the Catholic and Protestant Reformations the Catholic Church stood institutionally and pastorally strong and consolidated but without any very satisfactory theological solution of its problems. The Protestant Churches stood divided and generally closely tied to their State establishments but also consolidated. The religious wars that had resulted both between Catholics and Protestants and between the different denominations of Protestantism had, however, produced the situation in which the new religion of Humanism and later Marxism were to arise, as has already been described in an earlier chapter.

In the face of this unanticipated onslaught the Christian Churches at first reacted chiefly by traditionalism and fideism, arguing that Humanism was not only a subversive attack on the Church but also on the State. They found it difficult to meet Humanism's challenges positively, except by succumbing to them by compromise or complete loss of faith. Humanism originated in England and spread to France and Germany, then to Catholic countries and their New World colonies. The American and French Revolutions, followed by revolutionary movements in many countries, all sought to reduce the Christian religion to the private sphere and to erect a purely secular state. Such a secular state was supposed to be legally neutral to the diversity of religions but in fact became the sponsor of the spread of Humanism through public schools and the media of social communication.

The Churches reacted to this secularization by setting up parallel institutions to those of the state so as to perpetuate the Christian worldview and value-system. The Catholics attempted a revival of religious influence in the public sphere by the restoration of the monarchy in France after the collapse of the Revolution. Later the Protestant Churches supported the so called "Victorian Compromise" in England and the White Anglo Saxon Protestant (WASP) hegemony in the United States.

But these efforts proved transitional and, after each of the World Wars of our century, Humanism has advanced until it is now in full control of the Western democracies and their economic and cultural colonies. Humanism itself, because of the many disastrous social side-effects of the rise of industrial capitalism was soon confronted in the middle of the nineteenth century by the rise of the even more radical socialist or Marxist revolutionary movements.

The Orthodox Churches in the face of this modern onslaught generally have tended to survive as best they can by adherence to traditionalism. The mainline Protestant Churches have been tempted to compromise with Humanism through reliance on the dichotomy introduced by Kant between the public and private spheres, that confines religion to the private and subjective sphere. This has provoked the rise of fervent Evangelical and Fundamentalist sects that vehemently oppose modernity at the price of obscurantism, but it has also inspired the more intellectual Neo-Orthodoxy of Karl Barth and the ecumenical movement of the World Council of Churches.

Moreover, these Protestant Churches that originally had more an apocalyptic than a missionary attitude have become intensely missionary minded and thus have overcome much of their national narrowness. The result has been that the United States, Canada, and Australia have developed a remarkable pluralistic culture in that the state is neutral to religion. On the one hand this has left the Christian Churches free for their mission, but on the other it has privatized traditional religion and encouraged Humanist hegemony.

The Catholic Church has faced this challenge first by rejecting at Vatican I (1869-70) tendencies within the Church to accept Kantian rationalism and fideism, by maintaining the rational credibility of the Christian Faith, and by defining the infallibility of definitive papal teaching, thus cutting off "Modernism."[20] The Modernist movement at the beginning of this century was an attempt to circumvent this uncompromising stand that some scholars thought stood in the way of a necessary rapprochement with modern knowledge. "Modernism" is hard to define but tended to reinterpret the teachings of the Bible and Tradition as flexible symbols whose meaning can be accommodated to cultural change. Modernism was ruthlessly suppressed by Church authorities, but the problems that it had striven to meet by the manipulation of language still had to be solved in a more honest way.

Already at the end of the nineteenth century Pope Leo XIII laid the groundwork for a solid intellectual solution of the theological problems chronic since Trent. He called for a return to the sources, especially to Tradition as represented by the Fathers of the Church and to the great Medievals and for a renewal of biblical studies. He especially promoted the study of the philosophical and theological synthesis of St. Thomas Aquinas, but he also urged a positive but critical approach to the modern sciences.[21] The scholarly task of carrying out these papal recommendations led to a great theological and liturgical revival culminating in the Second Vatican Council in 1963-1965.

The implementation of Vatican II has produced decades of change and controversy in the Catholic Church, which has seemed to some disastrous. But these years have also seen the advance of the ecumenical movement that envisions a reunion of all the Christian Churches and a way to world-wide evangelization. This movement has already borne much fruit, and even, through "liberation theology," an assimilation of what is true in Marxism, as well as the formation of a new Christian culture that can meet the challenge of Humanism and the Enlightenment from which it sprang.

The great question mark that punctuates the hopes of Christianity today is whether there is time to carry out the implications of Vatican II. During the Cold War between the Humanism of the Western democracies and the Marxism of Russian and Chinese communism the possibility loomed of the destruction of all humanity in a nuclear war between these two great modern religions. This crisis has abated, but the threat of nuclear war as a result of other international crises and of local wars has not been overcome. Secular Humanism with its powerful modern technology and its weak grounding in the moral values and human rights it earnestly proclaims has made immense inroads everywhere in the world on the faith of the older religions. Amidst this pluralism Christians see the opportunity of playing a reconciling role.

Thus the history of the Christian Church shows that it has continuously struggled to maintain its essential structure, its independence of worldly powers, the continuity and integrity of its message, and its mission of evangelization. To do this it has had to endure many severe trials: persecution, internal divisions, failed leadership, popular indifference and desertion. Yet none of these trials has led to failures that can be shown to have altered the Church's essential fidelity to the mission entrusted to her by Christ.

4. The Indefectibility and Infallibility of the Church

Vatican II, reaffirming Vatican I, claimed, on account of the promise made by Christ to his Church of the guidance of the Holy Spirit, that the Church, unlike the older Israel, would be the ever faithful bride of Christ, thus implying both the indefectibility and the infallibility of the Church.[22] Some have recently attempted to separate the indefectibility of the Church from its infallibility, and to deny the latter not only on historical grounds but on the philosophical conviction that the human mind is incapable of certain truth. Nevertheless, it should be obvious that if the Church's mission is to preach and live the Gospel and if she is indefectible in this mission until the return of her Lord, she must also be infallible in her definitive teaching of the Gospel. To say that she cannot cease to preach the Gospel but can fail to preach the true Gospel is a contradiction in terms.[23]

According to Vatican II this infallible witness to the true Gospel is first of all a gift to the whole Church from the presence of the Holy Spirit and is reflected in the faith of all its members (the *sensus fidelium*) who as a community (but not as individuals) cannot be deceived by the lies of the world.[24] But this faith of the whole community achieves its authoritative expression only in the bishops in union with the pope or in the pope as the ultimate spokesman for the Church's faith, as Peter was for the Twelve in answering Jesus' great question, "But who do you say I am?"

History, of course, cannot demonstrate this infallibility since it cannot predict the future. History can, however, refute those who claim the popes or Councils or the faithful as a whole have in fact failed. Recent authors with all the resources of modern scholarship and with the vigor of bitter polemics have attempted to point out historic examples where the popes have *ex cathedra* (that is, using their full authority) contradicted themselves or the Gospel.[25] The examples they put forward are not new, because these have been thoroughly canvassed many times before by the opponents of the doctrine of papal infallibility. None will be found to be conclusive if two points are kept in mind. The first is that infallibility does not mean the popes are personally sinless, nor even that they exercise their office well, nor that they do not make mistakes in their government or in their teaching when this teaching is not intended by them to be definitive. Some popes have been personally vicious, others have been woefully negligent, imprudent, or mistaken in their official acts, others have made serious mistakes in non-definitive teaching. There is no guarantee that the Holy Spirit will relieve sinful men from all their faults, but only that the Church will not essentially fail because of failures by its leadership.

The second point to remember is the principle of the development of doctrine.[26] This principle is typical of Catholicism and distinguishes it from Orthodoxy and Protestantism in that the former accepts only the decisions of the first seven Ecumenical Councils, the latter only what is explicit in the Scriptures. Catholicism holds that under the guidance of the Holy Spirit the Church grows in its understanding of the Gospel through its historical experience. Nothing new can be added to the revelation given to the Church of the apostolic age, but the Church can grow (and sometimes retrogress) in its understanding of that revelation, making explicit what is only implicit in the Scriptures and Tradition. Thus Vatican II in stressing the historicity of theology was entirely in line with the Catholic conception of development. At the same time it rejected Modernist interpretation of development as a merely historical and analogical continuity of truth, rather than as the explicitation of truth already implicitly present in Scripture and Tradition.

Keeping in mind these two points, it is not difficult to show that the few cases of apparent contradictions in the history of the definitive teaching of the Church are explicable as negative failings by the popes or Councils in their teaching office, not positive assertions of errors. Or they may be seen as the explicitation of what was formerly implicit, or the better application of a general principle to some new situation. The reader can assure him or herself of this by studying any or each of the alleged contradictions. The simplest approach, however, is to read the documents of Vatican II that express the present faith of the Church and compare them with the standard accounts of the teachings of the great Councils of the Church back to Nicaea I. Such a comparison makes clear the unbroken continuity of the Church's faith, that is, its apostolicity. It was such evidence that led John Henry Newman in the nineteenth century to realize that historic Christianity is Catholic and to accept, as difficult as it was for him as an Englishman, the primacy and infallibility of the successor of St. Peter.

5. The Presence of Jesus Christ in His Church

The understanding of the historicity of the Church presented in this chapter need not lead to the replacement of Jesus Christ by the pope or by the Church. Rather it claims that the risen Christ is still present to us by his Holy Spirit in the Church (that according to St. Paul, 1 Cor 12:27 is Christ's "body"), making him visible and effective for us here and now in our times. Catholics in the teaching of Vatican II under the presidency of Pope John XXIII and Paul VI, the 259th and 260th successors of St. Peter, hear the voice of Jesus proclaiming the Kingdom of God, of love, peace, and justice for all humankind. The Council called for a reunion of all Christians, for the common pursuit of truth by all religions; invoking the rights of humanity and the good use of human talents in an appeal to Humanists and for a revolution in the unjust social order in an appeal to Marxists.

In Jesus' name the Council spoke of God's mercy and forgiveness, for the reconcilation of enemies. They invited all to join the risen Jesus in praise and thanksgiving to the Father, the principle and goal of all reality, in the faith, hope, and love that are the gift of the Spirit. They urged all to look forward to the eternal Kingdom at the consummation of history, a consummation for which the universe was created.

Thus the Catholic Church appears in its fourfold ecumenicity, its remarkable inclusivity and unity in the service of the integral fulfillment of human personal and communal gifts. It is no longer seen as a static institution but in its historicity as a pilgrim community organic in its structure and development as the Body of Christ making him visible and present in our world where we can personally experience him in his tangible reality. Thus we are confronted with the demands of faith. To believe in Jesus Christ as the communication, the self-revelation of God to us in the Son of God, we must make that act of faith that his disciples made two thousand years ago in Galilee.

Our experience and our intelligence tells us that here in the one, holy, catholic, and apostolic Church as the visible sacrament of the presence of Christ we have the certain sign that God is speaking to us. It is a sufficient sign. To ask more is to make the tragic error of the Pharisees who blinded by their own preconceptions kept demanding more and more signs that would compel their faith. But faith, since it is trust in a God who is our Creator and infinitely beyond our comprehension, must be a free act. Certain, trustworthy signs are only the needed condition not the formal motive of our faith. The motive can only be the trustworthiness of God himself. We must believe both what he says and that it is he who says it.

This act of faith in the Gospel requires on the part of the believer an act of self-renunciation, that is, a sacrifice of all opinions that contradict its truth, and of all desires that discord with its true love. But it does not require anyone to deny the truth and goodness they already possess. To become a follower of Jesus the Jew, Jews need not, indeed they cannot, renounce their heritage as Jews, because the covenant between God and Israel will never be repudiated by God (Rm 11:29). The Jewish Christian sees in Jesus the fulfillment of the Law and the prophets. Neither does a person who has made the submission to God that is Islam have to betray that submission, since Muhammad proclaimed the same God of Abraham, Isaac and Jacob that Jesus proclaimed. Muhammad also proclaimed that Jesus was a true prophet and therefore could not have claimed to be the Son of God in a physical sense or in the sense of a second god, and Christians must profess the same.

The Emanation Religions each in its own way proclaim that there is only One Absolute Reality. They agree that all our images of this Absolute must be transcended, yet they tell us to put faith in God's avatars or Buddhas by which he manifests himself in this world, so as to encourage us to enter the way of spiritual discipline and meditation on the One. The Christian is grateful for this ancient wisdom and discipline and can continue to practice it, while praising God as Creator and Savior who has manifested himself in many prophets, but uniquely in Jesus Christ his only Son in the plenitude of the Spirit.

Moreover, those whose religion survives from pre-literate times and who reverence the Great Spirit in nature and the spirits of their departed ancestors should not lose their sense of intimacy with the visible cosmos and the invisible spirit world. This sense of the spiritual milieu is retained in authentic Christianity in its sacramental understanding of creation and its conviction of the presence of the angels and the blessed dead still alive in Christ.

Nor do Humanists have to deny their reasoned convictions that humanity come of age must take responsibility for the earth and human society, and must overcome every form of injustice and oppression. Christians of course believe that reality is greater than human beings and their world. They also insist that the Creator made us to conserve and cultivate our garden earth and to bring the Reign of God on earth as it is in heaven. They realize today that science and technology are gifts of the Holy Spirit, talents that God will judge us for using well or ill in the service of humankind.

Thus authentic Christianity does not claim to dominate other religions or ways of life but seeks to serve them as Jesus sought to serve all humankind without discrimination. It finds in Jesus a God who has always cared for all his creatures and seeks only to bring them together into a single community with him. In this community the rich variety of human cultures can meet in one faith in him as a God who is Light and Love. Yet as we face this gentle challenge of Jesus to faith in him terrible doubts may arise in our minds and hearts. These must be examined in the next chapter.

Notes

[1] See Avery Dulles, *Models of the Church* (Garden City, NY: Doubleday, 1983). For an attempt to reconcile the organizational and charismatic aspects of the Church see Louis Bouyer, *The Church of God: Body of Christ and Temple of the Spirit* (Chicago: Franciscan Herald Press, 1982).

[2] See Albert Vanhoye, SJ, *Old Testament Priests and the New Priest* (Petersham, MA: St. Bede Publications, 1986); Jean Galot, *Theology of Priesthood* (San Francisco: Ignatius Press, 1984) and David N. Power, OMI, *Ministers of Christ and His Church: The theology of priesthood* (London: Geoffrey Chapman, 1969). There is a vast recent literature on the subject of Church office. For two poles of interpretation of the historical data see for example the very different reconstructions of Kenan B. Osborne, OFM, *Priesthood: A History of the Ordained Ministry in the Roman Catholic Church* (New York: Paulist Press, 1988) and Patrick J. Dunn, *Priesthood* (Staten Island, NY: Alba House, 1990). For a survey Daniel Donovan, *What Are They Saying about the Ministerial Priesthood?* (New York: Paulist Press, 1992). Jean Delorme, ed., *La ministère et les ministères selon le Nouveau Testament* (Paris: Éditions du Seuil, 1973) provides 14 essays by a wide variety of French scholars who cover the data very thoroughly but interpret it variously. For the canonical development see Alexandre Faivre, *Naissance d'une hiérarchie: Les premières étapes du cursus clérical* (Paris: Éd. Beauchesne, 1977) who treats of the early canons on the Sacrament of Orders.

[3] For this dating see Marie E. Isaacs, *Sacred Space: An Approach to the Theology of the Epistle to the Hebrews,* JSNT. Supplement Series 73 (Sheffield, England: University of Sheffield Press, 1992), and Paul Ellingworth, *The Epistle to the Hebrews: A Commentary on the Greek Text* (Grand Rapids, MI: W.B. Eerdmans, 1993), p. 31 f.

[4] An important Protestant study on this subject is R. Alastair Campbell, *The Elders: Seniority Within Earliest Christianity* (Edinburgh: T&T Clark, 1994) who argues that besides the traveling apostles, the local house churches were headed first by leaders ("elders," a term not of office but of dignity) often the well-to-do owner of a large house where the church could meet, then the leaders of several such house churches in a city formed a presbyterate under a leader (the overseer or protobishop), and finally this leader became the monarchical bishop of a city with several presbyters of second rank under him.

[5] *Ibid.* pp. 182-205 for a very thorough discussion of the opinions. Campbell believes that the Pastorals were written precisely to justify the emergence of the bishop as head of the presbyterium. If, as is the common opinion today, they are pseudonymous, they are dated between 80-100 CE. See Raymond E. Brown, *An Introduction to the New Testament* (New York: Doubleday, 1997), p. 668. A minority of scholars still hold they are by Paul and hence before 64 CE. It should be noted that though some think that Ignatius in his epistles emphasizes this development because it is recent, in fact he does not argue for it, but takes it for granted as well established and only urges unity with the bishop because of the situation of persecution. Thus the argument from ecclesial office for a late date for the Pastorals seems circular.

[6] The real issue for Christians is about whether the exercise of strictly priestly acts requires that they have apostolic authority. E. Schillebeeckx, *Ministry* (New York: Crossroad, 1981) and *The Church with a Human Face* (New York: Crossroad, 1985) argues that if necessary a local church has the power to ordain its priest. This has been well answered by the noted exegete Pierre Grélot, *Église et ministères: pour un dialogue critique avec Edward Schillebeeckx* (Paris, Les Éditions du Cerf, 1983). Grélot shows on New Testament evidence that apostolic authority, not simply congregational assent, was always required for church offices. See also Albert Vanhoye, SJ and Henri Crouzel, SJ, "The Ministry in the Church: Reflections on a Recent Publication," *The Clergy Review,* 5, 68 (May, 1983), 156-174; and Walter Kasper, "Ministry in the Church: Taking Issue with Edward Schillebeeckx," *Communio,* Summer, 1983, 185-195. The Congregation for the Doctrine of the Faith of the Vatican had a formal dialogue with Schillebeeckx on his position and asked him to correct it. This he attempted in the second of the books above, but the CDF declared his answer did not meet their objections. See Ted Schoof, ed. and introduction, *The Schillebeeckx Case* (New York: Paulist Press, 1980). Schoof is a friend and partisan of Schillebeeckx.

[7] *Epistle to the Trallians,* 2 and 3, etc. For authenticity of the Ignatian epistles see Johannes Quasten, *Patrology* (Westminster, MD: Christian Classics, 1992), pp. 73-74.

[8] *Didaché* 10, 7. Hervé Marie Legrand, "The Presidency of the Eucharist According to the Ancient Tradition" in R. Kevin Seasoltz, *Living Bread, Saving Cup* (Collegeville, MN: Liturgical Press, 1982), pp. 196-221 concludes that whoever had the right to preside over the community *ipso facto* had the power to consecrate the Eucharist. This is no doubt true, but how did the head of the community get his authority? See note 6 above.

[9] On the diaconate see Jean Colson, *La Fonction diaconale aux origines de l'Église* (Paris: Desclée de Brouwer, 1960). Colson concludes (p. 40) that the Seven chosen in Acts 6 to "wait on tables" for the Greek-speaking Jewish Christians in Jerusalem were not deacons but presbyters. This view has been widely accepted by exegetes. The only reasons given are that "table waiting" could mean presiding at the Eucharist, and later in Acts some of these Seven are shown preaching and baptizing. But if "table waiting" is understood, as has been traditional, to mean caring for the poor to free the Apostles to preach as the text explicitly says, this does not exclude that the Seven also preached. Moreover, it would be odd to think that it was celebrating at the Eucharist that hindered the Apostles from preaching! Colson's rejection of the traditional view has become widely accepted. Yet it seems to rest on a reconstruction of the account in Acts that supposes that the dispute between the Aramaic and Greek-speaking Christians led to a division into separate Eucharistic communities. In fact Acts says no more than that the Hellenists thought their poor were not getting a fair share of material assistance; it says nothing about Eucharist celebration.

[10] For examples see Raymond Brown, *Priest and Bishop* (Paramus, NJ: Paulist Press, 1970); André Lemaire, *Ministry in the Church* (London: SPCK, 1977); Edward Schillebeeckx, *Ministry* (New York: Crossroad, 1981) and Kenan Osborne's work, note 2 above.

[11] See Raymond E. Brown in Brown, SS and John P. Meier, *Antioch and Rome: Cradles of Catholic Christianity* (New York: Paulist Press, 1983), pp. 139-149.

[12] On this whole question see the recent work of Roland Minnerath, *De Jerusalem a Rome: Pierre et l'Unité de l'Église Apostolique,* Théologie Historique 101 (Paris: Beauchesne, 1995).

[13] *Ibid.,* vol. 1, pp. 42-53. A recent study emphasizing its rhetorical structure is Horacio E. Lons, *Der erste Clemensbrief* (Göttingen: Vandenboeck and Ruprecht, 1998). For an early date for the work (c. 70 CE rather than 95 CE) see Roland Minnerath, *op. cit.,* note 12 above, pp. 558-67 and T.J. Herron, "The Most Probable Date of the First Epistle of Clement to the Corinthians" in E.A. Livingstone, ed., *Studia Patristica* 21 (Leuven, 1989), pp. 106-21.

[14] In the interpretative sketch of the history of the Catholic Church that follows I have omitted detailed documentation. The reader is referred to the standard handbook with extensive bibliography edited by Hubert Jedin, Konrad Repgen and John Dolan, *History of the Church,* 10 vols. (New York: Crossroad, 1981).

[15] On the history of the development of Christology and Trinitarian doctrine see J.N.D. Kelly, *Early Christian Doctrines,* 5th ed. (San Francisco: Harper and Row, 1978). Also see Alois Grillmeier, *Christ in Christian Tradition* (London: Mowbray, 1975); and William J. Hill, *The Three Personed God* (Washington, DC: Catholic University of America Press, 1982).

[16] St. Augustine, *De Trinitate.*

[17] On this see Yves Congar, *I Believe in the Holy Spirit,* translated by David Smith, 3 vols. (New York: Seabury Press, 1983).

[18] For example, Henry A.F. Kamen, *The Spanish Inquisition: A Historical Revision* (New Haven, CT: Yale University Press, 1998) and B. Netanyahu, *The Origins of the Inquisition in Fifteenth Century Spain* (New York: Random House, 1995).

[19] See the summing up of Hans J. Hillerbrand, *Christendom Divided,* Theological Resources (New York: Corpus Books, 1971), pp. 283-306.

[20] For bibliography on Modernism see Thomas M. Loome, *Liberal Catholicism, Reform Catholicism, Modernism* (Mainz: Matthias Grünewald Verlag, 1970).

[21] See James A. Weisheipl, "Contemporary Scholasticism" in article "Scholasticism" in *New Catholic Encyclopedia* 12: 1165-70.

[22] *Dogmatic Constitution On the Church,* n. 25 with footnotes to Vatican I, Austin Flannery, OP, ed., *Vatican II: The Conciliar and Postconciliar Documents* (Collegville, MN: Liturgical Press, 1975) p. 375 f.

[23] See Francis A. Sullivan, *Magisterium: Teaching Authority in the Catholic Church* (New York: Paulist Press, 1983) with the critique of Germain Grisez, "Infallibility and Specific Moral Norms," *The Thomist* 49 (April, 1985): 248-287.

[24] On the meaning of *sensus fidelium* in Catholic Tradition see Hans Urs von Balthasar, *Elucidations* (London: SPCK, 1975), pp. 91-98, 42; John Henry Newman, *An Essay on the Development of Christian Doctrine,* ed. by J.M. Cameron (Baltimore, MD: Penguin Books, 1974); Jan H. Walgrave, *Unfolding Revelation: The Nature of Doctrinal Development,* Theological Resources (Philadelphia: Westminster, 1972).

[25] Hans Küng, *Infallible?* (Garden City, NY: Doubleday, 1981) raised the major claims for contradictions in defined Catholic doctrines. His arguments are criticized in John J. Kivan, ed., *The Infallibility Debate* (New York: Paulist Press, 1971). See also René Latourelle, *Christ and the Church: Signs of Salvation* (Staten Island, NY: Alba House, 1972).

[26] For further discussion see Jan H. Walgrave, *Unfolding Revelation,* note 24 above.

CHAPTER 10

COSMIC EVIL AND CHRISTIAN HOPE

1. The Subjective Aspects of Faith

At the beginning of our century a fierce controversy (already mentioned in Chapter 5) was waged between those who followed an "objective" or "rational" method in apologetics and those who followed a "subjective" or "existential" approach.[1]

The objective method attempted first to establish the rational motives of credibility of the Gospel. Then it argued the moral obligation of all who have become aware of that credibility to render obedience to the faith and to the Gospel by an act of the will moving their intelligences to assent to it. The subjective method (of which Karl Rahner is the most distinguished recent proponent[2]) began from the opposite end. It first established the human need for religion in order to live successfully, then deduced what kind of religion could satisfy this need, and finally attempted to show by a process of correlation that Christianity alone actually fulfills this need.

In this book I have argued that these two approaches are complementary but that the former should have priority if we are not to fall into a solipsism that hampers the sharing of faith. If the experience of faith is to be communicated or publicly witnessed it cannot begin from the experience of inner needs for that may very well not be felt by all, but must begin from public facts independent of subjective "experience." The term "experience," so much used today in religious discussions is, at best, highly ambiguous and provides only an insecure foundation for any ecumenical meeting of minds on such difficult topics.[3]

Back of the approach from the subject that in Catholic apologetics was first put forward effectively by Maurice Blondel and his school, lies the philosophy of Immanuel Kant who believed that modern science compels us to abandon hope of arriving at an understanding of noumenal reality.[4] Therefore, as we saw in Chapter 2, Section 1, Kant concluded that belief in God and transcendent reality must be purely practical, that is, we must believe in order to live well, but such belief rests on will rather than reason. It is necessary to face this Kantian point of departure critically, rather than accepting it as given, as Blondel seems to have done.

The Blondelians emphasize that Christianity is not merely a matter of intellectual assent to dogmatic propositions. Rather it is a way of life that involves the total human person. We do not believe and then act on our beliefs. We act and through acting come to believe. How many nonbelievers have experienced that when they were still nonbelieving, because they could find no other hope in life, they began to pray. Then, in praying without knowing whether they really believed they were doing more than talking to themselves, they came to the conviction that there was a God who was hearing them! Is not this the way we come to know that a friend is a friend — by common life together — not by some kind of objective, rational demonstration?

Yet this approach remains ambiguous. Are we saying that in taking on the life experiences of a Christian we are opened to the objective evidences for Christianity? That we come in contact with these evidences, and are supplied with practical motives for making the effort required to reflect on these evidences? That, finally, we come actually to believe in a reasonable and responsible way, just as we might come to commit ourselves to some political cause based on verified facts through intimate acquaintance with others of similar convictions? Or are we saying that Christian faith is simply a life-myth to which we permit ourselves to become habituated because we find it a source of personal security?

The real opponents of this kind of subjectivist apologetics are not conservative, rationalistic Catholics, but Humanist skeptics who point out derisively that if this be a true account of Christian faith, then verily "religion is the opium of the people"! Nor is it obvious that Hans Küng, for instance, has been able to avoid this accusation by his Pascalian apologetics. He grounds faith on the hope that "springs eternal in the human breast" which would be absurd if there is no God.[5] He seems to forget Jean-Paul Sartre's existentialist argument that since there is no God, the world *is* absurd! But not all Humanists accept existentialist despair and many are quite confident that human hopes announced not the Advent of God but the Revolution or at least a New Age of Progress.

We must remove this ambiguity in the subjective approach to apologetics by firmly asserting that the evidences for the truth of Christianity discussed in previous chapters must be established in a genuinely objective manner. They are valid or invalid independently of whether they provide an answer for my felt life needs or not. Of course such objective facts are of serious concern for my life projects and this motivates me to explore their implications. We should recall that the pressure to win the Second World War motivated the rapid development of our understanding of the physics of atomic fission and fusion, but the truth of these scientific laws is independent of any use made of the bomb. So also the truth of Christian doctrine is independent of whether anyone accepts and lives it or not. Living it may provide evidence, but it is the objective evidence, not the subjective experience that is decisive. To cover over this necessity of objective credibility in apologetics by the rhetoric of "life" and "experience" and "hope" is to appear dishonest to unbelievers and confirm their worst suspicions.

Nor is it helpful to rely too much on the arguments developed by Michael Polanyi to show that even the most systematic objectivity of physics rests on a kind of "tacit faith" in the reasonableness of the universe. Nor should we simplistically succumb to arguments of the sociologists of knowledge such as Jurgen Habermas that the subjective "interests" of the knower condition all human knowledge. Nor rely on the arguments of Marxists and the theologians of Liberation to show the necessity of a "unity of theory and praxis."[6] Pragmatic theories of knowledge ultimately self-destruct. Even if we recognize that our practical experiences and motives orient our thinking and profoundly condition it, the very fact that we can recognize this implies it is possible, at least in favorable circumstances, to transcend our subjectivity, so as to distinguish between science and ideology. If we cannot, then any philosophy of science, sociology of knowledge, or class analysis of ideology is itself nothing but another ideology.

Granted this unequivocal distinction between objective and subjective apologetics, and having sketched the former in previous chapters, it remains important to consider, as I will try to do in this chapter, the subjective factors that are favorable to religious objectivity. We have heard of the "judicial temperament" required of a just judge, and of the "scientific frame of mind" required of a sound scientist or scholar. In what frame of mind can the sincere searcher for religious truth overcome both the blind obstinacy of the Pharisee and the superstitious credulity of the deluded fanatic?

I have already discussed the difficulties that arose from the interpretation of science and critical history by the Humanism of the Enlightenment. I will deal here primarily with the difficulty that perhaps more than any other dissuades people of good will from accepting the Christian religion or indeed any form of monotheism. For example, nothing so alienates Jews today from a return to their religious traditions as the horror of the Holocaust[7] that seems to give the lie to any theistic explanation of the cosmos. Dostoevski expressed it in his question, "If there is a God, how can he look down on the suffering of one innocent child and do nothing to prevent it?"[8]

This is first of all, of course, a question demanding an objective answer, and I will attempt to give such an answer that is logical and philosophically necessary, but this answer will not overcome the subjective difficulty that must then be addressed in its own terms.

2. The Origin of Evil

In the Emanation Religions the misery of the world is explained as merely phenomenal: the enlightened person will recognize evil as illusory, a product of erroneous thinking to be overcome by true wisdom.[9] In Zoroastrianism and Gnosticism evil was attributed to a second ultimate principle coexistent with and independent of the first principle or Good God who would eventually defeat it. For Zoroastrians this second principle was personal, an Evil God; for Gnostics it was the impersonal reality of matter.

For Humanists evil is the inevitable consequence of a godless universe that can eventually be overcome by progressive human effort but will also eventually destroy us. For the process philosophers and process theologians evil is the result of the fact that God is finite in power and cannot prevent it, although once it has occurred he is able to integrate it into his own blissful vision of the world.[10]

For the Creation Religions, however, moral evil can only be the result of the sinful acts of free creatures, and physical evil would have been restrained by God from affecting human beings if they had not become liable to it as a punishment for freely committing moral evil. These religions proclaim that God in his mercy and justice has promised eventually to overcome all evil, moral and physical. They argue that he now permits such evil for a time in order to restore the order of justice by punishing crime and as a school of virtue for those of good will.

To see that Christianity does not evade this problem or seek to give it an easy answer one has only to look at its chief symbol, the Cross. Compare the Cross with the Star of Judaism or the Crescent of Islam, symbols of glory rather than tragedy. In the Cross we see starkly symbolized the dilemma that is the objection we confront. Here is the Innocent One (innocent not as a child, but as a free adult fully aware of his physical and moral torment) who claims to be the Son of God, yet whom that God has left naked to his enemies. He is dying in torture, shame, and failure in the sight of his mother and beloved but faithless disciples. How could an all-good, all-knowing, and all-powerful God permit his loving Son so to die? The Christian is forced to confront this mystery in the bleeding, agonized face of the Crucified. "*Eli, Eli, lama sabachthani?,* My God, my God, why have you forsaken me?" (Mt 27:46; Ps 22:2).

What is the logic of the Christian answer?[11] Evils are real, but they are the realities that are defects in some prior reality that is good. Thus a broken leg is all too real, but it is discontinuity in a bone that is otherwise healthy and serviceable. A fracture can exist only in something having the positive character of a living limb, because a fracture is a negation and defect in something positive. Similarly a sinful act is a human action of a positive character that is, however, an only apparent means to integral human fulfillment that in fact it blocks. Thus a lie can be a beautifully crafted narrative that would be admirable as an amusing story but when a perjury is a crime. The notion of an evil that is merely evil and not a defect in something positively good is a contradiction in terms, because it would be something that was nothing. Therefore, the existence of evil in the cosmos implies that the cosmos is basically good but has been perverted; and the greater the evil we perceive the more evident how great was originally the goodness of the cosmos that has been so distorted yet still survives.

Hence the existence of evil in the world, even if the evils appear to outbalance the good (for this can only be in appearance, as we have just seen) is not *per se* an argument against the goodness of the cosmos or its Creator. This truth holds if (1) the Creator is not the direct cause of the perversion of his own works, i.e., he permits but does not cause this perversion; (2) the Creator for a time tolerates evil only in order eventually to bring about a greater good.

The first of these conditions is met as regards moral evil in the cosmos because God in his goodness creates intelligent creatures who can share in his intelligence and freedom. If they freely accept his help they can avoid sin, but if they insist on going their own way their actions are defective and sinful. God cannot create beings whose nature is to be at the same time free and yet not liable to freely sin, since this would be contradictory. As creatures they are finite and therefore capable of defect, and as free they are capable of causing their own defection. Yet in spite of this possibility that his free creatures may go astray it is better that God include them in his creation, because only intelligent and free creatures can form a community with him and share in his happiness, the greatest good possible for creatures.

But in historical fact these free creatures have chosen to go their own way as is evident from the immense miseries of war, poverty, ignorance, and self-destructive hedonism that is everywhere about us. While it is true that much of this evil is not truly free but the result of evil social structures, nevertheless, these evil structures originated in free choices or in other determinisms that in turn go back ultimately to some original sin.[12] Today not all theologians understand this doctrine of "original sin" to refer only to the first sin at the beginning of human history. They reasonably argue that it includes the entire accumulation of the effects of all subsequent sins throughout history that further distort God's originally good creation. As I will show later, God has not merely permitted this growth of sin, but has constantly been at work inspiring free human acts of repentance, conversion, forgiveness, and reparation. These finally gained the upper hand in the redemptive action of Christ that has not yet fully triumphed, as ultimately it will.

But what of physical evils, of the earthquakes, thunderstorms, hurricanes, blizzards, floods, droughts, plagues, birth defects, contagious and generative diseases, famines, and accidents that fill the newspapers? Further, what of "nature red in tooth and claw" that the theory of evolution has exposed to us by its principle of "the survival of the fittest"? And what of the history of the cosmos that seems such a violent clash of blind forces, of such vast wastes of time and space, of the second law of thermodynamics and the inevitable death of the universe through entropy? Closer still to home: "Is not *my* death inevitable?"

The Christian Bible teaches plainly that death and by implication disease and accident and all physical evils have resulted from original evil. It even seems to say that, without moral evil, earth and no doubt the whole universe would have been a beautiful paradise in which "the lion" would "lie down with the lamb." As Jacques Maritain in his *St.Thomas and the Problem of Evil* shows,[13] Aquinas held that such physical conflict and death is inevitably a part of any created world in that there are material beings, because material things perfect themselves only by acting on (and thereby ultimately destroying) other material things. Hence, although moral evil cannot be attributed in any way to God, physical evil must be attributed to the Creator as First Cause. God indeed causes these physical evils, yet not as evil, but only as the inevitable consequences of the existence and development of physical things each seeking its own proper goodness for which he creates them and to which he carefully guides them.

The problem remains, however, to understand the biblical teaching that even physical evils are the consequence of moral evil and thus ultimately the responsibility of free creatures and not of God. Aquinas held that in order that this natural physical evil might not cause innocent humanity suffering and death God endowed the first human beings with "preternatural" health and placed them in a special paradisal environment.[14] Modern theologians tend to pass over this question because they consider Paradise not a historical reality but a symbol of the future Kingdom that because of human sin has never yet been historically realized. They point out that if there had been no sin, even if there had been natural physical death, it would have been acceptable as the necessary transition to eternal life and it would have been entirely peaceful.[15]

While both the traditional and the current theory of original sin are reasonable enough and are sufficient for the purpose of our general argument, I would suggest what seems to me a more satisfactory solution. According to Genesis, God created us in his image by giving us intelligence and freedom and a stewardship over his creation. If we had used this gift to care for and cultivate the paradise of earth that God gave us, we would have gained a control of nature that would have protected us from natural accidents. It would have supplied all our needs, and kept us in permanent physical and mental health, enabling us to live perpetually. No preternatural gifts would have been necessary, because the gift of our natural, creative intelligence, supported and elevated by grace would have sufficed for us to protect ourselves from all physical evils.

If it seems incredible that we could have gained this degree of control over nature and our own bodies, we have only to consider the unlimited promise of scientific technology. Times previous to our own had no notion of these possibilities. No doubt this is why theologians never saw this implication in the Genesis account. But today it has become entirely plausible that all these wonders can be accomplished if only we do not first destroy ourselves or allow human sin to prevent our pursuit of research and its wise application. This does not mean that even in principle we have the power, as Humanists think, to achieve the goal of human life by our own powers. Eternal life in the biblical sense of intimate life with God would not be gained even if we could forever protect ourselves from physical death. Life with the Trinity would still be possible only as God's free gift, but everything else he has given us virtually in making us in his image as intelligent and free.

But what is to be said of animal pain and of the tortuous, violent course of biological and cosmic evolution?[16] The struggle for the survival of the fittest existed long before the creation of humanity and its fall into sin. This question raises still another question often evaded by current theologians but nevertheless intrinsic to the Christian worldview as well as to that of Judaism and Islam. The Hebrew and Christian Bible, as well as the *Qur'an*, teach that humans are not the only, but simply the least, of the host of intelligent beings created by God. What then of the possibility of angelic sin? God has given to these superhuman intelligences or angels, who are an integral part of the created cosmos, a share in his governance of the universe.[17] The same arguments that lead to the proof of the existence of God lead also to the existence of angels, provided we also suppose that God acts through the ministry of created causes when this is possible.

Modern cosmological and evolutionary science have made even clearer than ancient and Newtonian astronomy that the natural events in the universe cannot be reduced to one simple law of development. They are the products of the historical concurrence of many causes that would not have produced human persons unless history had followed a wonderfully complex and exact sequence of events. As is now evident from the lifelessness of the other planets around our earth, it is only chance that our planet earth is so exactly placed that it is neither too hot nor too cold for the origin of life. Each step of the evolutionary process that ended in producing us might have run into a dead end or gone off in an entirely different direction.[18]

Consequently, the only adequate explanation of evolution is that this exact historical sequence of the concurrence of a multitude of natural forces is guided by a superior intelligence supervising this concurrence. The best analogy is the protocol of a chemist synthesizing a complex compound in his laboratory using the forces of nature but with a sequence and timing not completely determined by any one of these forces. Such guiding cosmic intelligence is not just that of God but of the many intelligences he has created and put in charge to give a historical direction to these processes. Human creativity is a part of this stewardship, but the least intelligent and effective. While this argument may seem fantastic to scientists, Alfred Russel Wallace, who with Darwin first proposed the theory of evolution through natural selection wrote a book called *The World of Life: A Manifestation of Creative Power, Directive Mind and Ultimate Purpose.* In this work he concluded "that evolution involved more than natural selection and was guided by creative intelligence, which he identified as angels."[19]

Such a theory does not substitute for scientific explanations of evolutionary processes but includes and completes them, while remaining entirely open to further exploration of the precise details of this historical process. If this proposal is granted, then the biblical conception of the "angels of the nations" (Dn 10:12) and the "dominations and powers" (Col 1:16) becomes quite intelligible. The recent study of this conception by Walter Wink demonstrates how important the "powers" are in Scripture, although Wink wants to explain them (very unsatisfactorily) as the spiritual essences of merely human realities.[20] According to the Scriptures, God entrusted the governance of history, cosmological and human, to these powers, but while some have remained faithful to him, others have set themselves up as autonomous, as "gods."

We may suppose, therefore, that if the good angels had governed the process of cosmological evolution it would have been smooth and gentle with much less waste and emptiness, and biological evolution would have come about by symbiosis, or cooperation, among living things rather than by their competition to survive. The history of evolution, therefore, might have been very different, but God would have insured that it would ultimately climax in the creation of intelligent, bodily humanity as supreme in the material world. Thus there seems no scientific reason, either physical or biological, that humanity might not have evolved very directly through an evolutionary line where animal pain could have been avoided, although this possibility staggers the imagination.

Those who laugh at the idea that evil angels have entered into human history must hold that the moral evils and tragedies that have occurred throughout history are exclusively our human work. Two great facts militate against this reductive explanation. The first is that the great tragedies of human history, including the Holocaust, have resulted from the concurrence of many factors not under human control. This has often tempted historians to adopt conspiracy theories that have in the long run been seen to be fallacious. Is it not more reasonable, then, to suppose that behind the human scene there are malevolent intelligences at work tempting humans to foolish and objectively (but not always subjectively) evil actions that have produced disasters of a magnitude and complexity beyond all human planning or anticipation.

The second fact, and I think even more evident, is that many of the greatest human tragedies (e.g., the division of Christendom, the threat of nuclear destruction resulting from the Allied determination to stop Nazi tyranny) seem to be produced by virtuous persons with good intentions. What could manipulate these good human acts so as to lead to the frustration of their noble purposes except a superhuman but malicious intelligence? If it is objected that this is mere "mythology," remember that in Chapter 2 I was quite willing to grant that we "moderns" still have much to learn from the universal human experiences expressed in the mythic view of the world.

Thus it is possible logically to reduce all the evil of the world, even its physical evils, to the sin of creatures, human and angelic, and to remove every implication that God has ever willed evil. But why has he permitted it? Is not a person who stands by while a crime he could stop is going on also responsible for it? This brings us to the second principle proposed at the beginning of this discussion: God has permitted no evil except so that he might bring a greater good out of it. But is this not the same as "doing evil that good may come of it"? Or "the end justifies the means"? By no means should one say that God does evil to achieve good, but that he permits humans and angels to do evil that he may bring about a greater good. That such permission is not necessarily immoral can be seen from a simple analogy. A good father could not rightly teach his adolescent son to smoke. Yet he might permit him to choose to try it out for himself in order that the boy may learn from experience that it makes him sick. In this way the boy may come to assume a mature responsibility for his own decisions and mistakes. This, no doubt, is why the loving Father in the Parable of the Two Sons

(Lk 15:11-32) allowed the Prodigal to take his inheritance and waste it "in riotous living." The Father knew that only in this way would his beloved son learn his lesson.

If the end of the universe and its greatest good is for intelligent and free creatures to come to share knowingly and freely in God's life of self-giving love, then it is understandable why a loving God may permit them to sin if they freely so choose. This will be true, if only in this way they can from their own experience come to know best what God's love means in their lives. Thus the whole of human history can be understood as a school of love in that the lessons are not taught abstractly but from the experience of life lived in freedom. Because human beings only learn perfectly from actual experience and experience means they learn best from the contrast of good and evil, it is clearer why God has chosen this pedagogy. Is it not a fact that for humans love in its fullest sense is never achieved without a struggle between the lovers, without offense and forgiveness?

But would it not be possible for an all-powerful God to have found a way to lead humanity to its goal by a smoother course? Since by his free grace God can move the free will without lessening its freedom but rather enhancing it, why could he not have moved Adam and Eve by his grace *freely* to resist sin? Couldn't God have inspired them with an understanding of his love gained not through bitter suffering but by mystical illumination? Does not the Catholic Church claim that Jesus and his mother Mary never sinned themselves, yet surpassed all sinners in the profound understanding of God's love?

To reply to this question is the most difficult part of our inquiry. Back of it lies the hidden assumption that God is obliged by his goodness to create "the best of all possible worlds." Voltaire in his *Candide* ruthlessly (and rightly) mocked this thesis attributed (perhaps wrongly) to Leibnitz. Yet Thomas Aquinas long before had already showed that the notion of a "best possible world" is self-contradictory.[21] Since God's power is infinite, it is contradictory to posit a best or most perfect world since that is to posit something finite (only God is infinite) that is at the same time and the same respect perfect, i.e., infinite. This is why creation is free, since the goodness of God cannot demand the production of something that in principle manifests the totality of his goodness.

No matter how perfect any universe God might create, he could always make it more perfect. Therefore, it suffices that any universe God creates should be good, or perhaps "very good" (Gn 1:31). Thus, we can admit that God could have made a world without conflict and therefore without suffering, but his goodness did not oblige him to do so, but only that if it involved conflict this conflict is not in vain, but leads to some good greater than the evil. This leaves open the question as to exactly what this greater good is, that will be discussed in a moment.

Our argument, therefore, shows that objectively speaking the physical and moral evil in the cosmos, immense as it is, cannot be attributed to God but must logically be explained as the result of the free choices of creatures. Thus the goodness of God cannot be impugned because he has permitted creatures in their freedom to work out their will, good or evil, on his creation because he knows how to bring a greater good out of this evil and ultimately will do so.

This explanation of evil, common to the Creation Religions of Judaism, Christianity, and Islam, does not contradict so much as it transcends and includes the theories of the origin of evil put forward by other religions. First, like the Emanation Religions it teaches that enlightened minds will understand that all evil is merely relative and will be transcended in eternity, and also (without admitting the transmigration of souls) that the evil of the present world is the effect of *karma*, original sin in a broad sense.

Second, this explanation admits with Zoroaster[22] that the present world is the result of dual powers, although it locates the origin of evil not in an ultimate Evil Principle but in superhuman yet created powers as well as in the human will. In this it agrees with the mythic and polytheistic view of the world.

Third, it admits with Humanism that the evil of the world is the result of the human misuse of the intelligence given us to turn this world into a paradise by scientific technology. Its superiority to these other theories is evident in that it does not deny the reality of evil or rely on the unprovable doctrine of reincarnation as do the Emanationist Religions. Nor does it posit the contradictory notion of an evil first principle, as did Zoroaster. Nor does it accept the groundless optimism of Humanism or the materialist determinism of Marxism in supposing that humanity by itself can solve all its problems.

3. The Subject and Evil

This logical objective answer is not likely to convince most people because their problem is not on the side of the object but of the subject. It seems to them impossible to imagine that a God of love would permit his children, whom they themselves love, to suffer, since if they themselves had the power they would never allow any harm to come to them. Nor is this difficulty relieved by claiming, as the Bible does, that eventually God will free from their suffering at least those who trust in him, because that will only shorten such suffering not prevent it altogether.

The weakest form of this difficulty but a very fundamental and persuasive one in our time is "the silence of God." If there is a God, why does he not communicate with us in some clear and unmistakable way? Why does he not make his presence felt in our lives? This objection is one of the chief bases of Humanism. Sometimes it takes a scientistic, rationalistic form in the demand that to be valid our knowledge of God must conform to the canons developed by science to verify natural events. At other times it takes a commonsense form as a healthy skepticism about stories concerning extraordinary events that cannot be fitted into our familiar, everyday world.

In both these cases I think all of us today feel subjectively more comfortable with an account of the cosmos that confines itself to the round of daily experience in our urban world. This world is largely the product of a technology that we know is of human making and thus humanly understandable — even if we leave this understanding to experts. We feel most at home in a world without mystery, except in fiction and film. Our everyday world is one that, full of pain as it may be, is in principle under human control and thus predictable. If it still has some "mysteries," these are in principle to be explored and understood by the same methods that have already eliminated so much mystery from our lives. Even when we try to imagine life on other planets in science fiction, we picture it as differing from our terrestrial life only in that the humanoids are after all not too different from us. Though they are more scientifically advanced than ourselves and are somewhat monstrous in appearance, they are hardly odder than are the apes one evolutionary step below us.

Yet from the beginning of the Enlightenment there has been another type of sensibility and imagination that has never been content with this hard headed scientism or commonsense comfort with the routine, ordinary, and predictable. The Romantic pole of Humanism has continued to insist that a rationalistic or merely pragmatic conception of the cosmos leaves out most of what life is worth living for. Humanity needs not only the security of the everyday world, but the excitement, the adventure, the yearning and dreaming of mysteries that can only be expressed in symbols, in art, poetry, fiction, and music.

Must we not abandon the attempt to fit this realm of the extraordinary, the creative, the adventurous, the ecstatic into the secure world of the daily routine or the scientific world of controlled fact? It is a world of risk and those dedicated to it typically lead lives of alternate ecstasy and despair, of psychological and moral conflict often ending in self-destruction. This kind of life seems out of control, or perhaps it is one of artistic control wielded so daringly that finally, after many triumphs, it overshoots itself, breaks down, and is carried helplessly away into the night.

In a culture dominated by a Humanism polarized between scientism and romanticism "God is silent." If he were to speak to those of scientistic or pragmatic temperament his voice would be discounted as background noise to be ignored in the search for the regular patterns of ordinary existence. Even for romantics if God were to speak to them they would be unable to distinguish his voice from the projections of their own creative imaginations and infinite longings. Thus it seems that if there is a God, he permits his creatures in their doubts and their suffering to live in a world in which he ignores them. He seems to remain indifferent to their cries for help, or at least for sympathy, for some personal reaction from him to their behavior. Certainly a God who is a stone wall to human pleas is a God of evil, even if it only takes the form of a cruel indifference.

A stronger form of this difficulty is the conviction of many people today, so eloquently expressed by the existentialists, that the world is absurd, meaningless, and indifferent to human concerns.[23] In the face of the account of the world given us by science does it not appear that we have been thrown into a universe that has come from nowhere and is going nowhere? As it is often said, our earth is only a speck of dust in a vast desert of space filled with trillions of other worlds which may or may not be inhabited by other rational beings who know nothing of us. Among them all this earth is insignificant and will inevitably be destroyed. While it exists it no doubt possesses much of beauty and delight for us, but there is mockery in all this, because human life is brief and for most of us full of pain, toil, and frustration. In the end it will all be forgotten, even the most magnificent human achievements. Thus human life in its brevity gives us the opportunity to create for ourselves moments of meaning and joy, but nothing more is possible. "Man is a useless passion."[24]

Still stronger is the form of this difficulty that arises from our experience of constant fear and conflict. Who in our world ever achieves security? Even the rich and powerful tempt the rival ambitions of others and the assaults of assassins; while the powerless live in terror of unemployment, homelessness, starvation, and enslavement by the powerful. Over us all hangs the threat of war, perhaps of nuclear war. The despair this brings to the young who must fight or who are widowed, to the mothers and fathers who lose sons, the humiliation and degradation of the defeated, the misery of those subject to famine has only been sketched by great writers like Tolstoy and great artists like Goya.

The tragic consequences of war for the victors are no less real. The climax of this horror of war is reached in genocide. History records the exterminations of whole peoples, men, women and children in the holy wars of the Old Testament, the imperial wars of the Assyrians, the invasions of Genghis Khan, the modern slaughter of the Armenians, or Hitler's genocide of the Jews, Poles, and Gypsies, the Hutus' genocide of the Tutsi, the Serbs' genocide of Bosnians and Kosovo Albanians. The Holocaust of the Jews was a special and unrivaled tragedy in that it was a deliberate effort to wipe out a people whose unique significance for the religious and moral history of the world I have emphasized in this book. Though Hitler was anti-Christian, a radical Humanist who based his views on romantic racist theories and the neo-paganism of Richard Wagner, he was able to exploit the anti-Semitism that had become endemic in nationalistic Christianity.[25]

The external conflict of nationalistic war is not the only kind of war. There is also civil and class war and finally the miserable "wars" within institutions such as universities, businesses, families, and between the sexes. The constant struggle for power and dominance that leads to the development of oppressed classes, including the oppression of women and neglect and abuse of the young, touches more human beings than any other kind of war. Almost any human biography reveals the sufferings of a neglected or exploited childhood, or the slanders and betrayals of those in whom love and trust were invested. Along with these injuries go the inner psychological conflicts that arise from our miseducation and traumatic early experiences. Where is the human heart to find peace?

Besides the misery of conflict there is the suffering of enslavement. Sometimes this is the enslavement to the boredom of the routine of crushing manual labor in country or factory, or the deadly routine of paper work, and of the make-work of army life, that deadens the human mind and blocks all human creativity. But more devitalizing still is the actual subjection of one's life and mind to the arbitrary or ignorant or dogmatic will of "authority" or "the experts." The history of the world is marked by this nagging restriction and enchainment of human potential by the authority of others, often much less able, jealous of their power. Here the oppression of women confined to domestic roles and to the abuse or entertainment of men and unable to use their gifts or choose their own way in life, is especially galling.[26] How many men and women who sought only to employ their talents to create beauty, improve the social order and environment, promote justice, search for or communicate truth have been frustrated and forced to see their work thwarted! But also how many ordinary people of ordinary talents have been forced to live their lives in ignorance and poverty of experience, illiterate or semi-literate, locked up in prejudice, superstition, fanaticism, or brute stupidity!

Finally, there is the immense burden of the experience of physical suffering and decay. Countless are those born with genetic diseases or other birth defects, those maimed by accident and disease who have to struggle through life often unable to accomplish the least daily task without enormous effort. Many are the young suddenly faced with devastating injuries, diseases, or imminent death. The latter part of life and its aging always knows the step by step disintegration of the body, the decline of energy, the dimming of the power to think and will. The experience of old age for very many is horrible and for all it is an entrance into the unknown night. While death is sometimes welcome, it is only because life has become intolerable, and it still remains, however stoic those who face it, a terrible inevitability, a great, black, question mark.

Thus from a subjective point of view life faces us as it did Macbeth, "a tale told by an idiot full of sound and fury, signifying nothing." Nor can this be fully compensated by the joyful, adventurous, serene, beautiful, and funny experiences of life. For many, probably most people, life is not rich with such experiences, but only very occasionally shows them bright spots in a fabric that is on the whole drab or filthy.

Yet even for those who can truthfully affirm their lives as rich with positive values, these seem never achieved without much that is anxious, painful, tedious, and always threatened with disaster. The very wonder of the great moments of life only makes the threat of losing everything the more ominous. We can understand why the great medieval pope Innocent III could have written with rapid pen his work *On the Contempt of the World: Or on the Misery of the Human Condition*, but never found time or energy to complete a planned sequel on human happiness.[27] With much less eloquence I have only pointed to the subjective miseries of the human condition that we all know only too well and that the classics of literature vividly depict. They are sufferings for which there is and can be, from a subjective viewpoint, no sufficient remedy. They can be mitigated but not escaped, and the very efforts to mitigate or escape them bring on other miseries. This in the final analysis is admitted even by Humanists who, in spite of all the hope they place in the power of human intelligence to solve human problems, in the end settle for a kind of Stoicism. They say, "Well, since suffering and death are inevitable, let us at least endure them with dignity and without the humiliation of false hope." The trouble is that, as the Holocaust shows, even dignity in death is beyond guarantee.

If this is the way it is with us, how can we accept subjectively the existence of a good God, or even of any meaningful Absolute, except blind Fate? Would not such acceptance be the worst of self-delusions? I quote again Jean-Paul Sartre's argument, "Either there is a God or the universe is absurd; but there can be no God, therefore the universe is absurd." That there can be no God he proved by saying that if there is an omnipotent God, then there can be no human freedom, but if we have no freedom, then we live in an inescapable hell of illusion, struggling always to be free and never able to be so — the ultimate absurdity.[28]

4. Compensation and Consolation

It might seem that the only answer to all this would be if our suffering could be shown to attain a fully compensatory reward. Certainly to a degree this is an answer. We all experience that sometimes our efforts and pains are rewarded. Then the pain is forgotten, or rather it enhances our victory. Because we human beings learn by contrast, it is certainly true that sunshine is more appreciated after the storm than if we lived in California. The silly story of the man who, when asked why he kept beating his head against a wall, replied that it was because it felt so good when he stopped, is really not very far from the facts of the human mode of experiencing. Good gained without painful struggle is hard for us to savor.

Consequently, all the older world religions promise their followers a reward for innocent suffering that will more than compensate for it. Humanism, however, can only promise that the reward can at best be satisfaction in having done well and in serving as an influence for good. Since the approach of death, the lack of appreciation, self-doubts, and the apparent destruction of one's efforts by others usually mar even our successes, such a promise is cold comfort. Nor is the notion put forward by some that a sufficient reward is the satisfaction of playing a role in the inevitable march of history toward a better society. If Utopia is inevitable, of what importance have one's efforts been in bringing about a state of things one will never share?

Yet even if the promise of the Creation Religions that God in his justice will more than compensate in our future life for every suffering in the present and will see to it that our efforts to help others will not have been in vain, the subjective problem remains. Why has an all-powerful God permitted us to suffer so much *here and now*? Why has he not eliminated the suffering and simply given us happiness that after all is ultimately his gift to give?

Judaism and Islam answer this hard question by stressing that since the believer suffers as a witness (martyr) to the cause of God he will receive a superabundant reward by sharing after death in God's victory over his enemies. Christianity agrees, but adds that the superabundant reward is precisely admission to the community of the Trinity, a reward infinitely beyond any compensation consisting in the abundance of merely human goods, even human spiritual goods. Nevertheless, Christianity also attempts to answer the subjective objection about present suffering.

The only consolation for human suffering that goes beyond the hope for a future reward and touches present suffering itself, is the sympathy of others, companionship in suffering. This we have all experienced from childhood. Nothing helped us so much to endure sickness or fear as a child as the reassuring and soothing presence of our mother or father. In maturity nothing can make suffering so endurable as the presence of a friend or lover. The reason for this is that this presence is an assurance of eventual compensation, an assurance that is, as it were, hope made present, rather than merely future.

This is the specifically Christian answer to suffering. Humanism like Stoicism can only emphasize the strength and consolation of human companionship in suffering. Yet this cannot offset the unreliability of human friendship that often willingly or not deserts us just when we most need it. The Emanation Religions and also the process theologians answer this difficulty by pointing out the abiding immanence of the Absolute in human life. The enlightened person knows that in his or her suffering deep within the suffering self the higher Self is ever at peace. But the mystical experience can be attained only by a few who have advanced to this state through countless reincarnations and is not continuously experienced except by the most advanced. Buddhism and *bhakti* devotion have to a degree met this difficulty by the their doctrine of the compassion of the Buddha or the graciousness of Shiva, Krishna, or the Mother Goddess. The Buddhas who have attained Nirvana remain for a time in the world of suffering to extend their mercy and consolation to those who have not yet arrived at Nirvana. Yet this only means that we are helped by others like ourselves to move more rapidly on our painful way to release.

The Gospel, however, proposes a further solution that does not negate but ecumenically includes the other answers. God the Father will wipe away our tears and give us ultimate and superabundant compensation in the future Kingdom. Yet he wishes us to achieve this not merely as a pure gift, but also as the just reward of our own achievements that because they are human necessarily involve pain and struggle. Human growth in knowledge, human growth in virtue, human transformation of the world must be in the human mode that works dialectically through contrasts, struggle, courage and patience. Yet God understands that subjectively it is very hard for us to accept and endure this fact of actual, even if necessary, suffering. The only way to make our suffering easier and ultimately to compensate it superabundantly is by sympathy not merely in the sense of appreciating our pain, but of experiencing it himself with us. Immanuel, "God with us," Jesus Christ, has chosen to suffer and to die with us and thus to enter into infinite delight through suffering with us.

Note how ambiguous is the term "compassion"![29] God and Buddha can have compassion in the sense of intimate understanding of what it is to suffer and profound desire to remedy that suffering and yet not suffer themselves. A Buddha does not himself suffer any longer. Nor can God as God suffer, since he remains forever in eternal peace. But the Christian doctrines of the Incarnation and the Cross teach that God has willed to suffer with us so that we might be strengthened by a hope that is subjectively present to us.[30]

Yet if God is to suffer with us, how can we be assured that in the end we will be victorious with him? Some process theologians have concluded that to suffer with us God must undergo change as God. By thus limiting God they take away his omnipotence and our certainty that he can surely help us. The doctrine of the Incarnation avoids this, since God the Father does not become incarnate, but only God the Son, and God the Son suffers with us not through his divine nature but through his assumed human nature that unlike his divinity is capable of suffering. But does not this mean that he does not really suffer, but only that his human nature suffers? No, because it is one and the same divine Person who is both God and human. The suffering of his human nature is his suffering, no one else's, just as my bodily suffering is my suffering although I am not just a body. Moreover, this incarnate Son is anointed with the Holy Spirit whom he sends upon the Church and the world as his infinite strengthening and consoling power, so that the God who truly suffers remains infinite in his power to save us.

Thus in Jesus Christ we see first the power of God in his miracles and his wisdom, the self-revelation of God. "Philip, whoever has seen me has seen the Father" (Jn 14:9), but we see God most perfectly revealed on the Cross, where the Son suffers subjectively all that we can suffer. Looking at him and believing that he is now at the Father's right hand sending the Holy Spirit upon us, our own present suffering is united with his. While it remains human pain, it is transformed by the hope of glory, a hope that is not merely future but present in the infinite power of God in Christ. And as Christ by his suffering saved the world, so by our suffering with him we save each other.

Moreover, this present hope is available not only to the mystic who experiences already something of that continuous peace that heaven will be, but even in the beginner. The thief on a cross repents and receives the promise of paradise at the very side of Jesus who suffers even more than the sinner because he feels the alienation of sin more profoundly.

Two objections can still be raised. First, is it true that Jesus experienced all that we suffer? He was on the Cross only a few hours.[31] How does that compare to the months and years of crucifixion some people undergo through sickness, enslavement, and rejection? How can we compare Calvary to the death camps of Auschwitz? Second, Jesus is no longer present with us. We may believe in his compassion, but he is not actually here to be our companion, since he suffered two thousand years ago. The answer to both difficulties is to recall that the doctrine of the Incarnation includes the Church as the Body of Christ in that Jesus continues to be present really, though sacramentally.

St. Paul says, "Now I rejoice in my sufferings for your sake, and in my flesh I am filling up what is lacking in the afflictions of Christ on behalf of his body, that is the church" (Col 1:24). Our consolation, therefore, is in the companionship of the suffering Christ present in our fellow Christians, the Church. We bear a common witness and carry on a common struggle that we believe and experience to be a share in Christ's sufferings, endowed with the power of transforming ourselves and the world. In the Church every mode of human suffering is experienced, though no single human being, even Jesus could actually suffer every kind of pain. Nevertheless in a very true sense, Jesus can be said to have suffered *all* suffering. For our sake he faced the totality of human evils, yet did not rebel against the Father for permitting them. In his suffering he knew that the Father is Love who would never permit even the least evil to one of his creatures except because he can and will bring out of it a greater good.

5. The Greater Good

What then is this greater good that God brings out of evil through sharing that evil with us in his Son? We cannot here and now know this greater good by direct experience. It can only be believed in and hoped for. The greater good is that the entire universe will be restored to its original purpose, freed from sin, not merely by God's gift, but by the efforts of angels and of human beings empowered by God's grace to cooperate with God in this ultimate perfecting of the universe. Moreover, this universe will be more perfect than it would have been if the road to its completion had not been through the fall and redemption.

It is an acceptable theological opinion in the Catholic Tradition that even if there had been no sin the Incarnation would have taken place in order to bring the universe to the most perfect possible union with God in its head, the God-Man.[32] This theological opinion although orthodox is purely speculative. What the Scriptures actually assure us is that God has chosen the way of the permission of sin to bring the universe to perfection. In his eternal wisdom he knows that out of this evil he can most fittingly bring the greater good of the Incarnation and thus reveal himself as the God of Love in a way most sympathetic to our human way of understanding.

In the universe as it actually exists God has permitted his creatures to use their free will to alienate themselves from him in order that they might learn through an experience in the mode proper to their own nature. They discover that they can be truly themselves only within his community, the Church; and he has mercifully provided a way back for them through the Incarnation. By doing so he has made the universe not merely his creation but has adopted angels and humans as his children in a most perfect personal union. Thus it is not only intelligible objectively how it is possible for an all-loving and all-powerful God to permit his creatures for a time to derail his creation and thus bring suffering on themselves and each other. This is also subjectively acceptable since the Son of God in person has come to share that painful lesson with us and to turn it into a marvelous victory in which we can fully participate.

The importance of emphasizing that through the Incarnation human cooperation with God becomes possible is that the Reformers in their anxiety to revive St. Paul's teaching on the gratuity of grace tended to deny human cooperation and to make our redemption purely passive on our part.[33] The result was that in that type of theology the Cross seemed to be God's Shylockean demand for a pound of flesh to revenge himself for the insult given him by his rebellious creatures. When to this notion was added the Calvinist theme of double predestination, that God created some for salvation, some for damnation, God became, as Pierre Bayle said,[34] hard to distinguish from the Devil. This theological nightmare accounts for the rejection of Christianity by many Humanists.

6. The God of Love

Once we have seen that God revealed himself on the Cross as the God of Love who is willing to suffer with us in order that we might understand his love and turn to him in love, we begin to see what the acceptance of Christian faith entails. It demands nothing less than the gift of self in love, the love of God and neighbor, the love of God's whole creation and especially of all other human persons, even our enemies.[35] This should not be understood as some kind of idealistic altruism. In loving God's creatures we first of all love ourselves for God's sake, with a love that seeks not immediate, partial satisfactions of a selfish sort, but with a love that seeks the common good in which our own good is included and completed.

The uniqueness of the Christian way of life is not in its glorification of love but in its insight as to what love is. For the Emanation Religions the concept of *bhakti* approaches this concept of the love of God. Yet because even in the theology of Ramanuja the human person does not stand in total distinction from God as in Creation Religions, this love cannot be more than a metaphor for the absorption of the creature into God. Hence also the love of neighbor is not seen as integral to the love of God.[36] In the Creation Religions of Judaism and Islam the notion of the love of neighbor is restricted to a love of the righteous, because love is not thought of as a gift of God, but rather as wholly human submission to God's will. In Humanism there can be a wonderful philanthropy and concern for the oppressed but it is restricted to a human relationship that does not extend to the cultural or class enemy.

Could it not be objected that Christian love also is limited since it only loves the enemy in view of his conversion and teaches that after death those who remain enemies of God will be punished forever in hell? The notion of hell seems to many Humanists the ultimate giveaway that exposes Christianity as, after all, an imperialism.[37] Don't Christians love only those they hope to control, and when they find they cannot control them, don't they hate the infidel or apostate with a remorseless hatred? Surely if God is a God of Love doesn't he still love those in hell and won't he ultimately redeem them?

In reply to this we must recall that love must be freely given. Moreover we have excluded the idea of literal reincarnation since that results in an idealistic dualism. We are not just spirits condemned to a body. As human persons the body we have is just as much ourself as the soul we have and in the resurrection we will regain that same body for all eternity. Each of us has only one life on earth in which to choose our ultimate relation to God and neighbor. This means that those who at death have by their own choice excluded themselves from the eternal Kingdom, the community of those who love and are loved by God, have also doomed themselves by their own choice to eternal alienation from God and humanity. The notion of hell as a place in which God torments his enemies and gloats over their suffering is a mistaken and misleading effort to express this alienation metaphorically and in imaginable terms. Hell is rather a state of alienation whose torments result from the self-imposed condition of self contradiction of those who were created to love but who do not want to really love anyone but themselves. Its "fires" are the remorse and loneliness of endless self-hatred.

God and the blessed still love those in hell for what they could have been, but the rejection by the damned of this love offered to them makes it definitively impossible that God and the saints could love what the damned have freely chosen to make of themselves. In justice God cannot deprive them of the existence that he gave them to use and to which in spite of their unspeakable misery they continue to cling since they are unable to will their own annihilation.[38] While suicides can will to annihilate themselves, the damned know they have no power to do so, yet cannot will that God should do so either, since that would be to submit to his sovereignty and their resistance to this sovereignty is the reason for their damnation.[39] This is precisely the source of their torment that they cannot help but will to exist and yet also are fixed in their proud will to be independent of the Source of All Existence. God remains true to his half of the bargain not to destroy what out of love he created, nor to violate the freedom of choice that he gave them.

But as long as any human being lives this earthly life the possibility of conversion lies open and Christians, who are commanded not to judge, must extend their love to their enemies hoping by that love to win their reconciliation and everlasting friendship in God.

Conclusion

We have searched for a world-view and way of life that not only meets all the ultimate concerns of human beings yet does so in conformity to objective truth accessible to human rational reflection over ordinary human experience. This search has arrived at Jesus Christ present in his community, the Christian Church, as that subsists in completeness in the communion headed by the successor of St. Peter, that poor sinner who said, "Lord, you know everything; you know that I love you" (Jn 21:17).

This answer does not mean that the other world religions, even the secular ones, are rejected as erroneous or "inferior."[40] As far as my admittedly limited acquaintance with and understanding of these religions goes, they are not excluded but included in the Gospel. This Gospel, I myself believe by a rationally credible faith, alone has the power to bring them into ecumenical dialogue with one another in mutual respect for the truth to which each strives to be faithful. Dialogue between world-views does not require anyone to submit to their partner as a superior; in dialogue all partners are equal. To the Christian's claim to possess the Truth, the other partners have the right to make the same claim. In the course of the dialogue it will gradually become apparent that all in large measure share much of the same truth, as we have seen in this book, but dialogue must continue to find reconciliation on the points of difference that seem to remain.

The Christian conviction is that in sincere dialogue Jesus Christ in his humility will himself shine forth as "the Light that enlightens everyone, coming into this world" (Jn 1:9) and it will become clear that all the other great prophets bear witness to him who dissolved all barriers. "For he is our peace, he who made both one and broke down the dividing wall of enmity, through his flesh" (Eph 2:14). I believe that Jesus, the Word of God, will be found hidden at the heart of every great religion as the one teacher before whom all humanity will be found equal in being taught (Mt 23:10), none of us having any claim to be superior to any other.

But this confrontation with Jesus Christ is a terrible one. No one can meet him and see him looking on us with a love that is ready to die for us, without beginning to tremble. To be so loved demands of us that we love in return, not merely out of fear or hope of reward, but in the gift of self in exchange for his gift of self to us. Such a gift requires us to let go of everything to which we cling, even ourselves. The first step and foundation of this self-giving is faith. Faith means to believe in God on his own word, not because of the signs that he has worked to reveal himself to us so that we might be able in our human way to believe. Yet these signs are given us not just in the remote past but in the living witness of the Catholic Church. Christ's Spirit maintains this community of faith, for all its human failings, faithful to God. Even today in this community of faith we can begin to practice the life of hope and love. Only this love can draw all Christians together in faith and make them a united witness so as to draw all the world to Jesus, and through him in the Spirit to the Father.

To be truly human we ought to open our eyes in faith to God's self-revelation to us lest we wander away into darkness. But we find we cannot make this act of faith except by yielding our alienated hearts. Only he can turn us back to himself, but he will do so if we ask in prayer, "Lord I believe, help my unbelief" (Mk 9:23).

Notes

[1] See Avery Dulles, *A History of Apologetics,* Theological Resources (New York: Corpus Books, 1971) and Tibor Horvath, *Faith Under Scrutiny* (Notre Dame, IN: Fides Press, 1975), pp. 7-78 for the historical development of the apologetic method; also Francis Schüssler Fiorenza, *Foundational Theology* (New York: Crossroad, 1984), pp. 251-84.

[2] Karl Rahner, *Foundations of Christian Faith: An Introduction to the Idea of Christianity* (New York: Seabury, 1968).

[3] On the meanings of "experience" in current foundational theology see Gerald O'Collins, *Fundamental Theology* (New York: Paulist Press, 1981), pp. 32-52. Following Rahner, O'Collins maintains that God is present in every human experience at least as its "transcendental ground."

[4] Maurice Blondel, *The Letter on Apologetics, and History and Dogma,* trans. by A. Dru and Illtyd Trethowen (New York: Holt, Rinehart and Winston, 1965) and *Action,* trans. by Oliva Blanchette (Notre Dame, IN: Notre Dame University, 1984).

[5] Hans Küng's principal apologetic works are *On Being a Christian* (Garden City, NY: Doubleday, 1976); *Does God Exist?: An Answer for Today* (Garden City, NY: Doubleday, 1980); *Eternal Life After Death?* (Garden City, NY: Doubleday, 1985); *Christianity and World Religions: Paths to Dialogue,* with Josef von Ess, Heinrich von Stietencron, Heinz Bechert (Maryknoll, NY: Orbis Books, 1996). For the serious questions raised by his erudite, lively but minimalizing apologetic method see *The Küng Dialogue* (Washington, DC: United States Catholic Conference, 1980).

[6] See Michael Polanyi, *The Tacit Dimension* (Garden City, NY: Doubleday, 1966); Jurgen Habermas, *Knowledge and Human Interests* (Boston: Beacon Press, 1971). For liberation theologians see Edward L. Cleary, *Crisis and Change: The Church in Latin America Today* (Maryknoll, NY: Orbis Books, 1985), pp. 51-103.

[7] See Chapter 5, note 9.

[8] Feodor Mikhailovich Dostoevski, *The Brothers Karamazov,* translated by Constance Garnett (New York: Random House, 1933) Book V, Chapter IV, pp. 246-255.

[9] See John Bowker, *Problems of Suffering in the Religions of the World* (Cambridge: Cambridge University Press, 1970).

[10] See the last two chapters of Alfred North Whitehead, *Process and Reality,* corrected ed. (New York: Macmillan Free Press, 1978).

[11] See John Hicks, "Evil, The Problem of" in *The Encyclopedia of Philosophy,* ed. by Paul Edwards (New York: Macmillan and Free Press, 1967), vol. 3, pp.136-141; Jacques Maritain, *St. Thomas on the Problem of Evil* (Milwaukee, WI: Marquette University Press, 1942). Also see Martin D'Arcy, *The Pain of the World and the Providence of God* (London/New York: Longmans, Green and Co., 1936); C.S. Lewis, *The Problem of Pain* (New York: Macmillan, 1943). Also see Austin Farrer, *Love Almighty and Ills Unlimited* (New York: Doubleday, 1961); Nels Ferré, *Evil and the Christian Faith* (New York: Harpers, 1947); Charles Journet, *The Meaning of Evil* (New York: P.J. Kenedy, 1963). Cf. John Hicks, *Evil and the God of Love* (New York: Harper, 1966); Paul Ricoeur, *The Symbolism of Evil* (New York: Harper and Row, 1967); Frederick Sontag, *The God of Evil: An Argument from the Existence of the Devil* (New York: Harper, 1970). On the origin of sin see Henri Rondet, *Original Sin: The Patristic and Theological Background* (Staten Island, NY: Alba House, 1972).

[12] See my *Theologies of the Body: Humanist and Christian,* 2nd ed. (Boston: National Catholic Center for Bioethics, 1997), pp. 381-85.

[13] Reference in note 11 above.

[14] Cf. St. Thomas Aquinas, *Summa Theologiae* I, q. 97.

[15] See my *Theologies of the Body* (note 12 above), p. 596 f.

[16] *Ibid.,* p. 419 f.

[17] *Ibid.,* pp. 652-659. See Mortimer J. Adler, *The Angels and Us* (New York: Macmillan, 1962); Claus Westermann, *God's Angels Need No Wings* (Philadelphia: Fortress Press, 1979); Jeffrey Burton Russell, *The Devil* and *Satan* (Ithaca, NY: Cornell University Press, 1977, 1981).

[18] See Stephen Jay Gould, *Ever Since Darwin* (New York: Norton, 1977) for the non-teleological character of evolution and John D. Barrow and Frank J. Tipler, *The Anthropic Cosmological Principle* (New York: Oxford University Press, 1986) for the teleological character of cosmology.

[19] From the not very critical book of Matthew Fox and Rupert Sheldrake, *The Physics of Angels: Exploring the Realm where Science and Spirit Meet* (San Francisco: Harper, 1996), pp. 22-23, I learned this important fact of which I was ignorant when, in my *Theologies of the Body,* I proposed the view that evolution requires the angels. Wallace's book was published in London by Chapman and Hall in 1911. It must be admitted, however, that Wallace was also a convinced spiritualist.

[20] Walter Wink, *Naming the Powers: The Language of Power in the New Testament* (Philadelphia: Fortress Press, 1984).

[21] See G.W. Leibnitz, *Theodicy,* trans. by E.M. Huggard (Edinburgh and London, 1952). Also see the discussion in Frederick Copleston, SJ, *A History of Philosophy* (Garden City, NY: Doubleday/Image), vol. 4, pp. 330-336. Schopenhauer was to maintain that "this is the worst of all possible worlds." St. Thomas Aquinas, *Summa Theologiae* I, q. 7 and *Contra Gentiles* I, c. 23-27, argues that while God is infinite, no creature can be essentially infinite. In I, q. 19, aa. 7-10, he shows that God creates freely. Thus God could always add

some reflection of his infinite perfection lacking to his freely but finite created world. Hence, the notion of the "most perfect possible world" is contradictory.

[22] See Chapter 3, note 32, for references.

[23] Since the word "meaning" generally connotes purpose or at least order, those who think that scientific explanation is non-teleological and non-causal have to consider the cosmos meaningless. Thus Bertrand Russell says, "Order, unity, and continuity are human inventions just as truly as are catalogues and encyclopedias," *The Scientific Outlook* (New York and Glencoe, IL: Free Press, 1931), p. 101.

[24] Jean-Paul Sartre, *Being and Nothingness,* Hazel Barnes trans. (New York: Philosophical Library, 1956), p. 615.

[25] See Richard Koenigsberg, *Hitler and Ideology: A Study in Psychoanalytic Sociology* (New York: Library of Social Science, 1975).

[26] Mary Daly, *The Church and the Second Sex* (NY: Harper and Row, 1968). In *Theologies of the Body* (note 12 above) and in *Justice in the Church: Gender and Participation* (Washington, DC: The Catholic University of America Press, 1996) I argue for a different diagnosis of this sexism and its remedies.

[27] *Patrologia Latina* (Migne) 217, col. 701-746.

[28] Sartre, *Being and Nothingness* (note 24 above), pp. lxviii, says that "Being in itself" is "Uncreated, without reason for being, without any connection with another being, being in itself is *de trop* for eternity." This is the theme of his novel *Nausea,* trans. by Loyd Alexander (London: New Directions, 1949). On Sartre and atheism see Corneho Fabro, *God in Exile* (Westminster, MD: Newman Press, 1968), pp. 939-957.

[29] See Henri de Lubac, *Aspects of Buddhism* (New York: Sheed and Ward), pp. 15-53 on the "charity" of Buddha and Jesus; and Alfred North Whitehead, *Process and Reality,* note 10 above, on process theology and compassion.

[30] See Jürgen Moltmann, *The Crucified God* (New York: Harper and Row, 1974); Gustaf Aulen, *Christus Victor: An Historical Study of the Three Main Types of Atonement* (New York: Macmillan, 1969); Romanus Cessario, *Christian Satisfaction in Aquinas: Toward a Personalist Understanding* (Washington, DC: University Press of America, 1982).

[31] Cf. St. Thomas Aquinas, *Summa Theologiae,* III, q. 46, a. 5-11.

[32] See Thomas P. Potvin, *The Theology of the Primacy of Christ According to St. Thomas and Its Scriptural Foundation* (Fribourg: University of Fribourg Press, 1973) and Juniper B. Carol, OFM, *The Absolute Primacy and Predestination of Jesus and His Virgin Mother* (Chicago: Franciscan Herald Press, 1981).

[33] See Harry McSorley, *Luther Right or Wrong?* (New York: Newman Press, 1969), and Erwin Iserloh, "Luther's Christ Mysticism" in Jared Wick, ed., *Catholic Scholars Dialogue with Luther* (Chicago: Loyola University Press, 1970), pp. 37-58.

[34] Daniel Walker, *The Decline of Hell* (Chicago: University of Chicago Press, 1964), pp. 195-200 (note on page 197 refers to Bayle's *Oeuvres Diverses,* p. 807).

[35] See John Piper, *"Love Your Enemies": Jesus' Love Command in the Synoptics and Early Christian Paraenesis* (New York: Cambridge University Press, 1979).

[36] On Ramanuja see Chapter 4, note 16.

[37] See the work of Walker in note 34 above.

[38] Some of the early Church Fathers seem to have held that the damned are annihilated, see H. Lassiat, *Jeunesse de l'église, la foi au 2e siècle,* 2 vols. (Paris: Mame, 1979), but at this time the Church's doctrine on future life was still in the process of dogmatic development.

[39] Another reason is that suicide can be willed by the living who hope somehow for a better state of existence even if it is only dreamless sleep. But the damned no longer can entertain any such illusion. At death the soul becomes directly aware of its own nature (known only indirectly and obscurely in this life) and cannot deny to itself its innate need to be.

[40] See Denis Lardner Carmody, *What Are They Saying About Other Religions?* (New York: Paulist Press, 1982) for a good summary of recent discussions.